Edward J. Cleary

BEYOND THE BURNING CROSS

Edward J. Cleary received his B.A. magna cum laude in political science in 1974 and his J.D. in 1977 from the University of Minnesota. He lives and practices law in St. Paul. This is his first book.

BEYOND THE BURNING CROSS

BEYOND THE BURNING CROSS

A Landmark Case of Race, Censorship,
and the First Amendment

EDWARD J. CLEARY

VINTAGE BOOKS

A Division of Random House, Inc.

New York

FIRST VINTAGE BOOKS EDITION, OCTOBER 1995

Copyright © 1994 by Edward J. Cleary

All rights reserved under International and Pan-American Copyright
Conventions. Published in the United States by Vintage Books, a division
of Random House, Inc., New York, and simultaneously in Canada by
Random House of Canada Limited, Toronto. Originally published
in hardcover by Random House, Inc., New York, in 1994.

The Library of Congress has cataloged the Random House
edition as follows:
Beyond the burning cross: Cleary, Edward J.
The First Amendment and the landmark R.A.V. case/
Edward J. Cleary.—1st. ed.
p. cm.
Includes bibliographical references and index.
ISBN 0-679-42460-1
1. Saint Paul (Minn.)—Trials, litigation, etc. 2. Hate crimes—
Minnesota—Saint Paul. 3. Hate crimes—United States. 4. Freedom of
speech—United States. 1. Title.
KF228.S23C54 1994
345.7302—dc20
[347.3052] 93-35882
Vintage ISBN: 0-679-74703-6

Manufactured in the United States of America
10 9 8 7 6 5 4 3 2 1

For my late father, Edward,
who proved to me the power of integrity;
my mother, Eleanor,
who taught me the necessity for compassion;
my late sister, Mary,
who showed me the true meaning of courage;
and my sister Kathleen,
who, through her devotion to teaching,
has reminded me of our responsibility
to the students of tomorrow

Free speech is about as good a cause as the world has ever known. But, like the poor, it is always with us and gets shoved aside in favor of things which seem at some given moment more vital.

—Heywood Broun
New York World,
October 23, 1926

Acknowledgments

———◼———

Writing is a decidedly different skill than litigating, being by nature more reflective. Working on this book has given me a chance to consider the support and assistance I have received since June 1990, when I was assigned the defense of R.A.V.

At my side from the beginning was Michael Cromett. Playing a crucial role outside the limelight, Michael proved once again both his loyalty as a friend and his ability as a lawyer. Also of great assistance were the lawyers and support staff from Bannigan & Kelly, in particular Pat Kelly and John Bannigan. Thanks also to Carol Eberhardt and Karen Jurney, who typed countless briefs and several drafts of this manuscript without complaint and often with helpful advice.

Thanks also to all the members and staff of the Ramsey County Public Defender's office, particularly those who encouraged me from the start at the Cedar Street Cafe, including Mike Fetsch, Jon Duckstad, Noreen Phillips, and Colia Ceisel. My thanks in addition to all those who offered moral support, in particular my uncle Tom Donlin, Michelle Ulrich, Kathi Leicinger, and Pat Diamond, as well as Scott Borchert, Bonnie Prawer, and Karen Paulson.

Professor Kathleen Sullivan, now of Stanford Law School and Professor John Siliciano, of Cornell Law School, helped by reviewing an early draft of the brief. Professor David Cole of Georgetown Law Center critiqued several chapters of the manuscript. Ellen Seesel deserves special mention for suggesting editing changes in the brief and the manuscript and improving the quality of both. My deepest gratitude to Nat Hentoff not only for the introduction but for being a friend and supporter both before and after the decision. His encouragement when few were encouraging and compliments when few were complimentary made all the difference in the world.

My mother, Eleanor, and my sister, Kathleen, rode an emotional roller coaster during these years and never complained. There are a number of other close friends and family members deserving of mention for their encouragement, and I thank them all rather than list them individually for fear of omitting anyone.

One of the great pleasures of this project has been the opportunity to work with the people of Random House, particularly my editor and my copy editor, Sono Rosenberg. Thanks also to Lawrence LaRose.

I would like to express my appreciation to those students who contacted me to discuss the case; I urge them to heed the words of George Eliot: "Decide on what you think is right, and stick to it."

—Edward J. Cleary
St. Paul, January 1994

Contents

Introduction

———◼———

The inflammatory case of *R.A.V. v. City of St. Paul,* which is the subject of this book, turned out to be an exceptional victory for everyone's First Amendment rights. Yet it was largely misunderstood and misinterpreted by the press as concerning whether cross-burning should be punished—particularly cross-burning outside the home of a black family, the only black family on the block of a working-class neighborhood.

The defendant's lawyer, however, had no difficulty in agreeing that cross-burning should be punished. Neither, ultimately, did the Supreme Court. As Justice Antonin Scalia said, "St. Paul has sufficient means at its disposal to prevent such behavior without adding the First Amendment to the fire."

It was the First Amendment, not cross-burning, that powered this case. At issue was a municipal ordinance so overbroad that its effect, if adopted by other cities and states, would have chilled the speech, both verbal and symbolic, of large numbers of protesting citizens. St. Paul had decreed that any expression on public or private property was unlawful if its perpetrator knew or had reasonable grounds to know that the symbol or writing "arouses anger, alarm, or resentment in others on the basis of race, color, creed, religion or gender." As Bruce Ennis said in his brief to the Supreme Court for the Freedom to Read Foundation, this ordinance "covers more than hate speech directed to minority groups. *There is no limitation on the subject of the speech so long as it arouses anger, alarm or resentment.*"

A pro-choice woman who placed a declaration on her lawn attacking the local Catholic bishop for his views on abortion could have been convicted under this ordinance. So could a black parent whose message on her property indicted the school board for being racist. Both forms of expression would surely have aroused "anger, alarm, or resentment in others on the basis of race, color, creed, religion or gender."

This story of how Ed Cleary, who had never argued a case before the justices, won a unanimous Supreme Court decision overturning the ordinance has all the drama of a movie, especially because his opposition included nearly every major civil rights organization, from the NAACP to the Anti-Defamation League. Moreover, at home in St. Paul he was treated as a pariah even after he won the case. As William Kunstler said when explaining the refusal of most blacks and most white liberals to understand the vital significance of *R.A.V. v. City of St. Paul,* "All they could see was the burning cross."

One of the values of Ed Cleary's book is that it illuminates, from the very beginning of the case, how the legal process works: the combat of the lawyers and supporting groups, the different levels of legal intelligence of the judges, and the often obfuscating role of the press.

While a few newspapers once used to follow a landmark Supreme Court case from beginning to end, this hardly happens anymore. Moreover, since television, when it does give time to an important case, summarizes the result in sound bites lasting only seconds, most Americans have little idea of how decisions are made that can change the lives of millions of us. The court system as a whole is unknown territory except to those unfortunates who become caught in its quicksand. Charles Dickens's *Bleak House* is still contemporary, but those mired in the legal process know only their own ordeals. Thus, how the Supreme Court makes the final decision on an important case—and what it took to get that case to its marble building—is a dark mystery to most Americans. What Ed Cleary has also done is to shed some light on the long, hard road to the Court and on what happens when you get there.

Fred Graham, a former Supreme Court reporter for *The New York Times* and CBS television, and now the host on *Court TV,* says, "The only groups who don't appear on television are the Supreme Court and the Mafia." The Court is the most mysterious branch of government. Oral arguments before it are seen only by those in the 230 seats for spectators (most of whom are rotated at short intervals) and in the press section. The Court resolutely refuses to allow oral arguments to be televised. Few of the justices give interviews, and then almost never about particular cases. Thus, among other dividends in this book, there is a sense of what it is like to be in that small courtroom being besieged by questions from the justices.

Along with the history of the case and the manifold obstacles Cleary had to face, including watered-down support from the American Civil Liberties Union, this is also a history of the evolution of the Supreme Court's understanding of the First Amendment. Further, since this is a book about Cleary's personal evolution, there is also a clear sense of who the lawyer was and is, which reveals why he became so obsessed with this case.

One of the most consistent themes of the book is Cleary's recognition of Justice Oliver Wendell Holmes's distinction between those who believe in the First Amendment and those who only say that they do. Said Holmes: "If there is any principle of the Constitution that more imperatively calls for attachment than any other it is the principle of free thought—not free thought for those who agree with us but freedom for the thought that we hate."

Cleary shows that he met this test by accepting his client. Robert Viktora was a racist, and Cleary, who is decidedly not, accepted the man's right to demonstrate his racism. However, Cleary did not regard the cross-burning only as pure speech. Viktora could have been charged with vandalism, arson, or terroristic threats, but he should not have been punished, his lawyer believed, for violating the St. Paul ordinance because that law subverted the First Amendment by encompassing a wide range of protected speech.

As the case went on, however, the author was confronted with another challenge to his First Amendment beliefs. In contrast with the large number of *amicus* briefs sent to the Supreme Court supporting the prosecution, Cleary had only a few. He was offered one by an attorney in Georgia acting on behalf of the Patriots Defense Foundation. This group spends much of its time and energy defending the Ku Klux Klan, but its lawyer claimed that in this case his basic concern was to prevent censorship. Cleary told the lawyer for this foundation that he would not refuse support in the form of an *amicus* brief from any organization, "since it was hypocritical to silence groups while defending the First Amendment."

But when the Patriots Defense Foundation's brief arrived, Cleary saw that it wanted "to protect the vital First Amendment rights of political activists and spokespersons who advocate the ideology that the United States should remain a predominantly Christian, Anglo-Saxon and European-derived nation, with all that proposition entails in terms of cultural, social and religious norms." As Cleary writes, this was a hard statement of support to welcome, but he did not send it back. Obviously he was the right lawyer for the case.

The Supreme Court agreed with Ed Cleary's First Amendment argument. On June 22, 1992, every justice struck down the St. Paul ordinance as being overly broad and therefore an unconstitutional violation of the First Amendment. Moreover, five members of the Court went further, ruling that legislators cannot say that only certain forms of offensive speech can be prosecuted under a statute. (As mentioned, St. Paul's ordinance limited sanctions to offensive expression based on race, color, creed, religion, and gender.) "Selectivity of this sort," Justice Scalia said for the majority of five, "creates the possibility that the government is seeking to handicap the expression of particular ideas. The point of the First Amendment is that majority preferences must be expressed in some fashion other than silencing speech on the basis of its content."

The *R.A.V.* decision did not impress Russ and Laura Jones, who, with their five children, were the targets of the cross-burning. They are Jehovah's Witnesses, and so, as Ruth Marcus noted in *The Washington Post,* are "especially sensitive to free-speech arguments." (Cases brought by Jehovah's Witnesses before the Supreme Court have notably and durably strengthened First Amendment protections.)

However, Russ and Laura Jones do not see *R.A.V.* as a First Amendment case. "If it was just a point of view," Laura Jones said, "it would be fine. But we took this as a threat, and all black people take cross-burning as a threat, just as all Jewish people take a swastika splattered across the wall as a threat."

Probably most people, including some academics who know about the case, agree with Russ and Laura Jones. On public television some law professors referred to *R.A.V.* as "the cross-burning case," with no further clarification. In talking with college students, I find hardly anyone who knows what the case was really about. This is also true in St. Paul, where I lectured twice a year and a half after the decision. Most of the audiences had only a faint memory of the appeal, and the rest were convinced that it had been wrongly decided by a racist Supreme Court.

This book, therefore, is the only complete and accurate account of a case that, as Rod Smolla, a law professor at the College of William and Mary, emphasizes, "will prove to be a long-term enhancement of free speech in America."

Up to this point, the story of Ed Cleary and his triumph before the Court could have been a Frank Capra movie, with a modern-day Jimmy Stewart showing that, despite the odds, justice can triumph. However, one subplot would require a more mordant director— Robert Altman, perhaps.

All the way to the Supreme Court, Ed Cleary was a person under suspicion at home. Although he had defended some highly unpopular black clients, once he took the case he was shunned by a number of black lawyers and civil rights activists, as well as by indignant white liberals. Furthermore, as time went on, he was accused of costing the taxpayers more than one hundred thousand dollars by taking the case. In point of fact there were no public funds available for Robert Viktora's appeal to the Supreme Court, so from August 1990 to the end of the case in June 1992, Cleary and Michael Cromett, a lawyer helping him, donated the time they spent on *R.A.V.*

All along the way there were threats—at work and on Cleary's home phone. Said one anonymous caller, "You can't trust lawyers. . . . They should burn on crosses. You should be burned on a cross."

Both the local press and much of the national coverage of the story focused on the fear and anger of the blacks, who had felt threatened by the burning cross. It would have been impossible not to feel empathy for them—all the more because the basic context of the incident was slighted or ignored entirely in news accounts.

After the Supreme Court agreed with Ed Cleary, there remained a widespread belief in St. Paul, he said, that "we . . . ignored the feelings of a black family for either financial or racist reasons. Even members of my family were confronted by people wanting to know how their relative could do such a thing."

Moreover, among a good many white liberals Cleary has been branded a turncoat. "One of the things I have learned," he says, "is that individual liberties may be threatened as easily by well-meaning liberals as by reactionary conservatives."

What the writer of this introduction has learned from all of this is that the division in this nation between civil rights and civil liberties advocates is greater than I had believed when it comes to a clash between free speech and codes or laws that punish offensive speech. This dissonance remains evident on college campuses, where minority groups, by and large, vigorously support speech codes while a smaller group of civil liberties students opposes them.

But it is not only minority groups that, with exceptions, wish to punish the expression of bigotry in words or symbols. In 1977, when American Nazis wanted to use their First Amendment rights of speech and assembly to demonstrate in Skokie, Illinois (which has a large Jewish population, including survivors of the Holocaust), the American Civil Liberties Union was alone in defending the Nazis' First Amendment rights. No other organization, including bar associations, supported the ACLU.

David Goldberger, the ACLU's lead attorney in the Skokie case, received some solace from a letter:

> I was one of the youth of Jehovah's Witnesses during World War
> II—stoned, spat upon, jailed without due process, urinated upon,

and reviled because my religion forbade me to salute the flag or buy war stamps in school. I resigned from the Jehovah's Witnesses in 1951, but eleven years was long enough to learn the value of the First Amendment to a person espousing an unpopular viewpoint.

Roger Baldwin, the founder of the American Civil Liberties Union, used to say that no civil liberties battle is ever won—not finally. There have been victories from time to time protecting freedom of speech, but there are always those—legislators, public officials, school boards, and indignant citizens—ready and eager to cut down the First Amendment, so the fight has to be waged over and over again.

But not all these victories are sufficiently chronicled to be of use to First Amendment paladins during the next round of conflicts. Ed Cleary, however, not only won this ringing victory but has also left a record for this and future generations. It is not a record only for lawyers, because he writes with passionate clarity of language and with devotion to Justice Louis Brandeis's advice that "sunlight is the best disinfectant."

—Nat Hentoff
New York, November 1993

———— ■ ————

The Road to Athens

The news reached the Hotel Apollo in Delphi, Greece, late in the afternoon of June 22, 1992. Two hundred and one days had passed since the United States Supreme Court had heard oral arguments in the case of *R.A.V. v. City of St. Paul.*

As I listened to the voice of the clerk in Washington, D.C., informing me of the decision, I watched the sun begin to descend behind the hills surrounding the town.

In ancient times, Delphi was believed by the Greeks to be the center of the world. From the seventh century B.C. until the end of the fourth century A.D., Delphi and its oracle were held in high esteem by all nations.

> In a way that was unique and very nearly inexplicable to people of our times, the Delphic contribution to wartime and peacetime enterprises, to political and civil controversies, to intellectual and religious pursuits, was always highly relevant and decisive in the context of the Greek world.

It seemed appropriate, then, that the news regarding one of the most controversial free-speech cases in American history, a case involving "political and civil controversy," reached me by phone as I gazed out over the valley below Delphi.

After sleeping fitfully for several hours, I found myself standing in front of the hotel with a faxed copy of the decision, waiting for a ride to a television station in Athens so that I could be interviewed on the *Today* show back in the United States and Canada. It would be my opportunity to explain to viewers in a few short minutes what I believed the decision meant to the country.

The taxi driver hired by the *Today* production staff pulled up in front of the hotel and we were soon speeding over the mountain roads toward Athens. Since he spoke only Greek and German, in neither of which I was conversant, I was left to my thoughts.

Two years and a day had passed since a makeshift cross had been set afire half a world away. So much had happened in such a short time. The case had led from a small juvenile detention cell in St. Paul to the court chamber of the majestic marble-columned Supreme Court in Washington, D.C., and now, finally, to a television studio in Athens.

After a harrowing two-and-a-half-hour drive conducted in three stages by three different drivers of three different vehicles, I arrived at the studio, only to find I could not penetrate the tight security surrounding the building. Having finally convinced the authorities that I really did belong there, I was ushered into the production area. I found that my Greek hosts could not comprehend the significance of a burning cross but knew that they would have quickly responded in anger at the display of a Nazi swastika, a symbol against which their countrymen had fought fifty years earlier.

While the producer conducted a sound check, I sat in front of the camera and considered the image of a burning cross. A symbol indigenous to America, it was etched into the national consciousness not only as a sign of our failure to unite as a family composed of many races but also as proof that we remained the only nation on Earth dedicated to the preservation of the individual right of self-expression, even when it hurt. The First Amendment would continue to have meaning only so long as the courage of the American people did not waver in the face of fear and anger. This case had severely tested that commitment, as it weighed so heavily on those who had already suffered so much as targets of intolerance.

As the voice of the announcer back in New York came over the headset, I remembered back two short years ago, to a hot summer night in St. Paul. . . .

BEYOND THE BURNING CROSS

Cross-Burning Doesn't Happen Here

If you hate a person, you hate something in him that is part of yourself. What isn't part of ourselves doesn't disturb us.

—Hermann Hesse (1919)

Contrary to later perceptions, it did not happen overnight. The campaign to intimidate and threaten Russell and Laura Jones and their five children began shortly after they moved into their home at 290 Earl Street on the east side of St. Paul, Minnesota, in a neighborhood known locally as Dayton's Bluff. In April of 1990, several weeks after the Jones family had settled into the mostly white working-class neighborhood, the tires on their car were slashed and later a window on their station wagon was shattered.

No previous event, however, had prepared the family for the sight of a small burning cross on their front lawn in the early morning hours of June 21, 1990. Later Mr. Jones would make it very clear that he had felt bewildered and threatened by this latest act of overt intolerance. Like thousands of other families across the nation, the Joneses were working parents doing their best to ensure a better life for their children. There is no record of any transgressions by the Joneses in the months that they lived at 290 Earl Street before June 21, 1990. Their only apparent offenses were the color of their skin and their audacity in choosing to live in the neighborhood of their choice.

No one was observed at the scene by Mr. Jones. Several other small crosses were burned in the same neighborhood that night. The cross that Mr. Jones had seen in his front yard was crudely fashioned from two wooden chair legs and wrapped in terry cloth measuring approximately two feet by two feet. This seemingly innocuous piece of charred wood conveyed an ugly and powerful message. Its image was to be observed by millions in the two years ahead.

The local police investigated the case and within the next several days made two arrests. One was an eighteen-year-old whose name was Arthur M. Miller III, who lived at 291 Earl Street, across the street from the Joneses' residence. The other individual arrested was a seventeen-year-old whose initials were R.A.V. Since he was a juvenile at the time of the alleged incident, his initials were used in court hearings because of the confidentiality of juvenile proceedings under Minnesota law.

Although statistics can be deceiving, they can also be helpful in understanding the forces at work in a community. The numbers reflect that although the population of Minnesota is becoming more diverse, the change has been a slow process. The most recent data from the 1990 census indicate that 7.9 percent of all United States residents are foreign-born, while in the Midwest the average is less than 4 percent. The cities of St. Paul and Minneapolis have one of the lowest percentage of foreign-born residents among major metropolitan areas. The same census shows that the population of the state of Minnesota is approximately 94 percent white, 2 percent black, 1.5 percent Asian, and 1 percent Native American. Twenty-nine counties in Minnesota have fewer than a dozen black Americans residing within their boundaries. Yet more than 50 percent of the population growth the last ten years in greater Minnesota consisted of African American, Native American, Asian, and Hispanic people.

Among the twenty-five largest metropolitan areas in the country, the Twin Cities area, the sixteenth largest, had the highest proportion of white residents in 1990, some 92 percent. Over recent years, St. Paul had fallen upon tough economic times as businesses left the city and the tax base fell. Competition for jobs became intense as families were dislocated and neighborhoods underwent change. Perhaps it should not have been surprising that evidence of intolerance among metropolitan residents would begin to surface, mirroring the experience of other major urban areas.

The Dayton's Bluff area on the east side of St. Paul, where the Jones family had taken up residence, was described in this fashion by a local newspaper:

> This is one of St. Paul's older neighborhoods, with a large stock of 19th century worker housing mixed in with a few old mansions. Like other neighborhoods around the downtown core, Dayton's Bluff has experienced an increase in minority population, a sharp rise in the percent of families headed by a single parent and a decrease in the amount of owner-occupied housing.

From 1980 to 1990 this neighborhood of approximately twelve thousand residents had witnessed an 11 percent drop in the white population with a 3 percent increase in black residents, a 7 percent increase in Asian residents, and a 1 percent increase in Native Americans.

A different type of integration had occurred in Minneapolis and St. Paul decades earlier. At that time the assimilation of diverse ethnic and religious groups had also resulted in unrest:

> The experience of other midwestern cities with the Ku Klux Klan varied considerably. In Minneapolis, where North Star Klan No. 2 began operations in August, 1921, the Invisible Empire never made much headway. . . . Negroes were rarely seen . . . but Catholics, particularly in neighboring St. Paul, were the object of growing concern.

The state of Minnesota generally and the city of St. Paul specifically are anomalous in that although the area has a liberal and progressive political tradition, this tradition has developed in the absence of some of the social forces that have torn apart other urban areas and states. The land of Humphrey and Mondale has always had an under-privileged Native American population; the black and Asian popula-tion had increased significantly only in the last two decades. Historically, Minnesota had not escaped earlier manifestations of intolerance, as shown by the activities of the KKK in Minneapolis in 1921. Seventy years ago the targets were the Irish and German Catho-lics of St. Paul. In the ensuing years, visible and bold acts of hate were unusual but did occur in the Twin Cities. However, it was the image of a burning cross that left a uniquely searing impression in the minds of most Americans, particularly black Americans, and to those famil-iar with the dark passages of American history.

As I read the morning paper on June 22, 1990, I reacted as I am sure a majority of St. Paul residents did: I was upset, angry, and embar-rassed for the city I had grown up in. Born thirty-seven years earlier, I had come of age in a different neighborhood of St. Paul, Highland Park. All four of my grandparents were Irish, making me a "four-corner Irishman," in the words of the late federal judge Edward J. Devitt. My parents were staunch Democrats, and I remember with fondness their pride in the election of John F. Kennedy to the presi-dency of the United States. Like Kennedy, my father had been well educated, had returned from the South Pacific campaign in World War II as a decorated naval officer, was Irish Catholic and proud of it, and was a man who had married late and fathered several children. Before World War II he had received his law degree in the midst of the worst economic depression our nation has ever seen. He had begun his career as a criminal defense attorney and then had become a career prosecutor.

When I was a child my father took me everywhere. The Ramsey County Attorney's Office, of which he was then a member, had a fascinating ethnic and religious mix long before diversity of personnel became mandated. There were Protestants, Catholics, Jews, men and women, white and black, young and old. All of them were counted among my father's friends. One in particular who had become a close friend was a young black man by the name of Stephen Maxwell. In 1961, the first year that the Minnesota Vikings played football in Minnesota, my father and Steve Maxwell bought season tickets together, and I remember the easy camaraderie they displayed as I sat at the games at the age of eight. It was clear they liked and respected each other and had a special friendship.

Several years later, I can remember my parents going with the Maxwells to a "fair housing" meeting at the local Catholic church. The reason I remember this meeting so well is that I didn't understand what "fair housing" meant. My father took the time to explain to me that for minorities it was not simply a matter of affordability when it came time to choose a neighborhood in which to live, there was also the problem of discrimination, which took place both overtly and covertly. He felt strongly that it was necessary for those concerned to organize to try to bring this practice to a stop.

Like many ten-year-old white boys of that era, I recognized that Americans were of diverse ethnic and religious origins. Most of my neighbors were Jewish or Catholic; Highland Park had the highest Jewish population in the city. I hadn't considered the fact that my neighborhood was not racially integrated at that time. I had not grown up around black children, but simply hadn't spent much time considering the reasons.

Perhaps my first enlightening experience was as an altar boy at the local Catholic church. Helping at the church was a visiting priest from an African country who was young and kind and who spoke only broken English. In those days, an altar boy during Communion was assigned to one of two priests. I was assigned to the visiting priest. As we walked down to one section of the church I noticed that the great majority of parishioners were in the other line. The line for this priest was much shorter, and it included my parents. After the young priest had given Communion to the people who had waited, we moved closer to assist the priest who was still giving Communion. Soon it became clear that many in line for the white priest were not going to move to receive the Host from the visiting priest. In my naïveté I didn't understand what was happening. It was only after the Mass was over and we returned home that my parents, to their everlasting credit, confronted the incident. They explained to me that racism was endemic to our society, that it was generally the uneducated and the insecure who acted in a racist fashion, and that I should not hold the actions of some against the Church.

After attending law school at the University of Minnesota in Minneapolis, I decided to return to St. Paul. Initially I practiced law with an attorney who later became the chief judge of the Minnesota Court of Appeals; later I began my own practice and the defense of indigent clients through the Ramsey County Public Defender's Office. The attorneys associated with this office are appointed to defend indigent clients. They do not choose their clients, but represent whomever the court appoints, whether juvenile or adult, charged with a misdemeanor or a felony. Defending indigents charged with crimes is often a thankless job. The hours are long, the pay is low, and the public generally views a defense lawyer as an evil necessity. Still, the quality of representation, while uneven, has improved dramatically over the years. In many areas, public defenders are among the best criminal lawyers available.

Six weeks before the Jones family found a cross burning in their front yard, a fellow public defender, Michael Cromett, and I had defended a black man charged with murdering his brother. On May 9, 1990, we had obtained an acquittal for our client. Several years before that, in late 1987, Michael and I had defended another black man who had been charged with shooting and killing a young white woman. The trial took almost a month and the community tension resulted in heavy security in the courthouse. One enduring memory of this case is that all the white observers in the courtroom sat on one side of the courtroom while all the black Americans sat on the other. During this relatively high-profile trial, several people had made some disturbing racist remarks to me about our defending such a client. Several members of the black community, however, were supportive and approved our efforts. Ultimately, after four days of jury deliberation, our client was convicted. One courtroom observer later accepted a leadership position with the local chapter of the NAACP, and led local opposition to our defense of R.A.V. four years later.

Such were the circumstances surrounding the morning of June 25, 1990. On that day I was assigned the representation of all indigent juveniles appearing in court in St. Paul. Between 8:30 A.M. and 11:30 A.M. I had handled some fifteen to twenty new files with the help of a law clerk. At approximately 11:30 the court administrator handed me a new petition. The petition charged one R.A.V., a seventeen-year-old, with "bias" assault under state and city laws. It was clear that the charges arose from the cross-burning incident, and I was not pleased to receive it at the end of a long morning. Upon reviewing the bias-motivated assault charged under the city ordinance, I did not like the language of the ordinance. Indeed, I had never seen the law invoked previously. I requested and received a twenty-four-hour continuance to review the law.

I immediately called Michael Cromett from the courthouse. He had previously been my co-counsel, was a close friend, and was more conversant with the state's appellate structure than I was. I told him that I did not like the wording of the law and that the prosecutor was considering amending the charge to another city ordinance involving "bias" disorderly conduct, a law I found even more appalling. Michael agreed with me, and I decided to challenge the city bias assault law, or, if the city chose to substitute, the city bias disorderly-conduct law. Within days, the Ramsey County Attorney's Office decided to substitute the city bias disorderly-conduct law, St. Paul City Ordinance section 292.02, for the city bias assault law. A petition was filed on July 5, 1990, charging R.A.V. with violation of section 292.02. (In the years since this hearing, many observers have wondered why the prosecutor chose to charge R.A.V. under this ordinance. The answer is simple: although the law had never been used before, it did specifically prohibit burning crosses. No one at this point saw this as a "test" case. The prosecutor simply wanted a charge she felt she could easily prove.)

Robert Anthony Viktora was seventeen when we first met. From the beginning, he was a cooperative client. Short in stature, with tattoos on each arm, he would sometimes grow his hair out and sometimes shave it back, although he denied that he was a skinhead. A high school dropout despite displaying obvious intelligence, he often wore combat boots, a T-shirt, and a leather jacket at our meetings. He was often sullen in disposition, and I couldn't help feeling that his anger at the world stemmed from a need to belong, in this case with the wrong people. The secretaries at our law office were never very happy to see him, partially because of the cross-burning allegations and also because of his apparent indifference and hostile attitude. The receptionist was often forced to share a room with one of his companions while I conferred with my client; the visitors mirrored the "rebel without a clue" aura surrounding those alleged to have participated in the cross-burning incident.

R.A.V. consistently denied that he believes people should burn crosses on other people's property and has denied any involvement in the events of June 21, 1990. While embracing the idea that increasing crime rates were at least partially attributable to minorities moving into his neighborhood, he later told a reporter that he had "written to and visited white power groups such as the White Aryan Resistance, the White Christian Patriots League and the National Socialists." Over the two-year period we remained in contact, he and I met at my office on seven or eight occasions and stayed in touch by telephone the remainder of the time. As the case progressed he took a keen interest in the ensuing constitutional debate and asked for and received copies of the briefs while appearing to understand the main issues involved. As his identity became known he appeared to enjoy his celebrity status; presumably it raised his standing among his peers. While we were able to convince him generally that talking to the media was not a good idea while charges were still pending, he nevertheless talked to members of the press after the decision and made comments that were not calculated to win any sympathy from members of the public. He never attempted to impose his views on me, and I made my views clear to him. However, he was my client. If I were to be unaffected by the ethnic, religious, or gender identity of my clients, I had a duty to defend political beliefs far from my own.

In the months ahead, I met both his mother and his father on separate occasions. The family continued to live in the same neighborhood as the Joneses after the cross-burning. During those two years of waiting, I often worried that a new incident would occur because another of the defendants lived across the street from the Jones family while the Viktora family was nearby. The media would have pounced on any new development and further adverse publicity was a daunting prospect. It never happened. Instead, Viktora worked hard doing manual labor, stayed out of trouble, and continued to meet with me periodically to be kept abreast of any progress with the case.

There was no question that his parents and sister suffered as a result of this case and the appeal. The day of the initial hearing in juvenile court, a local television crew filmed a news segment using the Viktora house as a backdrop, an apparent violation of juvenile confidentiality rules. Soon the family had to change its phone number. Throughout those two years the mother and father of Robert Viktora were always courteous with me in our dealings and strongly supportive of my efforts. Despite the fact that their lives would have been much smoother without the negative publicity, neither of them ever attempted to interfere with me. When it was over and the threats began, Mr. Viktora was one of the first to congratulate me, quoting from "The Impossible Dream" and telling me that I had "marched into hell for a heavenly cause."

All of that was in the future as I sat down and studied St. Paul City Ordinance section 292.02, which reads as follows:

> Whoever places on public or private property a symbol, object, appellation, characterization, or graffiti, including, but not limited to, a burning cross or Nazi swastika, which one knows or has reasonable grounds to know arouses anger, alarm or resentment in others on the basis of race, color, creed, religion, or gender commits disorderly conduct and shall be guilty of a misdemeanor.

Upon first review, my main objection to the ordinance was the sweeping breadth of a law that clearly attempted to censor expression that others found objectionable, effectively mandating the "proper" political viewpoint for the community of St. Paul. The *conduct* of threatening someone, whether with a gun, a knife, or a burning cross, can be prosecuted under more severe laws, such as felony terroristic threats. Had the county attorney's office charged R.A.V. with illegal *conduct* under a provision from the criminal code, the constitutionality of the law would not have been challenged. Instead, it chose to prosecute using a law that punished the *expression,* or viewpoint, itself, including expression that was neither threatening nor terrorizing but simply upsetting.

Unfortunately, the history of intolerance in our country is such that many Americans, particularly those without constitutional-law training, have difficulty thinking beyond an alleged factual situation to an examination of the horrendous laws often used to punish such offensive expression. Overt acts of hatred and prejudice seem to touch a nerve among most Americans, even though many individuals conceal bigoted viewpoints.

As David H. Bennett demonstrates in *The Party of Fear,* the United States has had a long and sordid history of intolerance over the past two centuries. Generation after generation of Americans has grappled with the continuing tensions present in a pluralistic and multicultural society. Previous generations have acted as though they lived in a nation under siege by what Bennett refers to as "alien intruders in the promised land." Whether it is a young white separatist on the east side of St. Paul in 1990, or a member of the Know-Nothing party a century and a half earlier pledging to work for "the removal of aliens and Catholics from all positions of authority and to deny them jobs and profits in private business or public office," the source of the nativist rhetoric is the same: economic insecurity, lack of education, and the pathetic need to demonstrate who "real" Americans are. Interestingly, according to the latest census involving major metropolitan areas, the residents of the Twin Cities area are the second least likely to "identify their ancestry as American." Those who reside in metropolitan areas in the South are the most likely to identify their ethnic heritage as "plain American." While we are all Americans, awareness of ethnic origins can offer a sense of identity. Yet overemphasis of group affiliations may lead to intolerance of others. We must hope that such knowledge may also serve as a reminder of the cost of bigotry.

Wanting to start a new life as an American, my great-grandfather emigrated to the United States from Ireland at the age of twenty-seven. The year was 1845. Since the Irish alone constituted "one-third of American immigration in the 1830s," many of his countrymen had already arrived. Yet the great boom in Irish immigration was to take place several years later, and from 1847 to 1854 almost three million new immigrants arrived in the United States, most of them German or Irish Catholics. Jeremiah O'Keefe, my great-grandfather, had left Ireland just before the potato famine devastated the largely rural population. However, once the native Irish arrived, "less than ten percent resettled on the land," even though 80 percent of the Irish immigrants came from rural backgrounds. He was one of the lucky and hardworking 10 percent who escaped the urban ghettos so prevalent in the major Eastern cities at that time.

Arriving in 1845, he walked right into the anti-alien upheaval of that year, capped by the founding of the Know-Nothing party, which was based on secrecy and intolerance. America found itself in an era of intolerance, a time of blind hatred, an age of nativist sentiments. Jeremiah O'Keefe's solution was to move to Minnesota, to work hard, to raise a family, and to try to assimilate as best he could. On March 17 (Saint Patrick's Day), 1860, shortly before the outbreak of the Civil War, he took possession of a farm that remains in my family to this day.

At the time O'Keefe was realizing his dream of owning his own land, nativism was contributing to the rending of the nation. As Bennett notes, the South was "the land of the native-born" and "had been insulated from the great European migrations" of the late 1840s and early 1850s. Consequently, the majority of the Southern states had fewer than 2 percent foreign-born residents, while the Eastern and Midwestern states had anywhere from 19 percent to 35 percent foreign-born population. In 1860 Minnesota was at the high end of this demarcation, with over a third of its population foreign-born. It is arguable that the War Between the States initially concealed an underlying conflict in which the foreign-born in the North fought to demonstrate their loyalty to their new country, while the Southern native-born felt that they were the true Americans and deserved to live independently. Once again, the coveted label of "true American" was at issue. For his part, Jeremiah O'Keefe survived the Know-Nothing anti-Catholic movement, which had ceased to be a viable political force after 1856. Ironically, the intolerant members of the nativist movement were split apart by the issue of slavery.

O'Keefe's brother-in-law, my great-great-uncle Daniel Patrick Ryan, enlisted as a volunteer for the Union army, and at the age of eighteen on May 31, 1861, was assigned to Company H of the First Minnesota Volunteers. On the late afternoon of July 2, 1863, he was one of the 262 members of the First Minnesota who were guarding an artillery piece less than one mile from Gettysburg, the site of perhaps the greatest conflict in American military history. As a member of a military unit soon to become legendary, he was assigned an impossible task at a pivotal point in "the largest battle ever fought on the North American continent," an engagement that turned the tide of the Civil War. The defense of the American flag by the First Minnesota stands out in the annals of military folklore, leading the commanding general to later conclude "there is no more gallant deed recorded in history."

> Winfield Scott Hancock . . . ordered a single, small regiment, the 1st Minnesota, to countercharge. . . . "Every man realized in an instant what the order meant," a survivor wrote, "death or wounds to us all, the sacrifice of the regiment to gain a few minutes' time and save the position."
>
> The tiny Minnesota force—just 262 men—raced down the slope at the oncoming 1,600 confederates with fixed bayonets. The astonished Southerners fell back and the gap in the Union line closed but only 47 of the Minnesotans survived unhurt—82 percent of them fell in less than five minutes, the highest percentage of casualties taken by any Union regiment in the war.

Surviving the battle, Ryan was mustered out of the Union army on May 5, 1864, and served as a Minnesota state legislator from 1875 to 1876 before his death at the age of forty-one in 1884. The sacrifices of Catholics like Ryan and of other immigrants silenced the nativist anger prevalent in the country at that time. Those who had voiced strong opposition to the incoming foreign-born population had done so in a misguided attempt to find stability and community in a time of social upheaval. "When it was over, the older anti-Catholic, anti-immigrant impulse was arrested; too many Catholic boys and immigrant sons had fought and died for the cause of union; the ethnic and religious hostilities of the past were tempered by the war fires of recent memory." Yet while the War Between the States helped the assimilation of Catholics and other immigrants, it merely loosened the chains of those who had been held in slavery.

While thousands had perished in the Civil War, thousands of others like Dan Ryan returned to their homes and farms. Jeremiah O'Keefe began to raise his family of eight children, and in 1874 he named his youngest son, my great-uncle Patrick Henry O'Keefe, after a famous American patriot. Consistently over the decades, minority groups have continued this patriotic tradition, perhaps in the effort to reach "true American" status.

Although Patrick Henry's attitude toward Catholics might have been less than tolerant, he was a great believer in individual liberty. Apparently fearless and known for his temper, Henry clearly distrusted monolithic government, whether British or American. An anti-Federalist, he fought bitterly against the Federalists, particularly James Madison, the chief architect of the Constitution. Consequently he opposed the ratification of the Constitution for fear that the colonists were replacing a monarchy with a dangerously centralized form of government. Wary of the potential for a tyrannical majority, Henry placed liberty above all other virtues stemming from self-government:

> You are not to inquire how your trade may be increased, nor how you are to become a great and powerful people, but how your liberties can be secured; for liberty ought to be the direct end of your Government. . . . Liberty the greatest of all earthly blessings— give us that precious jewel, and you may take everything else. . . . Guard with jealous attention the public liberty. Suspect every one who approaches that jewel.

Henry helped contribute to the early adoption of the Bill of Rights and ensured his place in history with the statement "Give me liberty or give me death!" in a speech delivered years earlier at Virginia's Revolutionary Convention. His "extremist" position on the issue of individual freedom balanced the opinions of those who tended to ignore the dangers inherent in centralized power. Madison recognized this danger in Federalist Paper No. 51 when he stated: "You must first enable the government to control the governed; and in the next place, oblige it to control itself."

Sometimes "obliging" the government "to control itself" is easier said than done. Although repressive laws often arise when our nation is threatened by outside forces, the easing of such foreign tensions does not necessarily translate into more tolerant behavior or more insightful leadership. In our own time we have seen the reduction of external threats occur simultaneously with increased acts of intolerance and fear in the United States.

In response to this perceived increase in intolerant behavior, the St. Paul City Council adopted several ordinances on March 9, 1982, aimed at "offenses directed to religious beliefs and racial origins." The first of these ordinances was the original charge filed in *R.A.V.*, section 292.01, and the second of these ordinances, section 292.02, was the amended charge, which we challenged.

In introducing the proposed ordinance on February 18, 1982, Councilman Leonard Levine read a statement describing "episodes of vandalism" that had occurred in the previous twelve months against a number of groups, including Asians, Jews, Koreans, Native Americans, blacks, and Hispanics. He stated that he had been assured by the city attorney that the ordinance was a "constitutionally sound" approach to this "growing problem." Other council members congratulated Councilman Levine; one said it took "courage to propose this legislation" and that he hoped it would be "enforceable." No mention was made of the criminal-code provisions that would have addressed vandalism or threats.

At the second reading of the ordinance on February 25, 1982, Councilman Levine responded to local newspaper criticism of the ordinance by suggesting that the writer had failed to contact anyone "knowledgeable about the specific law." In describing the city attorney's position on the law, one council member quoted the city attorney as saying that it was "defensable" [sic]. In less than one week, perceptions of the proposed ordinance had changed from a "constitutionally sound approach to the problem" to "defensable." Bill Wilson, a black councilman, indicated that he felt it was an excellent ordinance and that some state legislators had shown an interest in pursuing a similar law on a statewide basis.

At the third reading of section 292.02 on March 2, 1982, Councilman Levine once again stated his belief that the attorneys had drawn a "constitutionally sound ordinance." In response to a question from the audience, the city attorney said he believed that the ordinance did not apply to any verbal remarks.

Finally, on March 9, 1982, the city council unanimously adopted section 292.02, among other ordinances. Those present in support of the proposed ordinance included blacks, Jews, gays, and Native Americans. Councilman Bill Wilson reiterated his support, saying that St. Paul would be a "better place because of what is going to be done today," while Councilman Levine once again assured the crowd that the city attorney's office had drafted the law, and after "careful review" had indicated to the council that the area was "not covered under existing criminal law."

Later, after the United States Supreme Court had heard arguments on the ordinance, former councilman Levine and then current city council president Wilson indicated that they were "both surprised and pleased to see their work in the forefront of a national movement. Both say free speech is not put at risk by the ordinance." Levine, who is Jewish, indicated in retrospect that he had not had any personal experience of prejudice but had proposed the law because of the hate crimes he saw occurring in the city at that time. City council president Wilson had grown up in Indiana at a time when the Ku Klux Klan had been active there. He cited his participation in sit-ins and other civil rights protests in the early 1960s. He did not mention the importance of the First Amendment to the civil rights movement at that time. Further, before the Court's decision, he indicated that if the ordinance was upheld, he would "take it before the National League of Cities and seek to have it affirmed as a model ordinance recommended for all cities."

There is no record of St. Paul City Ordinance section 292.02 having been enforced against a citizen from its adoption on March 9, 1982, through April 3, 1990, when a councilwoman, an attorney, inquired about a further amendment to add the language of "gender" to protected subjects. The city attorney raised no objection, and on April 19, 1990, the ordinance was unanimously amended to include "gender."

The groups that had lobbied the St. Paul City Council in 1982 for passage of this ordinance, including Asian, black, Hispanic, Jewish, gay, and Native Americans, were clearly correct in suggesting that they had not been treated equally by society. However, their collective solution to continued inequality was to repeat the mistakes of history. A look back at the American experience demonstrates not only the changing identity of the victims of discrimination but the passage of repressive laws in response to widespread fear. By the late nineteenth century, the primary targets were Italian immigrants, Eastern European Jews, and Asian Americans. The last were particularly targeted on the West Coast, where they were seen as a threat to the American labor movement. The anger was so widespread that both the Democratic and Republican parties became hostile to "cheap Chinese labor," and supported the Chinese Exclusion Act of 1882, which suspended immigration from China for ten years. By the turn of the century the United States was hardly the melting pot so many believed it to be. While America looked abroad toward its enemies as World War I approached, a new wave of nativist sentiment arose, this time against German Americans. A terrified and angry nation passed the Espionage Act in June 1917, outlawing speech that obstructed the war effort or aided the enemy. A year later Congress passed the Sedition Act, which further mandated that disloyal speech or statements generally critical of the American form of government could be punished by up to twenty years' incarceration.

During this same period, another of my ancestors confronted the issues of ethnic intolerance and freedom of expression. On February 10, 1919, my great-uncle Patrick Henry O'Keefe found himself embroiled in an election contest. O'Keefe had been elected to the position of county attorney in Dakota County, an area immediately southeast of the Twin City metropolitan area. In the election of 1918, while World War I continued to bleed a generation of its youth, O'Keefe was opposed by A. E. Rietz. Rietz was of German heritage, and although there were many German Americans in the county, it was a difficult time for him to run for elective office. His brother, Edwin Rietz, had been indicted less than a year after passage of the Espionage Act on May 8, 1918. He was tried in Aberdeen, South Dakota, on May 9 and 10, 1918, and was convicted and sentenced to five years in the United States Penitentiary at Fort Leavenworth, Kansas. A. E. Rietz, who ran in the election for county attorney held in the fall of 1918, attended the trial in support of his brother. No record remains of what Edwin Rietz's transgressions were under the act, but speech that obstructed the war effort or aided the enemy was prohibited, and since Rietz was charged in a time of war hysteria, it would appear that statements remotely critical of the government resulted in a conviction.

As Anthony Lewis has pointed out, "hundreds of people were prosecuted under the act for merely speaking or writing in negative terms. The most innocuous criticism of government policy or discussions of pacifism were found to be violations of the Espionage Act. Judges told juries to convict if they found a defendant's words had been 'disloyal.' It was the Sedition Act (of 1798) reborn." Laws of this kind soon led to a reaffirmation of First Amendment principles, found in the opinions of Judge Learned Hand, Justice Oliver Wendell Holmes, Jr., and Justice Louis Brandeis.

The rebirth of freedom of expression was yet to come when the Honorable W. W. Bardwell sat in judgment of this bitter election contest in Hastings, Minnesota, in February 1919. A. E. Rietz challenged the election in part on the basis that defamatory statements had been made against him. The dispute was more ironic when one considers that each party to the lawsuit was a member of a group that had been the target of intolerance during much of the nineteenth century. As the Irish American witnesses testified against the German Americans, issues of loyalty, disloyalty, and offensive ethnic speech constantly reappeared.

A. (O'Keefe): Now, the inference was there . . . that I was one of the politicians for county office that branded the opposing candidate as a "Pro-Hun," which was absolutely a falsehood. I never used that term about Mr. Rietz in my life.

Q. (Rietz attorney): Never called him a Hun, without the "pro"?

A. (O'Keefe): No, nothing of that kind.

Q. (Rietz attorney): Had you never said that any supporters of Mr. Rietz were Huns or Pro-Huns?

A. (O'Keefe): I don't think I have.

Q. Have you never used that phrase?

A. Oh, I have used it in talking.

Q. Didn't you use it today when these witnesses of German descent were being called up; didn't you say "More Huns"?

A. (O'Keefe attorney): Objected to as not proper cross-examination.

The Court: Objection sustained.

On direct examination, A. E. Rietz's attorney attempted to establish the loyalty of his client to the court's satisfaction. It is disturbing to read such a transcript; the interrogation is a precursor of the loyalty oaths required thirty years later.

Q. (Rietz attorney): I will ask you whether you have stated at any time during the time we have been at war, the United States at war with Germany, anything reflecting upon the Government of the United States or in any way hostile to the interests of the United States?

A. (Rietz): I have not.

Q. (Rietz attorney): I will ask you whether or not at any time, during the time we have been at war, or since, you have done anything injurious to the cause of the United States?

A. (Rietz): I have not.

Q. (Rietz attorney): I will ask you whether or not you did anything in the way of talking in behalf of the cause of the United States during the war?

A. (Rietz): Yes; I made several speeches.

Q. (Rietz attorney): With reference to what?

A. (Rietz): About the war; called upon the people to sustain the country in the war against Germany.

Q. (Rietz attorney): I will ask you whether you ever said anything to the contrary?

A. (Rietz): Absolutely nothing.

The petition for a new election was denied. Six months later the United States Supreme Court decided a case involving the same Espionage Act that had resulted in the incarceration of Edwin Rietz. In *Abrams v. United States,* Justice Oliver Wendell Holmes, Jr., dissenting, joined by Justice Louis D. Brandeis, questioned the prosecution of four Russian refugees who had distributed leaflets urging a general protest strike against Allied intervention in Russia. Holmes, commenting on the theory of the United States Constitution, stated:

It is an experiment, as all life is an experiment. Every year if not every day we have to wager our salvation upon some prophecy based upon imperfect knowledge. While that experiment is part of our system I think that we should be eternally vigilant against attempts to check the expression of opinions that we loathe and believe to be fraught with death, unless they so imminently threaten immediate interference with the lawful and pressing purposes of the law that an immediate check is required to save the country.

Abrams and the other refugees lost their case but they had planted the seed that would later result in the rebirth of the First Amendment.

A hearing date of July 13, 1990, in St. Paul was set by the court for the parties to argue the constitutionality of St. Paul City Ordinance section 292.02. The eloquence of Justice Oliver Wendell Holmes, Jr., would be put to the test once again.

2

"The Pervasive Threat Inherent in Its Very Existence"

To make a government requires no great prudence; settle the seat of power, teach obedience and the work is done. To give freedom is still more easy. It is not necessary to guide; it only requires to let go the rein. But to form a free government, that is, to temper the opposite elements of liberty and restraint in one conscious work, requires much thought; deep reflection; a sagacious, powerful and combining mind.

—Edmund Burke

The Brown Wood Preserving Company of Tuscaloosa County, Alabama, maintained a quintessential "company town" in the rural South of the late 1930s. There is no record of what finally led to the breakdown between the local union and the company, but a strike order was issued and a number of employees joined a picket line that was maintained around the plant twenty-four hours a day.

One of these employees, Byron Thornhill, approached Clarence Simpson, a nonunion member reporting for work during the strike—in common parlance, a "scab." By all accounts, Thornhill was courteous and acted in a nonthreatening manner in asking Simpson not to work for the company during the strike.

Nevertheless, the company frowned upon such behavior and Thornhill was charged under section 3448 of the Alabama State Code of 1923. The statute prohibited virtually all picketing and charged Thornhill with picketing the company "for the purpose of hindering, delaying or interfering with or injuring [its] lawful business." Thornhill was convicted in the inferior court of Tuscaloosa County despite his complaint that such a law was repugnant to the Constitution of the United States. He appealed to the circuit court and was convicted there as well. The circuit court sentenced Thornhill to imprisonment for seventy-three days and default payment of a fine of one hundred dollars and costs. He did not offer any evidence at the circuit court level, and later his judgment was affirmed by the court of appeals in Alabama and a petition for certiorari was denied by the supreme court of the state. The United States Supreme Court agreed to hear the case and issued its decision on April 22, 1940.

With only Justice James McReynolds dissenting, Justice Frank Murphy wrote for the Court and began the opinion with the inspiring words used by Justice Louis Brandeis in a decision issued thirteen years earlier: "Those who won our independence had confidence in the power of free and fearless reasoning and communication of ideas to discover and spread political and economic truth." The Court went on to support a "facial" challenge by Thornhill disregarding the state's position that Thornhill could not complain of the deprivation of any rights but his own. In decisive fashion, the majority laid out the parameters of what has come to be known as the "overbreadth doctrine":

> It is not merely the sporadic abuse of power by the censor, but the pervasive threat inherent in its very existence that constitutes the danger to freedom of discussion. . . . The existence of such a statute, which readily lends itself to harsh and discriminatory enforcement by local prosecuting officials, against particular groups deemed to merit their displeasure, results in a continuous and pervasive restraint on all freedom of discussion that might reasonably be regarded as within its purview.

The Court concluded that peaceful picketing, which the law addressed, was speech within the context of the First Amendment. However, perhaps because Thornhill had not offered any evidence in his defense and since the prosecution, in charging the defendant, had used the actual language of the law itself, the Court turned to a "facial review" of the law, that is, a review of the law itself as it could be applied to anyone, without regard to the facts alleged in Thornhill's case. The Court recognized the "standing" or right of Thornhill and people like him to challenge laws that would affect others not before the Court, regardless of whether or not Thornhill's conduct might have been charged under another law. The theory of the doctrine was that such a law would deter free expression by virtue of its very existence. As Justice Thurgood Marshall once described it, such an overbroad law "hangs over [citizens'] heads like a sword of Damocles."

The overbreadth doctrine is widely misunderstood by the public as a "technical" defense or a lawyer's trick of some sort. The idea that someone could commit a crime and then "get away with it" because he was charged under an unconstitutional law is infuriating to many people. The case of R.A.V. is an example. It was alleged that with others he had entered someone else's property and burned a cross. Clearly, such *conduct* is not protected. R.A.V. could have been charged in state court with open-burning violations, trespass, or arson. None of those charges, of course, addressed the message of the burning cross. Few would argue with the proposition that a burning cross, when placed on the lawn of a black family, is more threatening than burning leaves. An obvious additional charge in this case would have been terroristic threats.

It is conceivable that laws punishing criminal conduct in a neutral manner, clearly constitutional "on their face," could be unconstitutional "as applied" to a specific defendant. A person may display a swastika, burn a cross, or burn an American flag, provided that the expression is not intentionally targeted at any individual, is not in violation of other provisions (e.g., trespass), and as long as all necessary permits have been obtained to comply with local regulations of time, place, and manner. A terroristic-threat law used to charge an individual under those circumstances might be constitutional on its face, yet may be unconstitutional as applied unless the expression constitutes a direct and immediate threat.

There is also the group of laws the embodiment of which is St. Paul City Ordinance section 292.02. They are unconstitutional on their face. Such laws, like the one in *Thornhill,* cannot be enforced against *anyone* unless and until the law is either rewritten by lawmakers or successfully narrowed by judicial action. Even when suspected of threatening others, R.A.V., like any other citizen, has a right to be charged under a constitutional law. When a court is faced with a law that is applicable to all types of controversial expression, it must consider (a) how much judicially recognized free expression is threatened by the law and (b) whether that expression is extensive enough to make it dangerous or impossible for the court to attempt to "narrow" the language of the law. For the moment, the alleged facts are irrelevant. In such a situation, the issue is *not* whether or not the defendant engaged in illegal conduct or whether it is likely that the local prosecutor would use the challenged law against protected expression, or even whether or not such prosecutions would be successful. The "very existence" of such a law is considered so dangerous in a free society that for over fifty years the Supreme Court has used the

First Amendment overbreadth doctrine to ensure that federal, state, and local governments do not infringe on the right of individual expression.

It is unwise for a community to attempt to enforce a political standard by passing a law that clearly infringes on the average person's right to express himself while applying it only in the most offensive factual situations. An average citizen may not feel threatened by a prosecution such as that in *R.A.V.*, but history demonstrates the danger in allowing communities, states, or countries to gradually establish a standard of political orthodoxy. Many of the founding members of our republic escaped nations that sought to impose on them religious and nationalistic beliefs. For this reason, among others, they enacted our cherished Bill of Rights.

Over the decades, the Court's dedication to the overbreadth doctrine has waned. In *Broadrick v. Oklahoma,* the Court reiterated that simply because a law can be applied to protected expression does not make the law itself unconstitutional. The test was changed to one of a requirement of "substantial overbreadth," meaning simply that if the law's legitimate applications outweigh impermissible uses of the law, it survives a facial challenge. The *Broadrick* majority seemed to justify a move away from true overbreadth analysis with the simple addition of the word "substantial." The Court treated the Oklahoma statute aimed at the political activities of civil service employees as any other law, purposely ignoring the danger inherent in government regulating political expression as opposed to conduct (i.e., trespass). By 1984, in *Brockett v. Spokane Arcades, Inc.,* the Court made it clear that anyone challenging the law on the basis of overbreadth would have to show "substantial" overbreadth whether or not his expressions constituted "speech" or "conduct." This then was the overbreadth standard at the time R.A.V. brought his challenge:

> An individual whose own speech or expressive conduct may validly be prohibited or sanctioned is permitted to challenge a statute on its face because it also threatens others not before the court. . . . If the overbreadth is "substantial," the law may not be enforced against anyone, including the party before the court, until it is narrowed to reach only unprotected activity. . . .

The core of the First Amendment overbreadth doctrine is twofold. First, the individual charged, as a citizen of the United States, has a personal right to be charged under a constitutionally valid law, regardless of the facts alleged. Secondly, the remaining members of the

American public also become a party to the challenge, since an over-broad law threatens their individual right of free expression under the First Amendment whether or not such a threat appears remote at the time. This is the "chilling effect" that is mentioned so often in the context of the First Amendment. It is properly evocative terminology, since laws that violate the First Amendment lead to a loss of personal liberty that could make the future "chilling" indeed.

These were among my thoughts prior to the hearing of July 13, 1990. Yet my objection to section 292.02 was not limited to its sweeping breadth. I recognized immediately that the ordinance was "the mother of all hate-speech laws," as later articulated by Nat Hentoff. Such a law could be applied to many types of expression far less objectionable than the burning of a cross in an innocent black family's front yard.

Freedom of speech embodies much more than just the right of American citizens to express themselves. It is countermajoritarian in nature. It was conceived by the Framers to protect the individual against the majority. As John Stuart Mill explained years later, "If all mankind minus one, were of one opinion, and only one person were of the contrary opinion, mankind would be no more justified in silencing that one person, than he, if he had the power, would be justified in silencing mankind."

The two hundredth anniversary of the Bill of Rights in 1991 re-minded all Americans of their precious birthright. Each citizen is granted the right at birth to be an individual, to think for himself and to live his life as he chooses. Few would disagree with that observation. Yet many Americans seem unaware that the frontiers of liberty are often delineated by society's outcasts. Part of the constitutional birthright in America is the right to dissent. It is how we respond to situations such as that in *R.A.V. v. St. Paul* which define us as a society. The words of Justice Felix Frankfurter written forty years ago ring true today: "It is a fair summary of history to say that the safeguards of liberty have frequently been forged in controversies involving not very nice people."

The First Amendment right of free expression has often involved the display of offensive symbols or symbolic speech. A decade after Justice Oliver Wendell Holmes, Jr., and Justice Louis Brandeis as-sisted in the rebirth of the First Amendment, the United States Su-preme Court granted review on such a case, *Stromberg v. California*.

Nineteen-year-old Yetta Stromberg was a member of the Young Communist League in 1930. She taught young teenagers that summer at a camp in southern California. The evidence showed that she owned a number of books described as "radical communist propaganda," but there was no evidence at her trial that she ever taught a child violence, anarchism, or sedition. She was charged with the supervision of the raising of a red flag at a daily ceremony. At the time the flag was a well-known symbol of the Communist party in the United States. She was convicted under section 403a of the Penal Code of California, which made such a display illegal.

When the Court decided the case of *Stromberg* on May 18, 1931, the nation was in the throes of the worst depression in its history. There were those who felt that capitalism had run its course and that the American form of self-government simply did not work. In response, nations around the globe were turning either to the far right or far left and embracing either fascism or communism. When the Court convened to announce its decision in *Stromberg,* only four weeks after arguments, it balanced classic First Amendment freedom of expression and thought against the prevailing economic chaos.

Nevertheless, the Court overturned the conviction of Yetta Stromberg. In doing so, it reiterated the right of free speech in American society, even when exercised with the display of a red flag.

> The maintenance of the opportunity for free political discussion to the end that government may be responsive to the will of the people and that changes may be obtained by lawful means, an opportunity essential to the security of the Republic, is a fundamental principle of our constitutional system. A statute which upon its face, and as authoritatively construed, is so vague and indefinite as to permit the punishment of the fair use of this opportunity is repugnant to the guaranty of liberty. . . .

Thirty-four years later, on December 16, 1965, thirteen-year-old Mary Beth Tinker wore a black armband on her arm as she entered her high school in Des Moines, Iowa. She and two other students were suspended from school for violating a recently adopted school policy banning such armbands. The children's families brought an action in United States District Court for an injunction restraining the school officials from disciplining the children. The local district court refused and the Eighth Circuit Court of Appeals split evenly before the United States Supreme Court agreed to hear the case in 1968.

At the time young Mary Beth Tinker wore her black armband the commitment of American troops to the Vietnam conflict was at its height. By the time the United States Supreme Court agreed to hear the case American casualties were soaring, the incumbent president had decided not to seek renomination, and the nation was bitterly divided on the wisdom of continuing such a war.

At the same time, however, the Supreme Court had acknowledged the uniqueness of the student environment. School authority was not absolute, as demonstrated in a case decided some twenty years earlier, *West Virginia State Board of Education v. Barnette*. There the Court held that under the First Amendment a student in a public school may not be compelled to salute the flag. The dilemma facing the Court in *Tinker* was to weigh the student's right to exercise First Amendment privileges against the right of the school's authority to control conduct in the schools. Writing for the majority, Justice Abe Fortas anticipated the student conduct codes that would be pervasive at the time *R.A.V.* was decided.

> In our system, undifferentiated fear or apprehension of disturbance is not enough to overcome the right to freedom of expression. Any departure from absolute regimentation may cause trouble. Any variation from the majority's opinion may inspire fear. Any words spoken, in class, in the lunchroom, or on the campus, that deviate from the views of another person, may start an argument or cause a disturbance. But our Constitution says we must take this risk . . . and our history says that it is this sort of hazardous freedom— this kind of openness—that is the basis of our national strength and of the independence and vigor of Americans. . . .

The Court once again concluded that displaying a given symbol, in this case an armband, was symbolic speech and protected by the First Amendment. The distinction between expression and conduct has always been a difficult one to grasp. Twentieth-century history shows that there are a number of powerful nonverbal symbolic expressions that the majority find offensive. American citizens in the 1990s might very well not be offended by a red flag or a black armband. The red flag would now lack historical significance to most Americans, and the black armband would signify to most citizens that the wearer is mourning an individual rather than American troops dying in a conflict. Other symbolic expression, however, like the burning of a flag or the burning of a cross, would be offensive to a certain group of Americans at any time in our recent history.

There are many types of expression that carry no message, and for the most part those forms of expression are unprotected and ignored. The more difficult case to resolve is the course of conduct that combines elements of speech and nonspeech. This was the dilemma the

Court faced in *United States v. O'Brien*. With three others, David O'Brien burned his selective service registration card on the steps of the courthouse in Boston on March 31, 1966. O'Brien was charged under a law that made it a crime for anyone who "forges, alters, knowingly destroys, knowingly mutilates or in any manner changes any such certificate. . . ." O'Brien acknowledged that he had burned the certificate but argued that his First Amendment right of free expression had been denied, since he had burned the certificate solely "to influence others to adopt his anti-war beliefs."

The Court ignored the communicative impact of such an act, and held that O'Brien was being punished for the noncommunicative impact of the conduct in that by burning the certificate he had willfully frustrated the governmental interest in maintaining a smooth and efficient selective service system.

O'Brien stands for the principle that the Court will not examine the motives of the actor, but will examine the interests served by the law in question. The fact that O'Brien intended to communicate antiwar opinion wasn't important to this Court because the government was able to justify its actions based on motives other than political persecution. Over twenty years later, *O'Brien* would be raised once again in an examination by the Court of two different laws, one addressing nude dancing and the other addressing cross-burning. A lawmaking body can justify a proposed law based on the conduct that is addressed (e.g., undermining the draft if registration cards are destroyed) even though the nonverbal symbolic expression (e.g., burning the card) carries a message (e.g., antiwar sentiment). Nevertheless, under *O'Brien*, it is still impermissible for a lawmaking body to pass legislation that is targeted at the "content" of the message without a separate non-content-based justification.

The Vietnam conflict produced another landmark First Amendment decision in 1971 in *Cohen v. California*. On April 26, 1968, Paul Cohen walked into the Los Angeles County Courthouse wearing a jacket bearing the words "Fuck the Draft." He was convicted under a disorderly conduct law that prohibited "maliciously and willfully disturbing the peace and quiet of a neighborhood or person . . . by . . . offensive conduct. . . ." Like O'Brien, Cohen acknowledged that by wearing the jacket he had hoped to clearly express his opposition to the war and influence others to share his opinion. In this case, the Court struck down the conviction because it was clear from the record that Cohen was being punished for the offensiveness of the words displayed on his jacket and that the only underlying "conduct" that the state sought to punish was "the fact of the communication."

Since *Cohen* was decided three years after *O'Brien,* it is arguable that a significant factor involved in this decision was the change in the public perception of the war. Nevertheless, the Court distinguished between Cohen's general displeasure with the war and O'Brien's conduct directly threatening the efficiency of the selective service system. In writing for the majority, Justice Harlan established a very significant principle for First Amendment jurisprudence:

> One man's vulgarity is another's lyric. . . . Much linguistic expression serves a dual communicative function: it conveys not only ideas capable of relatively precise, detached explication, but otherwise inexpressible emotions as well. In fact, words are often chosen as much for their emotive as their cognitive force. We cannot sanction the view that the Constitution, while solicitous of the cognitive content of individual speech, has little or no regard for that emotive function, which practically speaking, may often be the more important element of the overall message sought to be communicated.

Writing in a manner that belied his conservative philosophy, Justice Harlan stated a truism that continues to influence First Amendment jurisprudence to this day. Stromberg's red flag was more powerful than mere speech; Tinker's black armband stated more than mere words; Cohen's obscenity laid out his opposition to the war in a way that intellectual argument never could. In more recent times, the burning of the American flag has been more hurtful to those who cherish it than simple words of anarchy, and the burning of a cross carries a more visceral message than statements of racial or religious bias.

There are those who would deny that the emotive impact of a symbol or its destruction is any different from the "cognitive content" of a statement made to a similar effect. Robert Bork has criticized the Rehnquist Court for its decisions on the flag-burning cases for this very reason. He has argued that the Texas flag-burning law did not prohibit "desecration of the American flag because the idea expressed was offensive, but because the mode of expression was." Bork believes that the burning of the flag conveys the same message of hate, and since there are other ways for the flag-burner to express his sentiments, a person should not be allowed this method of expression. The colonists could have protested "taxation without representation" without dumping tea into Boston harbor. Yet the "emotive function" of such symbolic expression was certainly more powerful than the "cognitive content" of the same sentiment put into mere words.

Although the censoring of flag-burning on this basis has great appeal to many Americans, it is intellectually dishonest. The very reason that Bork would prefer to have a flag-burner state his position rather than burn a flag is that he finds the flag-burning so offensive. Others, further to the left in the political spectrum, might not find the flag-burning as offensive as Robert Bork. Yet, many of these people would adopt Bork's argument in suggesting that a person should not be allowed to display a swastika or burn a cross, since he has the option of putting his sentiments into words.

If we ignore the "emotive impact" of symbolic expression and adopt the alternative "mode of expression" test that Bork proposes, we could seriously undermine the First Amendment guarantee of freedom of expression. If symbolic expression isn't allowed because verbal expression is available, then why permit paintings, books, music, and other forms of art, since there are definitely alternative "modes of expression" available to the artist? Who decides what the proper mode of expression is? The government would become the final arbiter of acceptable expression as well as the mode for that expression, and the author, painter, musician, and sculptor would be held to a standard of orthodoxy. Realizing this, the Court in 1974 rejected an attempt by the Washington Supreme Court to punish "improper use" of the American flag on the basis that the defendant had "other means available . . . for the dissemination of his personal views." The Court cited a case decided over three decades earlier that "one is not to have the exercise of his liberty of expression in appropriate places abridged on the plea that it may be exercised in some other place."

Robert Bork has pointed out that while he and Justice Antonin Scalia were on the D.C. Circuit Court of Appeals, they voted the same way 98 percent of the time. Fortunately for the nation, Justice Scalia and Robert Bork differ significantly on freedom of expression. In both of the flag-burning cases and later in R.A.V., Justice Scalia took a position in protecting the First Amendment that Robert Bork clearly would not. Justice Anthony Kennedy was eventually appointed to the position that Robert Bork had sought and later agreed with us that the ordinance was unconstitutional.

As the time approached for the hearing to determine the constitutionality of section 292.02, which was scheduled for July 13, 1990, I formulated my argument that the law was unconstitutionally overbroad, that although it had addressed nonverbal symbolic expression, such expression was clearly guaranteed under the First Amendment, and any attempt to "narrowly construe" this law would result in unconstitutional vagueness, since it would be left up to police, judges, and juries to decide whether or not an expression was offensive enough to result in conviction.

I recognized section 292.02 for what it was: a political statement made by a community's lawmaking body defining acceptable expression within the city limits. It was an attempt to merge the criminal code with a liberal political tradition without recognizing the inherent potential danger to the First Amendment. In challenging this effort at ideological orthodoxy, I knew that I was burdened with overwhelmingly unsympathetic factual allegations. I needed to find a way to persuade the judge who would hear the case to take my argument to heart. The solution was provided by none other than Justice Anthony M. Kennedy.

3

A "Constitutional Moment"

> The case before us illustrates better than most that the judicial
> power is often difficult in its exercise. . . . The hard fact is that
> sometimes we must make decisions we do not like. We make
> them because they are right, right in the sense that the law and
> the Constitution, as we see them, compel the result. . . . Though
> symbols often are what we ourselves make of them, the flag is
> constant in expressing beliefs Americans share, beliefs in law and
> peace and that freedom which sustains the human spirit. The case
> here today forces recognition of the costs to which those beliefs
> commit us. It is poignant but fundamental that the flag protects
> those who hold it in contempt.
>
> —Justice Anthony M. Kennedy

A twenty-year odyssey of flag-burning cases led to the landmark decision of *Texas v. Johnson*, decided on June 21, 1989. It
began on the afternoon of June 6, 1966, when a young black man
heard over the radio that James Meredith, a pioneer in the civil rights
movement, had been shot while walking in the state of Mississippi.
Outraged at what he considered the failure of the government to
protect minorities, Sidney Street carried an American flag to an inter-
section of New York City, lit the flag with a match and dropped it
on the pavement as it burned. As a crowd gathered, a police officer
heard Street say, "We don't need no damn flag."

Charged with the crime of malicious mischief for defiling and
casting contempt upon the American flag, Street challenged the constitutionality of the law on the grounds of overbreadth, vagueness,
and that the damaging of an American flag as a means of protest is
protected expression under the Constitution. Resisting the impulse
"to decide the Constitutional issues involved in this case on a broader
basis," the Court held the law unconstitutionally overbroad *as applied*. By considering the constitutionality of the law as applied to
Street, the Court never reached the issue of the constitutionality of the
law "on its face." Avoiding a determination of whether the burning
of the flag was proscribable, the Court instead held that the words

Sidney Street had uttered were protected and may have been the sole basis for his conviction. Finding that "any shock effect of appellant's speech must be attributed to the content of the ideas expressed," the Court noted that "under our Constitution, the public expression of ideas may not be prohibited merely because the ideas are themselves offensive to some of their hearers." Specifically declaring that it was not ruling on the issue of the flag-burning itself, the Court noted that as of April 21, 1969, the date of the decision, "disrespect for our flag is to be deplored no less in these vexed times than in calmer periods of our history."

As the "vexed" times continued, less than a year later a young man named Goguen walking down a public street in Leominster, Massachusetts, was seen wearing a small cloth version of the United States flag attached to the seat of his jeans. Charged with violating the same type of law under which Sidney Street had been convicted, the man was found guilty of publicly displaying contempt for the United States flag and sentenced to six months in jail. After the Supreme Court accepted the case, Justice Lewis Powell, writing for the majority, held that the law was unconstitutionally vague for the simple reason that "contemptuous" was subject to numerous interpretations. As a result, "men of common intelligence must necessarily guess at its meaning and differ as to its application," and such a law is subject to "arbitrary and discriminatory enforcement" by law enforcement officials because the guidelines are not reasonably clear. In an observation that would be equally applicable to the St. Paul ordinance involved in *R.A.V.*, the Court noted that "statutory language of such a standardless sweep allows policemen, prosecutors, and juries to pursue their personal predilections."

Several months later, on May 10, 1970, only days after several Kent State students had been shot by National Guardsmen, a college student in Seattle hung the United States flag upside down with a peace symbol attached to it. The student, Spence, was charged under an "improper use" statute involving the American flag, as opposed to a desecration law. The law punished the "improper" display of the flag rather than an alleged desecration of it. The student initially received thirty days in jail; he appealed, and the United States Supreme Court heard arguments on January 9, 1974.

Citing the red flag displayed by Yetta Stromberg, and the black armband of Mary Beth Tinker, the Court noted the "pointed expression of anguish by Appellant." Once again, the Court was able to avoid the greater issue of flag desecration itself by simply holding that Spence was plainly and peacefully protesting the fact that the government did not endorse his viewpoint. The decision in *Spence v. Washington* was handed down on June 25, 1974, by a predominantly liberal court. In a series of decisions, the Court had avoided deciding the underlying issue of whether or not states could constitutionally proscribe the burning and/or mutilation of the American flag.

The Court went to great lengths in *Spence* to note that "no interest the State may have in preserving the . . . flag was significantly impaired on these facts. . . ." Considering the tumultuous reception of *Texas v. Johnson* and *U.S. v. Eichman* almost two decades later, perhaps it is not surprising that the majority of the Court avoided such a controversy. If a conservative president could manage to open the doors to China and the Soviet Union as Nixon had done, it is not surprising that a conservative Court directly addressed the issue of flag desecration a decade and a half after *Spence v. Washington*.

When Gregory Johnson burned a flag in protest at the 1984 Republican National Convention, the commitment of American society to First Amendment freedoms was once again tested. Like Street, Goguen, and Spence, Johnson "was not a philosopher" and may not have appreciated "the enormity of the offense he gave." His actions were calculated to receive media attention and to offend as many people as possible. Charged under a statute designed to protect the American flag, Johnson was convicted of desecration of a venerated object and his case was argued before the United States Supreme Court on March 21, 1989.

Acknowledging that Johnson's act invoked the First Amendment, the Court finally faced the issue it had avoided for years. Put simply, the issue before the Court was whether or not the "unique" nature of the American flag as a symbol of national unity justified the suppressing of expression that undermined the flag's symbolism.

Long a defender of civil rights and civil liberties, Justice William J. Brennan, Jr., had a difficult task in trying to form a majority to protect the First Amendment. Twenty years earlier, in *Street v. New York,* Brennan had been in the majority when the liberal Warren Court had avoided the underlying issue of the constitutionality of flag desecration statutes. This time there was no sidestepping the issue. Based on past decisions, Brennan could count on the votes of Justices Marshall and Blackmun. Although considered a "liberal" vote, Justice Stevens was a true maverick regarding First Amendment issues, as he was to show again three years later in *R.A.V. v. St. Paul.* Justice Brennan knew he needed to obtain two votes from among conservative Justices Scalia, Kennedy, Rehnquist, O'Connor, and White. Stevens, Rehnquist, and White were World War II veterans and were particularly sensitive to the issue of desecration of the American flag.

On March 21, 1989, the day oral arguments were held, Brennan sat silently at the bench and listened as Justices Scalia and Kennedy questioned the attorney for the state of Texas. Scalia challenged the state's basic premise:

> *Justice Scalia:* Why did the Defendant's actions here destroy the symbol? His action does not make it any less a symbol . . . you don't want just a symbol, but you want a venerated symbol.

Justice Kennedy chose the cross as another venerated symbol, and perhaps, unwittingly, foreshadowed the case of *R.A.V.*:

> *Justice Kennedy:* Over the years, over the centuries, the cross has been respected. I recognize [that] one's a religious symbol, the other's a national one, but there's no legislation that has appeared necessary to protect, say, the cross.

Later, Justice O'Connor, another unpredictable vote in this case, referred to the rebellious nature of the nation's founders:

> *Justice O'Connor:* Do you suppose Patrick Henry and any of the founding fathers ever showed disrespect to the Union Jack? . . . You think they had in mind when drafting the First Amendment that it should be a prosecutable offense?

Justices Scalia and Kennedy joined with Justices Brennan, Marshall, and Blackmun to find the Texas law unconstitutional, thereby protecting the First Amendment and setting off a prolonged national debate. The eloquence of Justice William J. Brennan, Jr., will be remembered for decades to come by those who treasure individual liberty:

> If there is a bedrock principle underlying the First Amendment, it is that the Government may not prohibit the expression of an idea simply because society finds the idea itself offensive or disagreeable.

Citing the oft-quoted words of Justice Robert Jackson from *West Virginia Board of Education v. Barnette,* Justice Brennan continued:

> Justice Jackson described one of our society's defining principles in words deserving of their frequent repetition: "If there is any fixed

star in our constitutional constellation, it is that no official, high or
petty, can prescribe what shall be orthodox in politics, nationalism,
religion or other matters of opinion or force citizens to confess by
word or act their faith therein."

Finally, Justice Brennan addressed the nation concerning the meaning of freedom and the American flag:

Our decision is a reaffirmation of the principles of freedom and
inclusiveness that the flag best reflects, and of the conviction that
our toleration of criticism such as Johnson's is a sign and source of
our strength. . . . It is the Nation's resilience, not its rigidity, that
Texas sees reflected in the flag—and it is that resilience that we
reassert today.

Predictably, many citizens and politicians expressed outrage at the
Court's decision in *Texas v. Johnson*. A constitutional amendment to
outlaw flag-burning was proposed but defeated. Congress eventually
enacted a statute attempting to protect the flag without violating First
Amendment principles. One year later, on June 11, 1990, the Court,
by the same vote, in *United States v. Eichman*, rejected this action by
Congress and found the Flag Protection Act of 1989 unconstitutional.
Once again, Justice Brennan spoke for the Court and admonished
Congress for failing to recognize the true meaning of the First
Amendment:

We decline the Government's invitation to reassess this conclusion in light of Congress' recent recognition of a purported "national" consensus favoring a prohibition on flag burning. . . . Even
assuming such a consensus exists, any suggestion that the Government's interest in suppressing speech becomes more weighty as
popular opposition to that speech grows is foreign to the First
Amendment.

Constitutional commentators have noted that at various times in
our nation's history we have passed through "constitutional moments." Unlike ordinary times, constitutional moments capture the
attention of the public and require reexamination of fundamental
issues of constitutional government. "We consider what sort of government we want to have, we consider what kind of limits we want
to place on that government, and, most important, we recognize that
the arrangements we put in place will persist for a relatively long

time." The line of cases leading to *Texas v. Johnson* resulted in a constitutional moment capping the distinguished career of Justice Brennan.

U.S. v. Eichman finally ended the nation's attempt at banning flag-burning and was decided ten days before the cross was burned in the front yard of the Jones family. The reverberations from *Texas v. Johnson* arguably culminated in the Court's decision in *R.A.V. v. St. Paul,* decided three years later.

On July 10, 1990, I submitted a short legal memorandum to the Ramsey County District Court with copies of relevant cases attached. Because of time constraints, Judge Charles A. Flinn, Jr., the presiding district judge, had requested each side to submit a brief summary. Argument remained scheduled for July 13, 1990.

As any practicing attorney knows, it is very important to be familiar with the judge presiding over a case. This is particularly true when arguing a dispositive motion challenging a law on constitutional grounds. I had to find some way to convince Judge Flinn that a true understanding of the First Amendment led inexorably to the striking down of this ordinance. It is easy to deny a motion to strike down a law on constitutional grounds. Once denied, such a motion is seldom overturned on appeal. The burden to be as persuasive as possible was magnified in this case by the political outrage that threatened any decision.

Charles A. Flinn, Jr., the son of an outstate judge, had come of age in rural Minnesota. He remembers traveling with his father to many local communities, but like many rural citizens of our nation, he had had very limited contact with members of minority races or religions during his youth. After graduating from Yale University in 1962, he returned home to attend law school and began practicing in 1965. In 1966 he joined the Air Force Reserves and remained a member for twenty-four years. After fathering two children, he and his wife adopted a Korean child in the late 1970s. A self-described "conservative," he was appointed to the Ramsey County District Court bench in 1980 by a Republican governor. Far from being an ideologue, Judge Flinn was "conservative" only in comparison with Minnesota Democrats. Nationally, he would probably be described as a moderate Republican.

I had appeared before Judge Flinn on numerous occasions. When I informed him that I intended to challenge the constitutionality of this law, he was cooperative and appeared interested in hearing a motion on a constitutional issue of substance. It was ironic that both Judge Flinn and I had volunteered to transfer to the juvenile court division from the adult court division of the Ramsey County court system. Many judges and lawyers avoided juvenile court because they felt that it was a forum in which little of legal significance occurred. I had transferred because I represented indigent clients only on a part-time basis and the juvenile court assignment allowed me more time for my private legal practice. I had just finished a homicide case in the spring of 1990 and I was looking forward to a less stressful work environment. Unlike others on the bench, Judge Flinn had volunteered for the assignment in disregard of the public perception of that court.

Having appeared before Judge Flinn on both civil and criminal matters prior to 1990, we knew each other and respected each other's abilities, yet as July 13 approached I was anxious to capture his attention in a favorable way.

Reading the eloquent words of Justice Kennedy's concurring opinion in *Texas v. Johnson,* it occurred to me that Justice Anthony M. Kennedy was a man that Judge Charles A. Flinn, Jr., would greatly admire. Born within a year of each other, both men were political conservatives and had come from small-town backgrounds. Kennedy, confirmed in February of 1988, had been on the Court for one term when he cast a vote in favor of the First Amendment in *Texas v. Johnson.* Confirmed on the heels of the failed nominations of Robert Bork and Douglas Ginsburg, Kennedy's nomination had been a compromise, but he would not have received the appointment had he not received strong conservative backing. Although Justice Scalia had also voted in the majority, Kennedy was the new man on the block and he must have known how many former supporters he alienated when he sided with the remaining four justices.

Although in my initial research I found many moving passages written by Justice Brennan, I decided that the words of Justice Kennedy would be much more persuasive to Judge Flinn because of their similar backgrounds. At the hearing, Judge Flinn indicated that he had examined our memorandums and the cases we had cited and "they [were] not clear." Although he indicated that he did not feel that it would be necessary to make argument, I insisted ("your honor, on behalf of [my client], I would like to make argument primarily because it may be important to have a record here at a later time"). Citing the flag-burning cases, I also noted *Collin v. Smith,* a case commonly known as the "Skokie case." In that case the Seventh Circuit Court of Appeals had decided that the village of Skokie, Illinois, home to a number of Holocaust survivors, could not ban the display of the Nazi swastika. Although Judge Flinn listened attentively, he became particularly interested when I ended my argument with Justice Kennedy's concurring opinion, which acknowledged the difficulty of decision-making in a controversial case.

Over the weekend of July 14 and 15, 1990, Judge Flinn considered the arguments as well as the cases and memorandums that had been submitted. On the morning of July 16, 1990, the Court reconvened for a ruling on the constitutionality of section 292.02. In striking down the ordinance, Judge Flinn reasoned that

> The Court feels that the ordinance is quite clearly unconstitutional and so rules. I do that having full mind of Justice Kennedy's great agony in the *Texas v. Johnson* decision dealing with the flag burning. . . . When you look at the line of cases cited, cited by the respondent here, I think they follow almost to a tee the issue that is raised by the respondent. . . . They also show remarkable to me at least a bright line leading to my finding this ordinance unconstitutional."

Since the respondent was a juvenile, he was entitled to confidentiality under state law, and was not mentioned in a newspaper article written about the ruling the next day. Realizing the potential for misunderstanding, I indicated in my first public statement to the press that by contesting the ordinance I did not condone cross-burning, and pointed out that other laws were available to prosecute such individuals. The article stated that the judge's ruling "cast doubt" on the case of the eighteen-year-old, Arthur Miller III, whose pretrial was scheduled for July 23, 1990. Miller, however, represented by private counsel, pleaded guilty to violating section 292.02, a law that had been found unconstitutional less than one week before. He was sentenced to thirty days' incarceration.

In response to the order of Judge Flinn, the Ramsey County Attorney's Office had several choices. It could have accepted his order and gone to trial on the remaining charge of bias assault against R.A.V. It could also have added other charges against R.A.V. that addressed his alleged illegal conduct rather than his viewpoint. Since Judge Flinn's order was not binding on other district judges, as seen in the case of the codefendant, his ruling would have had minor impact. The other charges available in prosecuting R.A.V. were of a more serious nature and would have sent a "community statement," the motive for which was used as an excuse to appeal. The prosecutors chose to file an appeal in the Minnesota Court of Appeals on July 20, 1990.

Once the prosecutor had made the decision to appeal, we faced several choices. The Ramsey County Public Defender's Office, with whom Mike Cromett and I had a contract to perform twenty hours of legal-defense work per week, had no funds available for appeals. We would be responsible for a continuing caseload and our respective law practices in addition to the appeal if we chose to keep the case; this would involve substantial financial hardship. Further, we couldn't ignore the fact that the public had already indicated a misunderstanding of the case; we would be subject to a great deal of anger and criticism. The public defender's office was severely understaffed; with some exceptions, we expected little support from our fellow attorneys. I had attended an office meeting on July 11, 1990, at which time I indicated that I was considering handling the appeal after a decision was rendered. I was promptly subjected to a hysterical diatribe from another attorney in the office who felt that I should not handle the appeal. Since my doing so would have had no effect on his workload, I can only speculate that his anger resulted from the emotional subject matter involved. He has never explained or apologized for his bitter invective that day. Several days later I was approached by a black probation officer who was furious with me and with the court's ruling. Repeated attempts to explain our challenge to the law failed. At this point, reason was a poor match for emotion. Before the case was over, I was often to experience such anger directed at me.

Since we knew R.A.V. had no funds to hire private counsel, our only other option was to drop the appeal and allow an unconstitutional law to remain. This we refused to do. Mike Cromett agreed to donate his time toward the appeal as well. Even if Judge Flinn had ruled for the government, we had decided earlier to go forward. Michael's support and assistance were crucial. I had helped him in several homicide cases when he had requested it, and when I turned to him for assistance he responded in kind. From the very beginning he stood by me and supported me while a great majority of others, including other lawyers, didn't comprehend the issue or its importance.

After we gave notice that we would handle the appeal, the prosecutor's office petitioned for "accelerated review" to bypass the Minnesota Court of Appeals for an expedited hearing before the Minnesota Supreme Court. On August 3, 1990, the Minnesota Supreme Court granted the request. In an extraordinary response, less than two weeks after Judge Flinn's order, the Minnesota Supreme Court served notice that the matter was important enough to be heard before numerous other cases. We doubted this was a favorable development; by acting in such haste the court appeared to be taking issue with Judge Flinn's ruling. We had made the decision to proceed. Little did we know what that determination would entail for R.A.V. and his attorneys.

4

———◼———

Words That Injure;
Laws That Silence

> There are certain well-defined and narrowly limited classes of
> speech, the prevention and punishment of which has never been
> thought to raise any Constitutional problem. These include
> . . . "fighting" words—those which by their very utterance inflict
> injury or tend to incite an immediate breach of the peace. It has
> been well observed that such utterances are no essential part of
> any exposition of ideas, and are of such slight social value as a
> step to truth that any benefit that may be derived from them is
> clearly outweighed by the social interest in order and morality.
>
> —*Chaplinsky v. State of New Hampshire*

Less than two months after the attack on Pearl Harbor, the
United States Supreme Court heard arguments in a case involving
Walter Chaplinsky. Chaplinsky, a Jehovah's Witness (as was the
Jones family in *R.A.V.*), had chosen a busy Saturday afternoon in
Rochester, New Hampshire, to denounce organized religion. After a
crowd had gathered and become "restless," Chaplinsky was led away
from the scene by a police officer whom Chaplinsky called a "damned
Fascist." Charged under a law that made it illegal to address a person
with "any offensive, derisive or annoying word," Chaplinsky argued
that his constitutional rights had been violated. He was convicted; the
New Hampshire Supreme Court affirmed the conviction but "narrowed" the scope of the law to the proscription of only those words
that were likely to cause an average addressee to fight.

By construing a law "narrowly," a state supreme court attempts to
save a law that is overbroad as written. A local lawmaking body
(such as a city council or a state legislature) occasionally enacts a law
that is unconstitutional in that it applies to a substantial amount of
protected expression. This problem has become particularly acute
because few members of such lawmaking bodies are conversant with
constitutional law. Further, even when a local lawmaking body has

lawyers among its members, those lawyers often remain silent when they know they should speak up. There are a variety of reasons for the failure of these lawyers to go on record against unconstitutional legislation. It could be that they have failed to examine the proposed law or to recall general constitutional principles, but more than likely the reason for silence is political expediency as the lawyer/lawmaker chooses a politically advantageous position over a constitutionally sound one.

In the half century since *Chaplinsky v. New Hampshire* was decided, the United States Supreme Court has on occasion encouraged state supreme courts to narrow the scope of offensive speech statutes by construing them narrowly to punish only fighting words. Sometimes the state courts have been successful; more often such a narrowing construction has raised additional constitutional issues. As a matter of public policy, state supreme courts should not allow local lawmakers to enact unconstitutional laws. A cynic might observe that this allows politicians to take the high moral ground by passing politically popular but constitutionally suspect laws, leaving the burden of responsibility on an appellate court. The result is a rewriting of the law by a reviewing court, though the function of the judiciary is to review laws, not to write new ones.

After the New Hampshire court in *Chaplinsky* tried to save a bad law with a narrow construction, the United States Supreme Court affirmed the decision in dramatic language that would perplex constitutional scholars to this day. Since the state court had narrowed the application of the law to instances of reflexive violence, the United States Supreme Court had only to decide whether this was a constitutionally sound result. Instead, the Court wrote a brief dissertation on the parameters of unprotected speech. Referring to fighting words which "by their very utterance inflict injury" or "tend to incite an immediate breach of the peace," the Court opened the door to widespread censorship of expression. The language prohibiting speech that incited an immediate breach of the peace addressed the fundamental interest of a free society in preventing physical violence. Depending on one's personal viewpoint regarding the tension between individual liberty and societal order, the parameters of breach of the peace can always be debated.

The phrase "inflict injury" is considerably more elastic and demonstrably more dangerous than "breach of the peace." As one constitutional scholar has observed, the latter phrase addresses the external condition of order that generally "can be given an objective fixed meaning, and there can be agreement that certain acts clearly threaten that interest." The "inflict injury" language, on the other hand, refers to an internal emotional reaction which

> creates a much more difficult evaluative problem for those wishing to incorporate it into the law's protected interests. Unlike the more tangible quality of order, the interest of protecting "sensibilities" has no physical component. The only manner in which an individual's "sensibilities" are known to be affected is by the individual's statement to that effect.

Historical cycles during the past fifty years have been a barometer by which to measure freedom of expression. *Chaplinsky v. New Hampshire* was decided during a war while our country sought order in the midst of chaos. Our nation has been particularly unwilling to tolerate unpopular expression and political opinion when threatened by external forces (such as World War II, the postwar Communist scare). A nation at war or suffering hard economic times has considerably less patience with free expression than a nation at peace or a prosperous country.

Several years after the end of World War II, a defrocked priest named Terminiello took the stage at an auditorium in Chicago and addressed a sympathetic crowd of approximately eight hundred while one thousand protesters demonstrated outside. Attacking the protesters, Terminiello "criticized various political and racial groups whose activities he denounced as inimical to the nation's welfare." He was convicted of "breach of the peace" and the United States Supreme Court agreed to hear arguments on February 1, 1949. As in *R.A.V.* over forty years later, the case split traditional allies; the American Civil Liberties Union filed a brief in behalf of Terminiello, while the American Jewish Congress supported the city of Chicago.

In a stirring affirmation of the principles of free expression, Justice William O. Douglas spoke for the majority in a badly divided Court. Ignoring the issue of whether or not Terminiello's use of speech constituted fighting words, the majority attacked the jury instruction that led to the conviction, which defined "breach of the peace" as that speech which "stirs the public to anger, invites dispute, brings about a condition of unrest, or creates a disturbance. . . ." Such a review was unusual, as the dissents pointed out, since the petitioner's attorney had not objected to the instruction at the time it was given. Nevertheless, the language of that decision was a natural extension of the eloquence of Justices Holmes and Brandeis delivered to a previous generation. Douglas reminded the nation of how fragile individual liberty is and how the American commitment to free expression set our nation apart from such governments as Nazi Germany, Fascist Italy, and Communist Russia: "The vitality of civil and political institutions in our society depends on free discussion. . . . The right to speak freely and to promote diversity of ideas and programs is therefore one of the chief distinctions that sets us apart from totalitarian regimes."

By this time the horrors of the Holocaust were well known. Douglas was aware that in this instance the American Jewish Congress had voted in favor of censorship by filing a brief in support of the conviction. Nevertheless he and the other members of the majority recognized the danger of censoring selected political viewpoints in the name of social progress:

> Accordingly a function of free speech under our system of government is to invite dispute. It may indeed best serve its high purpose when it induces a condition of unrest, creates dissatisfaction with conditions as they are, or even stirs people to anger. . . . There is no room under our Constitution for a more restrictive view. For the alternative would lead to standardization of ideas either by legislatures, courts, or dominant political or community groups.

By modifying the decision in *Chaplinsky,* decided seven years earlier, the Court gave notice that it once again would protect political speech even if that speech could arguably result in reflexive violence. The world had changed dramatically in those seven years. By the time *Terminiello* was decided, it would have been a greater insult to label someone a "damned Communist" than a "damned Fascist." Yet now that the threat of war had receded, the Court once again recognized the political importance of protecting speech, whether offensive on the basis of political opinion, racial or ethnic background, or even religious belief.

Several years later, expediency overcame intellectual honesty once again as the nation was gripped by the paralyzing fear of Communism. With the Korean conflict and McCarthyism on the horizon, Americans traded reason for repression and stood quietly by as the First Amendment came under a fierce attack led by government officials. The factual circumstances of one case, *Dennis v. United States,* moved Justice Hugo Black to include the following passage in his dissent:

> Public opinion being what it now is, few will protest the conviction of these Communist petitioners. There is hope, however, that in calmer times, when present pressures, passions and fears subside,

this or some later Court will restore the First Amendment liberties to the high preferred place where they belong in a free society.

Shortly after *Dennis,* the Court heard a case that remains unique in the annals of First Amendment jurisprudence. A bitterly divided Court upheld a "group libel" law from the state of Illinois. In upholding this provision, the Court sanctioned a law that made it a crime to engage in expression that exposed "citizens of Negro race and color to contempt, derision, or obloquy. . . ." Prior to this case, libel of an individual had been a common-law crime and such expression had never been protected under the First Amendment, as noted in the *Chaplinsky* case. Yet when Joseph Beauharnais distributed his white separatist literature on January 6, 1950, on the streets of Chicago, he acted in violation of a law that went far beyond libel of an individual.

The Court had previously recognized that one who libeled an individual would be subject to civil or criminal penalties, but now it broadened that prohibition to include the outlawing of expression that would offend a "group":

> If an utterance directed at an individual may be the object of criminal sanctions, we cannot deny to a State power to punish the same utterance if directed at a defined group. . . . We are precluded from saying that speech concededly punishable when immediately directed at individuals cannot be outlawed if directed at groups with whose position and esteem in society the affiliated individual may be inextricably involved.

As is often the case with laws that are contrary to First Amendment principles, the language of this law seemed reasonable to many citizens and politically attractive to more than a few politicians. Yet the blistering dissents of Justices Black and Douglas peel back the unobjectionable layer of the law to reveal the danger beneath.

As Professor Harry Kalven, Jr., said of Justice Hugo Black in 1967, he "inherited the mantle of Holmes and Brandeis" because "to begin with, he passes a major test for a great judge on free speech issues. He displays the requisite passion. The requirement is not so much a question of arguing for the preferred position thesis; it is rather that the judge respond to the fact that this is not just another rule or principle of law."

And respond he did. In a vitriolic answer to the majority opinion authored by Justice Frankfurter, Justice Black took the Court to task for suggesting that states have the right to enact laws encroaching upon the right of free expression.

The Court's holding here and the constitutional doctrine behind it leave the rights of assembly, petition, speech and press almost completely at the mercy of the state legislative, executive, and judicial agencies. . . . We are cautioned that state legislatures must be left free to "experiment" and to make "legislative" judgments. . . . My own belief is that no legislature is charged with the duty or vested with the power to decide what public issues Americans can discuss. In a free country that is the individual's choice, not the state's. State experimentation in curbing freedom of expression is startling and frightening doctrine in a country dedicated to self-government by its people.

Arguing that the First Amendment exception for libel had always been a narrow one, the former senator from Alabama and New Dealer continued:

For here it is held to be punishable to give publicity to any picture, moving picture, play, drama or sketch, or any printed matter which a judge may find unduly offensive to any race, color, creed or religion. In other words, in arguing for or against the enactment of laws that may differently affect huge groups, it is now very dangerous indeed to say something critical of one of the groups.

As I read Justice Black's dissent in preparation for writing the brief to the Minnesota Supreme Court, I was struck by how his wisdom was equally applicable to St. Paul City Ordinance section 292.02:

No rationalization on a purely legal level can conceal the fact that state laws like this one present a constant overhanging threat to freedom of speech, press and religion. . . . Moreover, the same kind of state law that makes Beauharnais a criminal for advocating segregation in Illinois can be utilized to send people to jail in other states for advocating equality and nonsegregation. . . .
If there be minority groups who hail this holding as their victory, they might consider the possible relevancy of this ancient remark: "Another such victory and I am undone."

Although Justices Jackson and Reed also dissented, Justice Douglas perhaps best expressed what it means to have absolute faith in the First Amendment. Referring to the recently decided *Dennis v. United States,* Douglas outlined the dangers of encroaching on the right of free expression:

> Recently the Court in this and in other cases has engrafted the right of regulation onto the First Amendment by placing in the hands of the legislative branch the right to regulate "within reasonable limits" the right of free speech. This to me is an ominous and alarming trend. The free trade in ideas which the Framers of the Constitution visualized disappears. In its place there is substituted a new orthodoxy—an orthodoxy that changes with the whims of the age or the day, an orthodoxy which the majority by solemn judgment proclaims to be essential to the safety, welfare, security, morality or health of society. Free speech in the constitutional sense disappears. Limits are drawn—limits dictated by expediency, political opinion, prejudices or some other desideratum of legislative action.

As Anthony Lewis lucidly outlined in *Make No Law,* twelve years after *Beauharnais* the Court significantly eroded the concept of group libel in *New York Times Co. v. Sullivan*. There a unanimous Court upset an Alabama libel judgment in a landmark opinion authored by Justice William J. Brennan, Jr. By protecting the right to criticize public officials, the Court gave new life to the free speech clause of the First Amendment.

Five years after *Sullivan,* in 1969, the Court again expanded the scope of freedom of expression by holding in *Brandenburg v. Ohio* that even speech advocating violence was protected unless and until that advocacy was "directed to inciting or producing imminent lawless action and is likely to incite or produce such action." Brandenburg, like Terminiello and Beauharnais before him, believed in the superiority of the white race. His arrest and conviction differed significantly from Chaplinsky's. Chaplinsky had been convicted on a reflexive violence theory, the belief that a hostile audience would take exception to his expression and become violent. Such a law appeared to be a type of protective custody open to abuse. The idea that the arrest of a speaker could result because an audience could not hold its collective temper when confronted with his viewpoint seemed perverse fifty years ago and remains a dangerous proposition. The holding in *Brandenburg,* however, dealt not with a hostile audience but with a sympathetic one. The Court now suggested that it was permissible to advocate violence to a sympathetic group, but if that group was incited to violence, one could be held responsible for the act.

Recognizing the need to balance individual liberty against the need for order in a civilized society, the court set the limits of free speech in *Chaplinsky* and *Brandenburg*. In *Brandenburg,* by suggesting that the expression must be "likely to *and* directed to produce imminent lawless action," the Court seemed to move away from the *Chaplinsky* standard. By maintaining a requirement that the speaker direct his expression and cause violence, the Court appeared to relieve the speaker whose views were unpopular but who did not intend to incite violence. By suggesting the action had to be "imminent," the Court put a heavy burden on those who would censor expression deemed to have gone past the mere advocation of violence. As the Supreme Court overturned several state court decisions involving fighting words in the early 1970s, it appeared that the Court had repaired the inroads made on First Amendment freedoms in *Chaplinsky* and *Beauharnais*.

However, the expansive language used by the Court in *Chaplinsky* remained a threat to individual liberty under the First Amendment. Indeed, Justice Frankfurter's majority opinion in *Beauharnais* a decade after *Chaplinsky* gave added weight to the notion that government may censor expression when the words used could, "by their very utterance, inflict injury upon the recipient." By incorporating the *Chaplinsky* doctrine into the group libel holding of *Beauharnais,* the Court now held that government could censor expression when it "inflicted injury" on a group. This went considerably beyond Chaplinsky's angry statement aimed at a police officer.

A quarter century after *Beauharnais,* legal scholars were divided as to whether the concept of group libel and the "inflict injury" language from *Chaplinsky* remained good law. Certainly *New York Times Co. v. Sullivan* had limited the effect of *Beauharnais*. It was unclear how the Court would react to a group that argued that it had been libeled by expression that had inflicted injury upon them. When the case was decided in 1952 the nation was suffering from racial and religious intolerance. By 1977 the flash points of intolerance remained race and religion. The stage was set for a case that would be seared into the nation's memory, much like the cross-burning case fifteen years later. This time it was not a burning cross but a Nazi swastika displayed in Skokie, Illinois.

Much has been written about the case of *Collin v. Smith*. Frank Collin and the National Socialist Party of America announced on May 1, 1977, that they sought a permit to march in the village of Skokie, Illinois, a northern suburb of Chicago, which encompassed a large Jewish population, including several thousand survivors of the Holocaust. To further aggravate the situation, the members of the NSPA wore brown shirts and carried swastika flags. Refused a permit, Collin and his cohorts turned to the courts.

On May 22, 1978, the Seventh Circuit Court of Appeals handed down its decision. Ruling that the demonstrators must be allowed to march, the court reminded the parties that "First Amendment rights are truly precious and fundamental to our national life. . . . It is, after all, in part the fact that our constitutional system protects minorities unpopular at a particular time or place from governmental harassment and intimidation that distinguishes life in this country from life under the Third Reich."

Striking down the village ordinance prohibiting the display of swastikas because they "would promote hatred towards persons on the basis of their heritage," the court rejected the village's reliance on the "inflict injury" or "psychic harm" language from *Chaplinsky* and reiterated the words of Justice Douglas from *Terminiello*:

> It would be grossly insensitive to deny, as we do not, that the proposed demonstration would seriously disturb, emotionally and mentally, at least some, and probably many of the Village's residents. The problem with engrafting an exception on the First Amendment for such situations is that they are indistinguishable in principle from speech that "invites dispute . . . induces a condition of unrest, creates dissatisfaction with conditions as they are, or even stirs people to anger." . . . Yet, these are among the "high purposes" of the First Amendment.

Although Skokie officials sought review by the United States Supreme Court, the Court denied the petition for certiorari despite votes from Justices Blackmun and White to hear the case. Since there is a requirement that four out of the nine justices vote to accept review of a case before it will be granted, it would remain for another day for the Court to hear its first "hate speech" case. Back in Skokie, the NSPA decided not to march, after all, even though its right to do so had been vindicated. One could reasonably speculate that these extremists would have preferred to lose in the courts, thus obtaining the mantle of the martyr.

The public reaction to the Skokie case was swift and furious. A number of constitutional law scholars raised questions about the wisdom of the decision. The nationwide public reaction would be repeated when the symbol displayed became a burning flag or a burning cross. The case touched a nerve close to the national psyche since the end of World War II. Contrary to its actions in the cross-burning case, the American Civil Liberties Union worked hard to defend the right of free expression for a group whose beliefs members of the organization personally loathed. As was to be the case fifteen years later, numerous groups, including the National Lawyers Guild and the Anti-Defamation League, lined up in favor of censorship. Partially in response to their perceived setback in the *Collin* case, the ADL began drafting model "hate crime" legislation, which "it proposed for introduction into state codes."

Aryeh Neier, the national executive director of the ACLU at the time of the Skokie case, wrote a very moving account of his experience. Neier lost family members in the Holocaust and now found himself in the position of defending the individual liberties of citizens who espoused beliefs that had resulted in the deaths of those he loved. Despite the intellectual honesty and courage of those who defended the NSPA, the ACLU lost a substantial part of its membership, who quit in protest over the efforts of the ACLU lawyers to protect the First Amendment in the Skokie case. Noting that "if violent actions could stop civil rights demonstrations, the movement for racial equality would have been defeated at the start," Neier pointed out that the "pretext of listener hostility was employed constantly by opponents of the black civil rights movement of the 1960s to suppress its demonstrations." As I was to argue in *R.A.V.* for intellectual honesty and adherence to principle, Neier spoke from a position of authority to those who had abandoned him on the left as he protected the First Amendment by defending the far right. Rejecting the group libel concept from *Beauharnais,* Neier quoted legal philosopher Edmond Cahn, who described the necessity for vision in considering the consequences of such laws:

> The officials could begin by prosecuting anyone who distributed the Christian Gospels, because they contain many defamatory statements not only about Jews but also about Christians. . . . Then the officials could ban Greek literature for calling the rest of the world "barbarians." Roman authors would be suppressed because when they were not defaming the Gallic and Teutonic tribes, they were disparaging the Italians. For obvious reasons, all Christian writers of the Middle Ages and quite a few modern ones could meet a similar fate. . . . Then there is Shakespeare who openly affronted the French, the Welsh, the Danes. . . . Dozens of British writers from Sheridan and Dickens to Shaw and Joyce insulted the Irish. . . . Literally applied, a group libel law would leave our bookshelves empty and us without desire to fill them.

Foreshadowing St. Paul City Ordinance section 292.02, Neier encapsulated the danger of an exclusionary ordinance whether it be in St. Paul, Minnesota, or Skokie, Illinois:

> The arguments against permitting the march have fostered the impression that a community can assert that those whose views are anathema to it can be forbidden to enter its boundaries. It is not the first time a town or neighborhood has asserted such a power to exclude views it dislikes from its own "turf."

Nor was it to be the last.

5

Death and Decision

Not that Europe or other parts of the world are ready to follow the American theory of free speech to the end of protecting even the most hateful speech . . . A distinguished French constitutional lawyer, Roger Errera . . . rejected for other countries the American willingness to tolerate such "extreme forms of political speech." . . . Americans, he suggested, have a quality, that given their experience, the Europeans cannot have—"an inveterate social and historical optimism." . . . Americans *are* optimists. Madison had to be an optimist to believe that democracy would work in a sprawling new federation. . . . Martin Luther King, Jr., had to be an optimist to believe that speech, appealing to conscience, could undo generations of racial discrimination.

—Anthony Lewis

Several weeks after the Minnesota Supreme Court had granted the state's motion for an accelerated review of Judge Flinn's order, I contacted the local chapter of the American Civil Liberties Union. Although I had never been a member of the organization on either the national or the local level, I had great respect for many of the volunteer attorneys who had contributed their time and had often defended unpopular causes. When I called the offices of the Minnesota Civil Liberties Union, a recording directed me to send a letter outlining my reason for contacting the office. Accordingly I wrote on August 29 to say that I was seeking assistance in preparing an appeal to the Minnesota Supreme Court on a First Amendment case.

The next week I was contacted by the man most closely identified with the MCLU, Matthew Stark. I explained the situation to him as well as my belief that a number of interested groups would be filing briefs on behalf of the state. Such briefs are referred to as *amicus curiae* briefs, Latin for "friend of the court." Various parties file such briefs on behalf of organizations sympathetic to one party to the appeal. The theory is one of friendly intervention by a group interested in the issues before the court who wants to bring certain aspects of those issues to the court's attention. The more controversial the case, the more *amici* briefs it generally attracts.

Stark requested me to send him all the police reports and information pertinent to the case along with a letter stating why this case was important to the MCLU. Holding my temper in check, I suggested that if this case wasn't important to a civil liberties organization, then perhaps that organization had no reason to exist. Stark reiterated his request, and then said that he was going on vacation and that he would get back to me upon his return. I sent the information he requested in a letter that said, "This is a classic 1st Amendment–Free Speech case. I am disturbed by the lack of interest or resources [provided] by the MCLU thus far. We need help on an important case," and waited for a response.

Weeks later, Stark told me that the organization was in too much disarray to help. He said it was in the process of hiring personnel and at this point it had no one available to assist us.

Turning to the parent organization, I got in touch with the national headquarters of the ACLU in New York City. It initially expressed interest and asked me to send copies of all documents to them. I did so with an accompanying letter on September 15 ("All help you can [provide] us would be greatly appreciated"). After reviewing the documents, an attorney for the organization called me and told me to request assistance from the MCLU. When I reminded him that the MCLU had already said it did not have the resources to help, he had no response. This from a civil liberties organization "armed with a $30 million budget, a national staff of 150, an affiliate in every state and hundreds of volunteer lawyers." We appeared to be caught in a catch-22 with the First Amendment at stake. I was angry at both organizations, but at this point I was willing to believe that scarce resources provided the basis for their rejection. Later, I had reason to doubt that this was the sole reason for their failure to assist us.

As we had anticipated, several organizations filed *amici* briefs for the state. The NAACP filed a brief that contained twenty pages of argument, with a sixteen-page appendix entitled "Terror in Our Neighborhoods," published by the Klanwatch Project of the Southern Poverty Law Center. The Anti-Defamation League of B'nai B'rith also filed an *amicus* brief, which included the stunning pronouncement that "the First Amendment is not implicated in this case." Even the city of Minneapolis filed a brief on behalf of the prosecutor before the Minnesota Supreme Court.

We had known that we would receive no financial assistance and that we would be responsible for maintaining our caseload as well as our respective private practices. Now it became clear that we would not receive any professional assistance, even from the organizations that presumably exist to protect the civil liberties of all American citizens. Without such assistance, it might very well appear to the public that ours was an isolated crusade and our motives arguably would become suspect. The sixteen-page appendix filed by the NAACP detailed ugly acts of racial intolerance with accompanying photos. What was ignored was that our challenge was to the law, and was not a justification of such intolerance; there were other more serious laws available to deal with such ugly incidents. We would have to work alone, without public support, appearing to lack compassion for victims of intolerance. We had only thirty days to write and file our brief.

In mid-September, we received a copy of the government's brief. Since our challenge was to the law itself, the factual allegations were not relevant. However, there is an old courtroom truism that if the law is not on your side, argue the relevant facts, and that if the facts do not support your position, argue the law; if you have neither the facts nor the law on your side, pound the table. Foreshadowing its strategy in the months ahead, the government engaged in its own form of "table pounding" by writing four full pages of irrelevant, inflammatory factual allegations. Approaching the ordinance as simply another disorderly-conduct provision, the appellant ignored the breadth of the ordinance and the selectivity of the proscribed subjects. Arguing the need for laws of this kind, the state took the position that anyone who engaged in such "behavior" must understand that the majority did not condone his actions. What the appellant actually hoped to establish was that the majority could punish an unpopular viewpoint, since the "behavior" itself could be punished by various provisions of the criminal code. The argument by the state ignored the nature of the First Amendment.

The Framers of the Constitution experienced the oppressiveness of rule by a single tyrannical individual, and many risked their lives and livelihoods to escape the British monarchy. When it came time to create a new democratic form of government, they intuitively knew it was essential to separate the powers bestowed upon the new leaders, ensuring that no single branch of government would reign omnipotently. Brilliant in its simplicity, the plan balanced the power of Congress with that of the president, and the power of the Supreme Court with that of both the legislative and executive branches, lest they stray from the constitutional principles that provided the framework for democratic rule. The power of the Supreme Court was theoretical until 1803, when *Marbury v. Madison* held once and for all that it was the province of the courts to interpret the meaning of the Constitution.

While some of the Framers felt threatened primarily by the possibility of a single tyrant seizing power, others worried about the creation of a monolithic federal government and what it could mean for individual freedom. They understood that tyranny can stem from rule by the one over the many or rule of the many over the one. This threat of the "tyranny of the majority" has been recognized by a number of individuals, including John Stuart Mill, who wrote in *On Liberty*:

> Like other tyrannies, the tyranny of the majority was at first, and is still vulgarly, held in dread, chiefly as operating through the acts of the public authorities. But reflecting persons perceived that when society is itself the tyrant—society collectively, over the separate individuals who compose it—its means of tyrannizing are not restricted to the acts which it may do by the hands of its political functionaries. . . . Protection, therefore, against the tyranny of the magistrate is not enough: there needs to be protection also against the tyranny of the prevailing opinion and feelings; against the tendency of society to impose, by other means than civil penalties, its own ideas and practices as rules of conduct.

If an individual tyrant can subjugate all his subjects, then the majority of people can set a standard of orthodoxy that imprisons the human spirit. A democratic society is not necessarily a free society. This, then, is one reason why many of the ratifying states to the Constitution insisted on a Bill of Rights. If the First Amendment's guarantee of freedom of the press exists to prevent tyranny imposed by those select few who hold power, then its guarantees of freedom of speech and religion exist to protect the individual against the tyranny of the majority.

The sky was a deep blue while a cold wind came from the north as the morning of December 4, 1990, dawned. As I drove to the Minnesota Judicial Center I thought about my argument and the likely outcome of the case. Although I had successfully briefed a Fourth Amendment case before the Minnesota Court of Appeals, I had never argued before the Minnesota Supreme Court. Since I was primarily a trial lawyer, I had spent the fall of 1990 learning appellate practice. Although I had done the majority of the brief writing, I looked to Mike Cromett for suggestions on the oral argument, as he had argued a number of cases before the Minnesota Supreme Court. I had observed several arguments in the days preceding December 4, including a case argued by Mike, so I felt I was ready. At the same time, we both knew that since the court had accelerated review on this case, it was likely that the court had taken issue with Judge Flinn's ruling. We were hoping for an affirmance of the lower court's decision, but we did not expect such an outcome.

By December of 1990 the Minnesota Supreme Court had three white female members, Justices Jeanne Coyne, Rosalie Wahl, and Esther Tomljanovich, and three white male members, Justices Lawrence Yetka, John Simonett, and Chief Justice A.M. "Sandy" Keith. The following year, with the appointment of Justice Sandra Gardebring, the Minnesota Supreme Court would become the first supreme court in the nation with a majority of female members. Justices Coyne and Simonett had been appointed by a Republican governor, while the other justices had been appointed by Democratic administrations. The most recent appointment to the court at that time was Associate Justice Esther M. Tomljanovich.

An attorney since 1955, Justice Tomljanovich had remained out of the public eye while raising her son and working as an attorney for the Revisor of Statutes Office for the state of Minnesota. Although she had become an expert in legal draftsmanship while reviewing laws for the revisor's office, she had little courtroom experience at the time she was appointed a district judge for the Tenth Judicial District in 1977 by Governor Rudy Perpich. Gifted with a winning personality and an incisive mind, Judge Tomljanovich proved to be a hardworking and capable jurist. Although diminutive in stature, she clearly controlled her courtroom and soon gained a reputation as a diligent and popular member of the bench. A staunch liberal, she supported a number of progressive causes and became a role model for women lawyers in Minnesota. Although I had appeared in her courtroom on a number of occasions, I did not become personally acquainted with her until 1988 and I have since considered her a friend.

By the time Justice Tomljanovich was appointed to the Minnesota Supreme Court in September of 1990, she became the only sitting supreme court justice with trial-bench experience. I applauded her appointment, and when I saw her at a social event in the fall of 1990, I mentioned to her that I would be appearing before the court on December 4. At 9:00 A.M. on December 4, 1990, as the six justices of the Minnesota Supreme Court entered the courtroom, Justice Tomljanovich caught my eye, smiled at me, and gave me a slight wave. Understanding the unpopularity of my position, she was attempting to make me feel at ease. At that time, I had no idea that she would be authoring the court's opinion or that we had diametrically opposed viewpoints on this issue.

Representing the government was the Ramsey County attorney. Since my father had been an attorney in that office for over three decades before his retirement in 1974, I was well acquainted with most of the attorneys there. Arguing for the state was Steven De-Coster. DeCoster had engaged in appellate work for Ramsey County since I was in high school, and he had argued before the Minnesota Supreme Court on many occasions. Though a respected appellate lawyer, he was to consistently underestimate the strength of our position in this case.

Although I had been involved in the trial of several high-profile homicide cases, and this was the first time that I would argue before the Minnesota Supreme Court, my father had never observed me in court and chose not to do so now. Retired and in good health, he could easily have attended the argument. He did not because he felt his presence would distract me. Instead, he sat by the phone and waited for my call after the argument. No family members were present, but a number of close friends and fellow attorneys attended to show support. Sitting next to me at the table as he would through-out the case was Mike Cromett. DeCoster began the argument by discussing the ugly factual allegations rather than the legal issues before the court, a pattern the government was to repeat over the next year. In citing the need for hate-crime laws, DeCoster argued that if the court found the ordinance overbroad, it should construe the law narrowly to cover only "fighting words" in order to save it.

Twelve years earlier, in another case argued by DeCoster involving a juvenile, this same court had saved the state disorderly-conduct statute with just such a narrow construction. In the *SLJ* case, the court had acknowledged that the language of the disorderly-conduct statute was unconstitutionally overbroad. That law applied to ex-pression generally and did not mention either "burning crosses or Nazi swastikas," and did not select certain subjects for censorship as this ordinance did with "race, color, creed, religion or gender." Since *SLJ* had not been heard beyond the state supreme court, it left two questions for consideration: Should state supreme courts continue to rewrite laws, and if so, should they do so with a law that singled out certain viewpoints and subjects for proscription?

The government continued its argument that the act alleged was an act of terror and a threat aimed at the Jones family, intentionally confusing the issue by arguing the threatening nature of the alleged conduct while proceeding under a law that failed to address such activity. The only explanation for this obfuscation was that the pros-ecutor now joined with the city council in attempting to set a stan-dard of political acceptability for the citizens of St. Paul.

Regrettably, the threats and the terror felt by the Jones family were not addressed in the charge. The public would be manipulated into thinking that the feelings of the Jones family were ignored by our side and by the court's; in truth, the government had disregarded their feelings from the very start by charging R.A.V. with a law that failed to address either the threats or the terror felt that night. From this moment, the government cowered behind deceptive arguments emphasizing the horror of the allegations, purposely ignoring the fact that it could have directly addressed that detestable conduct without jeopardizing the First Amendment.

As I rose to address the Minnesota Supreme Court for the first time, I sought to return the court to the true focus of our challenge: the language of the ordinance itself. Acknowledging the temptation to respond to the allegations viscerally, I reminded the court that the issue did not require a factual or political determination on the appropriateness of such activity. Noting the differences between this ordinance and the disorderly conduct statute of *SLJ,* I argued that this law was directly aimed at selected messages conveyed by certain ugly but powerful symbols. Arguing that the ban on unpopular expression applied to public property and to private property with the permission of the owner, I noted that the most serious impact of such a law would be the potential for prosecution of unpopular political expression, even if displayed on the steps of the state capitol, a stone's throw from the chambers of the court. Beyond the parameters of easily identifiable hate symbols, such as the burning cross and swastika, were other controversial symbols, several involving the issue of abortion. A picture of a fetus or a hanger could easily offend a member of the public, depending on his or her position on abortion. The display of such powerful and upsetting expression would be punishable under laws of this type.

Having grown up in Minnesota, I acknowledged the proud and progressive tradition of Minnesota politics. Yet I argued that it was a mistake to encroach upon the First Amendment even with honorable intentions, setting a constitutional precedent for other states that might not have such a progressive tradition. Returning to the issue of demonstrations on the steps of the state capitol, I considered the political events that I had witnessed on these steps while growing up in St. Paul. I thought of all the controversial and unpopular symbols that had been displayed there as a means of political protest. These steps were the quintessential public forum; all Minnesota citizens were allowed to express their opinions there subject only to reasonable restrictions on time, place, and manner. Such restrictions applied to all citizens equally in theory, and regulated only where, when, and how one expressed oneself; they did not regulate who could do so or the content of the expression. The list of topics debated had been endless and had covered the political spectrum. Antiwar or pro-veteran benefits, pro-life or pro-choice, pro–civil rights or pro–white separatism, pro–women's movement or pro–men's movement, the only common denominator of the expression was its controversial nature.

I asked the court to recognize this ordinance for what it was, a subterfuge by a lawmaking body to establish an orthodox political sentiment at the cost of individual liberty. By upholding the lower court's order striking down the ordinance, the court would not condone cross-burning but rather it would send a clear message that well-intentioned overbroad laws would not be allowed to suppress politically unpopular expression under the guise of keeping the peace. By narrowly construing the ordinance, the court would send a dangerous message to lawmaking bodies that they could pass unconstitutional laws restricting the right to dissent.

A decision of this nature would do little to encourage responsibility on the part of elected officials. The few questions I received from Justices Simonett and Wahl seemed to indicate that since the court had succeeded in rewriting the law in *SLJ,* it would attempt another such constitutionally suspect maneuver.

After I sat down, DeCoster was given a few minutes for rebuttal. When Justice Yetka expounded on the history of cross-burning since the Civil War, Mike Cromett and I knew that at least some members of the court were not focusing on the issue. The justices appeared unable or unwilling to look past the ugly factual allegations, and failed to see the danger in rewriting a law while allowing a community to maintain a politically popular but unconstitutional law on its books.

As I left the courtroom with friends and supporters, I felt I had done reasonably well, but I also knew it was unlikely that I had convinced the court to adopt our position. As the holidays came and went and I celebrated my thirty-eighth birthday on New Year's Eve, I had a troubled feeling that the year would begin with an unfavorable decision by the court. What I had not expected was the manner in which the court rejected our position. Although the court had months to issue its decision, it chose to do so on January 18, 1991. The court had taken only six weeks, and that brief period had included a number of holidays.

In an opinion written by Justice Tomljanovich, the court unanimously overturned Judge Flinn's order. The language of the opinion left the unmistakable impression that the court had not even found the decision difficult. The tone of the opinion, combined with the early release date and unanimous vote, gave the public the impression that we had no true understanding of First Amendment jurisprudence. The court held that "although the St. Paul ordinance should have been more carefully drafted, it can be interpreted so as to reach only those expressions of hatred and resorts to bias motivated personal abuse that the first amendment does not protect," in effect rewriting the law and begging the larger question of which expressions were not protected. Although we were disappointed that we had lost, the timing of the release hurt even more. January 18, 1991, was the Friday of the Martin Luther King, Jr., holiday weekend. Perhaps this was a coincidence, but it had a pronounced effect on us just the same. I have always had a great deal of respect for Dr. King; I don't believe that he would have welcomed a decision that imperiled the First Amendment. He would have understood that one does not win by silencing the enemy; any law that threatens individual liberty and the right to dissent will eventually be turned against the powerless of society. Regardless, we had lost swiftly and decisively.

We kept our disappointment to ourselves, and Twin City residents who opened their papers on the morning of January 18, 1991, were told only that it was "likely that [we] will ask the U.S. Supreme Court to accept the case for review." That statement must have been amusing to any lawyers who read the article because they would have understood how rare it is for the U.S. Supreme Court to accept review of a case.

I visited my father the night of the decision and found him quietly sympathetic. As the years went by we had gained a great deal of mutual respect. I was his only son and his youngest child. As he was almost forty-three when I was born, he had initially been a distant figure to me, but wanting only to please him, I had worked hard over the years to impress him. I attended a Catholic military all-male high school during the Vietnam conflict (as did Mike Cromett), and when I was seventeen in 1970, my father and I argued about everything from the war to the hours I was keeping. But by the time I graduated from law school at twenty-four, we had become close friends, and it is only in hindsight that I understand how unique our relationship was. I told my father that Mike and I were right about this case, contrary to the decision of the Minnesota Supreme Court and to public opinion. A man of few words, he said that if I felt that strongly about our position I should not give up.

On February 2, 1991, my mother called to tell me that my father was not feeling well, apparently suffering from the flu. The next day I went to visit him, and although he seemed better during the day, he started feeling ill as the evening wore on. He refused to go to the hospital, so I went home with the understanding that my sister would spend the night at the house and call me if he got any worse. The call came at 4:00 A.M. on Monday, February 4, 1991. He had finally agreed to go to the emergency room, but he did not want an ambulance so my sister and I brought him to the hospital. I sat by him as the emergency doctor examined him, and because of his high white-blood-cell count the attending physician decided to admit him to the hospital. One month short of his eighty-first birthday, he had previously spent only one night in the hospital. Once he was comfortable I returned home to catch a few hours of sleep, and I made a quick court appearance at 1:30 P.M.

Looking back, I think I knew. I arrived from the courthouse at his room at approximately 2:30 P.M. When I entered the room and saw my father, I knew that this was the day he would die. His color had changed drastically and he complained of pain in his legs. Trying to maintain my composure, I massaged his legs while calling for a nurse. Once the nurse came back into the room, I ran to get the attending physician. Since I was not able to locate him, I returned to the room and found four other doctors working on my father. Because my father was a devout Catholic, I immediately asked the nurse if there was a Catholic priest on the premises. The priest was nowhere to be found. I eventually reached his parish priest, who agreed to come to the hospital immediately. The head surgeon asked to speak to me, and looking into my eyes asked me if I understood the gravity of the situation. I assured him that I did, that a priest was on his way, and that, if possible, I wanted five minutes with my father before he was taken into surgery. When I reentered the room, my father saw me and asked me to take him home. I took his hand and explained to him that what was happening was serious, that he needed to have surgery, and that he might not make it. There was no whimpering, no denial, and no tears. Instead he clenched his jaw as I had seen him do hundreds of times before and he became very quiet.

Literally seconds before the operating surgeons and nurses would attempt to move my father, the priest appeared. Even though my father was in immense pain, when he saw Father Mitchell enter the room he smiled warmly and greeted him as though it were another day at church. As the priest gave him the last rites I held his hand and squeezed, and he squeezed back. By this time my tears were flowing freely but I did not make a sound. His responses to the priest were the last words he ever spoke. There was no hint of fear or sadness in his voice as his faith sustained him in his last moments.

After the last rites were finished, the surgical nurses moved him to an elevator. I was the only one with him, since my mother and sister could not get there in time. As we reached the doors to enter surgery, the operating physician turned to me and said, "This is where you say good-bye to your father." For the last time in my life I looked into my father's eyes, held his hand, kissed him on the cheek, and told him that I would be there when he came out of surgery. He never regained consciousness and died that night.

Memories of time my father and I spent together occupied my thoughts in the days following his death. As a young boy, I would sit quietly in my father's law office and proudly watch him work. In the lobby of the Ramsey County Courthouse in St. Paul, where he had his office, stands a three-story marble Indian chief locally known as Onyx John. While waiting for my father to finish working on his files, I would often sit and stare at this huge statue from the third floor of the courthouse. For many years, both as a child and as a teenager, that is how I saw my father: strong, honest, and unyielding. In his last years he would often drop into my law office to have lunch with me and quietly watch me work as I had watched him decades earlier. Now I would look at the empty chair across from my desk and miss his gaze, or I would find myself picking up the phone to call him and ask his advice only to replace the receiver as reality set in.

At 10:00 A.M. on February 7, 1991, I walked past my father's casket as I approached the podium to give the eulogy at his funeral Mass. I knew that he would have wanted a quiet, simple ceremony. After working at the county attorney's office for over thirty years, he had refused a retirement dinner for this very reason. Now that I had written the eulogy, delivering it would be the hardest single act of my life. But I needed to do it for myself as much as for him.

As I looked out at the packed church, I thought of how effortlessly my father had been "politically correct." His friends were men and women, white and black, Jewish, Catholic, and Protestant, and although he had appeared to be a gruff Irishman, he was actually the most compassionate man I had ever met. It was my father who had given me the strength to fight uphill battles, and he had quietly taught me what was important in life.

During the sixties the local movie theater had three admission prices: child, junior, and adult. Upon turning thirteen, one became a "junior," and the admission charge increased. One day after I had turned that age, the ticket seller sold me a child's ticket and I saved fifty cents. When my father overheard me boasting to my sister about my good fortune, he promptly drove me down to the theater and instructed me to pay back the fifty cents. A simple lesson, perhaps, but the message of doing the right thing regardless of what you can get away with remains with me to this day.

When I was a boy he would take me to the Twins and Vikings games at the old Metropolitan Stadium, where the Mall of America now stands. A big man, he towered over me as we made our way through the crowd. Once in a while we would be separated and I would feel a growing terror known only to children. Then I would catch a glimpse of him up ahead, he would turn and smile when he saw me, and I knew that everything would be all right.

That is how I see him to this day. Although we are separated, he is up ahead, saving the best seats.

6

Fascism from the Left: Speech Codes and Political Correctness

> Moderates who would prefer fending for themselves as individuals are bullied into going along with their group. Groups get committed to platforms and to we-they syndromes. Faculty members appease. A code of ideological orthodoxy emerges. The code's guiding principle is that nothing should be said that might give offense to members of minority groups. . . . The code imposes standards of what is called, now rather derisively, "political correctness." What began as a means of controlling student incivility threatens to become, formally or informally, a means of controlling curricula and faculty too.
>
> —Arthur M. Schlesinger, Jr.

Following closely behind my feelings of loss upon the death of my father was the knowledge that irrevocable changes in my life had occurred. My sister and I had inherited the farm homesteaded by our great-grandfather Jeremiah O'Keefe over 130 years earlier, which my father had purchased from his brother and sister. Though neither of us knew much about farming, we felt a closeness to the land first settled by our ancestors and we knew that it had become a part of us. Selling it was out of the question. In addition to feeling emotionally spent and physically exhausted, I found myself preoccupied with estate matters.

Nevertheless, Mike Cromett and I never seriously considered not filing a petition for certiorari. We were still smarting from the decision of the Minnesota Supreme Court, and we knew we must seek review from the United States Supreme Court. We were also aware that our appeal time was running out, and we agreed to meet a week after the funeral to begin work on the appeal.

There is confusion among members of the public over the American judicial system generally and the appellate process specifically. The only occasion upon which an appeal may be filed to the United States Supreme Court is after a person, corporation, or governmental agency has exhausted its lower-court options by losing a case in a state supreme court or a federal appellate court. There are numerous state, district, and appellate courts, fifty state supreme courts, many federal district courts, and thirteen federal circuit courts of appeals; there is only one United States Supreme Court. Once the lower court has ruled, as it did in our case, a party has a right to petition the United States Supreme Court for review of the case. This is the petition for certiorari. The likelihood of success in obtaining the Court's agreement to review a case is small and the obstacles are formidable, often insurmountable:

> The justices have no obligation to hear these appeals; they pick only those that raise important, disputed issues involving federal law or the U.S. Constitution. Big law firms charge clients, hoping to attract the eye of the justices, as much as $30,000.00 to prepare a 25-page petition. Few succeed. On average, about three percent of the appeals win a *review,* which means that the cases will be argued before the justices and decided with a written opinion.

Obviously, Mike and I had better things to do than to engage in a futile exercise. In addition to estate matters, my law practice was in need of close attention. These factors, and the continued lack of funding, the unanimous decision of the Minnesota Supreme Court and the odds of having a juvenile court case heard by the highest court in the land seemed to favor an acceptance of the decision. Yet we both felt that we were right and that the reasoning of the Minnesota Supreme Court was flawed. If we failed to appeal, the law would stand and the First Amendment would suffer. Under our system of common law and precedent, the decision of the Minnesota Supreme Court could be cited as authority in other jurisdictions as well. The First Amendment would not cease to exist, but we believed its key guarantee of freedom of speech would erode over time. For that reason alone, we felt that we should at least draft the best possible petition for certiorari and hope that from among the thousands of petitions ours would somehow be selected for review.

We would proceed *in forma pauperis.* This simply meant that our client was indigent and that we would file an affidavit signed by him indicating that he had no resources. The advantage of this procedure was to save a substantial filing fee and printing costs; the disadvantage was the increased likelihood of being overlooked, since there are thousands of *in forma pauperis* petitions filed every year. Mike and I briefly considered paying the filing fee ourselves to avoid this procedure and to increase our likelihood of success but decided against it.

The more Mike and I read the Court's history and discussed the drafting of a petition, the clearer it became that the Court placed a premium on cases involving issues of national significance. Out of necessity the justices avoided local, state, or regional disputes. In drafting the appeal, we would need to demonstrate that the Minnesota Supreme Court had misinterpreted earlier First Amendment cases and that the resulting decision could have a broad impact on all fifty states. The Court placed a great emphasis on brevity and clear, concise writing. Our final draft of the petition as filed with the Court was a mere seventeen pages.

Each petition contains a cover sheet with a second page including what are known as Questions Presented, which are of crucial significance because their phrasing will often determine whether the law clerk who initially examines the petition deems it worthy of consideration. The petitioner is allowed to pose several questions, while the Court may grant review on one or all of the questions presented. We decided to pose two questions. The first question we raised was as follows:

> 1. May a local government enact a content-based, "hate-crime" ordinance prohibiting the display of symbols, including a Nazi swastika or a burning cross, on public or private property, which one knows or has reason to know arouses anger, alarm, or resentment in others on the basis of race, color, creed, religion or gender without violating overbreadth and vagueness principles of the First Amendment to the United States Constitution?

With this question, we intentionally returned to the ordinance as written rather than to the "narrow" construction of the Minnesota Supreme Court. We wanted the Court to understand how overbroad the law was (it covered any offensive expression), how it selected topics for censorship ("race, color, creed, religion or gender") and how vague it was in describing a violation of its terms ("arouses anger, alarm, resentment in others"). It was our belief that such a law could never be narrowly construed. To do so would be to rewrite the law, which is the function not of the judicial branch but of the legislative branch. The narrowing construction had left most of the original terminology intact, clarifying little and confusing a great deal. Since the legislative branch has the power to enact laws, we believed that such lawmaking bodies should be held responsible for such laws and remain accountable to the electorate.

Having framed the first question in terms of the law as written, we phrased the second question to suggest that because the law selected certain subjects and viewpoints for proscription, it could not be narrowly construed in the same manner as a law that was "content-neutral," that does not censor expression based on the content of the message.

> 2. Can the constitutionality of such a vague and substantially overbroad content-based restraint of expression be saved by a limiting construction, like that used to save the vague and overbroad content-neutral laws, restricting its application to "fighting words" or "imminent lawless action"?

A law that punishes expression leading to an immediate breach of the peace may be permissible. It is another matter entirely to suggest that expression based on certain topics (race, religion, gender), may be punished if the speech leads to an immediate breach of the peace or inflicts "injury" on the recipient of the expression. Lawmakers may not punish expressive conduct based on the viewpoint conveyed. Provisions addressing expression must apply neutrally without regard to the message given or the subject addressed.

In the first instance, the government does not censor only that expression deemed offensive by some on selected subjects. It is arguable that an "immediate breach of the peace" standard still gives the government too much latitude to censor expression and that *Chaplinsky v. New Hampshire* should be overruled. Yet law enforcement officials across the country would argue that when someone targets expression (loud swearing) at an individual to precipitate a fight, officials need a tool to prevent such occurrences. Unfortunately, this "fighting words" concept has been used often by police officers to justify the arrest of unruly citizens who verbally abuse the officer but pose little threat. This is the "reflexive violence" theory upon which the *Chaplinsky* decision rests, and has been the law of the land for the past half century. We chose not to attack that decision, as we felt that the Rehnquist Court had demonstrated its sympathy for law enforcement and would be reluctant to overturn *Chaplinsky*.

We recognized the danger in allowing local governments to select certain topics for censorship, giving law enforcement the discretion to arrest when, in the officer's opinion, the expression violates an offensiveness standard related to controversial issues. Although *Chap-*

linsky and its "fighting words" theory has existed for over fifty years,
a more recent development was the selection of certain topics for
censorship based on the likelihood of the expression offending someone or inflicting emotional injury. Perhaps the theory was conceived
with the best intentions, in an attempt to foster social equality. Few
believed an extension of the guarantee of equal protection under the
Fourteenth Amendment to be in conflict with the First Amendment
when applied to expression. As a child of the sixties, I knew that the
First Amendment had protected civil disobedience, led to the passage
of progressive social legislation, and helped to end an unpopular war.
If the First Amendment had hastened the promise of the Fourteenth
Amendment, those who had relied on its guarantees now repeated the
historical pattern of censorship based on the dogma of those in
authority. Political correctness swept the land, and laws similar to
section 292.02 were enacted on campuses across the nation.

> Imagine places where it is considered racist to speak of the rights
> of the individual when they conflict with the community's prevail-
> ing opinion. . . . Imagine institutions that insist they absolutely
> defend free speech but punish the airing of distasteful views by
> labeling them unacceptable "behavior" instead of words—and then
> expel the perpetrators. . . .
>
> Where is this upside down world? According to an increasing
> number of concerned academics, administrators and students, it is
> to be found on many U.S. college campuses. And it is expanding
> into elementary and secondary school classrooms. . . . A troubling
> number of teachers at all levels regard the bulk of American history
> and heritage as racist, sexist and classist and believe their purpose
> is to bring about social change.

In the first section of our petition, we directly addressed the effort
to legislate racial, ethnic, and religious sensitivity both in local communities and on campuses. We now focused on the campus speech-
code context in which political orthodoxy had reached its zenith.

Historically, the First Amendment has been the lifeline for the
disadvantaged. In recent years this legacy has been widely ignored.
Censorship has flourished in the name of civility; orthodoxy has been
embraced in the furtherance of "progressive" principles. One commentator has noted:

> The radical ideas of the day often become the orthodoxy of
> tomorrow, and, in the process, take on a quite different political
> valance. I refer to this phenomenon as "ideological drift." Although

this drift can move either from right to left or left to right, the most common examples are comparatively liberal principles that later serve to buttress comparatively conservative interests.

For over a decade, many students and professors on campuses have embraced a doctrine known euphemistically as "deconstructionism." Put simply, proponents of this theory believe that the meaning of a text is subjective, based on "privileging" one interpretation over an opposing but equally justifiable viewpoint. Depending on one's opinion, Shakespeare is either the greatest playwright the world has ever known or simply a representative of a racist and sexist society that existed four centuries ago in England.

In the legal community this outlook is related to another theory, allegedly based on legal realism and popular for more than a decade, called "critical legal studies." The chosen targets of these theorists include legal education, legal reasoning, and the importance of precedent. According to this doctrine, a judge's decision in reviewing a statutory provision is again subjective, and often a function of his or her nonlegal and political preferences. "Crits" feel that the right to speak is "ephemeral"; when the hierarchy finds the exercise of this right threatening, it limits this right. Presumably, many of these proponents have no objection to eliminating this "ephemeral" right when exercised by those whose expressions they consider offensive.

Related is the theory of some legal scholars that a guarantee of liberty and equality generally favors the powerful, who have access to the "means of communication," including access to places to speak (private as well as public property), and to "modes of communication" (publishing houses, television stations, etc.). Viewed in this manner, those without power or property have a significantly diluted right of free expression. Although this may be an accurate observation, it is nevertheless a good argument for an expansive interpretation of the First Amendment to ensure that the less powerful have the "means" (i.e., public forums) and "modes" (i.e., public access cable television) available to them as well.

It is on campuses and in law schools throughout the nation that the battle is often waged over the wisdom of imposing an orthodox political standard. There is serious division among those to the left politically who have traditionally agreed on many controversial social issues, and liberals, civil libertarians, and minorities disagree about the appropriateness of speech codes regulating student expression. Traditional allies, such as the ACLU and the NAACP, have found themselves in dispute over these issues. Such traditional liberals as former JFK aide Arthur M. Schlesinger, Jr., Nadine Strossen of the ACLU, and Alan Dershowitz of Harvard Law School have aligned themselves in opposition to others on the left and right, including Mari Matsuda of Georgetown Law Center, Charles R. Lawrence III of Stanford Law School, and Stanley Fish of Duke School of Law. Many liberal individuals and organizations are uncomfortably allied with conservative commentators, such as Dinesh D'Souza, Charles Fried of Harvard Law School, and even iconoclastic conservative commentator Rush Limbaugh, who criticize speech codes as tools of political correctness.

Researching the petition for certiorari, our focus had changed from traditional First Amendment case law to the debate over the repressive climate of a political-acceptability standard prevalent on campus. This research led inexorably to the extremely overused lexicon of the times: political correctness and multiculturalism on one side of the debate, balkanization and cultural separatism on the other. Since the language of the ordinance reflected both student speech codes and a political standard set by a community, this phenomenon would be our focus, demonstrating the national significance of the issues we raised before the United States Supreme Court. The divisiveness on the left and the opposition from the right that permeated discussions of political correctness would be repeated in our case as the months passed.

> The central tenet of P.C. is that Western civilization, and, more specifically, American law and culture, is inherently unfair to minorities, women and homosexuals. From that belief springs a variety of stances.
>
> It is P.C. to be in favor of affirmative law review actions and admissions, faculty appointments and prestigious slots in the name of diversity and remedy. Women's studies, gay and lesbian studies, African-American studies are P.C., as is support of hate-speech codes and multi-culturalism.

In spreading this message, particularly regarding racial politics, commentators such as Mari Matsuda have gained national prominence in the legal community. Matsuda, with law professors Charles R. Lawrence III, Patricia Williams, and Richard Delgado, has steadfastly maintained that the silencing of offensive expression based on race is necessary. Separating the dangers of McCarthyism from the censorship of racist speech, Matsuda argues that the two are distinguishable; Marxist speech is not "universally condemned," while "racial supremacy" has been "considered and rejected." Because of the danger that such laws may be used against the very groups who seek their protection, Matsuda's solution is to divide the population into the categories of "dominant group" and "subordinated group." Hateful speech used by a subordinated group member coming from an "experience of oppression" would be protected, while speech aimed at a subordinated group member "adopting a rhetoric of racial inferiority," would be censored. It is not clear who will define the terms "subordinated" and "dominant," or what provision might be made for changing economic status. Apparently, there will be a presumption that white males are dominant, while minorities and females are subordinated regardless of economic class. Any hateful expression aimed at white males will be permitted, since it stems from a climate of oppression. Offensive speech by white males, however, may be censored. Presumably Matsuda, a female Asian American, wants freedom of expression for herself, but sees no danger in silencing those who may express themselves in a way that she finds offensive.

Charles R. Lawrence III extends the Matsuda theory to virtually preempt discussion of the matter on the basis that "not everyone has known the experience of being victimized by racist, misogynist, and homophobic speech." While no one can dispute the accuracy of this observation, not everyone has been victimized by intolerant speech based on other characteristics (e.g., mental and physical handicaps, economic status, religious beliefs).

Further, Lawrence's targets are transparent: those guilty of being "racist" are white, of being "misogynist" are men, and of being "homophobic" are heterosexuals. White, heterosexual males can never be sufficiently sensitive to understand the horrors of intolerance. This facile generalization makes as much sense as suggesting that minorities, women, and homosexuals can never understand the feelings of a disabled veteran who sees an American flag burned. While both statements may be true in many cases, neither observation furthers the debate. We do not succeed in combating intolerance by silencing some and blaming others. We do more damage to social progress by inhibiting free expression.

As John Stuart Mill noted over a century ago:

> With regard to what is commonly meant by intemperate discussion, . . . the denunciation of these weapons would deserve more sympathy if it were ever proposed to interdict them equally to both sides. . . . The worst offense of this kind which can be committed by a polemic, is to stigmatize those who hold the contrary opinion as bad and immoral men.

Nadine Strossen of the ACLU has argued that "combating racial discrimination and protecting free speech should be viewed as mutually reinforcing, rather than antagonistic goals." While sharing Lawrence's goal of a more tolerant and progressive society, Strossen contends that there is a "risk that such a speech restriction will be applied discriminatorily and disproportionately against the very minority group members whom it is intended to protect." This is a continuing danger of such proposals; the enforcement of such restrictions is left to those in power, while historically the right of free expression has been a tool of the powerless.

Addressing the larger issue of ethnic awareness, Arthur M. Schlesinger, Jr., outlines the historical cost of the current trend of cultural separatism:

> The cult of ethnicity has reversed the movement of American history, producing a nation of minorities—or at least minority spokesmen—less interested in joining with the majority in common endeavor than in declaring their alienation from an oppressive, white, patriarchal, racist, sexist, classist society.

Citing Theodore Roosevelt (who said that "the one absolutely certain way of bringing this nation to ruin, of preventing all possibility of its continuing to be a nation at all . . . would be to permit it to become a tangle of squabbling nationalities. . . .") and secure in his liberal and progressive past, Schlesinger takes issue with those who would engage in revisionist history to disparage the European heritage of America and the continuing importance of America in the world:

> Whatever the particular crimes of Europe, that continent is also the source—the *unique* source—of those liberating ideas of individual liberty, political democracy, the rule of law, human rights, and cultural freedom that constitute our most precious legacy and to which most of the world today aspires. . . . The genius of America lies in its capacity to forge a single nation from peoples of remarkably diverse racial, religious, and ethnic origin. . . . The American Creed envisages a nation composed of individuals making their own choices and accountable to themselves, not a nation based on inviolable ethnic communities. The Constitution turns on individual rights, not on group rights.

Strossen and Schlesinger are the minority in speaking out against orthodoxy, particularly liberal orthodoxy, and in favor of individual freedom. Their motives became suspect to some and they were criticized by traditional allies. Soon I was to understand the experience of being attacked by many of those who had supported me in the past.

Conservatives, steadfast in their opposition to speech codes, historically have been less willing to extend First Amendment protection to obscene expression, flag-burning, and offensive rap music. As I researched and read in preparation for the filing of the petition, I realized that conservatives regarded the right of free expression differently than in the past. They had become the target of censorship. If a conservative is a liberal who has been mugged, a civil libertarian, as Alan Dershowitz has argued, "is a conservative who has had his magazine censored."

Conservative commentators, such as the ubiquitous Dinesh D'Souza, verify that there is a newfound respect for the First Amendment by the right. Referring to the "enormous artificiality of discourse among peers" as a result of student speech codes, D'Souza cites Troy Duster, a Berkeley sociologist, whose findings reflect that multiculturalism on campus has in fact become cultural separatism leading to the balkanization among such groups:

> Students from different backgrounds came to college thinking of themselves as "individuals" or "Americans," but, once at Berkeley, began to think of themselves as "African-American, Asian-American or whatever." . . . "Each group accuses other groups of being closed and not receptive" and "each group complains about being stereotyped."

Former solicitor general Charles Fried, now of Harvard Law School, has pointed out that although the campus codes may have been enacted in the name of civility, they are hypocritical in that "not all breaches of courtesy and good manners fall under the ban." As Fried puts it:

> Is it unreasonable for me to conclude that one who shrinks from banning from the campus extreme and distressing verbal abuse generally, but will punish insults directed at "blacks, Latinos or gays," seems more interested in making a political statement and showing political solidarity than in protecting the civility of discourse in the academic community?

Although a minority of the left and a majority of the right appeared to agree on the issue of free expression, there remained the question of how the courts would approach student speech codes. In *Doe v.*

University of Michigan, the United States District Court for the Eastern District of Michigan struck down the University of Michigan's speech code, holding that it violated the First Amendment based on principles of overbreadth and vagueness. The court was particularly concerned that school officials were invariably invested with too much discretion in the enforcement process as they chose which incidents to discipline. Taking some comfort in Judge Cohn's opinion from 1989, I was disturbed by an addendum to his opinion. He indicated that he had received a copy of Mari Matsuda's article supporting speech codes after he had filed his opinion, implying that his decision might have been different had he read Matsuda's article first. There were no other federal decisions on student speech codes at the time we prepared our petition.

It is no secret that the Rehnquist Court has been known for its conservative stance on constitutional interpretation. It was within the context of student speech codes specifically, and political correctness generally, that we saw our chance. Although we would use the flag-burning cases to obtain a hearing before the Court, we would avoid those cases later, since both Justices Marshall and Brennan were now retired. Flag-burning is a flash point for many conservatives, as the display of hate symbols is a flash point for many liberals. We concentrated on censorship of conservatives on campus, reasoning that a majority of the Court might find such efforts offensive, in both a constitutional and a personal sense.

Having completed the research for the petition, I dictated a first draft for review. After three more drafts Mike and I were satisfied that the petition was ready for filing. We ended the petition with a quote from retired Supreme Court justice William J. Brennan, Jr.: "A certain amount of expressive disorder not only is inevitable in a society committed to individual freedom but must itself be protected if that freedom would survive."

We filed our petition for certiorari with the United States Supreme Court on April 11, 1991. On May 16, attorney Mark Anfinson filed an *amicus* petition on behalf of the MCLU in support of our position. Matthew Stark of the MCLU had contacted me in late March and apologized for the failure of the organization to get involved seven months before, when I had requested its assistance. On the theory of better late than never, I welcomed the help, after making it clear to Stark that I was still angry at the failure of the Union to take a stand earlier. Mark wrote a well-reasoned piece joining in our argument. I wasn't sure how the United States Supreme Court felt about civil liberties organizations, as they had often decided against the position of the parent organization, the ACLU. Still, for the first time Mike and I had allies and we welcomed the support.

Since both sides must consent before an *amicus* brief may be filed, the county attorney's office had to agree before the MCLU could get involved. Most parties agree to such intervention. The Court usually allows the filing of the brief if the respondent (in this case the county attorney's office) refuses to consent, so the respondent who refuses appears to be an obstructionist. The government refused to consent, so the MCLU was forced to bring a motion and in the process made the county attorney's office look petty.

The prosecutors compounded this mistake by filing a perfunctory response in opposition to our petition on May 7, rehashing the ugly factual allegations and ignoring the important constitutional questions involved. It appeared that they viewed our petition as little more than a nuisance, and were confident that we would fail in our attempt to secure a review of the decision.

The Court takes approximately sixty days to determine whether to accept a petition. We were careful not to become overly optimistic about the outcome of their decision, but as each day passed we found ourselves believing that all the factors necessary for granting the petition existed: a controversial lower-court decision, a concise and well-documented (we hoped) petition for certiorari, and, most important, timing. Newspapers and periodicals continued to document the fight over political correctness and student speech codes. We believed with all our hearts that this law was unconstitutional and felt that the issues presented were sufficiently serious for the Court to grant review. We knew that the law clerks for most justices screened the petitions and then made a recommendation to the Court regarding review; the justices personally reviewed petitions in the most promising cases. Approximately one fourth of the filed petitions make the "discuss list" compiled and reviewed by the judges at their conference. Those remaining (the "dead list") are directed out by the Court prior to any discussion concerning the issues raised. Then the Court meets to go over the discuss list.

At 9:25 in the morning, a buzzer sounds on the first floor. The conference will begin in five minutes. For new justices, the routine of marching to the time of buzzers recalls their high school days. The nine of them meet alone; no clerks, secretaries, or aides are allowed in the meeting. By tradition dating to the nineteenth century, they begin by shaking hands and greeting each other.

On June 6, 1991, Lyle Denniston of the *Baltimore Sun* called my office. A dean of the Supreme Court press, Denniston informed me that the file on *R.A.V.* had been checked out. He said that this meant the petition had probably made the discuss list and that by Monday, June 10, we would find out whether our case was one of the few granted review. He suggested that another possibility was that review would be denied by the Court but a dissent would be written by one or more justices who objected to the failure of the Court to grant review. For a case to be granted review, four justices would have to agree to accept it. I answered Denniston's questions about the petition and thanked him for the call. He seemed to believe we had succeeded; I hoped his instincts were accurate.

At 9:01 A.M. on June 10, 1991, Tim O'Brien of *ABC News* called my office to tell me that the Court had granted our petition.

The Eyes of the Country:
The Supreme Court Agrees
to Hear *R.A.V.*

The Supreme Court yesterday agreed to decide whether "hate-crime" laws . . . violate the constitutional guarantee of free speech. . . . Hate-crime laws, along with campus speech codes, have become a popular tool in recent years to combat racial and religious bigotry. . . . In asking the high court to review the case, . . . Edward J. Cleary said "displays of racial, ethnic, religious or gender intolerance reflect varied political viewpoints within our pluralistic society and are not susceptible to constitutionally valid restrictions."

—*The Washington Post*

This is a very important case, at a time when people in so many contexts—hate speech on campus, feminists against pornography, political correctness—are making the argument that you can suppress certain kinds of speech just because it does so much harm. . . . The First Amendment is almost always tested with speech that is profoundly divisive or painful. But if you start making exceptions, and suppressing speech that is hurtful, those exceptions will swallow free speech, and the only speech that will be left protected will be abstracted, emotionally lightweight speech that doesn't pack any wallop.

—Laurence Tribe

On the day the United States Supreme Court agreed to consider a law prohibiting the display of offensive symbols, hundreds of thousands of citizens lined the streets of New York City waving American flags in a ticker-tape parade for returning Gulf war veterans. In a brief national orgy of self-congratulation, citizens across the country cheered the outcome, perhaps as thankful that the nation had avoided another Vietnam as elated over the result of the short struggle in the Middle East. Although there was virtually unanimous relief that America had escaped serious casualties, many citizens were uncomfortable about the endless parades and flag-waving that surpassed the homecoming for veterans of less popular wars.

The huge parade in New York City on June 10, 1991, epitomized the differing viewpoints that had made banning offensive expression a dangerous proposition. On the same day that the Supreme Court announced its decision to review the cross-burning case, counter-demonstrations at the parade urged a focus on the ailing economy and decaying cities, a focus to which the nation would later return in ousting an incumbent president.

> Anti-war protesters dotted the route. "Operation Desert Massacre" proclaimed one sign mocking the march. "Jobs, health care and schools—Not war!" said another. "This parade and the millions of dollars spent on it to celebrate the evil destruction of Iraq is obscene."
>
> At least 25 protesters were arrested and 13 officers were injured in two clashes. . . .

Many Americans are angered by the sight of a burning flag; others are offended by excessive waving of the same flag. A cross alone upsets some non-Christians; a burning cross terrorizes some and offends nearly everyone. Powerful symbols elicit powerful reactions. Many observers, particularly in the media, saw an analogy between a burning cross and a burning flag. This was understandable, since we had relied on the flag-burning cases to support the argument that offensive symbolic expression could not be banned on the basis of its offensive nature. *Texas v. Johnson* and *U.S. v. Eichman,* the flag-burning cases, had been decided by 5–4 votes. After those votes were cast, Justice David Souter had replaced Justice William J. Brennan, Jr. Since Justice Brennan, a champion of the First Amendment, had written the majority opinions in those cases, many predicted that his retirement would erode established freedoms. Justice David Souter's position on laws prohibiting offensive symbolic expression was unknown.

On June 10, 1991, the *ABC Evening News* announced that the Supreme Court would hear *R.A.V.,* showed a protester burning a flag, and speculated that the new vote of Justice Souter might overturn the flag-burning cases. The most popular theory of the press at the time to explain the Court's decision to accept review, it accompanied speculation that this conservative court would uphold the lower-court decision.

Two observations seriously undermined these initial interpretations. Although the Rehnquist Court was not shy about overturning previous rulings of the Court, there remained the doctrine of *stare decisis*. Latin for the "decision stands," this doctrine forms the core of common law, as it places a premium on the continuity of legal interpretation over time, providing the stability that has remained the foundation of Anglo-American jurisprudence. Over the past thirty years, liberal and conservative Supreme Courts alike have appeared activist to Court observers, and stagnant to an impatient public. The upcoming 1991–92 term would demonstrate that certain justices were reluctant to overturn precedent, though they may not have voted with the majority at the time the original controlling decision was announced. Justice Souter may not have voted with the majority in *Roe v. Wade* or *Texas v. Johnson,* but his belief in the rule of law and the necessity for continuity may have so moderated his views that he was reluctant to overturn precedent.

Texas v. Johnson had been decided in 1989 and *U.S. v. Eichman* in 1990. The reaction that followed taught the American people the meaning of freedom in a democratic society, regardless of continuing anger toward flag-burners. To retreat now, within two years of the original decision, would demonstrate that the Court was more politicized than even detractors had imagined and would lead to further inconsistency in the interpretation of the First Amendment.

The flag-burning cases were submitted in an "as applied" posture, relevant primarily to the defendant; our challenge was to the law itself "on its face" as applied to all citizens. While to a nonlawyer that distinction may not seem significant, procedurally it meant that the Court would focus on the language of the ordinance rather than on the offensive factual allegations. A *Washington Post* editorial appeared that supported our position. It was the first editorial printed by any newspaper that shared our viewpoint:

> There is a hope in some quarters that the Supreme Court will not only sustain the kind of broad restriction of speech being challenged in the Minnesota case but will reverse the flag burning rulings as well. . . . That would be a tragedy not only because it would be wrong on constitutional grounds but because the First Amendment reasoning on which those decisions were based, and which was at first wildly unpopular, has through debate been understood and accepted by the public. This new challenge must be met with the

same concern for free speech and the same resolve, on the part of
the court, to protect it.

While many in the media seized on the flag-burning analogy to
explain the Court's action, other more seasoned observers offered
other explanations. The most popular of these was the "end to
overbreadth" argument. The Rehnquist Court, unlike the earlier
Warren Court, was widely known to be pro law-and-order in its
interpretation of the Fourth Amendment. Chief Justice Rehnquist
had clearly indicated a strong aversion to the overbreadth doctrine in
past decisions, and several major publications, including *The New
York Times* and *The National Law Journal,* saw this case as a
mandate on the doctrine itself. Under this doctrine, one who had
committed an obvious wrongdoing might escape punishment if the
prosecution resorted to a constitutionally defective provision. This
result would offend a court strongly supportive of law enforcement.
To avoid this outcome in the future, the Court in *R.A.V.* could
confirm the lower-court decision by striking down the doctrine, limiting future constitutional challenges. This result would appeal to
liberals because of the cross-burning incident and to conservatives
because of its lasting impact on judicial review.

The reasoning here was that the Court was being more subtle in its
approach and wasn't concerned about whether it was a flag or a cross
that was being burned but rather was interested in deciding whether
or not anyone should be allowed to challenge a law when he or she
had allegedly engaged in criminal conduct.

Another theory was that the Court had accepted the case to review
the "fighting words" doctrine of *Chaplinsky v. New Hampshire.*
American society had evolved in the half century since the decision;
the hope was that the Court was disabused of the doctrine and was
seeking a way to overturn it. This was discounted by most constitutional scholars; I, too, was skeptical that this Court would expand
free speech in that fashion.

More problematic was the issue of federalism. Since our nation
was founded two centuries ago, tension has existed between the belief
in a strong central government and the belief in autonomous state
governments, subject to little federal intervention. In articles and
speeches still powerful after two centuries, the competing political
philosophies that led to our present form of government diverged in
their outlook on the nature of man and on the meaning of self-
government. Federalists, believing in a strong central government and
the separation of powers, hoped to avoid not only the rise of a single

tyrant but also the problem of intersectional rivalries and conflicts. The anti-Federalists, believing in the primacy of the individual, were not convinced that a strong central government would prevent another form of tyranny, the tyranny of the majority. They preferred a loose confederation of colonies.

After the Civil War, "states' rights" took on new meaning. One section of the country inevitably wished to return to the "loose confederation" theory of government once in discord with the policies of the federal government. Segregationists like Strom Thurmond and his Dixiecrat party in 1948 were states' rights advocates. As the civil rights movement gained momentum in the 1960s, the Democratic party and the Kennedy administration used federal authority to enforce integration in the South, fulfilling the promise of *Brown v. Board of Education,* decided less than a decade earlier.

A quarter century later, conservatives still believe in strong state government, while liberals generally have more faith in the federal government. Closely allied with the conservative position is the belief that the United States Supreme Court should rarely review state court decisions and, when possible, narrow the scope of federal rights. Chief Justice Rehnquist and Justice O'Connor had been particularly reluctant to intervene in state court decisions. Justice White, having served in the Department of Justice during the Kennedy administration, had been an interventionist with regard to the use of federal authority. Both Justices Marshall and Brennan (as well as other members of the Warren Court) espoused the role of the federal constitution in ensuring basic rights for all citizens. In more recent years, many state courts that are more liberal in their interpretation of constitutional provisions have rested their decisions on state constitutions, rather than on corresponding federal provisions, in an effort to prevent review by a more conservative Supreme Court. As Justice Brennan has pointed out, state courts alone cannot ensure individual rights:

> Federal courts remain an indispensable safeguard of individual rights against governmental abuse. The revitalization of state constitutional law is no excuse for the weakening of federal protections and prohibitions. Slashing away at federal rights and remedies undermines our federal system. The strength of our system is that it "provides a double source of protection for the rights of our citizens. Federalism is not served when the federal half of that protection is crippled."

With the weakening of federal constitutional rights, citizens of this country have more constitutional protection in some states than others. The Minnesota Supreme Court generally interprets state constitutional provisions more liberally than does the state of Louisiana. Nevertheless, the United States Constitution continues to serve as a guarantee below which states may not infringe upon constitutional rights. While state courts are free to bestow greater constitutional rights than those guaranteed by the United States Constitution, they may not interpret state or federal constitutional provisions in such a way as to endanger the guarantee of the Bill of Rights. Consequently there have been a series of United States Supreme Court decisions throughout the past thirty years culminating in the flag-burning decisions in which the authority of the Bill of Rights was upheld despite state challenge.

Our case similarly challenged such established principles and foreseeable responses. Would the belief of liberals in the power of the federal government to intervene in state affairs to guarantee basic constitutional rights for citizens endure when the prohibited expression involved a hateful political viewpoint originating on the right? Would conservatives continue to oppose federal-government interference in state decisions when the challenged ordinance addressed offensive expression, often conservative in nature?

In the days immediately following the granting of review by the United States Supreme Court, my law office was deluged by the media with requests for interviews. Since the defense of indigent clients was only a portion of my practice, I maintained an office with a five-member law firm, Bannigan & Kelly. We shared secretaries, a library, and a conference room. We had maintained this arrangement for over a decade and I had become close friends with the partners and employees of the firm. From the outset, they were among my strongest supporters and demonstrated great patience as this case severely disrupted their operations for over a year.

As the media attention subsided, drafting the brief became our primary objective; all other considerations were put aside. Fortunately, my clients were patient in accepting my delays in returning their calls while a number of lawyers assisted me by covering court appearances for the following six weeks.

Arrangements were made with the county to pay for some typing and travel costs while the federal government handled printing fees, which was customary for an indigent appellant. No funding was available for attorney's fees, but neither Mike nor I had expected that there would be any available. Our immediate concern was to persuade constitutional-law experts to review drafts of the brief and to make suggestions as the matter progressed. With such a high-profile case we believed many law professors would willingly become involved. We had not foreseen that some law professors, who disagreed with our argument, would be reluctant to assist us. Others, in my opinion, did not want to become associated with such a politically incorrect position. We sought someone qualified to review a draft of our brief, a sacrifice of only a few hours' time.

We began our search for help at our alma mater, the University of Minnesota Law School. I contacted two professors, both of whom had clerked at the United States Supreme Court and were well known for their scholarship in the area of constitutional law. Professor Phil Frickey, a former clerk to Justice Marshall, had a conflict of interest and was unable to assist us. He did provide me with the name of a local lawyer who had clerked for Justice Scalia and whom Mike and I spoke to later. Professor Daniel Farber, a former clerk to Justice Stevens and a prolific legal writer, was unavailable. I did not contact the other area law schools; several professors at one of those schools assisted the government.

I did reach a friend of mine who was teaching legal writing at the University of Chicago, Pat Diamond. Pat suggested that I get in touch with Cass Sunstein, a professor at the law school who had written extensively on First Amendment cases. Sunstein, like Farber, was well known in the legal community as a prolific author of law review articles. I wrote him a letter on June 17 and awaited a response.

In the meantime I thought of John Siliciano. Nineteen years earlier, in the summer of 1972, I had enrolled in a summer session at Stanford University in Palo Alto, California. At the time I had hoped—unsuccessfully—for my miraculous admission to Stanford University Law School in 1974. I had relatives in the area and I knew how beautiful the campus and Bay Area were—a pleasant setting for a nineteen-year-old spending the summer relaxing, obtaining transferable credits for his degree. John was my assigned roommate from Elmira, New York. Although the session lasted only eight weeks, we became fast friends. As often happens in such situations, we corresponded after the summer and then lost contact.

In April of 1981 I was in the basement of the United States Supreme Court getting a cup of coffee before attending a ceremony where I would be sworn in as a member of the bar. Although to become a member of the United States Supreme Court bar one need not appear at the Court, I had arrived with a number of University of Minnesota law graduates to be sworn in as a group; it was no coincidence that the event was scheduled simultaneously with the arrival of the cherry blossoms. Pouring my coffee, I did a double take as I recognized John across the room. We visited briefly as he explained to me that he was clerking for Justice Thurgood Marshall. We had dinner the next night, but a decade later I had lost track of him once again.

Unable to locate him in the Washington, D.C., area, I remembered that his father was a practicing physician in or near Elmira, New York. The receptionist at his father's office told me that John was now a law professor at Cornell.

After John had returned my call, we reminisced about the simpler lives of college students. I explained why I was calling and the case I was working on. The discomfort in John's voice was apparent. He had clerked for Justice Marshall and he sensed the anguish that Justice Marshall would feel in deciding this case. I too had considered how difficult this case would be for Thurgood Marshall. With Justice Brennan now retired, Marshall remained the sole champion of the First Amendment. He had also been the single most influential legal figure in advancing civil rights in America in the twentieth century. It was hard to predict how he would vote on a case of this nature. Although I was confident that he would be appalled by the ordinance, I could only imagine how he would react to a case involving a burning cross. Since John and I had little contact over the years, I realized during our conversation that I must explain my motivation for handling this case.

Friends and associates in St. Paul knew my politics, knew that I had actively helped minorities in both private and public practice, and knew that I was appalled by a burning cross and any symbols of racial and religious hatred. In interviews with the media, I was quick to explain my background, fearing that the public would misunderstand me. Later I became irritated by the continual questions concerning my political beliefs, since I found them irrelevant to the defense of a client. I had represented clients charged with homicide, and no one had asked me whether or not I believed that murder was acceptable behavior. Yet members of the media repeatedly inquired about my position on burning a cross and on racism as though I were a closet Nazi. I held my temper in check, but soon tired of having to display my progressive credentials.

Now I had to tell an old friend that I had not changed, that I had not become a bigot and that I was pursuing this case because of my belief in the First Amendment. John responded as I had hoped he would, agreeing to review a draft of the brief and asking a constitutional law professor at Cornell for further input. The professor refused to assist, but John kept his promise and reviewed our draft.

I next sent a letter to retired Supreme Court justice William J.

Brennan, Jr. At the time of his retirement a year earlier, Justice Brennan had completed over three decades of distinguished service to his country and had influenced the American judicial system as extensively as any justice in the twentieth century. Over the last thirty years no justice had been a bigger champion of the First Amendment. Justice Brennan had long been an advocate of competent legal representation for indigents as well. He helped decide *Gideon v. Wainwright,* holding that indigent defendants charged with serious state criminal offenses must be provided with legal representation. That we were representing *R.A.V.* as an indigent was directly related to the recognition in *Gideon* that the Sixth Amendment mandated the right to counsel. As a result of the Court's interpretation of the Sixth Amendment in *Gideon,* we were now defending the First Amendment before the Court in *R.A.V.*

When asked his favorite part of the Constitution, Justice Brennan had recently responded: "The First Amendment, I expect. Its enforcement gives us this society. The other provisions of the Constitution merely embellish it." When asked "what he would do about the speech codes proliferating at colleges around the country," Brennan replied, "I can tell you what I think they ought to do . . . they ought to just abolish them."

In my naïveté, I had hoped to discuss the First Amendment with retired Justice Brennan as I worked on the draft. He graciously responded by letter and wrote that as an active member of the judiciary (retired status) he felt that it would be inappropriate to discuss a pending case. I was disappointed, but I understood his position; I only regretted that I would not be able to meet a man I so greatly respected.

On the day I heard from Justice Brennan, June 27, 1991, the last day of the 1990 term, Justice Thurgood Marshall announced his retirement while Justice Brennan was in the audience. The two strongest advocates of the First Amendment on the Court in the past quarter of a century were now retired. Two votes were now absent from the majority in the flag-burning cases that had upheld the First Amendment. One had been replaced by Justice David Souter, an unknown; the identity of the other would not be revealed until after the briefs were filed.

Two days earlier, I had participated by telephone in a radio talk show on WBZ in Boston. Expecting a debate, I was pleasantly surprised to learn that Alan Dershowitz supported our challenge to the law. He noted that a similar law had been "used in Leeds, England, a couple of years ago to ban the Star of David as a 'racist symbol' under the U.N. declaration equating Zionism with racism. . . ." He suggested that it was very hard to predict how the case would be decided.

Taking a call from a listener at the end of the program, I was amused to recognize the voice of a friend of mine, a Vietnam veteran who now lives in Concord, New Hampshire. I had called him to let him know I would be on the show, but I was surprised that he phoned in. Careful not to acknowledge our friendship on the air, he said that the flag-waving resulting from the Gulf war was militaristic and disturbing to him. I knew that he had returned his medals to the Vietnam Veterans Memorial in Washington, D.C., yet I was taken aback at the anger in his voice. Although he had phoned mainly to greet me, he also had to register his opinion.

Dershowitz, knowing nothing of my background, initially commented that he hoped I was defending the case on a "civil liberties basis." He later concluded that my motives were pure and that I was "acting in the highest tradition of the Bill of Rights in defending this person." I thanked him for his support and returned to my work on the brief the next day.

Mike and I had agreed that since I was arguing counsel I should be primarily responsible for the research and writing of the brief. Every law student is taught constitutional law and is examined in that area as part of the bar exam. Few attorneys ever return to constitutional law because constitutional issues seldom surface in their practice. Those knowledgeable about the First Amendment usually are found either at law schools or among the very few lawyers who represent newspapers and other media organizations.

It was clear that I would have to immerse myself in First Amendment law before beginning the brief. Since we had no clerks to do research, I secluded myself in the law library and began photocopying numerous law-review articles. These articles led to more articles; recommended books led to more books. I drove to Itasca State Park in northern Minnesota and read in a cabin for three days, taking notes hour after hour, interrupting the routine only to sleep, eat an occasional meal, and bicycle around the lake.

As I began to outline the first draft of the brief, I focused on the summary of argument. The summary appears at the beginning of the brief and is designed to be a short and concise summation of one position. It is most effective when it encompasses the position of the appellant while assuming some of the characteristics of a written final argument. The goal is artful persuasion leading the reader into the legal arguments.

Contemplating various approaches, I remembered an exchange between film characters. The movie was *A Man for All Seasons,* the fascinating story of Sir Thomas More, lawyer, philosopher, and martyr. My father, who was both a lawyer and a Catholic, had taken me to see the film when I was thirteen. I distinctly recalled an exchange between Thomas More and a young lawyer in which More declared he would defend the devil. To a thirteen-year-old that statement seemed the wrong sentiment for a presumably courageous and religious man to express.

Remembering that the movie had been adapted from a play, I went to a bookstore in St. Paul and found an old Vintage paperback edition yellowed with age. Scanning through the pages I found the scene on page 38.

> Roper: So now you'd give the Devil benefit of law!
>
> Thomas More: Yes. What would you do? Cut a great road through the law to get after the Devil?
>
> Roper: I'd cut down every law in England to do that!
>
> Thomas More: Oh? And when the last law was down, and the Devil turned round on you—where would you hide, the laws all being flat? . . . If you cut them down . . . d'you really think you could stand upright in the winds that would blow then? Yes, I'd give the Devil benefit of law, for my own safety's sake.

The playwright Robert Bolt had both captured the essence of Thomas More and articulated the principles of our case eloquently. Sir Thomas More was lord chancellor under King Henry VIII in sixteenth-century England; William Roper was a young lawyer and More's son-in-law. A man who loved life, his family, and the law, and who was loyal to both king and country, More was executed by Henry VIII for a matter of conscience. Bolt explains in his preface to the play that More was an average and worldly man, yet for the lord chancellor an oath before God was "not merely a time-honored and understood ritual but also a definite contract." An oath before God became an integral part of self; to break the oath was to destroy oneself. Wanting to live, he died rather than submit to the authority of the Crown. The theme of this dialogue—the protection of the most hated to ensure the protection of the many—was the foundation of our argument. History had shown that allowing the majority to decide which group was "unworthy" was to engage in systematic repression of all.

Familiar with the facts of the case, the firm's secretary, Karen, was reluctant to type the numerous drafts of the brief, but agreed to do so when Pat Kelly, an attorney in the office, told her that she would be "making history." As I gave her each draft, her reaction became a litmus test of the effectiveness of our advocacy. As the hours of typing grew, she appeared to become more and more convinced after considering our arguments. I was to see this reaction many times during the next year.

After the first draft, I received a call from the dean of the University of Chicago Law School, Geoffrey Stone, who had a reputation as an accomplished legal scholar. I appreciated the call because I had hoped that he would review drafts of our brief and offer suggestions on the basis of his knowledge in this area of the law. Although I was not shocked by the tone of his call as it progressed, I was disappointed and somewhat angry. After indicating that he was prepared to become involved in the case, he suggested that I should consider relinquishing my right to argue the case to a friend of his, Michael McConnell, a law professor at Chicago, who had previously worked in the Justice Department during the Reagan administration and had argued before the United States Supreme Court.

Stone suggested that since he himself had declined opportunities to argue before the Court, I should do the same. He went on to observe that this was "not the Minnesota Supreme Court." (Since I had lost 6–0 in that court, I hoped he was right.) He told me that this would be a close decision and that my inexperience could result in defeat. When I assured Stone that I had no intention of relinquishing my right to argue the case, he said he would review sections of my brief, but only if I "acted responsibly." Presumably that meant "doing it his way" and adopting the proper tone. Finding his manner altogether astonishing, I thanked him for his interest but looked elsewhere for assistance.

Cass Sunstein, also of the University of Chicago, contacted me and adopted an entirely different approach. Apologizing for not calling earlier, he told me that after having read more about the case, he was too busy to assist. Later, reviewing a number of his law-review articles, I realized that he probably opposed our position. Nevertheless, he suggested that I contact Kathleen Sullivan, then of Harvard Law School. I spoke to Professor Sullivan, who graciously agreed to review a draft of the brief at no expense when she realized that I was working *pro bono*.

By the first week in July, Mike and I had written two drafts and I had completed a third. Although we were close friends, we became irritable with each other because of exhaustion and pressure, and on one occasion we argued vociferously in a hallway outside a law library. We continued work on the next draft, mindful of the stress we both felt. Several people had argued against the inclusion of the passage from *A Man for All Seasons,* but both Mike and I were convinced that the power of the passage outweighed the unconventionality of its inclusion.

After faxing the brief to John Siliciano at Cornell and Kathleen Sullivan at Harvard, various groups asked for my consent to filing *amicus* briefs. Eventually, four briefs sponsored by seven organizations were filed in support of our position. Ten briefs sponsored by fifty-one organizations were filed in behalf of our opponent, Ramsey County.

The entire political spectrum was represented by the groups filing the four briefs in our behalf. The organizations sponsoring the first brief, including the American Civil Liberties Union, the Minnesota Civil Liberties Union, and the American Jewish Congress, would be considered politically left of center. The Association of American Publishers and the Freedom to Read Foundation, both active proponents of the First Amendment, also filed a brief. The Center for Individual Rights, a two-year-old conservative public-interest law firm, filed a brief representing a position right of center. Representing the far right was a brief from the Patriots Defense Foundation.

The circumstances surrounding the submission of the last brief were unusual. On July 11 I received a call from an attorney in Georgia who asked for consent to file a brief in behalf of the Patriots Defense Foundation. It was a call that I had hoped to avoid, coming as it did from an organization with which I had little in common. The attorney for the foundation was straightforward and told me that his group did most of the "Klan defense." Apparently familiar with my background, he said that our personal beliefs were probably dissimilar. I agreed and told him that I had spent much of my career defending indigents. He said he understood and that his primary concern was the prevention of censorship. Had he stopped there, all would have been well. But in discussing the dangers of censorship, he said that such laws in Canada had resulted in the removal of books arguing that the Holocaust was a hoax. I told him that we were in agreement about the First Amendment, and perhaps we should leave it at that. Noting the tone in my voice, and with obvious reference to my heritage, he said his organization generally had no quarrel with the Irish and that retired Justice Brennan, though imperfect, had authored some acceptable decisions. I made no comment. He told me that his ancestors had fought for the Confederacy. I told him that I had an ancestor who had fought for the Union against his ancestors at Gettysburg. There remained little to say. I told him that we would not refuse consent to any organization because it would be hypocritical to silence groups while defending the First Amendment. I suggested that since the Center for Individual Rights was already writing a brief and was politically conservative, he might call them to see if they could address his concerns.

John Siliciano had returned a copy of our brief with some written suggestions, and I talked to Kathleen Sullivan over the phone about her suggestions. Two professors, only one whose field was constitutional law, had taken the time to review a draft and make some general suggestions. This would be the only review we would have. Both felt that the quote from Thomas More, though unorthodox, was effective and should remain. Both felt that the law was obviously overbroad, that the Minnesota decision was defective, and suggested that we emphasize the vagueness of the law after the Minnesota Supreme Court decision. Both professors, particularly John, seemed relieved that our arguments appeared to be well thought out and not rooted in sympathy for the hateful.

Neither offered an opinion as to why the Court had taken the case, but John reminded me that the Court seldom took a case simply to affirm the lower court's decision. As a result of their advice, I shortened the first section of the brief regarding overbreadth and expanded the second section regarding the Minnesota Supreme Court decision.

While working on the next draft, we heard from the Rutherford Institute. A conservative organization primarily concerned with religious freedom and located in Virginia, the institute had contacted me earlier for consent to file a brief. They now did not have the resources to complete the brief on time. Instead, they proposed to sponsor our brief by paying an undetermined amount toward fees for the right to appear on our brief. I quickly turned down this arrangement. They thanked me and never filed a brief.

Soon I heard again from the attorney for the Patriots Defense Foundation, who said that his organization had decided to file a brief. Adhering to our agreement not to refuse consent, I nevertheless felt it necessary to clarify our position to the attorney. I told him that we had worked hard and believed very strongly in the promise of the First Amendment. Observing that our backgrounds and beliefs were entirely dissimilar, I noted that we shared the same goal in upholding First Amendment freedoms. I said that the worst mistake he could make would be to engage in hateful rhetoric, for such rhetoric would either distract from or undermine the arguments in support of our position. He assured me that he had no intention of acting in such a manner. Several days later I received a copy of his brief; it was short and did not break any new ground. Nevertheless, it was hard to accept the organization's stated "interest" in the case. The Foundation sought "to protect the vital First Amendment rights of political activists and spokespersons who advocate the ideology that the United States should remain a predominantly Christian, Anglo-Saxon and European derived nation with all that proposition entails in terms of cultural, social and religious norms." This was the stereotype of those who opposed hate-crime laws.

It would be melodramatic to say we experienced a crisis of conscience. Although we did not waver from our position on the First Amendment, I could not help thinking back to how the Klan had targeted Irish Catholics in the nineteenth century and well into the twentieth. I checked the legal directory and found that the lawyer with whom I had discussed the case was my age. He embraced an ideology totally alien to me but here we were on the same side of this issue. Perhaps because of their sheer number or perhaps by virtue of their white skin, Irish Catholics were now rarely targets and seldom had crosses burned in their neighborhood. The same could be said for the Italians. The burden of intolerance was now being borne primarily by Asian, African, Hispanic, and Native Americans. It was no surprise that members of these groups would wonder about people like me, particularly when we were allied with openly reactionary groups. But the truth of the matter was that we did not have the luxury of choosing the source of our support.

After we had filed our brief on July 23, 1991, I started receiving other briefs from groups that had supported us. I was particularly pleased to receive the brief from the Association of American Publishers and the Freedom to Read Foundation, a nonprofit organization established a quarter century ago by the American Library Association. Knowing that those who loved books and understood the dangers of censorship were on our side provided great comfort. The attorneys for these groups felt that the threat to the overbreadth doctrine put freedom of expression in jeopardy and they focused on that issue. Fearful that publishers and librarians who provided controversial books might be prosecuted under overbroad laws like section 292.02 in the future, these organizations supported our challenge to the ordinance.

The brief sponsored by the Center of Individual Rights was well written and correctly cited the reasoning of a conservative hero, Judge Richard A. Posner of the Seventh Circuit Court of Appeals.

Judge Posner had written an opinion involving an obscenity statute in which he recognized the danger in allowing any state to forbid some "disfavored" obscenity and not all obscenity. Posner's reasoning provided the basis for a significant portion of my oral argument.

The joint brief from the American Civil Liberties Union, the Minnesota Civil Liberties Union, and the American Jewish Congress was another matter. These were the groups from whom we had expected our strongest support. While drafting our brief, I had called Mark Anfinson, the attorney for the MCLU, and had asked for a copy of the first draft of the brief. Upon receipt and review, I was disappointed and extremely angry. The first section of the draft of the joint brief caused me great concern. It reflected the ACLU's apparent belief that the Court would go too far in protecting First Amendment freedoms, and did little to explain why the First Amendment was in danger. The second section, drafted by the MCLU, was similar to their earlier argument. The brief was disjointed, the latter section clearly in support of our position, the other section nonsupportive.

I called the offices of the MCLU and indicated my displeasure in no uncertain terms. I learned that the MCLU was in agreement with me, and that a major breach had occurred between the local and national chapters. I suspected that the ACLU had become politicized and that john powell, the national legal director (who doesn't use capital letters in his name), was probably responsible. Charles R. Lawrence III, of Stanford Law School, had cited powell as a "good friend" and quoted powell in his article in support of his position on the regulation of hate speech. Eventually a compromise was reached between the MCLU and ACLU wherein the MCLU's section became the first portion of the brief and the ACLU's the second portion. The failure of the ACLU to back our position fully is a continuing disappointment. While I respect the work and the opinions of Nadine Strossen, I was nevertheless disappointed in the brief filed by the ACLU and signed by Steven Shapiro and john powell. I sent a letter to the MCLU thanking them for their assistance, and once again registered my displeasure with the section contributed by the ACLU.

By late July I was inundated with requests by organizations seeking my consent to the filing of opposing briefs. We never considered withholding consent because the Court generally grants motions to intervene, and because it would be inconsistent with our position that censorship is not allowed under the First Amendment. Two of the organizations to which we consented never filed briefs. The first organization that chose not to file a brief was the Minnesota Lawyers International Human Rights Committee, of which I was a member.

I was disappointed when an attorney for the committee, a former law school classmate, asked my consent to file an opposing brief. Although I was not conversant with the entire international experience of hate-crime laws, I was confident that an examination of the international experience would further our position rather than that of those who opposed us. Indeed, as a British author pointed out,

> in most countries, hate speech laws either have been used to a substantial degree to suppress the rights of government critics and other minorities or else have been used arbitrarily or not at all. To the extent that the laws have served a beneficial purpose it has been to improve the tone of civility in liberal democracies. In those countries the laws do not seem to have improved underlying conditions of discrimination and hatred and, in some of the countries, may have justified inattention to those conditions. The possible benefits to be gained by such laws simply do not seem to be justified by their high potential for abuse.

I learned later that the board for the committee was deeply divided and had finally voted not to file the already completed brief. Another organization, the National District Attorneys Association, likewise received our consent in late July and eventually declined to file a brief. My father had been an active member of the association for over thirty years, and I had attended many national meetings of the association with him. The association did not file because they felt another *amicus* brief addressed their concerns.

I began receiving the eleven briefs filed against us in mid-August. The respondent's brief, filed by Ramsey County on behalf of the city of St. Paul, seemed to misconstrue the thrust of our argument. Noting that we had directed the first section of our brief to the wording of the ordinance and not to the construction given to it by the Minnesota Supreme Court, the respondent urged the Court to find this argument "irrelevant." We had acknowledged that under our federal system a state has a right to interpret its own laws, but an examination of the law revealed that it was not subject to such narrowing without being entirely rewritten, violating settled constitutional precepts. While the United States Supreme Court would focus on the Minnesota Supreme Court's decision, most of the language of the law as written remained even after the narrowing construction.

Negligently or intentionally, the brief also argued that the First Amendment did not protect the alleged facts in this case. Our challenge did not defend the alleged criminal activity; rather we questioned a law that did not address threats or intimidation, but did address the expression of an unpopular and offensive opinion, thereby threatening everyone's First Amendment rights. The ordinance was on trial before the United States Supreme Court. The facts of the case were irrelevant, which confused the public and provided political mileage for the prosecutor. The government even asserted that the law was "content-neutral," and was not aimed at any political viewpoint. This argument would haunt the respondent at oral argument. Finally, the brief quoted extensively from *United States v. Lee,* a decision from the Eighth Circuit that had been vacated (set aside for reconsideration) by the time we had received the brief. We were unimpressed with the quality of the respondent's brief.

There were ten more briefs to read. Three of them were from government organizations. The first, from the League of Minnesota Cities and the cities of Minneapolis and St. Paul, argued that the cities throughout the state of Minnesota needed the authority to enact laws of this nature to enforce the peace. The brief stated that the Minnesota Supreme Court had acted within its power and had successfully narrowed the law. It did not explain why cities could not effectively enforce the criminal code without resorting to laws of such a sweeping nature. The next brief was filed by a group of governmental entities, including the National Governors Association and the U.S. Conference of Mayors. This brief, defending the extensive use of hate-crime laws by state governments, also argued that the Minnesota Supreme Court had successfully construed the law, concluding with a recitation of the ugly factual allegations.

Next was a brief filed by seventeen attorneys general throughout the country. Since this position involved little political risk, I was surprised that almost two thirds of the states had apparently refused to sign. The West was represented by Arizona, Idaho, and Utah (California conspicuous by its absence). The South was represented by Alabama, Oklahoma, South Carolina, Tennessee, and Virginia (Texas and Florida conspicuous by their absence). The Midwest was represented by Minnesota, Illinois, Kansas, Michigan, and Ohio. The East was represented by Connecticut, Massachusetts, Maryland, and New Jersey (New York and Pennsylvania unaccounted for). The brief asserted the need for hate-crime laws generally, ignoring that this case involved a law directed at speech, not crime, and that the criminal code could adequately punish wrongdoers without endangering the First Amendment.

The next brief filed against us was sponsored by a California organization known as the Criminal Justice Legal Foundation. Apparently a conservative law-and-order organization, it exists to "bring the constitutional protections of the accused into balance with the rights of victims and of society to rapid, efficient, and reliable determination of guilt and swift execution of punishment." The brief's sole purpose was to persuade the United States Supreme Court to ban the right of a citizen to challenge a law "on its face," leaving only the challenge of "as applied." Superficially appealing to advocates of strong law enforcement, the result sought would have been disastrous for a nation that believes in individual freedom. Penal laws that clearly threatened protected expression would remain on the books. Citizens would express opinions at their own risk, hoping that the law would be found defective as applied to their case. The result would be a sliding scale of protection, buffeted by political winds, protected only by majority whim. This was not what the Framers intended in drafting the Bill of Rights.

Another brief was filed by four Asian-American organizations. Each group, less than two decades old, was concerned with reports of hate violence aimed at Asians and Pacific islanders. Detailing how racial bias has extended to a different immigrant group, the brief did not explain why such acts of violence could not be prosecuted effectively under existing laws.

A brief was filed by thirteen organizations, including the Center for Constitutional Rights, the YWCA, the National Lawyers Guild, and the National Coalition of Black Lesbians and Gays. This brief had an impact on us for two unrelated reasons. First, the key sponsoring organization, the Center for Constitutional Rights, was co-founded by William Kunstler. A well-known civil rights advocate, Kunstler had argued both of the flag-burning cases successfully before the United States Supreme Court. It seemed incomprehensible that Kunstler would now abandon the First Amendment. Only later did I learn that he disagreed with the center's position and supported the First Amendment.

Secondly, I was surprised and disheartened by the shortsightedness of so many liberal groups that allegedly were interested in freedom for the individual. The brief was extremely angry in its tone and strident in its rhetoric ("Every 18 seconds, a woman is beaten, and every three and a half minutes, a woman is a victim of a rape or an attempted rape"). Violence toward women is an increasing social problem in our country, and people who assault others or engage in criminal sexual conduct should be prosecuted under considerably tougher laws than this ordinance. These organizations seemed oblivious to the disingenuousness of their argument. Though they depended on the First Amendment for their very existence, they were prepared to sacrifice that freedom in order to silence those whose expression they did not want to hear.

To the surprise of no one who follows the debate over the First Amendment, Catharine A. MacKinnon requested my consent to file an opposing brief on behalf of the National Black Women's Health Project. Over the years, MacKinnon had actively supported legislation that seriously threatened freedom of expression. Whatever one thinks of MacKinnon, she and her co-author Burke Marshall, a high-ranking Justice Department official in the Kennedy administration, are highly regarded in legal circles, making their position on the First Amendment all the more puzzling.

Arguing to eradicate discrimination and social inequality based on race or gender, MacKinnon regards the Fourteenth Amendment as a steamroller and the First Amendment as a bump in the road. Millions of Americans would agree that we have not done enough to achieve social equality, but the debate is whether censorious laws bring us any closer to that goal. It is reasonable to argue in favor of strict enforcement of civil rights legislation to protect citizens from harassment or discrimination on the basis of race, religion, or gender. It is another matter to suggest that citizens who express offensive opinions on these issues should be subject to criminal prosecution.

The last three briefs were filed by organizations that Mike and I referred to as the "big three," the Anti-Defamation League, the NAACP, and People for the American Way. For over seven decades the ADL has been known as a progressive organization committed to fighting racial and religious discrimination while promoting and protecting the Bill of Rights. In this case they were opposed by the American Jewish Congress, an organization that has focused for more than seven decades on progressive social issues, particularly as they relate to Jewish Americans. Over the past ten years the balance between fighting discrimination and protecting individual freedom had tipped against freedom for the ADL and it had become the major proponent nationwide of hate-crime legislation. The legislation the League promoted were "enhancement" hate-crime laws, under which someone who had committed an assault, trespass, or burglary, "motivated by bias," would be punished more severely than someone who had committed the same crimes without the bias motivation. Those laws were distinguishable from the St. Paul law. Enhancement laws prohibit criminal conduct and enhance the sentence based on motivation; the St. Paul law made the expression itself illegal. The ADL engaged in a rearguard action with this case, cognizant of the constitutional flaws in the ordinance but fearful that enhancement laws were jeopardized.

Although erudite in tone, the NAACP's brief was flawed in several serious respects. It noted that the allegations indicated an intent to terrorize, but offered no explanation for the failure to use the more serious terroristic threat law. More surprising was the brief's recommendation that the Court "reassess the overbreadth doctrine." I wondered what Justices Brennan and Marshall would think about a civil rights organization urging a conservative court to limit a doctrine long used by the disfranchised to obtain judicial review. The two cases cited by the NAACP to demonstrate the "serious problems of the overbreadth doctrine" involved black Americans prosecuted for swearing at white police officers. The NAACP would not be satisfied with eviscerating the First Amendment; the organization also sought to limit the access of groups seeking facial review of repressive laws, laws that historically had been used to subjugate the dispossessed, including those citizens the NAACP ostensibly represented.

We received a brief from People for the American Way, an allegedly nonpartisan organization founded a decade earlier and devoted to the promotion and protection of civil liberties. Their failure to protect and defend the First Amendment was a bitter disappointment to us. Attorneys for this group had filed briefs in support of the First Amendment in the flag-burning cases. They now abandoned that position as they argued to uphold an unconstitutional law by saying that the law was not viewpoint discriminatory and that the burning cross and swastika were mere "examples" of prohibited expression.

As People for the American Way continued to be quoted by the press, it was difficult for me to understand how this organization could claim to be apolitical and nonpartisan. My cynicism increased a year later with the controversy over rap singer Ice-T's controversial song "Cop Killer." In releasing the record, Time Warner maintained that the song was protected by the First Amendment. A number of organizations sponsored an advertisement in *Variety* in support of Time Warner for "resisting efforts to ban the song." Among the groups signing the ad was People for the American Way. It is surely hypocritical, to say the least, to defend hateful rhetoric aimed at one group (police officers), while condemning hateful expression aimed at another (minorities).

As Labor Day approached, we began to outline our reply brief and formulate a strategy for the oral argument. In reviewing the concluding paragraph in our brief, I continued to believe that the other briefs submitted by fifty-one organizations had failed to undermine the core of our argument.

Restrictions might curtail some offensive expression but only at the cost of chilling a great deal of protected speech. The result may well be the silencing of political debate, the encouraging of orthodoxy, and the endangering of the individual's right to dissent. To enforce a notion of civility to the point of forbidding unpopular minority expression is to underestimate the citizens of this country at the cost of our basic right of self-expression.

8

Thought Control in the Marketplace: Progressive Censorship, Sexual Harassment, and the Pornography Debate

When men have realized that time has upset many fighting faiths, they may come to believe even more than they believe the very foundations of their own conduct that the ultimate good desired is better reached by free trade in ideas—that the best test of truth is the power of the thought to get itself accepted in the competition of the market, and that truth is the only ground upon which their wishes safely can be carried out. That, at any rate, is the theory of our Constitution. It is an experiment, as all life is an experiment.

—Justice Oliver Wendell Holmes, Jr. (1919)

Every idea is an incitement. It offers itself for belief and if believed it is acted on unless some other belief outweighs it or some failure of energy stifles the movement at its birth. The only difference between expression of an opinion and an incitement in the narrower sense is the speaker's enthusiasm for the result. . . . If in the long run the beliefs . . . are destined to be accepted by the dominant forces of the community, the only meaning of free speech is that they should be given their chance and have their way.

—Justice Oliver Wendell Holmes, Jr. (1925)

In the fall of 1919 Justice Oliver Wendell Holmes, Jr., delivered his dissent in the case of *Abrams v. United States* in open court. A thirty-one-year-old anarchist, Jacob Abrams, had thrown leaflets out of a third-floor window in New York City that severely criticized the Wilson administration for having sent troops into Russia in 1918. He was convicted of sedition and sentenced to twenty years in prison. Holmes had voted with the majority in such cases as *Schenk v. United States,* upholding the conviction of individuals who had obstructed the war effort, but he now changed his mind. In the fall of 1919, at the age of seventy-eight, he dissented from the majority despite concerted efforts by three of the justices and his own wife to dissuade him from doing so.

Using a marketplace metaphor, Holmes outlined the parameters of modern free speech. He reaffirmed the principle of free expression tested by other expression without censorship by the majority. After a lifetime of experience, Holmes had concluded that enforced truth was not truth at all but only governmentally imposed orthodoxy. History had shown, and experience had confirmed, that in a climate of fear, well-intentioned leaders would enact legislation eroding individual liberties, undermining a free and democratic society.

Six years later, in *Gitlow v. New York,* Holmes posed the ultimate challenge to a free society. In a dissent joined by Justice Brandeis, Holmes raised the question of whether a free and democratic society is capable of tolerating the dissenting viewpoint. Speaking to a citizenry that had suffered through one world war and would soon suffer through another, along with the worst economy of the century, the eighty-four-year-old Holmes reminded America of the true meaning of freedom of expression. Born more than twenty years before the start of the Civil War, when the Bill of Rights was only a half century old, Holmes had lived through severe military and economic upheaval, but had not lost sight of the essential quality of freedom.

Those who criticized his "marketplace of ideas" doctrine of free speech argued that some speech is not answerable, that ultimately some speech could destroy the very marketplace it relied on. Holmes reminded those critics that such offensive speech, even that which threatens the foundation of democratic government, must be allowed in a free and representative society. He believed that courage and vision were vitally important virtues in a democracy and would counter fear and repression. The nation could then withstand challenges to accepted beliefs, even the challenge of anarchy during wartime.

Over the last twenty years some disfranchised groups, including minority and feminist organizations, have lost faith in the First Amendment. Discounting the fact that free discourse fostered the civil rights and antiwar movements of the sixties and early seventies, they have grown frustrated with their perceived inability to accelerate social change. They believe that the promise of those movements has dissipated. It is true that although progress has been achieved by minorities and women, much more needs to be done to eradicate racial and sexual discrimination. Freedom of expression will aid this effort unless it is eroded in the manner advocated by proponents of censorship.

Those who would censor offensive speech disagree. Some disfranchised groups take issue with Holmes's marketplace metaphor and suggest that access to power is the issue. They rely on the belief that there is constitutional room available for "progressive censorship," whereby subordinated groups may express "progressive" ideas while censoring others. Proponents of this theory believe that racism and sexism are endemic to the marketplace, rendering the marketplace an anachronism. Frustrated that the Fourteenth Amendment has not eradicated racial and sexual discrimination, these individuals argue that it is not censorship to silence what is bad or hurtful. Well-meaning in principle, such an elastic standard could well be disastrous in practice. It could easily be used against antiwar protesters in wartime ("Extraordinary times call for extraordinary measures"), or to justify the persecution of anarchistic Communists ("They would destroy the marketplace if given the chance").

Many of the arguments used to justify offensive-speech regulations have been used by those who would ban pornography, defined broadly. If the debate over hate-speech restrictions has divided the civil liberties and civil rights communities, the struggle to ban pornography has united such disparate groups as radical feminists and conservative religious organizations.

As James Davison Hunter writes in his study *Culture Wars: The Struggle to Define America,* old alliances have fallen and new ones been created. Orthodox Catholics, Protestants, and Jews now have more in common culturally than the more liberal groups within the same religions. According to Hunter, a more accurate depiction of the cultural division in America would contrast an orthodox viewpoint with a progressive one. The same schism exists in the feminist movement; those led by Catharine MacKinnon, of the University of Michigan Law School, philosophically oppose such groups as Feminists for Free Expression. The orthodox traditions of established religions agree with MacKinnon on the issue of pornography, but little else. Both orthodox and liberal groups in American culture demand censorship of the other, asserting their own validity. Hunter notes, as did Gary Wills before him, the distinction between censure and censorship:

In the contemporary culture war, regard for rights to the freedom of speech has become a matter of "whose ox is being gored" at the moment. The fact is, both sides make a big mistake when they confuse *censuring* (legitimate mobilization of moral opprobrium) with *censoring* (the use of the state and other legal or official means to restrict speech).

If some on the right seek to censor an art exhibit in Cincinnati based on its perceived obscenity, others from the left, given the chance, would censor offensive expression on selected topics such as race or gender. Although these forms of censorship reflect a division between orthodox and progressive thought, the efforts of MacKinnon and her partner, Andrea Dworkin, to ban pornography, as well as offensive speech based on gender, blur these distinctions as this movement joins some on the left to favor campus censorship, and joins others on the right to ban pornography.

Many American citizens would welcome the day that pornography ceases to exist. Many Americans would celebrate an end to obviously offensive racial or religious expression. The sight of materialistic pornographers or fanatical racists waving American flags and proclaiming their rights is upsetting. But as Edward de Grazia has said, "Sexual dissent and political dissent are siblings: both defy old orthodoxies and de-stabilize fixed beliefs." Just as racial intolerance may lead to oppressive laws enforced against those who sought the law's protection, some would argue that "pornography cannot be separated from art; the two interpenetrate each other, far more than humanistic criticism has admitted. . . . 'Great art is always flanked by its dark sisters, blasphemy and pornography.' *Hamlet* itself, the cardinal western work, is full of lewdness." There are obvious cases in which pornography may be banned, such as child pornography. Yet when loosely defined, "pornography" is often what offends those most easily offended, a definition that threatens books, music, art, and theater. Minority groups have often raised the national consciousness through works offensive to some.

For MacKinnon, the imposition of selective censorship is nevertheless a worthwhile risk; she sees such censorship not as an application of a subjective moral viewpoint, but rather as an effort to mitigate harm done to the ability of women to participate equally in the marketplace:

> So while the First Amendment supports pornography, believing that consensus and progress are facilitated by allowing all views, however divergent and unorthodox, it fails to notice that pornogra-

phy (like the racism, in which I include anti-Semitism, of the Nazis and the Klan) is not at all divergent or unorthodox. It is the ruling ideology. Feminism, the dissenting view, is suppressed by pornography. . . . Liberalism has never understood that the free speech of man silences the free speech of women.

To follow this argument logically, the free speech of whites silences the free speech of blacks; the free speech of Catholics silences the free speech of Jews; the free speech of heterosexuals silences the free speech of homosexuals, etc. For MacKinnon, the First Amendment should benefit only subordinated, not dominant, groups. If "dominant" groups were silenced and "subordinated" groups given complete freedom, wouldn't such arbitrary labeling result in widespread censorship? MacKinnon and her followers would find this unlikely. They see no constitutional dilemma in silencing speech based on its objectionable content, and in silencing groups based on their perceived status. The argument is that "American society is a patriarchal system that enshrines a male perspective and relegates women to subordinate roles. Notions of logic, objectivity, equality under the law, and the common good are all regarded as reflections of this patriarchal bias. . . . The 'gender-neutral' person, feminists argue, is a patriarchal artifact intended to perpetuate male power."

The problems of discrimination and intolerance are real and pervasive in society. Silencing those who disagree does not eradicate such problems. By establishing a framework for the erosion of personal freedom for members of selected groups, such advocates fail to grasp the dangerousness of the precedent they are embracing. Once a group labels itself "subordinated," it is free to ignore the constitutional framework that "dominant" groups must honor. It is a selected rejection of individual liberty for some citizens and appears particularly disingenuous against the backdrop of the politics of abortion.

Those feminists who believe in banning pornography as well as the proscription of offensive speech based on gender ignore the fact that such a result would undermine the constitutional foundation for the individual liberties they cherish, including the liberty of choice. Justice Brennan addressed this issue in dissenting from a majority decision involving an obscenity statute:

Like the proscription of abortions, the effort to suppress obscenity is predicated on unprovable, although strongly held, assumptions about human behavior, morality, sex and religion. The existence of these assumptions cannot validate a statute that substantially undermines the guarantees of the First Amendment, any more than the existence of similar assumptions on the issue of abortion can validate a statute that infringes on the constitutionally protected privacy interests of a pregnant woman.

The logic of Justice Brennan is unassailable, particularly when one considers the arguments usually presented by those who would ban such expression. One contention is that pornography is closer to conduct than it is to speech and is thus subject to regulation. Even if one accepts this argument, the Court has already spoken on the "emotive function" of such speech as opposed to its "cognitive content." Recognizing that the most powerful expression provokes a nonintellectual reaction, the Court weakened the distinction between conduct and speech, and endorsed a broad definition of speech, including speech apparently devoid of intellectual content.

Another argument involves the concept of harm to women as a group. "Group libel" has fallen into disfavor in the forty years since *Beauharnais v. Illinois.* In subsequent cases the Court has disapproved of laws that silence expression while seeking to protect group reputation. Laws that would punish expression deemed to "harm" a group would inevitably result in self-censorship and selective enforcement of the law by those who controlled political power. Both sexes, as well as all races, religions, and ethnic groups, would suffer because all expression deemed offensive on such topics, even expression not targeted at an individual, would be prohibited. Controversial opinions would be replaced by politically acceptable speech, thus eroding individual liberty.

Since 1983 a movement has been led by MacKinnon and Dworkin to pass sweeping antipornography legislation in various communities across the nation. The movement began in 1983 at my alma mater, the University of Minnesota Law School, within the same time period that the St. Paul City Council enacted St. Paul City Ordinance section 292.02. At that time the First Amendment was under siege in the Twin Cities. As a practicing attorney at the time, I remember the newspaper and television coverage of the often emotional debates conducted by the Minneapolis City Council. Enveloped in the hysteria of political correctness, the council enacted a draconian antipornography measure less than six weeks after it had been presented to them by MacKinnon and Dworkin. Secure in his progressive credentials, Mayor Don Fraser vetoed the ordinance a week later. Six months later he once again vetoed a modified ordinance.

Dworkin and MacKinnon moved on. Having failed to persuade a

liberal community to agree with their censorship position, they focused on the more conservative community of Indianapolis, Indiana. This time they succeeded in passing an ordinance, perhaps because they lowered their public profile. The ordinance was challenged immediately by the American Booksellers Association, and in November 1984 Judge Sara Evans Barker of the U.S. District Court of the Southern District of Indiana struck down the law. Judge Barker's comments were equally relevant to consideration of St. Paul City Ordinance section 292.02:

> To permit every interest group, especially those who claim to be victimized by unfair expression, their own legislative exceptions to the First Amendment so long as they succeed in obtaining a majority of legislative votes in their favor demonstrates the potentially predatory nature of what defendants seek through this Ordinance. . . .

After the city of Indianapolis appealed, Judge Frank Easterbrook of the Seventh Circuit confirmed Judge Barker's ruling and foreshadowed the consideration of the St. Paul Ordinance in *R.A.V.* years later. Accepting the premise in the legislation that subordination of a group could perpetuate subordination, Easterbrook nevertheless held that it was not constitutionally permissible to suppress speech based on its power to influence opinion. Noting that pornography did not fit comfortably into the "marketplace of ideas," he wrote that "the Constitution does not make the dominance of truth a necessary condition of freedom of speech. . . . A power to limit speech on the ground that truth has not yet prevailed and is not likely to prevail implies the power to declare truth. . . . If the government may declare the truth, why wait for the failure of speech?"

> Racial bigotry, anti-semitism . . . influence the culture and shape our socialization. None is directly answerable by more speech, unless that speech too finds its place in the popular culture. Yet all is protected as speech, however insidious. Any other answer leaves the government in control of all of the institutions of culture, the great censor and director of which thoughts are good for us.

The law was held unconstitutional because it impermissibly discriminated between viewpoints. A year later the United States Supreme Court refused to hear the case, thereby affirming the decision of the Seventh Circuit. Two years later, in 1988, a similar ordinance was proposed in Bellingham, Washington. Although the Bellingham statute eventually failed, in December 1990, when asked whether her continual defeats reduced her confidence in the future enactment of such legislation, MacKinnon stated, "Not at all. We'll be in the courts again and again until we win."

Viewpoint neutrality in our laws is critical to our form of government. Public officials must not allow the silencing of one view on a subject in favor of another. As Donald Alexander Downs concludes in his study of the MacKinnon/Dworkin efforts, *The New Politics of Pornography:*

> The development of cultural pluralism in the twentieth century has made state neutrality toward the content of speech even more desirable. Were state action to unduly favor one side over others, it would jeopardize the speech of those who are unable to command the state's approval. . . .
>
> Whatever the limitations in the marketplace of ideas, there is significant difference between a dominant discourse enforced by the unparalleled power of the state and a dominant discourse that must compete with other discourses, however unequally. This is the difference between political freedom and non-freedom in a world in which absolute freedom and equality have never and probably cannot exist. Given the course of history, the freedom we have managed to attain is too valuable to risk.

Yet some ignore the lessons of history. On February 27, 1992, the Supreme Court of Canada upheld an anti-obscenity provision in the Canadian Criminal Code. The Court ruled that while the antipornography law infringed on freedom of expression, it was permissible because the law suppressed materials harmful to women. The code provisions defined an obscene publication as one that has, as a "dominant characteristic," the "undue exploitation of sex." Since the guarantee of freedom of expression in the Canadian Charter of Rights and Freedoms was not passed until 1982, the Canadian courts lack our tradition of First Amendment jurisprudence. Whether reviewing an obscenity case or a hate-crime case, such courts focus on the groups "harmed" by the expression and the "consensus" of the Canadian people regarding "morality." Such concepts seem reasonable and attractive with respect to offensive pornography and ugly hate speech. Yet our nation has a history of protecting the individual against the majority, in recognition of the fact that the consensus changes, often as a result of being challenged by an unpopular minority (as in antiwar demonstrations, civil rights marches, etc.).

The debate over pornography restrictions in the United States has shifted from proposed city ordinances to Senate legislation and cases involving Title VII of the Civil Rights Act of 1964.

In 1986, in *Meritor Savings Bank v. Vinson* the United States Supreme Court held that a claim of "hostile environment" sexual harassment was a form of sex discrimination actionable under Title VII of the Civil Rights of Act of 1964. Five years later the United States District Court for the Middle District of Florida, in the case of *Robinson v. Jacksonville Shipyards, Inc.,* found that pornographic pictures and verbal harassment were not protected speech because they constituted discriminatory conduct by creating a hostile environment. Previously, pornography had been used as evidence of discrimination in the workplace. Now it was held to constitute discrimination itself. The court further held that the regulation of discriminatory speech in the workplace constituted nothing more than a regulation of time, place, and manner. The ACLU disagreed initially with the prohibition of suggestive and offensive written materials in the employment setting, reasoning that by barring "suggestive" materials the court had gone too far. The case balanced individual liberty with the need to protect employees in the workplace.

On March 1, 1993, the Supreme Court agreed to hear the case of *Harris v. Forklift Systems, Inc.* The case involved a woman supervisor who filed suit against her employer under Title VII, alleging that a "hostile work environment" had forced her to quit her job. While the Court had previously indicated that such claims were permissible, it had never decided whether a litigant could prevail by showing that a "reasonable woman" would have been offended by the alleged harassment or whether proof of severe psychological injury was required.

Harris was only the second case involving sexual harassment to be accepted for review by the Supreme Court. Seven years earlier the Court had attempted in *Meritor Savings Bank* to narrowly define sexual harassment in the workplace by requiring egregious behavior, "severe or pervasive" harassment, that poisoned the working environment to such an extent that it altered "the conditions" of the victim's employment. In the ensuing years the lower courts had been inconsistent in their interpretation of that standard while American society and attitudes toward sexual harassment had changed substantially.

Five years after the *Meritor Savings Bank* decision, the issue of sexual harassment in the workplace entered a new era; Anita Hill's allegations of misconduct on the part of Clarence Thomas ignited a national debate on the subject. The result was an avalanche of complaints filed with federal and state agencies. In the first eight months of 1993, leading up to the oral argument in *Harris*, twice as many complaints of sexual harassment were filed as in all of 1990, the year before the Thomas confirmation hearings.

Acrimonious debates ensued over the issue of "sexual correctness" as well, removing the dispute from the confines of the employment setting. Proponents of a new standard for communication between the sexes argued that women had been demeaned for too long and were only seeking equal treatment. Others felt that an "offensiveness" standard applied to expression between men and women was too elastic to be enforceable and led inevitably to a "victimization" syndrome among some. Those who offered solutions to silence "street harassment," attempting to extend workplace safeguards against offensive speech to the "street," often seemed oblivious to the First Amendment.

Many men felt that they were being blamed for the language, conduct, and attitudes of a relatively small number of misogynists and social misfits. Many women believed that most men continued to harbor paternalistic and sexist attitudes whether or not they acted on such beliefs. Attitudes toward "date rape," sexual harassment, and relations between the sexes proved divisive even to feminists.

Nevertheless, sexual harassment in the workplace was indefensible, even if agreeing on a clear definition of such behavior remained elusive. As the Supreme Court heard oral arguments in the *Harris* case on October 14, 1993, it appeared that the justices would find it difficult to reach a consensus on a more workable definition of such conduct. The addition of Justice Ruth Bader Ginsburg, who had replaced Justice Byron White at the beginning of the term, ensured that for the first time in history, two female justices would help define acceptable expression between the sexes in an employment context.

Less than four weeks later, on November 9, 1993, "with astonishing speed and brevity," the Court handed down a unanimous opinion in *Harris* that one observer described as "short, polemical and hastily written," reading "like the worst sort of opinion journalism."

Perhaps the "speed and brevity" of the opinion was more crucial to the members of the Court than the language of the decision. Arguably the justices, realizing their inability to further define a "hostile work environment," chose instead to send a clear message to the lower federal courts that litigants were not required to submit proof of "severe psychological injury." That said, the Court gave little guidance on what claimants did need to show to proceed under

Title VII ("so long as the environment would reasonably be perceived, and is perceived, as hostile or abusive, there is no need for it also to be psychologically injurious").

It appeared that the Court intended to erase an unreasonable hurdle for claimants without embracing too elastic a standard (apparently applying the reasonable "person" standard, "rejecting by inference the . . . reasonable woman construct"), taking "a middle path between making actionable any conduct that is merely offensive and requiring the conduct to cause a tangible psychological injury." Both female justices wrote opinions; Justice O'Connor wrote the majority opinion while Justice Ginsburg submitted her first (albeit brief) concurring opinion. Justice Clarence Thomas joined in the unanimous opinion without comment. Justice Scalia, in a concurring opinion, criticized the majority opinion—it "lets virtually unguided juries decide whether sex-related conduct engaged in (or permitted by) an employer is egregious enough to warrant an award of damages"—while acknowledging the Court's inability to arrive at a clearer standard saying, "Be that as it may, I know of no alternative to the course the Court today has taken").

While few would deny that the plaintiff, Teresa Harris, was subjected to the type of sexual harassment that clearly created a hostile or abusive work environment, Scalia's warning about "unguided juries" in the future was well taken. Although First Amendment concerns must give way to a certain degree in the employment context, its guarantees do not stop altogether at the workplace door.

Already, "many companies are . . . trying to avoid having their workplaces branded 'hostile environments' by banning broad categories of speech or expression: reproductions of classical nude paintings or sex-based job titles like 'draftsman' and 'foreman.'" Even proposed guidelines from the Equal Employment Opportunity Commission strayed dangerously close to banning speech or expression that merely offends ("providing that epithets, slurs, negative stereotyping" and "written . . . material that denigrates or shows hostility or aversion toward an individual or group . . . creates a "hostile environment"). Allowing "unguided juries" to punish expression in the workplace deemed "offensive," without more, is to allow censorship predicated on notions of political correctness to spread from the campuses to the working environment. Punishing "street harassment" (offensive expression in public outside of campuses and the workplace) cannot be far behind. The principle of freedom of expression even for that expression that offends continues to come under broad attack. The impact of *Harris* on First Amendment cases that arise outside of the workplace remains to be seen.

A different type of threat to the First Amendment organized by antipornography forces was the Pornography Victims Compensation Act of 1991 (S. 1521). No other single alliance of antipornography forces demonstrated the "strange bedfellows" coalition more clearly than that formed by proponents of this legislation. The sponsor was Senator Mitch McConnell (R., Ky.), who "gets no stars as a friend of feminism." The co-sponsors included Orrin Hatch, Arlen Specter, and Strom Thurmond. Referred to as the Bundy Bill for serial killer Ted Bundy (who credited pornography with inspiring his horrific acts), it might better have been titled Bundy's Revenge. Opposed by the ACLU and the Feminists for Free Expression, the legislation would "allow the victims of sex crimes to sue the authors, producers and distributors of any work—from hard core books to Playboy to rap records—deemed to have 'caused' an offender to do what he did." As one national newsmagazine observed, "Advocates of the anti-porn bills seem blithely indifferent to the crippling cultural impact of legislation that places so much emphasis on the subjective views of crime victims. Porn, like beauty, may be in the beholder's eye. But it is a bad perspective for building good law." As another observed, "We don't permit lawsuits against Marx's publisher when *Das Kapital* is found in a terrorist's back pocket."

Perhaps the best argument against repressive laws in the area of pornography is twofold. One inevitable defect in these laws is ambiguous terminology. What is offensive, what is demeaning, and what reflects dominance are subjective determinations for the individual viewer. Antipornography provisions often threaten other areas of artistic endeavor, including literature, music, paintings, and sculpture: "One man's vulgarity is another man's lyric." Another problem with such legislation, which feminists like Catharine MacKinnon seem to ignore, is the issue of enforcement. Kathleen Sullivan of Stanford Law School points out that "if the MacKinnonites' claims about the male-dominated power structure are true, then it is simply naive to suppose that it would actually commit the cultural suicide they prescribe. . . . That's what happens when you try to change culture before power in a greatly unequal world."

This does not mean that we are powerless to combat pornography. Just as the criminal code can effectively address targeted threatening or terrorizing hate speech, so it can punish the exploitation and abuse of women. Viewpoint-neutral child pornography legislation, protecting those too young to consent, has already been upheld by the United States Supreme Court. We can continue to subject pornography to constitutionally permissible regulations of time, place, and manner, controlling access to such materials.

Women like Catharine MacKinnon deserve credit for bringing the issues of harassment, discrimination, and sexual abuse to the forefront of the American consciousness. Laws prohibiting criminal sexual conduct, assault, harassment, and discrimination should be effectively prosecuted throughout our nation. The Fourteenth Amendment, guaranteeing equal protection for all, can and should be the primary weapon in the fight against discrimination in our society, short of countermanding individual liberty under the First Amendment.

Through education and example we must teach our children the responsibility of liberty. Together with effective prosecution of existing criminal laws, education, not indoctrination, will have long-term benefits in addressing these issues without endangering freedom of expression. While we may guide our friends, relatives, and neighbors to an understanding of discrimination, we must not succumb to fear. Where the First Amendment is threatened, we must have the vision to remember the words of Justice Holmes. We may attain social goals without sacrificing individual liberty. As Donald Alexander Downs concludes:

> Liberal doctrine constrains our passions, so it naturally arouses resistance in difficult cases. This is why difficult cases are so important, for tolerance like freedom has meaning only in contexts of tension and temptation, where its exercise depends on reason and self-control.

Racial Politics:
Clarence Thomas, David Duke,
and *R.A.V. v. St. Paul*

During the sixties, the dream, so long deferred, was by way of becoming the awakening. Marches, gatherings, voices from below, and a stirring of national conscience led to the passage of civil rights laws. It appeared that this nation, white and black, was on the threshold of overcoming.

—Studs Terkel

Late in the summer of 1991, Mike and I were contacted by a professor at a local law school. A number of the professors at this school gathered at times to discuss pending Supreme Court cases. They had chosen our case for a roundtable discussion and invited us to listen, if not to participate. Since one of the professors at this meeting had spoken to me earlier and requested copies of all the briefs, we decided that it would be interesting to attend. Presumably this professor was now well informed about our case. Apparently he was writing a law-review article on the issues involved and he appeared to be in support of our position.

When Mike and I arrived at the law school, I noticed that another professor taking part in the roundtable discussion was the one who had taught me ethics in my third year at the University of Minnesota Law School. He had transferred to this law school shortly thereafter and I had lost touch with him. Before the meeting began I introduced myself and reminded him that he had been my ethics teacher fourteen years earlier. He looked at me and said, "It takes with some, and not with others," and walked away. I was stunned, so taken aback that I was speechless. When I later told my friends about the remark, they were incredulous and said I should have challenged him. I saw no purpose in doing so, since those who hate intolerance are often intolerant themselves. On another occasion, a lawyer I had known for years angrily admonished me for challenging the law and asked if I was "running for governor of North Dakota."

As the meeting continued I was surprised to find that the professor who had appeared to support our position actually opposed us, as did the majority in attendance. I learned later that this professor had assisted our opponents in preparing for the argument in December. Mike and I left the meeting quietly. It was hard not to feel alone and isolated as each new day seemed to bring further opposition to our defense in R.A.V.

Shortly after Labor Day, on September 10, I had a phone call from Charles Fried. A former solicitor general in the Reagan administration, Fried had argued before the United States Supreme Court on a number of occasions and was now a law professor at Harvard. He had been contacted by an attorney for one of the conservative organizations that had filed an *amicus* brief in our behalf. This attorney felt that since I was inexperienced at arguing at this level and was not a conservative, he would try to persuade me to relinquish my right to argue the case so that Fried could do so. His plan had been to speak to me first and then have Fried contact me, but before he could do so, Fried called.

Professor Fried began by saying that he felt strongly about the issue involved and that he was available to help, "gratis." I told Fried that I knew him by reputation as a skilled advocate and that I appreciated his support. I knew what Professor Fried meant by "support," but I thought I would let him come to the point. After an awkward pause, he reiterated his interest and his "very conservative" leanings, and made it clear that he was available to argue the case. I thanked him for his interest, said that I was not a conservative, and that I would be arguing the case. That was the end of the conversation. It appeared as though when we did receive support, it always stemmed from self-interest and was conditioned on our "cooperation."

Geoffrey Stone, dean of the University of Chicago Law School and Charles Fried, professor at Harvard Law School and a former solicitor general, were the only two individuals who asked me to relinquish my right to argue the case. Stone felt that my inexperience could mean the difference between winning and losing. Fried's attitude appeared to be that I should simply step aside. While recognizing Stone's reputation for scholarship and Fried's for effective advocacy, I had no intention of giving up my right to argue the case. The briefing was done, and from a personal and professional standpoint I wanted the ultimate career challenge of arguing before the United States Supreme Court.

There was another reason why I felt it was important that we should continue with this case. Mike and I had spent much of our careers defending indigent clients, and our political beliefs were left of center. Both Michael McConnell (Stone's choice) and Charles Fried were former members of the Reagan administration. The legal community and the media had focused on conservatives' interest in the outcome of the case, and had ignored the support of those on the left who insisted on consistency in the application of the First Amendment. We felt that if a well-known conservative argued this case before the Rehnquist Court, a successful outcome might appear to be a political, not a constitutional, triumph, and leave the impression that the left no longer believed in an expansive interpretation of First Amendment freedoms. Of course, if I argued the case and the outcome was not successful, we would be criticized for not having stepped aside.

Although our challenge was to the ordinance and not to the factual situation, the underlying issue that permeated all discussion was race. Shortly after the Supreme Court granted review, I wondered how Justice Thurgood Marshall would vote. John Siliciano, who had clerked for him, believed it would be an extremely hard issue for Marshall to confront. Marshall's past eloquence in cases concerning freedom of expression usually involved minorities. Here he would have been forced to apply the First Amendment to a law aimed at the far-right hate groups that he had so effectively combated as an attorney and as a civil rights advocate. The man who had done more than any other individual to end apartheid in America would now be criticized whatever his vote. He resigned several weeks after review was granted, so we will never know how he would have voted on this case. But I am confident that he would have voted on our side.

After Marshall's resignation, President Bush nominated Clarence Thomas to the D.C. Circuit Court of Appeals. When he insisted that race had played no part in his selection and that Judge Thomas was the best man available, Bush not only was being disingenuous but did a disservice to Clarence Thomas as well. Though Thomas was more qualified than some he was less qualified than others. He was selected primarily on his race and political beliefs. His nomination, Shelby Steele argued, touched

> the very soul of the debate in black America, which is a debate between using the principle of self-sufficiency as a means to power as opposed to using our history of victimization. We have taken our power from our history of victimization, which gave us an enor-

mous moral authority and brought social reforms, to the neglect of self-reliance and individual initiative. And now, any time you talk about self-reliance in relation to black problems, you are automatically considered a conservative.

While many black Americans were willing to give Clarence Thomas the benefit of the doubt, they could not help wondering about a man who had been endorsed by former segregationist Senator Strom Thurmond of South Carolina, Senator Jesse Helms of North Carolina, and even former KKK leader David Duke. Prior to Anita Hill's allegations, he was supported by many in the black community who felt that if he was not appointed, another (presumably not black) conservative would be appointed. As Maya Angelou then argued, he deserved support for no other reason than that there was a reasonable chance that he would become more sensitive to his ethnic roots once he had been appointed to the lifetime position.

As the Thomas hearings began in the second week of September, race again had become the key topic of discussion throughout the nation. Many felt that after Ronald Reagan took office in the fall of 1980, covert racism had become socially acceptable. As the tax cuts took effect in the eighties, the income disparity between the affluent and the poor increased steadily. The racial tension that resulted was pervasive throughout the nation. In the white community, many felt that the economy of the eighties rewarded individual initiative and left behind only those unable or unwilling to take care of themselves. Many seemed to feel little obligation to those not fortunate enough to benefit from the changes in the economy. Others, particularly those in the middle class, favored equality for all, but not at the expense of their own well-being. Some believed that drugs and crime followed integration of white working-class neighborhoods. Still other Americans felt that the government was at fault for failing to raise the standard of living for all Americans because they believed that society would benefit from a government more interested in seeking equality in living standards for all its citizens. Years after the death of the Reverend Martin Luther King, Jr., a vast majority of both white and black Americans believed race relations in the United States were "generally bad."

The black community too was divided as the American dream became a reality to more members of the minority community, however slowly. A number of black men, championed by white conservatives, criticized a "victimization syndrome" they believed had been embraced by much of the minority community, mirroring the historical division found between rich and poor white Americans. By mid-September of 1991 it appeared that a majority of black Americans felt they had been betrayed and that the promise of the sixties had been illusory. Even those members of the community who had "made it" found that the color of their skin remained a barrier to true social acceptance. This was the climate that had led "progressive" or "liberal" communities like St. Paul to pass laws like section 292.02. Motivated by frustration or fear, campuses and communities resorted to the final weapon available, the criminalization of bigoted opinion and expression.

Like many other Americans, I avidly watched the Clarence Thomas nomination hearings. Unlike others, I watched the proceedings primarily to get a sense of Clarence Thomas and his political philosophy for purposes of my oral argument. He appeared to be as he had been described, a young black conservative who had arrived on the Republican fast track. He did not appear to have any discernible First Amendment philosophy or experience in First Amendment interpretation. The hearings bogged down in discussions of "natural law," but I noted with interest that Senators Biden and Grassley made reference to the same quotation from *A Man for All Seasons* that we had in our brief.

As the date for oral argument approached, we were given the name of a former clerk for Justice Scalia who now practiced law in Minneapolis. I contacted him, sent him copies of the briefs, and set up a meeting to discuss the case. Although there were other attorneys in the Twin Cities who had clerked for Supreme Court justices, he appeared to have the most recent experience and therefore would be the most knowledgeable about the current members of the Supreme Court. On September 25, Mike and I met with him at a cafeteria for lunch. Candid and helpful, he indicated at first that he thought we would prevail and that we might even receive a unanimous opinion. After a few minutes he qualified that prediction with the observation that we could also lose 8 to 1. By way of explanation, he said that he thought that we would obtain Justice Scalia's vote, but he could make no other predictions. He thought that we had "pushed the right buttons." Specifically, he told us that the passage from *A Man for All Seasons* was a favorite of Justice Scalia's. I worried that Justice Scalia would think that I was playing to him by including this passage, but he told me not to worry, since few knew that Justice Scalia was fond of it. He said that our quotation from Judge Silberman of the D.C. Circuit would be well received by Justice Rehnquist. I had inserted a quotation from Judge Silberman about the campus speech-code situation at Dartmouth College, not only because it was appropriate but because I knew that Clarence Thomas had worked with Judge Silberman's wife at the EEOC. I had also added several quotations from Dinesh D'Souza's *The Illiberal Education* not only because they were relevant to the campus speech-code issue but also because D'Souza had noted in a *Wall Street Journal* article that he was a close friend of Clarence Thomas.

As an aside, the former law clerk advised us to be familiar with the location of the cross-burning incident. When I said I already knew where it occurred, he advised me to note precisely how far the location was from St. Paul landmarks, such as Mounds Park or I-94. When I asked him why this was necessary, he said that Justice Blackmun had a habit of asking St. Paul attorneys to describe the precise locations of St. Paul relevant to their case. Because Justice Blackmun had grown up on the east side of St. Paul, he could not resist illustrating his familiarity with the area. Although I found this recommendation unusual, I did map out the precise location of the cross-burning in relation to other areas of St. Paul in case the issue arose at oral argument.

The next day we filed our reply brief with the Court. In its brief, the government had been critical of how much time was spent on an examination of the language of the ordinance. The implication was that the only matter for review before the Court was the earlier decision of the Minnesota Supreme Court and its constitutionality. We focused our reply brief on the ordinance as written and its importance to an understanding of how the Minnesota Supreme Court decision had failed in its attempt to narrow the ordinance. We reminded the members of the Court that they were the final arbiters of the constitutionality of legislation. Our position was that while states may interpret their constitutions in a more liberal fashion, this Court must maintain "a floor" of constitutional rights for citizens of all fifty states, below which no state court may venture. We wanted to persuade the Court that fighting words could not be censored on an ideological basis, a recurring issue that would become crucially significant. It was not enough to classify certain expression as "unprotected" and then select certain topics within that unprotected area to censor. A local government that punishes fighting words related to some topics but not to others betrays neutrality as the government imposes an orthodox standard. Authorities can enforce progressive social legislation (as in the effective use of civil rights laws), but it should not punish personal opinion by setting a standard of "political correctness" that must be adhered to at the risk of incarceration.

The government had also quoted extensively from *United States v. Lee*. After the city's brief had been filed, *Lee* was vacated by the Eighth Circuit. Numerous pages of the brief filed by the city no longer had any legal validity. This prompted the attorneys for the city to file affidavits with the United States Supreme Court noting that they were unaware that the opinion had been vacated at the time they had used it in their brief.

The three-judge panel from the Eighth Circuit which heard oral arguments in *Lee* issued its decision on June 10, 1991, the same date that the Supreme Court granted review on *R.A.V.* Lee had been found guilty of constructing and burning a cross on a small hill approximately a block away from an integrated apartment building in a suburb of Minneapolis. He was convicted of conspiracy against civil rights in violation of 18 U.S.C. section 241. He challenged the law both on its face and as it applied to him. The law makes it a crime to

> conspire to injure, oppress, threaten, or intimidate any inhabitant
> of any State, Territory, or District in the free exercise or enjoy-
> ment of any right or privilege secured to him by the Constitution
> or laws of the United States, or because of his having so exer-
> cised the same. . . .

In a 2–1 decision, the panel held that this law was "content-neutral," required the "specific intent" to threaten or intimidate and did not prohibit the burning of a cross. St. Paul City Ordinance section 292.02, even as narrowly construed, was content-based, did not require an intent to threaten or intimidate, and did, effectively, prohibit the burning of a cross. The dissent, written by Judge Richard Arnold, now chief judge of the Eighth Circuit Court of Appeals, noted that the law as applied to *Lee* was ineffective unless and until a jury found that the threats and intimidation involved an imminent use of force. *U.S. v. Lee* focused on a law constitutional on its face but unconstitutional as originally applied to *Lee*, while in *R.A.V.* the law was unconstitutional on its face, while the facts alleged were clearly punishable.

A threat aimed at the exercise of constitutional rights, such as interfering with housing rights, can be punished by local authorities with terroristic threat statutes, or by federal authorities (under 18 U.S.C. section 241 or possibly, 42 U.S.C. section 3631), provided that the expression involves intentional threats or is made with the intent of creating a reasonable fear of imminent force or violence or, finally, is done with the intent of advocating the use of force or violence and is likely to produce such action. Section 241 is aimed at protecting individual rights and privileges in a content-neutral manner. Section 3631 requires the use or threat of force to willfully injure or intimidate a citizen based on his status (race or religion, etc.) and his engaging in a protected act (seeking housing). Unlike the St. Paul ordinance, neither of these provisions punishes the mere expression of an unpopular viewpoint. These laws were available to both state and federal authorities in June of 1990 to address the allegations in *R.A.V.*

Shortly after we filed our reply brief with the Court, the media began to focus on the upcoming 1991–92 term beginning on the first Monday in October. At the end of September, *U.S. Law Week* and the *National Law Journal* listed *R.A.V.* as one of only a handful of notable cases appearing on the upcoming docket (which at that time numbered sixty-nine cases). My office received calls from national television programs, radio programs, periodicals and newspapers.

During the fall term, several justices of the United States Supreme Court traveled to law schools and became jurists-in-residence. I had heard that Justice Blackmun spoke at a college in southern Minnesota in the fall. He had mentioned *R.A.V.* and offered the opinion that the case would result in a significant decision. I later learned that Justice Anthony M. Kennedy would be visiting the University of Minnesota Law School from the twentieth to the twenty-third of October and that Justice Stevens would be speaking at the University of Chicago Law School on October 25. I had read everything available regarding the backgrounds and opinions of the justices I would address, and was determined to hear both Justices Kennedy and Stevens speak. I got in touch with Dean Robert Stein at the University of Minnesota Law School, who arranged for Mike and me to attend a dinner honoring Justice Kennedy on October 21. Pat Diamond of the University of Chicago Law School made it possible for me to attend the First Amendment Seminar and to hear Justice Stevens's speech on October 25.

Chief Justice Rehnquist and Justices O'Connor and Blackmun had visited the University of Minnesota Law School as jurists-in-residence in previous years. The justices teach several classes, participate in various law-school programs, and attend a dinner as the keynote speaker. I was particularly interested in hearing Justice Kennedy's speech because I knew that he had taught constitutional law and I had been impressed by his concurring opinion in *Texas v. Johnson,* the first flag-burning case.

Following the rancorous Senate debates over the Robert Bork nomination and the short-lived nomination of Douglas Ginsburg to the Court, Anthony Kennedy was sworn in without controversy as a Supreme Court justice in February 1987. He was then viewed as the "fifth vote," allowing Chief Justice Rehnquist to solidify a conservative majority. Two years later in *Texas v. Johnson* he had found himself voting with liberals Brennan and Marshall in opposition to conservatives Rehnquist and O'Connor. For both Justices Scalia and Kennedy, voting with the majority in such a controversial case could not have been an easy decision. They knew the result would undoubtedly anger many conservatives who had been essential to their nomination and confirmation.

R.A.V. might never have reached the nation's highest court but for Justice Kennedy's concurring opinion in *Texas v. Johnson.* Judge Flinn had been visibly affected by Kennedy's words, making numerous copies of the one-page concurring opinion and distributing it to a number of judges. The opinion had addressed the difficulty in the exercise of judicial power. Had Kennedy not written this concurring opinion, and had I not used it as part of my argument, it is doubtful that Judge Flinn would have found in our favor. Although we would have appealed, the procedural posture and timing of the case would have been significantly different. It is probable that the United States Supreme Court never would have heard the case.

On the evening of October 21, 1991, Mike Cromett and I went to the dinner for Justice Kennedy at the University of Minnesota Law School. After I had finished eating and before the keynote speech, I walked down the long hallway to the men's room. The restroom was empty when I entered it. Shortly thereafter, Justice Kennedy came in, smiled and mentioned that he needed to use the facilities before he gave his speech. I thought of all the things I would have liked to say to Justice Kennedy, but felt that since I would appear in front of him within a matter of weeks, it would be wise to avoid any legal discussions. As I started to leave, I indicated to him that I would be appearing before the Court in December. I do not remember his response, but as we left the men's room and walked the long hallway back to the banquet, we discussed the World Series (ultimately won by the Minnesota Twins), which he had attended the night before and enjoyed, and he talked about his teaching of constitutional law before he became a justice and how that had often interfered with his students' ability to watch *Monday Night Football,* and his general enjoyment of his stay in Minnesota. When he went to the podium he was introduced by Justice Simonett of the Minnesota Supreme Court.

Justice Simonett had received a copy of Justice Kennedy's concurring opinion in the flag-burning case from Judge Flinn, who was also in attendance. In his introduction, Justice Simonett referred to the language of the opinion as he introduced Justice Kennedy.

Justice Kennedy is a very effective public speaker. Without notes, he discussed the aftermath of *Texas v. Johnson* and the resulting controversy regarding the constitutional amendment to ban flag-burning. He admitted he had been approached by many citizens who were outraged by the adverse public reaction to the Court's decision, but said he did not share their outrage because part of the democratic process is the debate and consideration of controversial First Amendment issues. The proposed constitutional amendment to prohibit flag-burning had failed, and by the time *United States v. Eichman* was decided there was much less controversy about the decision. He felt that First Amendment guarantees, though controversial, were the very fabric of our society, and are ultimately accepted by the public after reflection. Mike and I left that dinner feeling that Justice Kennedy would agree with our position in *R.A.V.*

Four days later I sat in an auditorium at the University of Chicago Law School and listened intently to constitutional scholars debate aspects of the Bill of Rights, including freedom of religion, speech, and the concept of unenumerated rights. As Pat Diamond and I listened to Geoffrey Stone, we were sitting only a few seats away from Charles Fried. I considered introducing myself to the two men who had asked me to relinquish my right to argue the case, but since both of the earlier conversations had been uncomfortable, I chose to remain anonymous. The only lecturer to whom I introduced myself was Kathleen Sullivan. She was friendly and charming and an engaging speaker. During our brief meeting, she made reference to the "Bill of Rights" issue of *Life,* which was then on the newsstands and in which an article about the *R.A.V.* case had appeared.

The article stated I was a self-described "liberal Irish-Catholic Democrat," mentioned the death of my father, and noted that we had proceeded "with little help and no money." Although I appreciated the article, I was irritated with the "liberal" label. I had told the reporter that I was an Irish-Catholic Democrat but felt I was more moderate than liberal. The term "liberal" had become misleading to many Democrats and to most of the country. I had been quoted as saying "that individual liberty may be threatened just as readily by well-meaning liberals as it has been by reactionary conservatives." Since the entire issue was devoted to the Bill of Rights, I felt that the justices of the Court (or their clerks) would read it. Eight of the nine justices were Republican appointees and the lone Democrat, Justice Byron White, would not be considered liberal by most observers. Consequently, when I stood before the Court on December 4, I would appear as an attorney with "self-described" party and political affiliations quite different from their own. Such a designation would not be crucial, but I wondered whether such labeling would affect the reception I would receive.

Before leaving for Chicago, I received notice from the Court that our argument would be held at 10:00 A.M. on December 4, 1991. After checking my calendar, I confirmed my suspicions: it would be one year to the day and to the hour that I had argued the same case before the Minnesota Supreme Court. I wondered whether this was a coincidence or whether someone at the Court was aware of the anniversary.

Mike and I contacted Professor William Greenhalgh of the Georgetown Law Center before I left for Chicago because we were both members of the National Association of Criminal Defense Lawyers and Professor Greenhalgh was in charge of U.S. Supreme Court moot-court preparation for the association. The professor had arranged an all-star panel to hear my practice oral argument in November. Moot-court judges included David Cole, Mark Tushnet, Steve Goldberg, and Vicki Jackson. Several had clerked for justices of the United States Supreme Court and all were teaching at Georgetown. When I returned from Chicago, I had a week to prepare for this practice argument.

Virtually every law school has a moot-court program for law students to argue hypothetical cases before lawyers or judges. Similar to exhibition athletic contests, the theory of such exercises is that the participants will be better prepared for the real thing. After law school, many lawyers never practice law. If they do, they often do not engage extensively in trial work or appellate practice. I had considerably more trial experience than most attorneys, but had minimal appellate experience. The two skills are decidedly different. While trial work emphasizes rules of evidence (i.e., objections, introduction of exhibits), direct- and cross-examination and argument to a jury, appellate practice involves legal research (drafting of the brief) and oral presentation to a panel of judges or justices. Perhaps the only skill useful in both trial and appellate practice is quick thinking. Important in trial practice for making objections and in cross-examination of witnesses, it is important in appellate practice to maintain a dialogue with appellate judges. Answering the questions of the justices, particularly Justice Scalia, is similar to cross-examination. While answering the question, the attorney must anticipate the questions to follow so he or she is not trapped.

It is a difficult intellectual exercise, and perhaps the one area where trial experience is of assistance.

When a petition for certiorari is granted by the United States Supreme Court, one is often advised to do as many practice oral arguments as possible. Contacting other lawyers who had argued, I found that many had done so before a panel of attorneys, an experience I believed to be counterproductive in a case as complex as ours. Since most attorneys are not experts in constitutional law, their questions are often misleading and irrelevant to the actual oral argument. I did not agree that many practice oral arguments would be constructive. Some of these would probably involve inexperienced panelists, so I decided to schedule just one moot-court oral argument if I could persuade a qualified panel to hear the case. Professor Greenhalgh had seen to it that I had access to such a panel.

It is common for attorneys arguing before the United States Supreme Court to conduct practice arguments in Washington, D.C., within two to three days of the argument. This may be self-defeating for most attorneys dealing with complex constitutional issues. Professor Greenhalgh intended to schedule the moot-court argument only several days before the case would be heard. Since we had time available, I asked him to schedule it four weeks in advance so that I could build my argument with additional research and reflection. It is often a mistake to have too many practice arguments or to schedule a practice argument too close to the actual presentation. Such a procedure will often confuse the attorney or overwhelm him with differing opinions about how the presentation should be made.

November 1, 1991, was the one hundred fiftieth anniversary of the founding of the city of St. Paul. Nature celebrated by bestowing a twenty-four-hour record snowfall on the Twin Cities. The next day Mike and I flew to Washington, taking off from the only runway still open at the airport. After arriving and settling in, we had a beer at Kelly's Pub, near the Capitol, where, enshrined above the bar, was a familiar sign from an earlier time in our nation's history: NO IRISH NEED APPLY. It was a grim reminder of offensive attitudes and discrimination against ethnic groups. I thought once again about the anger, frustration, and hopelessness felt by earlier American immigrants subjected to ugly nativist rhetoric. But I remained convinced that in the long run such tolerance of the intolerant is a small price to pay for the freedom each citizen has to speak his mind.

As we left the pub I considered how freedom is not equally borne by members of our society. I, as an American with Irish roots, would never know what it means to be a black American confronted with a burning cross or a Jewish citizen who is demeaned by the display of the Nazi swastika. Many former targets of intolerance are now the most intolerant. The Irish American experience is indicative, as shown by the reactionary ranting of Pat Buchanan. One of my lasting memories of speaking to students about the *R.A.V.* case is how many of the minority students would look away when I tried to make eye contact with them. At times I would become defensive and seek out the moral support of those members of the minority legal community who understood the issue and agreed with my position: I was never insensitive to the black experience in America; I was sensitive to the lessons of history, which had shown that the repressive alternative of censorship was a mistake and would eventually be borne unequally by the very groups it had meant to protect. I further believed that the deeper issue was one of acceptance between different ethnic groups, and that intolerance in America was not limited to the white response to the black experience, although it was and is clearly the most egregious example.

On the morning of November 4, Mike and I listened intently for the first time to arguments made before the United States Supreme Court. It is a unique experience, as anyone who has observed such arguments will attest. My first impression was that Chief Justice Rehnquist and Justice Scalia were impatient and unforgiving interrogators and that Justice Souter was effective in reaching the underlying issues. I looked forward to hearing more arguments in December.

The next afternoon, Mike and I went to the Georgetown Law Center for my practice oral argument before the five law professors. The argument took place before a classroom of 250 students. (Also observing was an attorney who would be arguing before the Supreme Court several days later. The attorney, Bernie O'Donnell, successfully argued the case of *Dawson v. Delaware.*) Normally, such oral arguments are held just before the moot-court panel. I had agreed to the unusual arrangement because I enjoyed appearing before students generally. I felt that such a large crowd might re-create the tense atmosphere generated by such a controversial case before the United States Supreme Court. Although Professor Greenhalgh did not ask any questions, Cole, Goldberg, Jackson, and Tushnet were merciless, as I had expected. All challenged various facets of my argument. Although the Supreme Court argument is limited to thirty minutes per attorney, the practice argument went on for over an hour. Challenging my assumptions, the panelists interrupted my answers with increasingly complex questions, never allowing me to establish a rhythm. When it was over, each critiqued me as the class watched and listened.

Usually an arguing attorney gives the Court a brief factual background before beginning a substantive argument. The consensus of the panel was that a case like this did not require an introduction, and that my conclusion should be used at the beginning of my argument. The panel felt that this part of the argument was particularly effective, and that if I did not deliver this portion of my presentation first, I might not have time to do it at the end. One professor also noted my defensive body posture; I had crossed my arms during the argument. She suggested that I be aware of my posture and a tendency to shake my head on occasion. She pointed out that the justices would not approve of an arguing attorney who shakes his head while they are speaking—an observation that was difficult to take issue with.

David Cole was in agreement with the thrust of my oral argument. We had objected to the breadth of the ordinance and to the ineffective decision by the Minnesota Supreme Court. We had also objected to the application of the "fighting words" doctrine to ideological speech. We felt that if this ordinance had included "political party" as a protected topic—say, punishing Republicans who spoke angrily about Democrats—the constitutional ramifications would be obvious to everyone.

Cole recommended that I be prepared to emphasize this portion of my argument. This then became the focus: that the ordinance was in violation of First Amendment principles in that it punished a *subcategory* of unprotected speech. Although government can punish the greater, it does not follow that it can punish the lesser, since in doing so the government betrays neutral principles. The government may ban all fighting words, but it may not take a position on viewpoint and ban only those fighting words on subjects that it designates beyond the pale.

I disagreed with David Cole on his suggestion that I be prepared to ask the Court to overrule *Chaplinsky v. New Hampshire* in its entirety. The original "fighting words" case was now almost a half a century old and had become a legal anachronism. That a person could be punished as a result of the inability of another to control his temper never really became a viable exception to the First Amendment. However, the Rehnquist Court was conservative and clearly on the side of law and order. I was prepared to ask the Court to disavow the "inflict injury" language, since I felt that the emotional harm to an audience was too elastic a standard and would lead inevitably to censorship. I was not prepared to tell this Court to overrule that portion of *Chaplinsky* which punished expression leading to an immediate breach of the peace. While constitutionally suspect, this portion of the holding had historically been used as a law-and-order tool by law enforcement officials. Someday a more liberal Court may find this language unconstitutional, but I believed that this Court would be unwilling to do so. Later, two days before the argument, David agreed with me.

As the practice argument came to a close, the Georgetown students began to leave the classroom. One approached Mike and me and asked which one of us had attended Dartmouth. This Ivy League college had been the scene of heated exchanges between students and faculty over the issues of racism and intolerance. The school had come to symbolize the conservative response to the move among colleges and universities toward political correctness. We had quoted several conservative commentators with ties to Dartmouth in our brief (author Dinesh D'Souza and federal judge Silberman), believing that the members of the Supreme Court would look favorably upon such commentary. Although neither of us had any connection to Dartmouth, the student left unconvinced of this.

While we were busy preparing for the oral argument, my opponent, who had taken over the file from the appellate attorney in his office, was making his own preparations. Tom Foley had been Ramsey County Attorney since 1978. With time off for World War II, my father had served in that same office from 1939 to 1974. Foley's father was one of the original members of the Minnesota Court of Appeals, formed in 1983. Irish-Catholic Democrats, described by a local newspaper as "both liberal-leaning," Foley and I were descended from families in southeastern Minnesota who had produced several generations of lawyers. Seventy years earlier, while my great-uncle was county attorney in Hastings, Minnesota, Tom's grandfather had been county attorney in Wabasha, a town just south of Hastings. Foley had come from a more political tradition than I, and when he was elected county attorney a mere six years out of law school I had not supported him. I was loyal to the incumbent county attorney with whom my father had worked for sixteen years; I also felt he was inexperienced and thus not qualified for the position.

Until Foley's election in 1978 the county attorney was generally experienced in trial work, enabling him to personally prosecute high-profile cases. By 1991 the county attorney's position had become primarily political and administrative; Foley had not engaged in trial or appellate practice. Nonetheless, he had been reelected three times and was unopposed in the last two elections. When the decision was made in June 1990 to charge R.A.V. under this ordinance, Foley had not been consulted. No one in the office had foreseen the controversy that would arise.

After the decision to appeal, the case was routinely assigned to Steven DeCoster, the longtime appellate attorney in the Ramsey County Attorney's Office. After the Minnesota Supreme Court decision in January 1991 Foley had become involved. When the petition for certiorari was granted by the United States Supreme Court in June 1991, Foley decided to argue the case himself. He had hoped to split the argument with DeCoster, but the Court frowns upon this procedure, so he had decided to present the entire argument. Coming from a long legal and political tradition, he knew it was a lifetime opportunity that he could not pass up. He was criticized by attorneys in his office, who felt that DeCoster should have been allowed to argue the case, based on his experience.

To argue a case before the United States Supreme Court, one should be involved in the drafting and researching of the brief presented. I had had that opportunity. Now that Foley had decided to present the argument, he was forced to become familiar with this area of law while he prepared. A law firm in Minneapolis, the local representatives for the Anti-Defamation League, helped him. Local lawyers and law professors also sat on moot courts to hear his case. After I had finished my practice argument at Georgetown, I was grateful that I had four weeks in which to research, to reflect on the issues, and to restructure my argument. Conversely, Foley did what I had refused to do. He held a practice argument less than forty-eight hours before the actual case was heard before the Court. As I suspected would happen, this practice hearing did not aid Foley and only served to confuse the issues in his mind at the eleventh hour.

Returning to the Twin Cities from Georgetown, I learned of a recent case filed by the U.S. District Court for the Eastern District of Wisconsin. *The U.W.M. Post, Inc., et al. v. Board of Regents of the Univ. of Wis. System* had been decided by Judge Robert W. Warren on October 11, 1991. Judge Warren struck down the UW Rule, a speech-code provision, on the basis that it violated a student's First Amendment rights:

> The problems of bigotry and discrimination sought to be addressed here are real and truly corrosive of the educational environment. But freedom of speech is almost absolute in our land and the only restriction the fighting words doctrine can abide is that based on the fear of violent reaction. Content based prohibitions such as that in the UW Rule, however well intended, simply cannot survive the screening which our Constitution demands.

I called Sandy Nelsen, assistant clerk of the United States Supreme Court, and asked permission to submit recent additional authority, namely, a copy of this case, which had not been decided at the time the reply brief had been filed. After some jousting, Nelsen allowed me to file the case.

Most of the briefs that are filed in the United States Supreme Court are filed by government entities, large organizations, or prominent law firms. Often the attorney is insulated by law clerks, secretaries, and other support staff. Mike and I did not have this luxury. We did our own research, made our own copies of articles and cases, bought our own postage, opened and sent out our own mail, and generally tried to make up for our lack of resources with constant attention to the case. I was on the phone to Sandy Nelsen on many occasions. On one occasion, at the request of the MCLU, I had asked for a short continuance on the brief. As a matter of personal pride, I was unwilling to ask for the continuance on our own behalf because I was positive we would finish the brief on time. Recognizing this, she correctly refused the continuance. On another occasion, while I was reviewing the proofs (copies furnished by the Supreme Court printer), I noted that the caption had been removed from one of the pages. Nelsen explained patiently to me that this was commonly done to save printing costs for the Court. She pointed out that no one else had ever objected to the deletion. I decided there was a difference between hands-on and pushy. The deletion stood.

We filed the Wisconsin case as recent authority with the Court on November 20. I still had several weeks to prepare the argument. Knowing there would be a media frenzy immediately before we left for Washington on November 30, I set aside time early in mid-November to practice the argument. I took the time to examine and consider the constitutional issues surrounding "enhancement" hate-crime laws.

The St. Paul ordinance was directed at offensive expression itself, expression based on certain subjects that aroused anger in others. There was no requirement of criminal conduct. Section 292.02 was more similar to student speech codes than it was to enhancement laws, as it addressed "hate speech," not "hate crime." Many states have laws that punish a "bias" motive more severely than a crime based on other motives. If A assaults B without a bias motive, he could be incarcerated for up to ninety days; if A assaults B "because of" or "by reason of" B's race, he could be incarcerated for up to one year.

Such laws are based on model legislation originally proposed by the Anti-Defamation League in 1981 that sought to insulate them from constitutional challenge. Proponents of such provisions believe that the person who was assaulted is not the only victim in such a case, but represents all members of the targeted group (characterized by race, religion, gender, etc.). While this argument is similar to the justification offered for hate-speech restrictions—i.e., all members of the targeted group suffer—the enhancement laws apply only to the one charged under an existing criminal law.

If one has the right to think what one wishes and to say what one thinks, supporters of these laws believe that once one is guilty of criminal conduct, one loses First Amendment protection. Although we found this approach questionable, we had recognized that section 292.02 was much more objectionable, since it was aimed directly at a viewpoint without an underlying requirement of criminal conduct. We had not challenged the enhancement law cited in the second charge against R.A.V. Some observers felt that the Court might question the attorneys on these issues in *R.A.V.* even though section 292.02 was not an enhancement law. As it turned out, the Court did not inquire about these laws, saving that inquiry for another case at a later date.

As expected, mid-November brought intense media scrutiny as we prepared for the argument on December 4. Although many newspapers, including the *Chicago Tribune, The Wall Street Journal,* and *Kansas City Star,* conducted interviews by phone, both the *The Washington Post* and *The New York Times* sent reporters to do background articles. Many radio stations nationwide conducted interviews by teleconference, while each of the major networks sent camera crews and on-camera reporters for feature stories. Most interviewers wanted to talk directly to R.A.V. to address the "human interest" angle of the story. Feeling that this was not appropriate, since he might face charges depending on the outcome of the appeal, we decided that it was his decision to make after discussing the matter with us. The decision was made to try it on an experimental basis with strict ground rules.

The library in our law offices became a media center for the next ten days. One by one the camera crews set up and then dismantled their operations. We agreed to allow R.A.V. to go on camera with Tim O'Brien of *ABC World News Tonight* on the condition that there would be no inquiry about the events of June 21, 1990, that Mike and I would be present off-camera to prevent questions that we felt inappropriate, and that ABC would use only footage of questions and answers to which we did not object.

As the brief interview took place, R.A.V. answered the questions intelligently and somewhat evasively. When he praised his lawyers, O'Brien quickly ended the interview and turned to us and congratulated us on our "preparation of the client." The comment by R.A.V. regarding his attorneys had been spontaneous, and we knew it would not be aired on the program. (It wasn't.) Afterward, I sat and talked to O'Brien. I mentioned to him that I was becoming leery of seeing footage of a three-story-high burning cross surrounded by Klan members as an introduction to television features on this case. Although the message is the same, a two- by two-foot cross does not have the impact of a three-story cross, with the flames sweeping in the wind. O'Brien told me that he had obtained the footage years earlier when he had been stationed in New Orleans. I asked him if he had an opinion on why the Court had taken the case. He said he did not but that it may have been a mistake on the part of the Court, and he did not feel that we would prevail.

The next day I met with Tony Mauro of *U.S.A. Today* and *Legal Times* and Tamar Lewin of *The New York Times*. Mauro was writing a background article for *U.S.A. Today* and would be reviewing the argument for *Legal Times*. I had heard from another attorney who had argued before the Court that he had found Mauro acerbic and overly critical. Since I did not have this impression, I attributed this comment to dissatisfaction with the review of his performance. Mauro had taken part in a moot court in the Washington, D.C., area on *R.A.V.* and was knowledgeable concerning the issues before the Court. His reporting of the case was accurate and concise.

Tamar Lewin of *The New York Times* was a close friend of Ruth Marcus of *The Washington Post,* who would be coming to St. Paul several days later. Each reporter wanted to scoop the other one with an interview with R.A.V. Unfortunately for the media, R.A.V. would no longer be meeting with reporters, but both Mike and I were relieved at his decision. As an avid reader of the *Times,* I was familiar with Lewin's byline. An insightful reporter, she wrote one of the best articles about the case, which appeared as a cover story in the Sunday issue of *The New York Times* on December 1, 1991. The interview was held at night; as she walked through our law offices and realized that Mike and I were working on our own with little support and few resources, she seemed stunned and was full of sympathy for us. It was her opinion we would not win, and she had been told by other attorneys in New York that any decision would have little impact on hate-crime laws. With the exception of Nat Hentoff of *The Village Voice,* most reporters believed we would not prevail. Not wishing to undermine our confidence any more than it had already been, I no longer asked the opinion of media representatives.

Ruth Marcus of *The Washington Post* arrived on Monday, November 25, and interviewed me immediately after completing an interview with the Jones family, who had been victimized by the burning cross. She too was disappointed that she would not get a chance to interview R.A.V. She mentioned that the justices received *The Washington Post,* just as Lewin had mentioned that they received *The New York Times.* Her style was more confrontational than that of any reporter I had previously met. Expressing her sincere sympathy for the Jones family, she stared at me intensely. Perhaps because the interview took place on a long day that had involved seven interviews, I was confrontational as well. I said that I too was sympathetic to the Jones family, that as I had worked on the case, photographs of Mr. and Mrs. Jones and their children often haunted me, and that although it had not been their decision to use this law to prosecute the case, I had never felt that the Joneses truly understood that there were more severe and less problematic sanctions available. I told Marcus that I was often faced with reporters who had interviewed the Jones family and viewed me with hostile suspicion, and said that I was uncertain whether she could remain objective given her apparent attitude. She assured me that she could, and she did.

Later that same day I had a radio interview scheduled with Nina Totenberg of National Public Radio. Totenberg had recently been subjected to media scrutiny herself about her role in the Clarence Thomas hearings and Anita Hill's testimony. Now that Clarence Thomas had been confirmed, she too would soon be relying on the First Amendment because Congress overreacted in an attempt to find the "leak" that had led to the exposure of Anita Hill's sexual harassment allegations against Clarence Thomas. (The subpoena for Totenberg's and another reporter's phone records was eventually quashed on First Amendment grounds.) I was curious about what Totenberg's attitude would be toward me and toward this case. I was pleasantly surprised. She had done her homework, was familiar with the facts of the case, knew my role and background, and proceeded to conduct the interview in a precise and professional manner.

Finishing local media interviews, I spent Thanksgiving quietly and used the following Friday for rest and reflection.

As my plane taxied down the runway on the morning of November 30, I thought about what a shambles my life had become. My law practice was suffering, my personal life was in upheaval (a close relationship with a woman had recently been irrevocably shattered), and few understood what it was we were trying to accomplish with our efforts. Having coped with death so recently, my mother, fearing a hostile reception in Washington, D.C., seriously worried that I would not return. Because of her health, she was unable to attend the argument. I assured her that her worries were groundless and told her whom to contact while I was away. The case had not been easy on her, as many of her friends simply did not understand the issue before the Court. Many had to reconcile their memories of me as a boy with the image of an attorney who apparently felt that burning a cross on someone's front lawn was permissible behavior. To my mother's great pain, several of her friends, oblivious to the First Amendment issues, had confronted her, criticizing my position.

With a few exceptions, almost everyone I had talked to felt that we would lose this case, even though many believed we were right. Many found it hard to understand why we had embarked on this crusade because of the personal and professional price we had paid and the unlikelihood of prevailing. The answer was simple: Mike and I had been convinced we were right from the very beginning and this was enough to sustain us.

Washington was rainy and dreary the weekend we arrived. Nevertheless, as always, I enjoyed walking the Mall and visiting the monuments. As we had in November, Mike and I attended oral arguments at the Court on the morning of December 2. Our counterparts, Tom Foley and Steve DeCoster, were also present. The members of the Court were in a disputatious mood that morning as Chief Justice Rehnquist in particular challenged several of the arguing attorneys, leaving one attorney in particular confused and speechless. Both Foley and I left the Supreme Court building acutely aware of what we faced.

That afternoon we had both agreed to be interviewed by CNN and to appear on the *Sonya Live* show. Tom and I reported to the studio near the Capitol to be questioned on camera by Sonya Friedman stationed in New York. I had participated in a pre-interview for this show several days earlier. Such pre-interviews enable the host or hostess to be familiar with the underlying issues and the positions of the participants. We had become somewhat spoiled because radio, newspaper, and television interviewers, particularly on the national level, acted conscientiously and responsibly in obtaining background information and becoming familiar with the underlying First Amendment issues before interviewing us. This show would be different.

As Tom and I were fitted for earphones while we looked at a blank screen, I saw that what was happening did not bode well for this interview. I heard the hostess tell the audience that the next segment of the show would be a discussion on "how affairs can help a marriage," and immediately thereafter I heard the crackling of a blazing fire and knew that the film of the three-story burning cross was again being flashed on the screen.

It became clear that Sonya had not done her homework. First she asked whether I or my client had brought the challenge, which was a totally inappropriate question. We clearly had acted in our client's behalf and were in this together. What she was really asking was whether I was responsible for such an outrageous and, in her opinion, indefensible position. I explained to her that there were other, more serious charges available to address the alleged conduct; she accused me of using empty rhetoric and equated our challenge with an article that had appeared in *The New York Times* concerning a Klan meeting in Iowa. Friedman seemed unable to grasp that the law, not the underlying conduct, was being challenged. As she became more animated, I responded in kind. After I told her, "I don't think you understood what I said earlier," the interview became more heated. Interrupting both Tom and me before we could finish our sentences, Friedman then moved from an implied allegation of racism to an implied allegation of greed, suggesting that the taxpayers were "paying" for our challenge. I kept silent, although I was tempted to explain to her that we were not being paid. Her final attack once again implied that I was racist and unfeeling when she asked how I could proceed with this challenge "in good conscience." In response to her apparent inability or unwillingness to examine the real issues involved, I cited Alan Dershowitz's observation from the WBZ radio program in Boston in June that an earlier United Nations resolution equating Zionism with racism had led England (specifically Leeds, England) to ban the Star of David. Unconvinced, Friedman ended the program with the observation that "not all of our arguments ring true equally." It was easily the most unpleasant interview I participated in at any time on this case. (Two weeks to the day after this interview, the General Assembly to the United Nations repealed the offensive 1975 resolution characterizing Zionism as "a form of racism and racial discrimination" by a vote of 111 to 25, with 13 abstentions.)

While Foley spent the afternoon conducting a final practice oral argument before members of the Department of Justice, I spent the next thirty-six hours writing, thinking, and reorganizing my argument. Although Clarence Thomas had survived the allegations of sexual harassment made by Anita Hill and had taken his seat on the Court, his position on this case was far from clear. As the only black

American on the Court, would he feel an obligation to question me at the argument—or would his admitted lack of experience in constitutional interpretation of the First Amendment keep him silent? Like other new appointees to the Court, Thomas thus far had remained quiet on the bench, allowing the senior justices to conduct the interrogation of the attorneys at argument. At this juncture he was an enigma. He was, after all, a man who had come of age in the segregated South. No other justice on the Court would view the burning cross with the same life experience as Clarence Thomas. He had sat on the Court for only a number of weeks, and his approach to this case was simply unpredictable.

I was stunned and unhappy when I learned that David Duke had chosen to announce his quest for the presidency on the same day as our oral argument and in the same city. This was no accident, for we were being shadowed by a group whose interests could not have been further from our own. All of this would occur in the nation's capital, where minorities represented a majority of the population and where the contrast between the powerful and the powerless was open and obvious.

The next morning I would be faced with the specter of an intolerant demagogue while I argued before the United States Supreme Court in a case involving a burning cross. Duke's timing ensured that every major newspaper on December 5 would run a review of the oral argument next to an article reporting his announcement that he was running for president. Even television stations reporting on the argument would follow their report with news of Duke's press conference. The result would be further confusion among the public about our point. Many would equate our position with sympathy for white racists, whereas we had done everything we could to dispel that notion. In our own minds, we were defending the First Amendment rights of those who did not realize the danger.

As I fell asleep the night of December 3, 1991, I did not know what to expect the next day. Aware of the possibility of demonstrations outside the Supreme Court building and a hostile audience inside, I wondered how the members of the Court would approach the argument. All I knew was that I would never forget the morning of December 4, 1991.

The Price of Liberty:
Courage, Tolerance, and Vision

"Out of the crooked timber of humanity no straight thing was ever made." To force people into the neat uniforms demanded by dogmatically believed-in schemes is almost always the road to inhumanity.

—Isaiah Berlin (quoting, in part, Immanuel Kant)

Free speech is the whole thing, the whole ballgame . . . free speech is life itself.

—Salman Rushdie (December 11, 1991)

If free speech is an instrument of education, the St. Paul hate crime law is an instrument of ignorance, reaction and paranoia, the very maladies it ostensibly is designed to combat.

Chicago Tribune (December 3, 1991)

In late 1992, a year after *R.A.V.* was argued, the National Association to Protect Individual Rights announced the results of two recent surveys, one conducted by a Democratic polling firm and the other by a Republican firm. Asked to prioritize different issues facing our country in the years ahead, those polled listed the preservation of individual rights above "protecting the environment, holding down the cost of living or strengthening the country's defense." Fully 86 percent of those surveyed indicated concern that as citizens they would "lose some of the individual rights we enjoy in this country in the coming years."

That American citizens should treasure their individual rights in the abstract is hardly surprising. Willing to share with pollsters their fear of a loss of liberty, Americans nevertheless seem oblivious to the continuing threat to First Amendment freedoms that is posed by laws such as section 292.02. With only a few exceptions, reporters seemed unwilling or unable to explain the issues in this case in a manner that could be understood by the public. Still, by the eve of the oral argument, many national newspapers had finally published editorials that favored our challenge to the ordinance.

The public often remains silent when its precious individual rights are jeopardized by local lawmakers. Some would argue that society has only itself to blame for this lack of understanding; others would say it is a failure of leadership. Since the media owe their very existence to the First Amendment, the press has a heightened role in alerting the public to dangerous legislation and in holding erring lawmakers accountable.

On June 8, 1789, when James Madison introduced the proposed amendments that would later form our Bill of Rights, he brilliantly outmaneuvered those who hoped to change the structure of government as it was then proposed in the Constitution. By finding the middle ground between opposing factions, Madison and his supporters not only reached a compromise but erased the fear held by some that local majorities would threaten individual liberty through the tyranny of state government. By creating a strong centralized government held in check by these crucial amendments, Madison displayed the courage and the vision of true leadership. As the nation celebrated the two hundredth anniversary of the Bill of Rights in December 1991, we were reminded that in regard to the First Amendment, "no other forty-five words in the English language have brought so much spiritual, intellectual and material benefit to a people as these few phrases. They are the envy of the oppressed in every land."

In the month that oral arguments were heard in *R.A.V.*, numerous stories appeared extolling the first ten amendments to the Constitution. Some of the articles noted the ongoing dangers the First Amendment faces as it enters its third century. Columnist Ellen Goodman noted:

> Last spring, the American Society of Newspaper Editors presented a survey of attitudes toward the First Amendment. It found that Americans believe that we believe in free speech more than we do in fact.
>
> But the greatest inhibitor of free expression wasn't the fear of the state or even the boss, but the fear that we might offend someone else. The people polled worried most that "saying what's on your mind may harm or damage other people" and that "speaking your mind may hurt the feelings of those you care for." . . .
>
> The monsters in our living rooms do not carry placards that read

"tax policy." They are labeled race, gender, values, sexuality. Stuff that needs a good talking about.

Another story noted that a man who had produced an anniversary radio special for the Bill of Rights fifty years earlier had been unable to get funding for another anniversary special even though he solicited underwriting from "150 of America's largest corporations and foundations. . . . Not a single one was willing to lend its name or money to the program." Although he finally secured funding several months before airtime, Norman Corwin, eighty-one, had lived long enough to see the changing attitudes toward freedom of expression:

> There's something stiff and unbending about the idea of correctness. . . . I'm not gainsaying its values necessarily. But the Bill of Rights doesn't offer freedom from speech. To silence an idea because it might offend a minority doesn't protect that minority. It deprives it of the tool it needs most—the right to talk back. Exemptions are for the tax laws, not the Bill of Rights. Sure, it's a high price. But if you want a bargain-basement Bill of Rights, I know a lot of places you can get one. They are very quiet places because no one makes noise. Correctness silences noise. I say the more noise the better.

This was the climate in December of 1991 as the United States Supreme Court prepared to hear *R.A.V. v. City of St. Paul.*

A look back at earlier interpretations of the First Amendment confirms that freedom of expression was not a high priority of the Court prior to World War I. As Anthony Lewis has pointed out, "The speech and press clauses of the First Amendment lay essentially dormant" throughout the nineteenth century. In fact, the Supreme Court "was hostile to claims of free expression." It is generally acknowledged that Justice Holmes and Justice Brandeis ushered in modern First Amendment doctrine in a series of dissents commencing in 1919. The influence of these men on First Amendment jurisprudence is well documented. A closer examination of the forces shaping their reasoning may shed some light on the vision Holmes and Brandeis had for our nation in the decades to follow.

In 1917 a federal district judge for the Southern District of New York, Learned Hand, decided the case of *Masses Publishing Co. v. Patten.* In that decision, Hand courageously held that the government could not ban the circulation of a radical magazine under the World War I Espionage Act. As Gerald Gunther of Stanford Law School has noted, "it was a rare judicial effort to stem the mounting tide of suppression of dissent, in an articulation of first amendment values and an elaboration of free speech doctrine announced two years before the Supreme Court's first opportunity to grapple with the same issues." Hand's focus "on the speaker's words," as opposed to the likely consequences of those words, was a uniquely "speech-protective" interpretation of the First Amendment. Since Judge Hand was swimming against the tide with this liberal interpretation, the professional response was "painfully disappointing." Some observers felt that this courageous but unpopular decision hindered his professional advancement.

Hand's formulation—and subsequent correspondence with Oliver Wendell Holmes (documented fully by Gerald Gunther)—helped change the course of First Amendment doctrine, culminating over fifty years later in the case of *Brandenburg v. Ohio*. There the Court finally held that the "probability of harm" was "no longer the central criterion for speech limitations. The inciting language of the speaker—the Hand focus on 'objective' words—is the major consideration." In later years Hand worried that the unique test he had formulated would be viewed after his death as "some false coin." Yet as Gunther notes, "Learned Hand's analysis was precious metal, never 'false coin'; the problem always lay in the eyes of the appraisers." Though seldom mentioned in the same breath with Holmes and Brandeis, Hand had helped to ensure the strength of freedom of expression seven decades later.

While Holmes may have been influenced by the persuasive logic of Learned Hand, Justice Louis Brandeis was influenced by more classical forces. Chroniclers of the life of Brandeis have noted "the high esteem in which Brandeis held the Greeks of fifth-century Athens." With his concurring opinion in *Whitney v. California,* joined by Justice Holmes, Brandeis drew on his obvious affection for the ancient Greek world with his idealistic defense of First Amendment principles. For Brandeis, courage was the most critical of all human virtues. It was necessary to ensure personal liberty, and liberty provided the framework for a happy and productive life. Wary of those who would acknowledge only that a person should be allowed to think what he wants but not to speak his mind, Brandeis joined the two for posterity when he stated that "freedom to think as you will and to speak as you think are means indispensable to the discovery and spread of political truth."

As Vincent Blasi of Columbia Law School has noted, Brandeis avoided "the marketplace of ideas" metaphor formulated earlier by

Holmes. Perhaps anticipating later criticism of Holmes's metaphor, Brandeis was arguably more realistic. Aware that there were no guarantees that the marketplace would always function properly, Brandeis placed the burden on each citizen to respond creatively to threats to civilized society. As Blasi points out, Brandeis believed that "noxious doctrine is most likely to flourish when its opponents lack the personal qualities of wisdom, creativity and confidence. And those qualities, he suggests, are best developed by discussion and education, not by lazy and impatient reliance on the coercive authority of the state."

By emphasizing the role of the individual, Brandeis protected free speech in a way that others who followed failed to emphasize. His lifelong affection for Athenian democracy reflected his belief that individual courage led directly to the greater good. By maintaining intellectual independence, one could be both realistic and virtuous: "Others are brave out of ignorance; and, when they stop to think, they begin to fear. But the man who can most truly be accounted brave is he who best knows the meaning of what is sweet in life and what is terrible, and then goes out undeterred to meet what is to come."

Quoting the funeral oration of Pericles ("They believed liberty to be the secret of happiness and courage to be the secret of liberty"), Brandeis demonstrated a deep belief in the classical form of democracy. For Brandeis, civic leadership meant the sense of self based on a principled life, and the vision and sense of responsibility to foresee the needs of society in the future.

To Blasi,

> It is this quality of initiative—the willingness to take chances, to persist against the odds, to embark on novel ventures in the face of scorn and risk, to commit oneself—that provide the essential connection between Brandeis' regard for Athenian democracy, his emphasis in the *Whitney* opinion on the virtue of courage, and his lasting impact on first amendment thought.

In the decades since the legendary dissents and concurring opinions of Holmes and Brandeis, First Amendment scholars have debated the meaning of their words and the core of First Amendment values.

Zechariah Chaffee, Jr., was a major proponent of the Holmes "clear and present danger" test, which placed emphasis on the "imminent" danger of expression as a justification for proscription rather than on an "objective" examination of the words, as Hand had emphasized. Chaffee, the author of several famous constitutional treatises on the First Amendment, preferred the approach of Judge Hand but publicly supported the approach of Justice Holmes, perhaps hoping to influence the historical interpretation of a rather conservative standard.

Another noted First Amendment scholar, Alexander Meiklejohn, rejected Holmes's marketplace justification for freedom of expression and instead argued that "free speech is indispensable to an informed citizenry required to make democratic self-government work." Initially protecting only political speech, Meiklejohn later extended this protection to "novels and dramas and paintings and poems." By doing so, he effectively erased the underlying distinction between political and nonpolitical expression. Moreover, he continued to emphasize the governing powers of the people as opposed to their individual rights. His view of the First Amendment stressed the need for the education of the population so that they may be prepared for self-government. As he stated over three decades ago, "Our citizens are not educated for self-government. We are terrified by ideas, rather than challenged and stimulated by them. Our dominant mood is not the courage of people who dare to think. It is the timidity of those who fear and hate whenever conventions are questioned."

Other First Amendment theorists have noted that judicial construction of freedom of expression has been inconsistent throughout history, failing in its promise to be speech-protective at precisely the wrong times. The Framers provided that the federal judiciary would be insulated from public opinion through the mechanism of lifetime appointment. In return, this branch of the government was expected to interpret constitutional provisions in an independent manner, cognizant of the rights of the individual in the face of majoritarian opposition. This lifetime-appointment procedure is only one tool in ensuring that the First Amendment is protected in the years ahead.

Some scholars classify certain periods in our nation's history as being "pathological," as times when we as a people were particularly intolerant of unorthodox beliefs. They argue that First Amendment doctrines should be formulated with an emphasis on "how well they would serve in the worst of times," with the judicial branch interpreting the amendment in normal times "to promote an attitude of respect, devotion, perhaps even reverence, regarding those central norms." Setting the parameters of such a doctrine is easier said than done.

Those who see the First Amendment as an instrument for the greater good emphasize the collective political purpose of speech and downplay the individual right of self-expression. We maintain the right of free expression "not because people have an intrinsic moral right to say what they wish, but because allowing them to do so will produce good effects for the rest of us." Underlying such an approach is a majoritarian value judgment as to what those "good effects" may be, now or in the future. Such an approach is invariably tied to the collective morality of the moment. This morality often translates into fear that leads to censorship in the name of social good. Such outcries for silencing offensive expression will often come during "pathological periods," with the result that First Amendment values are pushed aside, as in times of economic upheaval and war when selected political groups are targeted for repression.

It does little good to relate free speech solely to the value of self-government, since such a valuation would seem to limit free expression to political topics. Protecting any political speech begs the question of what speech is political. As Meiklejohn discovered, once one extends the meaning of "political" expression to "novels and dramas and paintings and poems," as perhaps one must, then little is accomplished in defining political speech. Those who embrace this instrumental viewpoint of First Amendment freedoms would not necessarily object to an ordinance such as section 292.02, since the type of expression apparently prohibited by such a law would not further the public good.

Others, including myself, would emphasize that speech is an end in itself. As Ronald Dworkin of New York University Law School has argued, it is "an essential and constitutive feature of a just political society that government treat all of its adult members, except those who are incompetent, as responsible moral agents." Dworkin explains that this governmental responsibility has two dimensions:

> First, morally responsible people insist on making up their own minds about what is good or bad in life or in politics, or what is true and false in matters of justice or faith. Government insults its citizens, and denies their moral responsibility, when it decrees that they cannot be trusted to hear opinions that might persuade them to dangerous or offensive convictions.

Further:

> Government frustrates and denies that aspect of moral personality when it disqualifies some people from exercising these responsibilities on the ground that their convictions make them unworthy

participants. So long as government exercises political dominion over a person, and demands political obedience from him, it may not deny him either of these two attributes of moral responsibility, no matter how hateful the opinions he wishes to consider or propagate, any more than it may deny him an equal vote. If it does, it forfeits a substantial ground of its claim to legitimate power over him.

If Brandeis was right when he said that our country was founded by leaders who "valued liberty both as an end and as a means," then it follows that we must have the foresight to maintain this liberty in the face of offensive and even hateful opinions. Rodney A. Smolla of the College of William and Mary Marshall-Wythe School of Law, has said that "censorship is a social instinct" and "the conflict felt by most decent Americans is that we hate hate speech as much as we love free speech." Nat Hentoff, quoting a postcard he received, noted that "censorship is the strongest drive in human nature; sex is a weak second." Justice Holmes observed ironically that "persecution for the expression of opinion seems to be perfectly logical. If you have no doubt of your premises or your power and want a certain result with all of your heart you naturally express your wishes in law and sweep away all opposition."

Recognition of the powerful societal impulse to censor, particularly in the area of offensive or hateful speech, fails to provide any justification for such action while it does provide grounds for opposing this instinctive behavior. We may recognize that hateful expression should be punished fully when it poses danger of an immediate incitement to violence. When such offensive opinion crosses the line into discriminatory conduct, such as in the workplace, civil rights legislation should be actively enforced against those employers who allow such conduct to take place. When the display of bigoted attitudes creates a hostile work environment, such opinions are no longer protected. When bigoted opinion crosses the line and becomes a targeted threat of terror, as was alleged in *R.A.V.*, such conduct should and can be punished, but not with a law that ignores the illegal conduct and singles out the offensive opinion. While we may prevent threats and discriminatory conduct, we may not prohibit offensive opinions. Such opinions must be dealt with in a different manner.

Lee Bollinger, dean of the University of Michigan Law School, addresses some of these underlying issues in *The Tolerant Society*. Bollinger recognizes that it is human nature to defend the established order by suppressing any challenging viewpoints, including offensive expressions that threaten to undermine this established order. Rather than emphasizing the fragmented nature of the pluralistic society, Bollinger suggests that we focus instead on the "shared values" that we possess as a people. As those values become more widespread, we should be secure enough to also share a capacity for tolerating varied viewpoints. One hopes that the development of society may mirror the image of the development of the individual as he becomes more at ease in his own beliefs and thus more willing to accept a contrary viewpoint. If "fear breeds repression and repression breeds hate," as Brandeis suggested, then confidence breeds tolerance, and tolerance leads to a free and open society.

Recognizing freedom of expression as an evolving concept throughout the twentieth century, Bollinger confronts the challenge that appears to succeeding generations: "One generation may seek merely the right to speak, while another will take strength in tolerating bad speech acts. Each generation has its own agenda, as the conditions then prevailing will dictate what subjects are important for inquiry." While many of those who came of age in the sixties found their purpose in civil rights marches and antiwar demonstrations, others coming of age now may be called on to demonstrate a different type of courage by tolerating offensive speech aimed at the gains of the earlier struggles. In demonstrating a confidence to deal with even the most offensive expression, we provide a framework for succeeding generations of Americans whose defining moments may very well be attributable to the freedoms we protected so conscientiously years before.

In the meantime the challenge is to turn away from censorship and coercion, and toward education and example. The tolerance of different physical characteristics, religious beliefs, and lifestyles is learned behavior. Every American adult should consider that his or her attitudes communicated to the young will either prevent or contribute to the growth of tolerant attitudes. As Bollinger says,

> To a society that seeks to develop a certain capacity, especially one of security and control, toleration can help to establish and prove symbolically the arrival of that capacity. Often, the harder something is to do, the more symbolic in meaning the doing of it carries. For speech that attacks and challenges community values, the act of toleration serves to both define and reaffirm those values; the act of tolerance implies a contrary belief and demonstrates a confidence and security in the correctness of the community norm. Through toleration, in short, we create the community, define the

values of that community, and affirm the commitment to and confidence in those values.

Despite the disappointment of many with the pace of social progress, it is nevertheless accurate to observe that our society has come a long way in the past three decades toward a greater understanding of what our ignorance toward others has cost us as a nation. While racism, sexism, and other forms of intolerance are still pervasive throughout segments of society, many of those who came of age three decades ago moved away from the intolerant beliefs and attitudes of their parents or other role models. It is this ongoing evolution of social attitudes in which we must have faith. We should recognize ugly and offensive expression as a manifestation of the resulting friction that occurs as we move forward, remembering that civil rights and antiwar demonstrations in the sixties produced upheaval as well as positive results.

Bollinger's premise is that by tolerating offensive challenges to our accepted beliefs, each of us is forced to come to terms with his or her own value system. It is one thing to live in the neighborhood of the Jones family on the east side of St. Paul and to acquiesce to their move into the neighborhood. Such a passive acceptance of integration may appear to be a step forward, but it does little to address the underlying hostility that some members of the community may continue to feel. Residents of that area were forced to confront their own beliefs and values after that overt act of racism took place in the Joneses' front yard. As in other communities when such a hateful act has taken place, a sense of community was formed when many of the neighbors rallied to support the vicitimized family.

In addition to the example that can be set by members of a community, we have the continuing obligation to train our young to think for themselves, reminding them of our historical legacy as the only nation on earth that truly defends the individual right of self-expression. As one observer has noted, "Through lower educational standards, declining intellectual competence, diminished zest for debate and social sanctions against skepticism, our liberties can be eroded and our rights subverted." Studies show that the vast majority of hate-based crimes, both here and abroad, are committed by juveniles.

Presumably adults are more educated and consequently more tolerant or perhaps they are simply less overt in displaying intolerant beliefs. Some believe that ninth grade is the optimum level for teaching students about these issues; others suggest the fifth grade because at this point children are just beginning to understand that "adults are keeping things from them" and that there are issues they wish to know more about. For Abraham Lincoln, the time to educate was even earlier: "To the support of the Constitution, let reverence be breathed by every American mother to the lisping babe that prattles on her lap; let it be taught in schools, in seminaries and in colleges; let it be written in primers, spelling books and in almanacs. . . . Let it become the political religion of the nation."

Education and example will go a long way to protecting the guarantees of the First Amendment in the years ahead. The greatest continuing threat to these constitutional guarantees may not be the ignorance of the citizenry but the failure of leadership among our elected public officials. As Stephen Carter of Yale Law School wrote regarding the handling of Anita Hill's testimony, "Perhaps what we saw in last October's hearings was less a gender dynamic than a power dynamic: people with power will use it or abuse it to do what they think is right. The reason this frightens—or ought to—is that once those in power are convinced that they are right, standing in their path is a good way to get run over."

As Justice Kennedy noted in his remarks at the University of Minnesota Law School, after the United States Supreme Court decided *Texas v. Johnson* in 1989 there was a public uproar about the decision. There were a number of ways that our nation's leaders could have responded. They could have addressed the issue directly, explaining that they too found such expression offensive and hurtful, while pointing out there were more pressing issues facing our nation in 1989 than the isolated demonstrations of a few anarchists. In swearing to uphold and defend the United States Constitution, many would argue that members of Congress have an obligation to lead the people, not just to respond to the emotions of the moment. Instead, the administration attempted to secure an amendment to the Constitution to ban flag-burning, and when that failed, the Congress passed unconstitutional legislation. This series of events constituted a classic example of a bipartisan failure of leadership. History is replete with such well-meaning but ultimately misguided acts on the part of civic leaders.

When the Flag Protection Act of 1989 came before the United States Supreme Court, it arrived with "Congress' recent recognition of a purported 'national consensus' favoring a prohibition on flag burning." Considering the number of congressmen knowledgeable in the law, it is hard to understand how so many could reconcile this supposed "consensus" with the clearly established doctrine of the First Amendment that protects the individual against the majority viewpoint. Writing for the Court, Justice Brennan curtly responded, "Any suggestion that the Government's interest in suppressing speech becomes more weighty as popular opposition to that speech grows is foreign to the First Amendment."

The Senate passed a resolution after *Texas v. Johnson* criticizing the United States Supreme Court by a vote of 97 to 3. Congress, of course, was stating the obvious: a vast majority of Americans—and I include myself—are personally appalled and offended when our flag, the symbol of our nation, is desecrated. But even such an abhorrent expression is protected by the First Amendment. Our nation's leaders should find ways of maintaining public popularity other than advocating the sacrifice of constitutional guarantees. When the House of Representatives passed a resolution similar to the Senate's with only five dissenters, one of the dissenters stated, "We have nothing to fear from the flag-burners, but we have a great deal to fear from those who have lost faith in the Constitution."

An examination of local politics confirms the importance of leadership. A year after the St. Paul City Council passed section 292.02 by unanimous vote, the Minneapolis City Council passed an unconstitutional antipornography ordinance, which Mayor Don Fraser, in an act of political courage, vetoed. In criticizing the Minneapolis council members, Donald Alexander Downs notes:

> Without responsible leadership, the larger society does not always exhibit the political maturity envisioned by the modern doctrine of free speech. To those bent on reform, free speech may seem only an impediment to the realization of their desires. . . .
>
> According to the theory of democratic elitism, political leaders' stronger support for civil liberty should save the day when people at large fail to exhibit the virtues of a tolerant society. The frequent failures of both leaders and society suggest that free speech values are perhaps less well-established than is desirable . . . salvation by judiciary is not always the best practice for constitutional democracy.

Leadership has many facets. Elected officials have an obligation to serve their constituents in several ways, including promulgating legislation that will be met with approval by a majority of those voting. Yet the constitutional framework exacts a larger price. It is in this area that Brandeis's observation that "courage is the secret of liberty" becomes clearly illuminated. To obtain elected office, a candidate must appeal to a majority of the electorate, ideally by using his or her positions on issues. Once in office, all too often these same elected officials vote in a self-interested manner in an effort to retain office. A constitutional democracy demands more of them. True leaders must risk their self-interest and elected position to fulfill their obligation under the Constitution, particularly under the First Amendment. Downs is right: "salvation by judiciary" is not always the best method of sustaining the democratic state. As he notes, lower courts often fail to properly enforce the higher courts' decisions, perhaps out of the same fear felt by elected officials. Downs notes in the case of the Minneapolis ordinance:

> The episode revealed something all too common in political life—the reluctance of elected officials to be found on the wrong side of an emotionally charged issue which partisans have framed as a matter of good versus evil. The vulnerability of civil discourse to capture by single-minded advocates raises disturbing questions about the possibility of maintaining respect for legal forms and the rule of law.

It is the single-mindedness of political pressure groups, whatever their political affiliation, that leads to zealotry and the failure of leadership. As Isaiah Berlin put it in summarizing the state of mind of the zealot, "Since I know the only true path to the ultimate solution of the problems of society, I know which way to drive the human caravan; and since you are ignorant of what I know, you cannot be allowed to have liberty of choice even within the narrowest limits, if this goal is to be reached."

While Americans have witnessed stridency on both ends of the political spectrum, as some seek to "drive the human caravan" through the means of censorship, other countries less committed to individual liberty have embraced limitations on expression. Anthony Lewis noted in the conclusion of *Make No Law* that most countries have been reluctant to protect hate speech perhaps because they "have suffered too much, firsthand, from hateful ideas that gained power on their continent." He cites Roger Errera, a French constitutional lawyer, who has suggested that Americans "have a quality that, given their experience, Europeans cannot have—'an inveterate social and historical optimism.' "

Perhaps it is true that Americans are optimists. An equally plausible argument can be made that Americans are realists and suspicious of attempts to encroach upon their right of free expression. Perhaps in the final analysis, both Americans and Europeans fear the loss of individual liberty. Americans are optimists in that they believe in continuing a tradition of dissent while maintaining faith in the ultimate legitimacy of their government. Because of their recent history, Europeans are prepared to sacrifice individual liberty now to prevent the possible failure of their governing institutions in the future.

The attitudes toward free expression in countries such as France or Germany are rooted in the recent past. Errera believes that "laws against racial incitement and libel are necessary and that they are useful." He defends such laws on the grounds that they are "needed to defend the basic civility of our society" and that hateful speech is "directed against the whole body politic and its social and moral fabric." He notes, "The history of our society in the 20th century fully legitimizes the use of legal instruments against what is, and is meant to be, an aggression." If these arguments seem familiar, it is because they are often used to justify restrictions on offensive speech in the United States. Another observer of the French system finds these standards too elastic and wonders "what legitimate speech might be subjected to suppression and whether the growth and support for extreme right-wing parties might not be due in some part to the notoriety they have received from cases against them."

When it comes to the tension between individual freedom and fascism, the eyes of the world remain on Germany. No other government in the world must be as careful in avoiding overreaction to fringe political expression while remaining alert to the danger of widespread acceptance of such deviant beliefs. Perhaps American and German society can learn little from each other when it comes to free expression. While America has maintained a stable and democratic government despite (some might say because of) challenges to majoritarian thought given breathing room by the First Amendment, Germany has never had the dissenting tradition that Americans have been blessed with. As Bollinger notes, "While anti-semitism is a problem in American society . . . it is not of such magnitude, or so pervasive, as to transform toleration into an act of implicit condonation. This society is not in this sense in a situation like that of Germany, where even today that society maintains extraordinary restrictions on Nazi symbolism, no doubt because of a fear of what would be implied by tolerance."

With the fall of the Berlin Wall, the disintegration of the Soviet Union, and the reunification of Germany, perhaps it was inevitable that the former clash of political ideologies would be replaced by racial and ethnic intolerance. The very unification of Germany and the attendant economic dislocations contributed to this rise of ethnic violence. As one expert noted, although the violent episodes constituted fringe activity, the attitudes were not as isolated. "Since the economic problems of unification have become dominant, foreigners are used even more as scapegoats. The political crusade to change liberal asylum laws, 'has fed the latent aggression against foreigners of millions of citizens.'" The continuing unrest resulted in calls for a ban on extremist groups, huge rallies against intolerance, and an asylum accord that was attacked by both the right and the left.

Germany has discovered painfully over the years that it is a question not of how many "tough" laws are available to authorities, but rather of which group is in authority. "Germany's criminal libel law, on the books since the late nineteenth century, was used to protect Germans living in Prussian provinces, large landowners, Christian clerics, German officers and Prussian troops, but not once, before 1945, did it provide protection for Jews." Seventy years ago, while Holmes and Brandeis were drafting landmark dissents, the Weimar government in Germany passed an emergency Act for the Protection of the Republic. Aryeh Neier, in *Defending My Enemy*, noted that "the Weimar government demonstrated some vigor in prosecuting offensive speech. This produced conflict between the Reich (federal) government and the government of Bavaria, where the Nazis were strongest."

> On paper, the Weimar republic was a free and democratic socie-
> ty . . . but lacking a government with the will and the strength to
> enforce the provisions of the constitution and the laws against
> politically motivated violence, Weimar did not safeguard the liber-
> ties of Germans. The constitution itself was so lightly regarded that
> the Nazis didn't bother to repeal it when they took over. They left
> it in place but ignored it.

Once "offensive speech" was banned, the door was open for the Weimar government to "occasionally prosecute those who were publicly critical of the descent into Nazism" while allowing "hundreds of Nazi political murderers" to go unpunished. "Weimar Germany . . . attempted to combat Nazism by prohibiting the wearing of uniforms and emblems indicating political affiliation. Such prohibitions on uniforms, however, proved meaningless. Nazi political murders mattered, not Nazi uniforms." Neier makes the distinction between suppressing political opinion and symbolism and punishing political violence. This is a lesson in history that we must remember. Attempting to suppress expression and political opinion is a mistake; punishing violent acts, swiftly and decisively, is a necessity.

On February 14, 1989, the late Ayatollah Khomeini condemned *The Satanic Verses,* written by Salman Rushdie, who was sentenced to death for having written a book deemed libelous by a group, in this case the Muslims. Rushdie was cited for group libel, an offense not recognized in the United States since *New York Times Co. v. Sullivan.* Group libel laws are largely symbolic in nature and exist in some countries as a form of community censorship. St. Paul City Ordinance section 292.02 was similar in nature, albeit less punitive, because it made a well-meaning but dangerous statement in behalf of the community.

Sandra Coliver, the legal officer of ARTICLE 19, an international organization organized to combat censorship, has noted, "The U.S. commitment to free speech has resulted in a reduced commitment to laws which serve a primarily symbolic or educative function, and which may improve the civility of discourse. The U.S. has made the decision, however, to place a higher value on free expression than on its symbols . . . it is clear that intolerance and discrimination are no worse [in the U.S.] than in many parts of Europe and that dissent is offered greater protection in the U.S. than anywhere else in the world."

The United States approaches the right of free expression in a manner that is unique in the world. This can be explained partly by the fact that it has, for the most part, historically rejected the "balancing" approach. While the idea of balancing the right of free expression against the "harm" caused is seductive, Smolla believes that "the use of the balancing approach tends to result in relatively low protection for speech, because when balancing is employed, speech tends to be devalued as just another social interest to be considered in the mix." Such a balancing approach is similar to the "means to an end" view of free speech. Often the expression of those who are intolerant is upsetting, disturbing, and offensive. With a balancing approach, such expression will almost always lose to the majority's view of what is appropriate, resulting in the imposition of an orthodox viewpoint.

At the end of 1991, Freedom House reported that of the world's 5.4 billion people, "25% live in free countries, 43% in partly free countries and 32% in not-free countries." Of all the countries on earth, only the United States truly protects the right of individual self-expression. If that makes us optimists, so be it. Our optimism about freedom of expression makes us the envy of the world.

As morning dawned on December 4, 1991, I thought once more of Isaiah Berlin and his observation that "to be lonely is to be among men who do not know what you mean." This was the day I would discover whether the United States Supreme Court knew what I meant.

I I

———— ■ ————

"Each Generation":
The Court Hears Argument

There is more to oral argument than meets the eye—or the ear. . . . It forces the judges who are going to decide the case and the lawyers who represent the clients whose fates will be affected by the outcome of the decision to look at one another for an hour, and talk back and forth about how the case should be decided.

—Chief Justice William H. Rehnquist

Each generation must reaffirm the guarantee of the First Amendment with the hard cases.

—Edward J. Cleary
(Opening line before the United States Supreme Court,
December 4, 1991)

Exactly one year to the day and the hour I had argued the case of *R.A.V. v. St. Paul* before the Minnesota Supreme Court, I was about to step to the podium to argue once again. This time I presented my argument to the most powerful court in the world, the United States Supreme Court.

By the fall of 1991 the Court had completed its much heralded "conservative" transformation. It had been eleven years since Ronald Reagan had become president and during that time he and George Bush had filled six of the nine positions on the Court. Reagan had appointed Justices Sandra Day O'Connor, Anthony Kennedy, and Antonin Scalia, and had shifted William Rehnquist to the position of Chief Justice, while George Bush had appointed David Souter and Clarence Thomas. The holdovers on the Court after this realignment were Justices John Paul Stevens (a Ford appointment), Harry Blackmun (a Nixon appointment), and Byron White (a Kennedy appointment and the sole remaining Democratic appointee). The makeover had been so complete, and the shifting of political alignments so pronounced, that many observers believed the Nixon appointee, Harry Blackmun, was now the most "liberal" member of the Court. Justice Stevens was also considered to be left of the new center of the Court. This description was deceptive, since Stevens's apparent political leaning was "liberal" only relative to the "conservatism" of the others, and he was particularly idiosyncratic when it came to First Amendment litigation. Justice White, although a Democratic appointee, was considered by most to be conservative in nature, and was also unpredictable when it came to First Amendment issues.

The conservative juggernaut had never materialized to the satisfaction of the right wing of the Republican party. The ultraconservatives were not pleased at the appointments of Justices Kennedy and Souter, saving their praise for the irrepressible and iconoclastic Antonin Scalia. Kennedy and Souter were viewed as compromise candidates, selected primarily for their ability to avoid the acrimonious Senate confirmation hearings that had taken place in 1987, when Robert Bork had been rejected as a nominee, a circus event that was to be repeated in 1991, when Clarence Thomas was barely confirmed as a member of the Court. The underground heroes of the right, the "once and future justices" were men like Richard Posner and Frank Easterbrook, both federal circuit judges for the Seventh Circuit. These were the "keepers of the faith," whom the conservative wing of the Republican party wanted to serve on the Court. However, presidential and congressional politics had intervened and prevented this potentially radical transformation. Justice Antonin Scalia, although widely recognized for his intellect, had become known as much for the acerbic language of his many concurring opinions and dissents as for his apparent inability or unwillingness to consistently meet the "rule of five," the garnering of five votes among the justices to achieve a majority vote.

Although Scalia did not have the ability of retired Justice William J. Brennan, Jr., to forge a consensus, conservatives were relieved that at least both Brennan and Marshall had retired. Yet the continuing criticism aimed at the Court from the right suggested that it had not pursued a clearly ideological agenda.

The approach of the Court to First Amendment litigation appeared more inconsistent than ideological. Accepting conservative precepts, including the federalist belief in giving wide latitude to state courts, the Court often moved away from a "broad" ruling if a "narrow" decision would suffice. The Warren Court had been criticized for its judicial activism and the Rehnquist Court seemed intent on reversing this trend. This retreat from judicial intervention was not only reflected in the Court's preference for narrow rulings, but was likewise evident in the shrinking number of cases accepted by the Court for review. The Court had scaled back to such an extent that the 1991 term involved the fewest cases heard in over twenty years; the result was a decline in nearly one third from the number of cases the justices had heard in the 1980s. The Court never explains its reasoning in accepting or refusing to accept cases.

A journalist observed that the "lower federal courts, now dominated by Republican appointees, are more pro-government than they were a decade ago, producing fewer rulings of the kind that this Supreme Court feels obliged to review." The number of appeals reaching the Court continued to soar, so the shrinking number of cases heard was not due to a lack of interest on the part of litigants. It seemed strange that this Court would choose to review a case that involved a pro-government ruling issued by a state's highest court concerning a juvenile charged with a minor criminal offense. The Court normally reviewed cases after there had been a division in authority, as when state supreme courts or federal courts of appeal came to different conclusions involving the same issues of law. No such division in authority existed at the time the Court agreed to hear *R.A.V.* It seemed incontrovertible that it had selected *R.A.V. v. St. Paul* in an unusual manner.

Part of the explanation may have been the Rehnquist Court's attitude toward the First Amendment. Inconsistent on issues of free expression, some justices had apparently agreed with those "conservative intellectuals" who "had adopted the right to free speech as one of their own." They were convinced that the " 'free trade of ideas,' just like the free marketplace for goods, made for a thriving democracy." Influenced by the left's effort to enact student speech codes on campus, the right had discovered what the left had known for years— that limiting the power to censor was considerably more satisfying than being targeted for censorship.

At the beginning of the 1991 term, the Court was still searching for a consistent position in cases involving freedom of expression. Although it had protected the First Amendment in the flag-burning cases, it later appeared to have undercut freedom-of-speech guarantees in several other cases. In *Barnes v. Glen Theatre, Inc.*, the Court, in a 5–4 decision, had upheld the constitutionality of an Indiana law used to prohibit nude dancing. The opinion had a limited impact, however, because Justice Souter, although voting among the five who upheld the law, wrote a concurring opinion rather than agreeing with the other four justices that "society's moral views" could justify such laws. If he had joined with the majority, Meiklejohn's "novels and dramas and paintings and poems" would have lost constitutional protection to the extent that "society's moral views" forbid their dissemination. In *Rust v. Sullivan,* decided in May 1991, ruling on the federal funding of family-planning clinics, the Court held that there were strings attached to such federal financing. Holding that doctors who accepted government financing did not have a free-speech right to discuss the alternative of abortion with patients, the Court noted that government funding was contingent on the physician not discussing abortion. "The gag rule," as it came to be known, resulted in new questions regarding the Court's position on the exercise of freedom of expression.

The Court's inconsistent approach to First Amendment issues weighed heavily on me as I crawled out of bed at 5:30 A.M. on the morning of December 4, 1991. After breakfast in the lobby of the hotel with family members and friends, I reviewed the outline of my argument one last time. After three solid days of rain and overcast skies, dawn finally produced the sun. Although the day was chilly by Washington standards, it was virtually balmy in the opinion of the many Minnesota natives who had flown in to hear the arguments. Leaving the hotel, Mike and I flagged down a cab and asked the driver to take us to the Supreme Court building. As anyone who has used the taxicabs in the Washington, D.C., area knows, every trip is an adventure. Often the drivers either speak no English or else ask the passengers for directions. Since many of the people who use the taxis speak only English and are from out of town, this presents a problem. When the driver headed north from our hotel instead of east to the Mall area, I had visions of explaining to the Chief Justice why I was late for the argument, but he finally turned the vehicle in the right direction and headed back on Rock Creek Parkway. I relaxed when the Capitol came into view.

We knew that this case was one of a handful where public demand for admission was so intense that extra seating had to be made available, yet arguing counsel were still each allowed the traditional six seats for friends and family. I had allocated one of those seats to R.A.V. himself, who had said that he might be attending the arguments. Although he later changed his mind, I held the seat open in case he appeared at the last minute. Both Tom Foley and I had many requests for seats from friends and family members, and we had devised the same solution. There was special seating for those admitted to the United States Supreme Court bar, so those already admitted to the bar would simply come early and wait in line in the lawyers' section. The reserved seating would be used for friends and family. The rest of the lawyers, who had not yet been admitted before the Court, had arranged to be admitted immediately before our argument, which presumably guaranteed admission. Others had to wait in line. Although the argument was scheduled for 10:00 A.M., many had arrived and stood in the dark and cold at 6:00 A.M.

As the cab pulled up to the north side of the building, we could see the long line in the Oval Plaza in front of the building facing the United States Capitol. We had acknowledged the possibility of protesters, particularly because of the widespread media coverage of the case. None were in sight. It was only later that night that we remembered that David Duke had announced his candidacy for the presidency several miles away at approximately the same time as the argument, perhaps attracting many of those who would have protested in front of the Supreme Court building.

As we entered the building I considered what I had learned about delivering an effective oral argument. John Siliciano, who had clerked at the Court, had reminded me that arguing counsel are essentially actors and actresses in a play. The members of the Court are the casting directors and control the flow of dialogue. By the time of the argument, most of the justices have formed at least a preliminary opinion about the respective positions of arguing counsel. In contrast to trial practice, the attorneys make their case to a panel of justices rather than to a panel of jurors. At the same time, appellate practice before the United States Supreme Court is unique if for no other reason than that the stakes are so high and the justices so well prepared. Since 1970 each attorney has been allowed a half hour to argue his or her position. Thirty minutes may seem like a short period of time to argue a case, but for arguing counsel it can often seem to last a lifetime. Even Chief Justice Rehnquist has acknowledged that he was "drenched with sweat" after the one oral argument he made before the Supreme Court as a young assistant attorney general.

Almost all first-time observers of oral arguments before the United States Supreme Court are moved by the experience. Questions are directed to counsel by the justices in a fast and furious manner. One observer I know likened the image of arguing counsel to that of a lone tree on a prairie during a tornado. Another likened the experience to that of a storm-tossed ship on the high seas. For thirty minutes the attorney is alone before nine justices with the purpose of engaging them in dialogue on the issues.

Certain words of advice that were given to me are applicable to appellate practice generally. The first commandment before the

Court is not to be evasive in answering questions. While this may seem like obvious advice, it is extremely hard for attorneys to answer a question against their interest with a yes or no. Instead attorneys often try to explain why the question does not pertain to their case or why the answer is not important. In witnessing several arguments, we had seen attorneys answer questions in a nonresponsive and evasive manner. They had paid the price. Chief Justice Rehnquist and Justice Scalia particularly have little patience with attorneys who do not concede when they must. The best approach is to answer the question directly with a yes or no, and then explain why that answer is or is not relevant to the case before the Court. Being candid about weaknesses in one's case can be effective because it leaves the impression that arguing counsel is well aware of weaknesses but feels strongly enough about the case to make open concessions.

The second commandment is to be aware that answering the question asked is more important than arguing a prepared presentation. The attorney is not before the Court to give a speech. If he rarely departs from a prepared text, the Court may well ask few questions because the justices may feel that he is incapable of discussing the issues. As Chief Justice Rehnquist has noted, the Court is looking for counsel to depart from the text at will, to answer questions concisely, to cover main points—though not every point—and to present the argument in a manner that is responsive to the justices' concerns while indicating a depth of knowledge in that particular area of the law before the Court.

Many familiar with the Court have observed that justices ask questions primarily to tell fellow justices where their concerns lie. To that extent, the answer of the attorney is less important than his ability to perceive areas of judicial concern. In many arguments, only a few justices will ask questions. Justice Scalia is well known for aggressively interrogating counsel. Attorneys who are experienced in trial work often are inexperienced in appellate work, particularly in these days of legal specialization. Any attorney who appears before Justice Scalia would do well to master the art of cross-examination, since he will most likely find himself the object of such questioning. Having cross-examined a number of witnesses in both civil and criminal trials, I was about to learn what it was like for a witness to attempt to stay two steps ahead of the interrogator.

Some observers have pointed out that there are specific methods and strategies for arguing before the Rehnquist Court. Attorneys are admonished not to argue legislative intent, but to keep to the actual language of the legal provision at issue in the case. Several members of the Court, particularly the Chief Justice and Justice O'Connor, embrace the federalist belief that states are autonomous units of government whose authority should be acknowledged and seldom questioned. While I was more than content to argue the language of the flawed ordinance, I was in the unenviable position of asking a group of justices who strongly believed in state authority to overturn a state court decision.

While preparing for the argument we had learned of an article severely criticizing two Minnesota lawyers who had argued a high-profile case before the Court eight months earlier. Lyle Denniston had written an article for the *American Lawyer* taking issue with the oral presentations of the attorneys involved in the case of *Cohen v. Cowles Media Company*. *Cohen* was also a First Amendment case, and since *R.A.V.* had a higher national profile, both Foley and I knew that we would be critiqued by reporters who had heard numerous oral arguments and had recently found fault with two experienced Minnesota attorneys.

It was my own observation from other arguments that the Court would control how others would later perceive the oral argument and performance. If the members of the Court truly wished to humiliate a lawyer, there was little that that lawyer could do except maintain his dignity and defend his position in the face of obvious hostility. Most observers believed we would not prevail in this case. It remained to be seen how the members of the Court would approach arguing counsel.

As we entered the Supreme Court building and walked through the metal detector, among the first spectators I saw were Russell and Laura Jones, the couple on whose lawn the cross was burned. My sister had flown in on the same plane with the Joneses, so I had known they would be present at the argument. I wanted to walk over and introduce myself and tell them that I hoped they understood our position. Reporters who had interviewed the Joneses had told me that though they understood that we did not condone racial hatred, they found it difficult to understand why we had fought so hard. I wanted to tell them that the guarantee of freedom of expression was essential to the protection of the powerless. I wanted to say that what they had gone through was needless because there were other laws that could have punished the alleged conduct in a tough but constitutional manner, but mostly I wanted to tell them that I was sorry that it had happened and sorry that the appeal was necessary. I was not surprised, however, that they merely glanced at me and turned toward other members of the crowd. I wanted them to understand me and not to hate me. Perhaps we had that in common.

We saw some friends and family down the hall who greeted us with a wave. Tom Foley stood with his father, and I envied him. Judge Foley turned and, greeting me, told me that he had known my father. He reminded me that his son and I were getting an opportunity that very few lawyers had in their lifetime and mentioned that he had recently retired without ever having had the opportunity to argue before the Court. Then a television reporter for WCCO, the CBS affiliate in Minneapolis–St. Paul, approached me. The commencement of the oral argument was less than twenty minutes away. He introduced himself and asked me whether or not I had any thoughts about my father. Since he was unaccompanied by a cameraman, I believed that he was sincere and did not mean this as an invasion of privacy minutes before the argument. I smiled and told him that I did in fact have thoughts about my father, that I was sorry that he was not present, but that I was Irish enough to believe that maybe he was there after all.

I left my briefcase with Mike, excused myself and went down the hallway to the men's room. I splashed some water on my face, straightened my tie, and stared in the mirror as I thought of my father. Walking back down the hallway, I saw that the lawyers were being led through the back hallway to the office. I grabbed my briefcase and Mike and I went into the clerk's office along with Tom Foley and others. Mr. Suter, the clerk of court, gave us some last-minute advice. I couldn't help thinking that he sounded much like a trainer counseling a prizefighter; he told us to keep our chin up, answer the questions, and avoid being evasive with our answers. He reminded us that several attorneys had failed to heed this advice earlier in the week and had suffered the wrath of the Chief Justice as a result. Both Foley and I had seen the argument to which he referred, and nodded.

We were issued identification cards and started up the back stairway to the Court entrance. I glanced down the hallway and saw that there were folding chairs packed into an area normally not used by spectators. Separated from the Court chamber by curtains, those sitting there would be able to hear the arguments but would not be able to see the participants.

I am sure that all of the attorneys who have argued before the Court have felt the excitement of appearing before the most powerful judicial body in the world. We were no exception. The mood in the room was electric. Since this was the day chosen for taking the official portrait of the Rehnquist Court for the 1991–92 term, many of the wives and some of the children of the justices were present to observe the argument. My sister sat next to Clarence Thomas's wife, who with her husband had been through a great deal of emotional trauma in the last several months. Thomas had come of age in the Deep South during particularly intolerant times, and since he was married to a white woman, I could only assume that they had both been subjected to racial slurs. This case was bound to affect them.

As Mike and I sat down, there were approximately ten minutes remaining before the argument was scheduled to commence. The area where the attorneys argue is surrounded by the lawyers section. I turned and saw the young lawyers who had flown in from the Twin Cities to watch the argument and who would be sworn in minutes before it began. I also saw a young woman who I knew would be arguing a case for the first time before the Court the following week. Although we had never been introduced, I went over to shake her hand and wish her well, feeling an immediate bond with anyone who would experience what I was about to undergo.

Minutes before the members of the Court were scheduled to enter, Tom and I became involved in a heated discussion with the individual in charge of seating. We had been led to believe that the lawyers sworn in that morning would be able to stay there and watch the argument. On this assumption, a number of local attorneys had flown in at their own expense to support both of us. Now the marshal was asking those attorneys to leave before the argument began because of the demand for seating. Neither Tom nor I wanted to see this happen, and we were able to resolve the matter minutes before the justices entered from behind the heavy drapes that separated the private chambers of the justices from the Court chamber.

As I heard the gavel pound, I scribbled *carpe diem* on the scratch pad provided next to the white quill pen given to arguing counsel since the earliest sessions of the Supreme Court. Mike did the same. "Seizing the day," or at least the hour, was our only objective after the six long months of intense preparation that had brought us to this moment.

The Honorable, the Chief Justice and the Associates Justices of the Supreme Court of the United States, Oyez! Oyez! Oyez! All persons having business before the Honorable, the Supreme Court of the United States, are admonished to draw near and give their attention, for the Court is now sitting. God save the United States and this Honorable Court!

As we all sat down I noticed that from the moment she entered the Court chamber Justice Sandra Day O'Connor appeared troubled, as though there was something about our position that puzzled or worried her. As the Chief Justice conducted the proceedings for admission to the Supreme Court bar, whenever I looked at Justice O'Connor I found that she was staring at me. After the decision, I suspected the reason why she had appeared to be so intensely concerned about this argument.

After the Chief Justice announced the case and my name, I stepped to the podium. In the usual case, counsel begins with a statement of the facts. After the practice oral argument at Georgetown, we had become convinced that the general factual outline of this case—a cross was burned in the front yard of a black family in St. Paul—was already well known and that further facts were irrelevant. The Court interrupted attorneys with questions almost immediately, so I was determined to use my initial time to dwell on the larger issue before the Court rather than on the smaller:

> Each generation must reaffirm the guarantee of the First Amendment with the hard cases. The Framers understood the dangers of orthodoxy and standardized thought and chose liberty.
>
> We are once again faced with a case that will demonstrate whether or not there is room for the freedom for the thought that we hate, whether there is room for the eternal vigilance necessary to protect the opinions that we loathe.

The first line was my own. The second was a paraphrase of a passage in a dissent written by Justice Douglas in *Beauharnais v. Illinois*. It amused me to quote one of the most liberal justices of the twentieth century to a conservative court; it was further evidence that the principles of free thought and expression were timeless and apolitical. The next paragraph was an attempt to align *R.A.V.* with the very foundation of modern First Amendment doctrine, the dissents of Justice Oliver Wendell Holmes in *United States v. Schwimmer* and *Abrams v. United States*. My Jewish friends would describe what I was doing as *chutzpah*. Here I was, a young, unknown, Midwestern attorney quoting Holmes in a broad First Amendment dissertation to the United States Supreme Court. I felt like a football player who takes the field but has not yet been hit.

I acknowledged that the conduct alleged was "reprehensible" and "abhorrent." This observation was clearly gratuitous, since the alleged conduct was not relevant to my challenge, nor was my personal opinion concerning it. Bollinger has noted that the various judges who were involved in the Skokie case indicated their personal repugnance for the defendants. He attributed this to the need of the judges to reaffirm "the general norm"—that is, to identify with society rather than with the fringe group involved. He said that by publicly expressing their views, the judges' opinions acted as a type of "official censure and thus a kind of coercion and punishment, as well as the threat of other punishments." Perhaps it was gratuitous, but it was important to me to let the world know that my defense of the First Amendment did not involve sympathy for the hateful expression alleged. The issue of disavowing the underlying aims of those who conducted themselves in such a manner would arise once again upon the issuance of the opinion written by Justice Scalia.

After I had changed the focus to the Minnesota Supreme Court's interpretation, Justice O'Connor prepared to challenge me. Sixty-one years old, she had recently celebrated her tenth anniversary on the Court. She had been nominated by President Reagan, and in those pre-Bork and pre-Thomas days she had been affirmed by a vote of 99 to 0. She had raised a family and practiced law, but had only been a county judge for four years and an appellate judge for two years before taking her place on the Court to fill the position of retiring Justice Potter Stewart in 1981. Although she had been diagnosed with breast cancer three years earlier, she continued to work long hours and appeared to be well prepared for the oral arguments. In the recently completed 1990–91 term, she had written more majority opinions than any other justice. To many Court observers, she still did not appear to be physically well. Nevertheless, she had a deserved reputation for challenging both arguing attorneys with probing and pertinent questions.

Ostensibly conservative in nature, O'Connor's demeanor differed noticeably from the professorial style of Justice Antonin Scalia, and she often voted against his position. The fact that the ordinance listed "gender" among the groups selected for special protection was of some concern to me. Although I believed that such labeling would not be pivotal for Justice O'Connor, I felt that as the only female member of the court she would be especially aware that these laws addressed not only racial expression but offensive expression on a number of other highly volatile subjects, including gender.

By this time the Court had allowed me to proceed uninterrupted far longer than I would have predicted. By giving me this opportunity to speak about the First Amendment in such broad terms, it appeared the members of the Court were sympathetic to our position. Time would tell.

Justice O'Connor abruptly ended my dissertation and confronted me with a tough, though not unexpected, opening inquiry. The Court had jurisdiction to review the decision of the Minnesota Supreme Court. Rather than the actual language of the ordinance, the wording of that decision was of primary significance to the Court in reviewing its constitutionality. We had taken the calculated risk that a review of the ordinance as written, rather than as interpreted, was necessary to an understanding of the inability of *any* court to save it. The Minnesota Supreme Court may have held that this apple was actually an orange, but it was our position that it was still an apple—and a rotten one at that. We spent the first section of our brief discussing the ordinance as originally written and as it had been interpreted by the Minnesota Supreme Court. We knew this would subject us to criticism, but we believed the wording of the ordinance was significant even after the decision. This interpretation generally offends conservatives, who believe strongly in the right of a state to interpret its own laws. Justice O'Connor is a strong believer in this federalist system, so it was not surprising that we would draw questions in this area, and that they would come from Justice O'Connor.

Chiding us for changing the focus from the Minnesota Supreme Court decision to the ordinance as written, O'Connor elicited an agreement from me that the Court would need to examine the Minnesota decision. Since that court had narrowed the ordinance to the language from *Brandenburg* and *Chaplinsky,* Justice O'Connor took the position that in effect we were asking this Court to overturn opinions reaching back half a century.

Although the Supreme Court takes cases of only national significance, it will usually decide cases on the most narrow basis available rather than engaging in sweeping decisions. It is dangerous to ask the Court to overrule earlier decisions unless it is necessary to do so to achieve the result that the petitioner is seeking. We had made the decision that I would not ask the Court to overrule either of those cases, since such a request might make it harder for the petitioner to prevail. If the Court truly wanted to overturn those holdings, they would do so.

In response to Justice O'Connor's question, I argued that the Minnesota Supreme Court had misinterpreted the holdings in those previous decisions. The *Brandenburg* decision had been aimed at the speaker who attempts to manipulate a crowd by inciting them to imminent lawless action. It was a situation where the agitator attempted to cause a sympathetic audience to break the law. Fifty years of First Amendment case law had led to the *Brandenburg* decision, and it had finally drawn the constitutional line between simply advocating violence and inciting an audience in a manner likely to cause unlawful activity. Such a standard was the opposite of that imposed on a speaker talking to a hostile audience, where a heckler is allowed to silence the expression of the speaker if he objects to the speaker's opinion. Incorporating the *Brandenburg* holding into this ordinance did little to narrow the language of the law because it was aimed at silencing people who expressed themselves in an offensive manner before a hostile audience, not those who attempted to incite others to join them in unlawful activity before a sympathetic audience.

As I finished my answer to Justice O'Connor's last question, Justice Kennedy interrupted to question me about my reading of *Chaplinsky* and the "fighting words" doctrine. A California native, Justice Kennedy was fifty-five years old at the time. Sixteen years earlier, President Gerald Ford had appointed him to the U.S. Ninth Circuit Court of Appeals, making Kennedy at thirty-nine the youngest federal appeals-court judge in the country. Thirteen years later he had been appointed to the United States Supreme Court in the wake of earlier nomination fiascoes. He had been in the right place at the right time and had the right credentials to be elevated to the Court. His conservative background made him acceptable to the Reagan administration, and the lack of a tainted personal history and the absence of a "paper trail" of controversial opinions led to his nomination to the Court in February 1988. During the 1990–91 term Kennedy had voted with Rehnquist and O'Connor 84 percent of the time. Although the conservative wing of the Republican party would have preferred Robert Bork, it appeared that Justice Kennedy was almost as conservative as the earlier failed nominee.

Later it became clear that Justice Kennedy and Robert Bork disagreed on the meaning of the First Amendment. With his powerful concurring opinion in the *Texas v. Johnson* decision in 1989 Kennedy gave notice that, together with Justice Scalia, he was reluctant to allow his personal ideology to influence his responsibility to interpret and protect First Amendment freedoms. Since the *Johnson* decision in June 1989, and leading up to the oral argument in *R.A.V.* in December 1991, on a number of occasions Kennedy had reiterated his commitment to freedom of expression. He was to disappoint conservatives further by the end of the 1991 term in July of 1992, when he joined Justice O'Connor and Justice Souter in moving from right to center in a series of decisions culminating in the partial reaffirmation of *Roe v. Wade*.

Although Justice Kennedy and Robert Bork disagree on a number of issues, their differences on the scope of First Amendment freedoms are pronounced. Those in the Senate who had voted against Bork and in favor of Kennedy were rewarded by the latter's protective stance on freedom of expression. Bork would almost certainly have voted in favor of the state in *R.A.V.* and upheld St. Paul City Ordinance section 292.02. If he had been confirmed instead of Kennedy, he would probably have taken the same side as People for the American Way, one of the *amici* organizations that had worked the hardest to prevent his nomination. The Bork/People for the American Way alliance on this issue demonstrated dramatically how positions on First Amendment freedoms cross political boundaries.

As Justice Kennedy questioned me, his focus was similar to that of Judge Arnold of the Eighth Circuit, who had dissented in a 2–1 decision in *U.S. v. Lee* before the opinion was vacated. For Kennedy and Arnold, the key issue was whether the government could punish threatening speech if the threat was not immediate. The burning of a cross in someone's front yard is targeted and threatening behavior. The burning of a cross farther away from the apparent target is more problematical, as it was in *U.S. v. Lee*. In both instances the threat is not necessarily immediate but could be a precursor to violence at a later time. Judge Arnold felt that it was not enough to threaten or intimidate someone unless it involved the imminent use of force, and Justice Kennedy inquired about this issue. I answered that I felt that there were "viewpoint-neutral" laws that punished people who threatened or intimidated without directly punishing their opinions. Justice Kennedy seemed concerned about the immediacy of the threat; the Jones family could reasonably have believed that it was immediate, even if no one was seen in the area.

As we discussed this sub-issue, the Chief Justice changed the focus to the ordinance itself, inquiring into the language that would eventually form the core of the majority opinion. We had expected this line of inquiry and planned for it. I had intended to follow my initial remarks with this portion of the argument (tying the case to earlier First Amendment landmark decisions), but I had been diverted by the questions of Justices O'Connor and Kennedy. The Chief Justice returned the focus of the Court to an examination of the constitutionality of punishing subcategories of unprotected expression.

> *Chief Justice Rehnquist:* Mr. Cleary, isn't one of your complaints that the Minnesota statute as construed by the supreme court of Minnesota punishes only some fighting words and not others?

> *Mr. Cleary:* It is, Your Honor. That is one of my positions, that in doing so, even though it is a subcategory, technically, of unprotected conduct, [the government] still is picking out an

opinion, a disfavored message, and making that clear through the state. It's a paternalistic idea, and the problem that we have is that the government must not betray neutrality, and I believe it does, even when it picks out a subcategory.

With the First Amendment, it does not necessarily follow that if you punish the greater you can punish the lesser. If we had a law that banned the posting of signs, for instance, somewhat akin to *Vincent,* and if we had in there "including but not limited to signs regarding the Democratic Party symbols," now that might be a mere example, and it might be a subcategory, but I believe this Court would be offended by that.

I believe the Court would feel that that was betraying sympathy or hostility to a political viewpoint, and I believe the same principle is in course here, because I think the problem we have here is that we have—regardless of whether those symbols are mere examples—we have the possibility, the real possibility, that we have a government signaling its disagreement with a particular type of opinion.

Although I could have been more articulate, this was the answer the majority had been seeking, particularly Chief Justice Rehnquist and Justice Scalia. While other members of the Court were focusing on the language of the lower-court decision, these justices were interested in the original terms of the ordinance as written, particularly references to certain disfavored subjects of "race, color, creed, religion, or gender." This ban on controversial expression about particular subjects mirrored the student speech codes and reflected the general trend toward "political correctness." It is one thing for government to inform its citizens, "You must not cause an immediate breach of the peace"; it is another for government to warn the public that it must not cause an immediate breach of the peace by expressing disturbing opinions on certain subjects.

The favorable attitude of Chief Justice Rehnquist was surprising to both sides. As one Court observer has noted, "Rarely did Rehnquist vote for anyone asserting a constitutional right." Seen by many as doctrinaire, Rehnquist, confirmed in 1986 as Chief Justice, had achieved this position following a tally that had included the most Senate votes ever cast against a Chief Justice. A conservative, Rehnquist, like O'Connor, was a strong believer in federalism and the right of individual states to interpret their own laws. Generally he voted for the prosecution in criminal cases, taking the disconcerting position that the means justified the ends in law enforcement. The prohibition on illegal searches and seizures under the Fourth Amendment had eroded dramatically under Chief Justice Rehnquist's tenure. The Chief Justice had demonstrated a strong aversion to unpopular symbolic expression, including flag-burning, and had filed a vitriolic dissent from the majority opinion in *Texas v. Johnson.*

Although he showed equal hostility to freedom of the press, Rehnquist had written the unanimous opinion of the Court in *Hustler Magazine, Inc. v. Falwell,* upholding the right of a magazine publisher to publish an outrageous and offensive parody. The Court's rejection of an ''outrageousness'' standard for prohibited expression was encouraging, but Falwell involved a civil case and did not involve any law-and-order issues. Most First Amendment cases arriving at the Court challenged the criminal enforcement of a state or local law, and the result was usually unfortunate for the defendant. ''In most constitutional cases, an individual comes to the Court challenging the government, and in those cases, Rehnquist can be counted as a near-certain vote for the government.'' On a more personal note, the Chief Justice had suffered the death of his wife only six weeks earlier. The obvious pain caused by such a loss, combined with his chronic back problem, which forces him to get up and stretch his back during arguments, led me to wonder what kind of disposition he would have on the day of the argument.

Observing other arguments, Mike and I had both witnessed how tough both the Chief Justice and Justice Scalia could be with arguing attorneys. As I approached the podium to begin my argument, I had fully expected the Chief Justice to attack our position in a probing and potentially humiliating manner. He did not, and his tone and demeanor at this stage of the argument indicated that he was responding favorably to our position.

As the questions continued, Justice Scalia inquired pointedly, expressing his disapproval of the language of the ordinance and seeking from me an even stronger condemnation of the law. The government and the *amici* organizations had suggested that the language of ''burning cross or Nazi swastika'' provided mere examples of outlawed expression rather than evidence of viewpoint discrimination. Finding this distinction disingenuous, I asserted that even if such symbols were ''mere examples,'' the government was still ''signaling its disagreement with the particular type of opinion.'' Justice Scalia wanted me to disavow these ''mere examples'' and restated what I had argued: that only certain subjects involving fighting words were prohibited. Diplomatically suggesting that my earlier answer was consistent in spirit, if not in tone, I replied:

I'm simply suggesting the worst-case scenario, that if the Court were to believe that they were mere examples, that there are still problems with the narrow construction in that it does not address speech that would not be—that it would either be tolerant or intolerant in other areas, and in that sense it's betraying a viewpoint from the government that is no longer neutral. They're picking out certain categories in that sense.

Justice Scalia was seen by many observers to be an interesting study in contrasts. A former law professor, on and off the bench he was not a mild-mannered ivory-tower scholar. Sociable and gregarious by nature, he nevertheless appeared to enjoy striking terror into the hearts of arguing counsel and creating resentment among other justices. Despite the fact that he was cooperative, outgoing, and popular with the media, he believed in a restrictive interpretation of the freedom-of-the-press clause. He seemed to enjoy his reputation as the dominant intellect on the Court, and continued to be the hero of the conservatives. While Justices Kennedy and O'Connor, and later Justice Souter, might stray in the eyes of conservatives, Justice Scalia was considered a reliable voice for those on the right.

Scalia had been raised in an Italian Catholic family and had attended an all-male military high school run by the Jesuits. I had been raised in an Irish Catholic family and had attended an all-male military high school administered by the Christian Brothers. A superficial comparison, yet interesting when one considered that Scalia had come of age during the McCarthy years, and I during the Vietnam war. Even at an early age, Scalia was conservative, while I was not. Although I had great respect for his intelligence, I disagreed with a number of his opinions, and particularly took issue with his interpretation of freedom of religion. Justice Scalia's restrictive views of the establishment and free-exercise clauses failed to recognize the critical importance of a clearer division between church and state. Retired Justice William J. Brennan, Jr., also Catholic, viewed the separation between church and state very differently from Justice Scalia.

Although he was generally considered a model for conservatives, Scalia had been disappointing in several ways. It has been widely observed that due to his iconoclastic nature he was not a consensus maker. He preferred to write concurring opinions and stinging dissents rather than form a majority to establish a precedent. It was as if the justice had an uncontrollable desire to set himself apart from the other members of the Court, whether attacking counsel at oral argument or writing a strongly worded dissent. Often compared with

retired Justice Brennan in terms of intellectual ability and in light of
opinions supported by consistent ideological beliefs, after five years
on the Court he had also set himself apart from Justice Brennan.
Brennan often remained silent at the bench during oral arguments;
Justice Scalia reveled in his attention-getting cross-examination of
attorneys. Justice Brennan had used his personal charm behind the
scenes to overcome ideological differences and to reach agreement;
Justice Scalia seemed to prefer to emphasize differences publicly, even
if they were among fellow conservatives.

I Justice Scalia did disappoint the conservatives by voting with the
majority in the flag-burning cases. Uncharacteristically, he had quietly joined Justice Brennan's two majority opinions in both *Texas v.
Johnson* and *U.S. v. Eichman*. His vote once again demonstrated that
interpretations of the freedom-of-expression clause cut across ideological lines. His willingness to protect expression that he must have
found offensive and idiotic had encouraged us when we were preparing our case.

I finished by explaining to Justice Scalia that we were in agreement
that the ordinance discriminated among viewpoints rather than citing
"mere examples" of prohibited expression. Justice David Souter then
shifted the inquiry back to a detailed examination of *Chaplinsky v.
New Hampshire*.

The original "fighting words" case continued to vex legal scholars,
who remained concerned about its ramifications. Presiding over a
calendar while the nation was at war, the Stone Court had chosen to
carve out an exception to the First Amendment freedom of expression
using this New Hampshire case. The new expression created a Pan-
dora's box for freedom of speech because it held that words that led
to a reflexive and violent response from a target could be punished.
Such an exception, interpreted broadly, could silence any expression
deemed offensive by those who heard it. Chaplinsky had called a
police officer a "damned Fascist," a particularly offensive label while
American servicemen were giving their lives to prevent the spread of
Fascism. To that extent the decision was political; it was a recognition by the court that law-enforcement officers need tolerate only so
much abuse before making an arrest.

The decision had bedeviled the Court over succeeding generations.
Chaplinsky's statement, although obviously offensive, was political
rather than obscene or threatening, and even a restrictive First
Amendment analysis would protect political speech. This law-enforcement tool had been abused by law-enforcement officers. In a
series of decisions in the early 1970s, the Court had failed to sustain

"fighting words" convictions because they often involved minority defendants or witnesses and white police officers. The potential for abuse of such a doctrine, particularly by those in power, was recognized by the Court; police officers should be held to a higher standard when confronted with abusive language by an unarmed defendant. The *Chaplinsky* Court had upheld the conviction of the defendant based on the likelihood of an immediate breach of the peace. The standard was flexible, but less so than the dictum in *Chaplinsky* implying that words which inflicted emotional harm might also be punished. As courts were to recognize, speech is most powerful when it is unsettling and disturbing to others. It is an integral part of the dissenting tradition in America. If a person could have someone arrested because he felt harmed by the other's expression, there would be no more demonstrations on such controversial topics as civil rights, war, or abortion. When the Minnesota Supreme Court held that the St. Paul ordinance applied only to "fighting words," it did little to narrow the problem of prosecuting individuals who expressed themselves on the subjects of race, color, religion, or gender in a manner that others found harmful. It seemed unlikely that this "law and order" Court would abolish such a common law-enforcement tool as "fighting words."

This area now became the focus of Justice Souter's questioning. Perhaps it was a coincidence that Justice Souter was particularly interested in a case decided half a century earlier by the supreme court in New Hampshire, the state of his residence. Although he had been on the Court for over one year, he remained an enigma. He had been appointed to fill the shoes of William J. Brennan, Jr. By all accounts a decent man, he epitomized the cloistered life of a backwoods bachelor. He had risen quickly through the Attorney General's Office of New Hampshire, and had appeared on, but not argued, a case before the United States Supreme Court. The case, *Wooley v. Maynard* was interesting for several reasons. For years, New Hampshire state license plates have read "Live Free or Die," a patriotic sentiment from colonial times. One motorist taped over the motto and claimed that the state could no more force him to drive a car with that motto than it could make him recite the Pledge of Allegiance, a practice held unconstitutional years earlier. Souter had pursued the case for the state, which had argued that in requiring the license plates to remain uncovered, the state did not compel the motorist to affirm the slogan, and that this requirement was not as coercive as forcing someone to recite the Pledge of Allegiance. New Hampshire lost the case, and it appeared that Souter might have a restrictive viewpoint toward freedom of expression. After having served on the New Hampshire Supreme Court for seven years, and briefly on the U.S. Court of Appeals for the First Circuit, he had been appointed to the United States Supreme Court during the post-Bork and pre-Thomas days of 1990. In his first term he had voted with Justice Sandra Day O'Connor on 90 percent of the cases decided by the Court. Like Justice Scalia, he seldom agreed with Justice Stevens.

In November and December of 1991, Mike and I had watched five oral arguments before the Court. Our strongest impression had been of the incisive and deliberate line of inquiry conducted by Justice Souter. He questioned attorneys effectively and expeditiously in an evenhanded manner and made his point without humiliating counsel or belaboring the obvious. I felt that his skill as a jurist had been underestimated in the media.

I had just finished parrying the questions of Justice Scalia and was slow to recognize that Justice Souter simply wanted me to embellish the position stated in our brief that the punishment of "words that inflict injury" was too elastic a standard to be constitutionally permissible. Justice Souter brought the matter into focus:

> *Justice Souter:* Well, I agree, but aren't you really coming to the point of saying the *Chaplinsky* reference to words that injure was in fact, at least by today's standards, an erroneous reference and we should disavow *Chaplinsky* to that extent?
>
> *Mr. Cleary:* I am.
>
> *Justice Souter:* Okay.

After Justice Souter's questioning and some general pronouncements ("The debate in this case is not about the wisdom of eradicating intolerance; the debate is about the method of reaching that goal"), I was interrupted by Justice Harry A. Blackmun. Eighty-three years old at the time of the argument, he had grown up in a working-class neighborhood on the east side of St. Paul, only blocks from the home of the Jones family. The east side had changed a great deal since the days of Harry Blackmun's youth, but it was slow to integrate and had remained a white working-class neighborhood for many years.

Like Anthony Kennedy eighteen years later, Harry Blackmun had been appointed by a Republican president only after the chief executive's first two nominees had failed. Over the years, he had disappointed the right wing of the Republican party; he was not the consistent conservative they had longed for. His legacy as a Supreme Court justice would always be evoked by his majority opinion in the famous abortion decision of *Roe v. Wade*. Justice Blackmun understood dissent and protest because for many years he had been picketed at public appearances. His record on First Amendment litigation had been favorable. Now he asked me directly whether I felt that *Chaplinsky* had been incorrectly decided. Evasively I replied that *Chaplinsky* need not be overruled to find for the petitioner. I believed that the "words that inflict injury" language had led to a great deal of confusion. After a dialogue with Justice Kennedy about the parameters of "fighting words," I told Justice O'Connor that the law was "underinclusive" in that it applied to certain subjects but not to others. Then I discussed the national ramifications of the Court's decision:

> I believe that this is the hour of danger for the First Amendment in that there are many groups that would like to encroach upon its principles with well-meaning intentions, but in doing so, they are still punishing the content of the communication and they are doing so in a discriminatory manner, and the government is betraying a neutral principle in the sense that they are allowing that to happen and they are partaking in that.

Justice Scalia, who had noted the underinclusiveness of the ordinance, decided to cross-examine me about "fighting words per se." By categorizing some expression in this manner, clear limits would be set; particularly offensive speech would be outlawed without reference to the audience. A nonviolent individual, such as a Quaker (Scalia's example), would not be subjected to abuse for failure to react violently, while a person with a quick temper could not silence an individual simply because he was more easily provoked. A "reasonable man" standard could effectively undermine freedom of expression because such a standard would reflect majoritarian values. Since the First Amendment is meant to protect individual expression against orthodox opinion, "fighting words per se" would do little to ease the potential for community censorship.

Chief Justice Rehnquist, perhaps still smarting from the Court's opinion in *Texas v. Johnson,* the flag-burning decision, reminded Justice Scalia, by his comment to me, that the majority in that case (including Justice Scalia) had already decided that issue by holding that there could not be a "fighting symbol per se." It continued to appear that the Chief Justice was sympathetic to our position.

Aware that the Court had been divided in the flag-burning cases, and that Justices Marshall and Brennan from the majority were retired and replaced by two conservative appointments, I felt that those decisions should both be discussed and distinguished at oral argument. The flag-burning decisions recognized that unpopular symbolic expression was protected under the First Amendment. It was also important to distinguish the cases sufficiently to satisfy the dissenting justices. Reading the strongly worded dissents in *Texas v. Johnson,* particularly those of Chief Justice Rehnquist and Justice Stevens, I noted how often both justices described the American flag as "unique." The use of this adjective signaled that the dissenting justices were so angered by the burning of the flag that they sought a special exemption from First Amendment guarantees. If so, it followed that they did not seek a wholesale rejection of other unpopular symbolic expression. I decided to pursue this interpretation and to use the opportunity to link *R.A.V.* to earlier First Amendment cases involving unpopular expression:

> This Court put a great emphasis on the unique nature of the American flag and in doing so, I believe acknowledged the *Stromberg* red flag of the thirties, and the black armband in the sixties, in *Tinker,* and was mindful of the fact that once that door is opened, it could lead to a ban on symbolic behavior in such a fashion that a great deal of expression would be prohibited.

After a few questions from Justice Kennedy, I reserved my last five minutes for rebuttal and sat down. Only Justices White and Thomas had failed to question me. The courtroom remained completely still. There had been no coughing, no rustling of paper. Now it was my opponent's turn.

12

■

"The Rankest Kind of
Subject-Matter
Discrimination":
The Argument Continues

Oral argument . . . is the only time before conference discussion
of the case later in the week when all of the judges are expected to
sit on the bench and concentrate on one particular case. The judges'
questions, although nominally directed to the attorney arguing the
case, may in fact be for the benefit of their colleagues.

—Chief Justice William H. Rehnquist

As I sat down Tom Foley stepped to the podium. Before Foley
could even utter "May it please the Court," Justice Blackmun asked
him why a county attorney was defending the city of St. Paul. Foley
explained that the county had jurisdiction over juveniles. As mentioned earlier, when Mike and I met with a former clerk of Justice
Scalia's, he had warned us that Justice Blackmun often inquired
about the geographical location of a case that originated in St. Paul.
Heeding his advice, I had familiarized myself with the location of the
cross-burning incident. Justice Blackmun had not questioned me
about it, but now he asked my opponent, who had no idea of the
precise location of the incident. After establishing his familiarity with
the area, Justice Blackmun chided Foley for allowing the grass to
grow so high in Mounds Park, finishing with "Have your maintenance man cut the grass." As the audience laughed nervously, Justice
Scalia ended the exchange in a pointed manner, saying, "Mr. Foley,
if you are going to make all these concessions, you might as well sit
down now." Delivered in a humorous context, Justice Scalia's comment would assume new meaning in the majority opinion.

Foley began his argument with a statement that he would often use at our public appearances. Effective in summarizing public opinion regarding the case, it was misleading and inaccurate in terms of the First Amendment. "The First Amendment was never intended to protect an individual who burns a cross in the middle of the night in the fenced yard of an African-American family's home." Charged under a law that addressed the illegal conduct of terrorizing someone, a defendant in this case would not have found protection under the First Amendment. Charged with a law that unconstitutionally prohibited a great deal of other expression and was selective, an individual was protected by the First Amendment. It wasn't freedom of expression that had originally protected R.A.V.; it was the county that had protected him by resorting to an unconstitutional law, allowing him to invoke the First Amendment.

Foley told the Court that he would "touch on four propositions," and then outlined his oral argument. My immediate reaction was that he had not been well served by the moot-court panels that had critiqued his argument. The justices, not the arguing attorneys, steer the boat. Suggesting a framework for arguing, Foley was inviting a frontal assault by the justices, who were not interested in hearing what arguing counsel wanted to discuss but instead wanted answers to the issues they considered relevant. Justice O'Connor ignored the outline of the proposed argument Foley had just recited and drew his attention to what had become the main issue before the Court: the underinclusiveness of a law that punished only fighting words that aroused anger, alarm, or resentment on the basis of race, color, creed, religion, or gender. Foley denied that the ordinance was underinclusive and reiterated the right of the city to punish such illegal conduct. He found himself in further trouble when he denied that the ordinance was "content-based." The content of the communication (offensive words based on race, etc.) was the basis for its proscription. Upsetting words on other subjects were not prohibited by this law. Arguing that the ordinance was content-neutral was indefensible and inexplicable. Faced with Justice O'Connor's incredulous tone, Foley recovered to argue that even if the ordinance was "content-based," it was supported by a compelling state interest, specifically public safety.

To illustrate the problems in allowing a government to ban a subcategory of expression, I had used the example of a constitutional law banning signs for aesthetic reasons that unconstitutionally specified "including but not limited to signs of the Democratic party." Now Justice Scalia used his own example. Noting that one can ban all obscene pictures, he suggested to Foley that an ordinance banning only obscene photographs that advertised the Republican party would be "bad." The crowd laughed, but Foley responded with a serious answer, arguing that "bias-motivated" harm was more serious in its impact than other harm. Scalia rejected the response, labeling Foley's response "a political judgment" and observing that the ordinance involved subject-matter discrimination. Foley stated that the city of St. Paul would "add additional harms to be regulated as it finds them," and I shuddered. Although he referred to them as "harms," what he was really referring to was "subjects." Every political-interest group that lobbied local officials could get a new "subject" added to the list on the basis that their group would be harmed by offensive expression on that topic. Struck down by the federal court, the University of Michigan speech code had prohibited offensive expression on the basis of "race, ethnicity, religion, sex, sexual orientation, creed, national origin, ancestry, age, marital status, handicap or Viet Nam-era veteran status." I will never believe that this is what the Framers intended when they created the right of freedom of expression to protect the dissenting tradition against the weight of orthodoxy.

Justice Souter refined the area further by eliciting an agreement from Foley that he believed that government could prohibit offensive expression based on the subject addressed. Justice Scalia's example of punishing only those obscene photos that depicted members of the Republican party illustrated this. My example of a law that banned the posting of signs for aesthetic reasons was distinguishable from Justice Scalia's example. His example was of a subcategory of expression (obscene pictures of the Republican party) not protected by the First Amendment. My illustration had been a subcategory (signs of the Democratic party) incorporated into a constitutional regulation—that is, a restriction on time, place, or manner—generally neutral in its effect (banning all signs posted in certain areas for aesthetic reasons).

Foley informed Justice Souter that he disagreed with Justice Scalia. Justice Souter then asked Foley whether or not time, place, and manner restrictions could be limited to certain harms, which I had asserted would be unconstitutional. Initially confused, Tom stated that the government should be allowed to make these distinctions by having content-based time, place, and manner restrictions. It should be said in Foley's defense that the question was somewhat deceptive. Justice Souter's question "Since time, place, and manner restrictions are constitutional, why can't they, too, be limited to certain particular harms based on content?" could be answered with the observation that such restrictions would then no longer be time, place, and manner restrictions that are content-neutral by definition. A local government may refuse to issue permits for local demonstrations at 2:00 A.M. on the steps of the state capitol as a reasonable time restriction, but they may not prohibit only demonstrations held at 2:00 A.M. that advocate a pro-choice position. What was a constitutionally permissible time restriction applying equally would become a content-based restriction aimed at preventing the dissemination of certain viewpoints. Content-based time, place, and manner restrictions are not constitutionally permissible. Foley indicated that they were. When there was an audible gasp in the lawyers' seating section, he quickly changed his answer to "No." Justice Souter stated that if the Court adopted the position of the city regarding the punishment of certain categories of fighting words, it would be making new law. Foley disagreed.

Justice Blackmun and Justice Stevens followed with questions about the location of the burning cross. Blackmun's examples of a cross burned in front of a courthouse or a state capitol and Stevens's example of burning a cross on private property by the owner of the property highlighted the problems with the ordinance, since there was no element of *intent* to threaten or intimidate required for a violation of the law. Foley, of course, wanted to highlight the ugly factual circumstances of the case. Since our challenge was to the law, his suggestion that the other hypotheticals offered by the justices would constitute protected expression was not accurate. What he meant was that as chief prosecutor he would not be interested in prosecuting such cases because he would recognize that such expression was protected. The Court held in 1963 in *NAACP v. Button,* that "it makes no difference whether such prosecutions or proceedings would actually be commenced. It is enough that a vague and overbroad statute lends itself to selective enforcement against unpopular causes."

Justice Souter returned to the words "inflict injury" in *Chaplinsky.* I had asked the Court to disavow the "inflict injury" dictum, and Foley argued to the Court that such language was "still good, viable law."

Justice Scalia focused again on the "bias-motivated" label by noting that such a label depended "on what your biases are." Using the example of offensive expression directed at a home established for the mentally ill, Scalia asked Foley whether such a sign would be covered by the ordinance. Foley was forced to acknowledge that he didn't "believe under the facts that you described that it would." Scalia noted, "It's the wrong kind of bias." As if to explain away Justice Scalia's example, Foley noted that "there are other alternative criminal laws that may apply to that particular situation." This statement was accurate, but it did not go far enough. There were "other alternative criminal laws" that would apply to any of these situations without needlessly endangering the First Amendment. Justice Scalia jumped on Foley's answer and said that the ordinance appeared to him to be "the rankest kind of subject-matter discrimination." Although Scalia was not prepared to overrule *Chaplinsky,* he did appear to be greatly troubled by the language of the ordinance.

Justice O'Connor interrupted to bolster Foley's argument and prompt him further. She cited the case of *New York v. Ferber* in support of the city's position. Nine years earlier, in *Ferber,* the Court held that there was nothing unconstitutionally underinclusive in singling out child pornography for proscription. Although nonobscene pornography was generally protected, the Court had unanimously held that children subjected to such harmful practices deserved special protection as a class. *Ferber* was undoubtedly the strongest case in support of the city's position because a unanimous Court, including such First Amendment champions as Justices Brennan and Marshall, had found an underinclusive law constitutionally permissible. The Court noted that the applicable state law in *Ferber* provided that the prohibited conduct must be adequately defined. In contrast, the Minnesota Supreme Court had tried to impose limits on the ordinance, but had merely created a new and confusing law that constituted a much greater threat to freedom of expression than the law in *Ferber.*

After three quarters of an hour, only Justices Byron White and Clarence Thomas had remained silent. With his first question, White elicited an admission from Foley that the ordinance was unconstitutional as originally written. It was the first time that the city had acknowledged that section 292.02 was unconstitutional as originally drafted and approved by the St. Paul City Council.

Like David Souter, Justice White was a Rhodes scholar. Dour in appearance and manner, by December of 1991 he was the senior member of the Court, having served almost thirty years. In addition to his scholarly achievements, he had achieved fame as an outstanding athlete, later playing professional football. Long before the *R.A.V.* case, he had personally witnessed Fascism and the effects of racism. In 1939 the twenty-two-year-old White visited Munich, Germany, in the tumultuous days before World War II. Earlier in the spring he had met another twenty-two-year-old, the son of the American ambassador to the Court of St. James's at a reception at the embassy. In Munich he renewed his acquaintance with young Jack Kennedy. One night White, Kennedy, and a friend of Kennedy's were driving on the streets of Munich when strangers stopped the car White was driving. Kennedy's friend later gave an account of the incident:

> The storm troopers got "rough." We were yelling back and they started throwing bricks at the car. So we drove the car away for a while and I turned to Jack and said, "What in the hell was wrong with them, what's all this about?" We weren't doing anything, I mean, we weren't agitating people or doing anything. And Whizzer [White] explained the car we were driving in had English plates on it—and they were so agitated at the English people that they were throwing rocks at our car! And this is the first time I ever heard Jack say it: he said "you know, how can we avoid having a world war if this is the way these people feel?"

The oppressive atmosphere of prewar Nazi Germany must have left a lasting impression on young Byron White. His path again crossed that of Jack Kennedy, and as a lieutenant in the United States Navy in 1943 he wrote the intelligence report detailing the sinking of Kennedy's boat, P.T. 109. White described Kennedy as "very intelligent in the way he ran his boat, as well as cool and courageous under fire."

After Kennedy was elected president in 1960, he appointed White deputy attorney general under Robert F. Kennedy. (Also at the Department of Justice at that time was Burke Marshall, who submitted an *amicus* brief in *R.A.V.* with Catharine MacKinnon). In the spring of 1961, a year before Kennedy appointed him to the Supreme Court, White personally observed racism as well when he "led a contingent of 600 National Guardsmen sent to Alabama to protect the 'Freedom Riders' who were seeking to integrate the interstate buses." Thirty years later he was the only remaining justice appointed by a Democratic president. To the dismay of many liberals, he was considerably more conservative than Republican appointees Justices Blackmun and Stevens. Further, his approach to the First Amendment was generally restrictive. He was said to have acknowledged "privately that his biggest mistake was joining the majority in the seminal 1964 press-protection case of *New York Times Co. v. Sullivan*." As proof of his conservative stance, liberal critics could point out that in the most recently completed term, 1990–91, White had voted with Rehnquist 79 percent of the time.

Justice White confronted Foley with the case of *Lewis v. New*

Orleans. Lewis involved a confrontation between a white police officer and the black mother of a criminal defendant on a road in Louisiana in 1970. The mother had been arrested for allegedly swearing at the police officer, which she denied doing and alleged that the police officer had sworn at her and made racist remarks. She was convicted under a law that made it a crime to curse at a police officer "while in performance of his duties." The Louisiana Supreme Court had stated that the law could be limited to "fighting words." The United States Supreme Court sent the case back to Louisiana in light of *Gooding v. Wilson,* another "fighting words" case. Given a second chance, the Louisiana Supreme Court emphasized that they applied the law only to "fighting words," although other language in the decision indicated that they "contemplated a broader reach of the ordinance" than was constitutionally permissible. Put simply, the Louisiana Supreme Court thought that swearing at a police officer constituted a criminal offense, while the United States Supreme Court was concerned that such an interpretation of a "fighting words" standard could lead to selective enforcement and abuse of authority by certain law-enforcement officers. Underlying this interpretation was a recognition of the specific power imbalance between a minority defendant and a white law-enforcement officer in the South.

By citing the *Lewis* case in questioning Foley, Justice White demonstrated that he objected to the wording of the decision of the Minnesota Supreme Court. However, Justice White was signaling much more than just dissatisfaction with the lower-court decision. Justice Scalia had attacked the original language of the ordinance, appearing to agree that government violated First Amendment principles when it selected certain ideological viewpoints for proscription. Justice White had realized that certain members of the Court were leaning toward a rule of law that he thought would be broader than necessary. By raising the *Lewis* decision, he served notice to the other justices that he too found the ordinance objectionable, but only on the narrow ground that the Minnesota Supreme Court decision had failed to adequately narrow a badly drafted ordinance. White appeared ready to acknowledge that the ordinance was unconstitutional because it continued to be susceptible of being applied to protected speech. By this time, there were indications that his brethren had other ideas.

During my last few minutes of rebuttal, I once again pointed out the other options available to the prosecutor:

> There were other, more serious laws available that didn't make this kind of political statement.

This is not a question about whether anyone here approves of this alleged conduct. There were tough ways of dealing with it without implicating the First Amendment. . . .

In closing, I would ask the Court to consider this, that it would be a sad irony if we diminished the First Amendment right of free expression to American citizens in this way when the countries of Eastern Europe and the Baltic States and the Soviet bloc are returning their liberties to their citizens.

The Chief Justice thanked me and indicated that the questioning had ended. The vast majority of spectators, both lawyers and members of the public, rose from their seats to leave as the attorneys who had been waiting for the next case moved up to the table for arguing counsel. As the Chief Justice angrily admonished the crowd to depart silently, I took the white quill pen and turned to leave with Mike. When I looked into the eyes of my friends who had watched the proceedings, it seemed to me that they felt that the hour of argument had gone well.

On different grounds, it appeared that Justices Scalia, Souter, White, and probably the Chief Justice were sympathetic to our argument. Justice O'Connor seemed somewhat unsympathetic. The positions of Justices Kennedy, Stevens, and Blackmun were unclear. The newest justice and the only minority member of the Court, Justice Clarence Thomas, had not asked a single question at the argument. Several months earlier, Thomas persevered through electrifying Senate hearings and was confirmed by a narrow majority of voting senators in the closest confirmation of a Supreme Court justice in this century. On the Court since the first of November, he remained an enigma as he sat amid continuing allegations of sexual harassment. His confirmation hearings, like the case of R.A.V., had shattered old alliances and belied the significance of such labels as "liberal" and "conservative." It was strange to watch the NAACP oppose the nomination of a black man to the Supreme Court. Underlying the ongoing dispute between liberals and conservatives on the topic of race were other issues that promised to dominate politics into the nineties; gender attitudes and power sharing. Since the ordinance prohibited offensive expression on the issues of both race and gender, it was hard to predict how Justice Thomas would view this case.

Justice John Paul Stevens was also an unknown. Although he had asked several questions, he had given little indication of which way he was leaning. In the most recent completed term, he had written the most dissenting opinions, and a review of the decisions showed that he and Justice Scalia had the lowest rate of agreement between any two justices on the Court. With the Court's shift to the right, Stevens now found himself labeled a liberal along with Justice Blackmun. He was more accurately considered a moderate and a maverick, and his interpretation of the First Amendment appeared hard to pin down. He had been among the four dissenters in the flag-burning cases, and he had written a particularly acerbic dissent in *Texas v. Johnson* excoriating the majority for allowing the burning of the American flag.

As Mike and I greeted friends and family and started down the steps of the Supreme Court toward the press pool, I was amused to learn that Gregory Johnson, the flag-burning defendant, had been present for the argument and was now making a statement to the press that while he was in favor of flag-burning, he condemned cross-burning. The irony of someone who engaged in fringe political expression recommending the censorship of another was lost on him. Justice Kennedy's observation in his concurring opinion in *Texas v. Johnson* that Johnson "was not a philosopher" appeared to be an accurate observation.

Back home in Minnesota there were over two feet of snow on the ground but the sun was shining brightly in the nation's capital while I answered questions from the press after the argument. A few minutes later Laura and Russell Jones and Tom Foley met the press. The Joneses stated how important it was to them to have the law upheld, saying that the events of that night constituted a "threat." They still did not realize that there were more serious charges available that did not implicate the First Amendment. Perhaps they would never truly understand that this challenge was not evidence of indifference to their feelings but an effort to protect the right to dissent.

After having lunch with friends and family near the White House, Mike and I walked the Mall, replaying the argument in our heads, savoring the moment. Arriving back in Minneapolis the next day, we were greeted warmly by some and less warmly by others because the local media had covered the case extensively. Although most of the press still did not understand the underlying issues, local reporters had at least attempted to explain to the public that Mike and I did not favor cross-burning.

This message had not reached some members of the public. My law office had received several threats, including one from an irate man who said that he wanted my address so he could burn a cross in my front yard. Since there were over two feet of snow there, I concluded that this was a long-distance threat. I also received several threats at home on my answering machine, which I had fully expected; later my residence was "egged" on Martin Luther King Jr.'s holiday. Still, considering the complexity of the issue, the response had not been as severe as it might have been.

After appearing with Tom Foley on a local public television show, I flew to New York to appear on the *Today* show on the morning of December 9. The smell of roasting chestnuts on Fifth Avenue and the sight of the Christmas tree at Rockefeller Center towering over the skaters allowed me to forget burning crosses. As I sat on the *Today* show set flanked by Bryant Gumbel and Theodore Shaw, a black law professor from the University of Michigan, the events of the past week seemed unreal.

Only days earlier Katie Couric of the *Today* show had conducted a devastating interview with David Duke. Geoff Stephens, an assistant producer of the show, assured me that although Monday was Bryant Gumbel's first day back from vacation, he would review the pre-interview and be conversant with the underlying issues. I did not want a repeat of the Sonya Friedman fiasco. I had read that Gumbel's father had been a probate judge, which gave me added confidence that he would approach this issue responsibly. I was not disappointed; Gumbel was courteous to me both on and off camera. It was humbling to appear on national television during the week celebrating the anniversary of the Bill of Rights to explain to the nation why the First Amendment was threatened, and why cross-burning could not be banned.

On the flight back to Minneapolis, I saw an article in *USA Today* that I found encouraging. Retired justice William J. Brennan, Jr., had met the previous day with a group of journalists, five days after the oral arguments in *R.A.V.* He had given "a clean bill of health to the First Amendment," noting that the "public's affection" for it "hasn't diminished." I wasn't sure if Justice Brennan knew the results of the preliminary vote taken by the members of the Court several days earlier, but I chose to view his comments as a favorable sign.

After arriving back in St. Paul, I was called by *People* magazine. One of the reporters for the publication had approached me at the press pool at the Supreme Court and said she would be doing a story on the case. Considering how much media attention it had already received, there was no reason why the thought of another feature should have made me feel ill at ease, but I worried that *People* magazine was not the right "vehicle" for such a complex issue. While I cooperated with its reporters, I told them that I did not feel that they could explain such a complex issue in a magazine that often appeared to be the equivalent of written sound bites. I suspected they would focus on the Jones family and their trauma rather than on the underlying legal issue. The reporters agreed that there was some truth in my concern but said that they would do their best to be evenhanded. A photographer flew in on a weekend to take photographs of the Jones family and me. Against my better judgment, I put on a suit and tie and went to my law office on a Sunday morning for a series of photos, believing they would never appear because the story would focus on the Jones family. When the story appeared, it seemed I had been correct in my assumption, but the reporters kept their word by attempting to balance their coverage. At least the article was not placed next to a story about David Duke.

A few days later I picked up the local paper to see an editorial written by Tom Foley. I was upset that the paper had not contacted me for my views. On January 11, 1992, the St. Paul *Pioneer Press* printed my response:

> Under the guise of law enforcement, various politicians and political groups have argued that communities need special "hate crime" laws. . . . When communities are allowed to set a political standard as to what is acceptable expression, the First Amendment has no guarantee for any American.

I wrote that, understandably, Americans have little patience for flag-burners and cross-burners, but

> when that expression is combined with illegal conduct, as in this case, tough laws are always going to be available to prosecute these individuals.
>
> The more serious question is how laws of this type affect the average citizen. Virtually anyone who has ever opposed the majority on any of the major issues of our day (race, color, creed, religion or gender) stands in danger of being silenced. . . .
>
> Imagine how a law like this, that punishes expression on the basis of "race" if it "angers" others, would have been enforced thirty years ago in Alabama. How far would the civil rights movement have reached if George Wallace had had such a law at his disposal? Indeed, if demagogues reach power somewhere in this country in the future, what could they do with a law that allows them to punish unpopular expression simply because it is unpopular?

Due to the anniversary of the Bill of Rights, the intense media coverage of the case continued. Within a span of only a few weeks, radio interviews with me were aired by WABC and ABC Talk Radio (New York); KGIL (Los Angeles); WYLL (Chicago); and KLBJ (Austin, Texas). Most questions from the listening audience were hostile or disbelieving. When a friendly phone call was made by a listener, I was intensely grateful.

On January 22 I read an article that noted the ACLU had received a $1 million gift from benefactors "because the organization does the most to defend the First Amendment right to free speech." I found it hard not to be bitter, considering the lack of support we had received from the ACLU. We had spent hundreds of hours without compensation, protecting the amendment that they supposedly did "the most to defend." While they would still defend it in certain contexts, some members of the hierarchy seemed more interested in pursuing a political agenda than in conducting a nonpartisan defense of the First Amendment. I believe that some of the leaders of the ACLU are out of step with thousands of members and volunteer attorneys across the country. Many members of the organization believe in civil liberties for all American citizens regardless of political belief. The ACLU refused initially to lend us their support. Later, perhaps out of embarrassment or because they wanted to try to control the debate, they had filed a portion of a brief that reflected lukewarm support at best. I questioned whether this organization wanted the petitioner to prevail in this case, and I expected the leadership to undermine the decision if we succeeded.

Shortly after the first of the year 1992 I was asked by a black law students' association to speak at a local law school. The title of the proposed discussion was to be "Cross Burnings: Personal, Historical and Legal Perspectives." The title highlighted a continuing problem with the public's perception of *R.A.V.* The case was about the constitutionality of an ordinance that threatened the First Amendment because it prohibited dissent and selected subjects for censorship. As civil rights lawyer William Kunstler later pointed out, minorities simply could not get past the image of a burning cross to a consideration of the First Amendment. I was advised not to attend the discussion because no one appeared interested in the larger legal issues. However, I did attend and found it to be a stimulating evening, if for no other reason than having the honor of meeting Nellie Stone Johnson, an eighty-five-year-old black woman, who had been politically active in minority affairs and labor relations for over a half century. She had been the first black citizen elected to a citywide office in Minneapolis, in 1945, and years before that had been the first woman in the nation to serve on a contract-negotiations committee. With the benefit of her experience and wisdom, she reminded the audience that overt acts of racism, such as cross-burnings, distract society from an examination of the underlying causes, including economic issues and fair employment practices. She criticized the NAACP and told the audience that we must all be careful in supporting laws that would undermine the First Amendment, since the poor and disfranchised have historically relied on its guarantees.

I continued to accept speaking engagements at law schools and human rights organizations. I enjoyed speaking to audiences, even those who initially disagreed with my position. I found a deep satisfaction in hearing from members of the public that they had given serious consideration to the issues involved and now supported my position. I reminded listeners that important First Amendment cases often involved intolerant demagogues. Providing space for intolerant expression was the only way to protect the right of the powerless to seek redress for grievances. In the early sixties the United States Supreme Court had relied on an accepted understanding of the high purpose of the First Amendment to protect the early civil rights movement, when dissidents engaged in marches or sit-ins. The belief that expression based on a volatile topic like race could lead to a public disturbance could not justify silencing that expression. When Alabama state troopers broke up the civil rights march on the Edmund Pettus Bridge in 1965, the justification used by Governor Wallace was the inability of the onlookers to control their tempers. There are those who would justify the use of the First Amendment to protect civil rights marchers but not to protect those who preach intolerance. Such moral and political judgments have historically been too constitutionally tenuous to be entrusted to government officials.

On February 17 I watched a television program about the Bill of Rights called *The Delicate Balance*. This segment was about hate speech and had been taped only days after the argument in December. Justice Scalia was one of the panelists, and although I could not ascertain his position, it was apparent that he and Robert Bork, another panel member, disagreed on protecting unpopular expression; Bork criticized the flag-burning decisions while staring directly at Scalia.

When arguments are heard on Wednesday, as *R.A.V.* was, the initial vote is usually taken two days later, on Friday. Although the votes of the justices may change as the matter proceeds, the initial vote often reflects the final outcome. If the Chief Justice votes with the majority, he assigns the task of writing the majority opinion.

While Justice Scalia sat on the panel on the show he probably had been assigned to write the opinion in *R.A.V. v. St. Paul*. However, his comments on the program were subject to interpretation, so I felt little confidence at the time about the outcome of the case.

As Akhil Reed Amar of Yale Law School and Kathleen Sullivan, then of Harvard Law School, observed, the issues presented by *R.A.V.* were considerably more complex than those raised by the flag-burning cases, leaving a myriad of options open to the Court and making a prediction of the outcome of the case hazardous.

If the Court had chosen to affirm the lower court's decision, it could have done so in a number of ways. It could simply have affirmed the lower-court decision, an act that would have been consistent not only with the conservative makeup of the Court but also with the strong federalist beliefs of its members. For the Court to have acted in such a manner without conflicting state court decisions would have been unusual.

The Court might have affirmed the lower-court decision while effectively abolishing the overbreadth doctrine. The Court could have held that those who engaged in unprotected conduct were no longer allowed to make a challenge to a law on the basis that it could be applied in other cases involving protected expression. Since the allegations in the *R.A.V.* case were offensive and ugly, the public had trouble understanding why anyone charged with such conduct should be allowed to challenge the law. Many felt that overbroad laws should be challenged only by those who were unfairly prosecuted— that is, by citizens who had engaged in unpopular expression without committing a crime. The entire theory of overbreadth was that laws of this nature left on the books would remain as political statements inviting selective application by law enforcement, potentially chilling or suppressing the right of any citizen to dissent for fear of prosecution.

Liberals historically have championed the overbreadth doctrine. As Kathleen Sullivan observes, if the Court had eliminated overbreadth with this case, the "outcome would have culminated trends on the Court toward restricting overbreadth challenges and, more generally, toward restricting standing." The Court could have struck down the doctrine and in the process incorporated a type of "unclean hands" approach to First Amendment challenges. A defendant who had allegedly engaged in some type of criminal conduct and was charged under an overbroad law would not have been allowed to challenge the law because of the unsavory allegations. While this may seem reasonable, a number of cases that have extended the First Amendment's protection involved criminal conduct of some kind. The power of the First Amendment has emerged from cases involving extremely unpopular and disturbing expression.

Had the Court upheld the state-court decision and abolished the overbreadth doctrine, the result would have arguably satisfied both ends of the political spectrum. Conservatives would have been pleased to see the end of First Amendment challenges maintained by those charged with crimes or politically active groups engaged in protest, usually in support of liberal causes. In addition, conservatives would have approved of the Court reaffirming the federalist doctrine of allowing wide latitude to state courts.

Some liberals may have felt that losing the overbreadth doctrine was a price worth paying in order to uphold certain hate-crime legislation. To demonstrate this "strange bedfellows" alliance, a conservative organization (the Criminal Justice Legal Foundation) and a liberal organization (the NAACP) submitted *amici* briefs asking the Court to reassess or overrule the overbreadth doctrine. It is inconceivable to me that the NAACP could be so shortsighted as to jeopardize a principle that historically has provided the powerless access to the courts. Their position was and is inexplicable.

The possibility that we had come this far not only to lose the case but to undermine the very doctrine that had served to protect First Amendment freedoms for decades was both real and frightening. Several national publications had speculated that the overbreadth doctrine was in danger, and that perhaps the Chief Justice now had enough votes to overturn a doctrine that he had often faulted. I referred to this as the "cruel hoax" theory. It would have been cruel and a hoax to have fought this hard only to lose in a decision which foreclosed that avenue to others seeking review on similar grounds. Still, it was possible that the Court had accepted our challenge in order to limit access to petitioners in the future.

The Court might have affirmed the lower-court decision and given the government authority to eliminate expression that was "hateful" or "inflicted injury." This could have been done narrowly, by adding a new category of expression devoid of First Amendment protection or, more broadly, by articulating a compelling state interest served by these laws, disregarding alternative methods of addressing that interest. Finally, as Amar suggests, the Court could have extended the traditional interpretation of the Thirteenth Amendment, banning hate speech as a "badge of slavery."

On the other hand, if the Court reversed the lower-court decision in favor of *R.A.V.*, it could have done so in several different ways. As Sullivan notes, the Court might simply have overturned the decision on the basis that the narrowing construction of the lower court had failed. The Court had used this approach decades earlier in *Lewis v. City of New Orleans,* a case mentioned by Justice White during oral argument. This analysis might have left the overbreadth doctrine intact and broken no new constitutional ground.

The Court might have gone further and eliminated the "fighting words" doctrine by overturning *Chaplinsky v. New Hampshire,* the fifty-year-old case that created the law-and-order tool that remained constitutionally dubious, but this seemed unlikely.

Recognizing that the outcome of the case was hard to predict did not prevent me from considering the possibilities. I found it hard to concentrate on my law practice, but I had little choice. In March, my co-counsel Pat Kelly and I spent a week in northern Minnesota on a civil jury trial. In our absence, another cross was burned in St. Paul. Apparently a white student at a local college had been assaulted by two black students on a nearby campus; in retaliation, friends of the white student had burned a cross in the front yard of one of the suspected assailants. I received calls in my hotel room and realized that whenever an act of racial intolerance occurred in the Twin Cities, the focus would return to *R.A.V.*

More disturbing than the continued criticism of our position was the anger leveled at members of my family. My widowed mother, who did not have a drop of intolerant blood, was confronted and harassed, even by friends. Because she never complained, I did not learn of this until much later. I could sense that she was deeply distressed by the public reaction to the case, and I was grateful that I did not have young children, who would have been subjected to abuse.

At the end of April, I agreed to take part in a forum at an inner-city high school to discuss the issues of intolerant behavior among adolescents. Although the members of the mostly minority audience were angry about racism, they listened intently and seemed deep in thought. The date of the forum was April 28, 1992. The next day several Los Angeles police officers were acquitted of the beating of Rodney King.

If the Clarence Thomas hearings had riveted the nation and turned its attention to issues of gender and sexual harassment, the Rodney King verdict shifted the nation's attention once more to our apparent lack of progress made in race relations. The resulting riot was a scene from our past, a bitter reminder that the issues dividing us lay just beneath the surface, threatening to destroy our collective dream of a "multicultural" nation. Hours earlier, I had looked into the eyes of minority students and explained why violence was not the answer, how laws, prosecuted properly, could severely punish criminal conduct, and how intolerant expression was the price we paid for a freedom too precious to endanger. Now over fifty people were dead, and over one thousand buildings were partially or completely destroyed.

I worried about how the decision in *R.A.V.* would be interpreted by the minority community. The nation's leaders seemed powerless to heal the fragmentation of society. These riots would further strain individual liberty as calls for law and order would follow the riots as a final antidote to the nightmare of race relations in America.

On the day of the Rodney King verdict, I felt a dull pain in my leg as I walked to my office. Though familiar with muscle tears and pulls, I was aware that something else was occurring. One physician suggested that I had probably just strained my knee; I consulted another who soon had me admitted to United Hospital with a diagnosis of deep vein thrombosis. The physicians could not explain how a clot had formed in my leg. I had no previous medical history, I did not smoke, drank little alcohol, and exercised regularly. In spite of following all the health rules, I had suffered a major blood clot that could have led to a heart attack, stroke, or worse, and I was only thirty-nine years old. Fourteen months earlier my father had died in the very same hospital from a similar condition, without any previous medical history. Coincidental or not, events seemed to be spinning out of control.

While hospitalized, I waited for my office to call by 9:30 A.M. with news from the Court. I had been given a list of "decision dates" during each month on which the Supreme Court released its opinions. No one ever knew in advance when a decision would be issued. Since few opinions were released within sixty days, we knew only that the decision would be released after late February. No decision came, and I spent a week in the hospital. Hooked to an I.V., I watched the news coverage of the riots and thought of similar scenes from the sixties. Conservatives and moderates believed that social programs alone wouldn't solve the country's problems, and that the middle class had tired of paying for those programs. Yet the liberals correctly observed that simply building more jails to incarcerate ever-increasing numbers of criminals was not a long-term solution. The answer had eluded us as a nation, and each generation of Americans had been confronted with the age-old problem of maintaining a stable, free, and democratic society while holding widely diverse groups together.

Among my hospital visitors was Tom Foley, who sat on the bed next to me as we discussed the long wait for the Court's determination. Tom was the state campaign co-chairman of the Clinton for

President Committee, and was busy organizing a thousand-dollar-per-plate fund-raiser for him that week. Although we had been opponents many times, fate had brought us together in the case of *R.A.V. v. St. Paul,* and I sincerely appreciated Foley's visit.

After my discharge from the hospital, I decided to take a long-awaited trip to Greece. The last two years had taught me that there were no guarantees in life and that we are apt to regret what we didn't do when given the opportunity.

As my girlfriend and I boarded the plane for Athens on June 11 I knew that there were only a few decision dates left; on some of them I would be physically in Greece and mentally in Washington, D.C. Some people thought I should cancel the trip. Perhaps I would miss a bit of the excitement if we prevailed, but somehow celebrations no longer seemed so important. Besides, we would get a chance to see Justice Brandeis's beloved Greece, and I enjoyed the symmetry of receiving a decision about free expression in a country that had created the model for freedom and democracy.

On July 4, 1946, twenty-nine-year-old John F. Kennedy spoke to the citizens of Boston in Faneuil Hall during his first campaign for public office:

> Conceived in Grecian thought, strengthened by Christian morality, and stamped indelibly into American political philosophy, the right of the individual against the State is the keystone of our Constitution. Each man is free. He is *free* in *thought*. He is *free* in *expression*. He is *free* in *worship*. To us, who have been reared in the American tradition, these rights have become a part of our very being. They have become so much a part of our being that most of us are prone to feel that they are rights universally recognized and universally exercised. But the sad fact is that this is not true. They were dearly won for us only a few short centuries ago and they were dearly preserved for us in the days just past. And there are large sections of the world today where these rights are denied as a matter of philosophy and as a manner of government.
>
> We cannot assume that the struggle has ended. It is never ending. . . .
>
> May God grant that, at some distant date . . . the orator may be able to say that these are still the great qualities of the American character and that they have prevailed.

As we landed in Athens, Greece, on June 15, 1992, we knew that we would soon learn if these great qualities of the American character had prevailed.

"Without Adding the First Amendment to the Fire": The Court Decides

> Let there be no mistake about our belief that burning a cross in someone's front yard is reprehensible. But St. Paul has sufficient means at its disposal to prevent such behavior without adding the First Amendment to the fire.
>
> —*R.A.V. v. City of St. Paul*

The days passed quickly as we vacationed on the sun-drenched island of Mykonos in the Aegean Sea. Late on the afternoon of each decision date, I would retreat to the hotel room to call the United States Supreme Court in Washington, D.C. Relaxing was possible on other days, but on those days when I knew the release was imminent, I would feel my entire body tense as I made the phone call. Decision dates came and went, and on June 19 we headed for the windswept island of Santorini. Located farther south among the Cyclades, Santorini had been inhabited since approximately 2000 B.C., and legend held that it was the site of the lost continent of Atlantis. In the town of Oya we settled into one of the caves, euphemistically called "villas" by the natives, dug out of the black volcanic rock. We were struck by the remoteness and eeriness of an island paradise where time seemed to stand still.

On the day of June 19 the only phone I could find to make my call was a metered one located in a tiny room at the tip of the town on the cliff. As I waited my turn in line, I realized that if the Court decided the case that day, I would not have a chance to make other calls, nor to get a fax of the decision. As it turned out, the Court did not issue the opinion that day. There were now two remaining scheduled decision dates in the term. After spending the weekend on Santorini, we headed for the mainland.

On the morning of June 22, with only a few cases from the 1991 term unresolved, the Supreme Court issued its opinion in the case of *R.A.V. v. City of St. Paul.* Over a year had elapsed since the Court had agreed to hear the case and over six months since oral arguments. The summary of argument in our brief had begun with the words of Thomas More from *A Man for All Seasons.* Now a unanimous Court issued its opinion on the Catholic feast day of Saint Thomas More, the majority opinion written by Justice Antonin Scalia, a devout Catholic. By a 9–0 vote the Court had overturned the decision of the Minnesota Supreme Court, perhaps cognizant of More's advice that cutting "a great road through the law to get after the Devil" was a mistake and that in an imperfect world society must "give the Devil benefit of law" for its "own safety's sake."

While the decision was a stunning victory, sending, as some commentators said, "shock waves across the nation," it was also a sobering event. Thousands of miles away I sat in a television studio in Athens and waited for the questions of Katie Couric of the *Today* show. After the interview was completed, I was assigned a driver in a black limousine who took me back to Delphi. I was in a daze and recall very little of the long, leisurely ride. Both relieved and elated, I knew that although the decision would be hailed by most legal experts, it would be misunderstood by those who had opposed us.

The effect in St. Paul was immediate. The mayor and the county attorney quickly met with the press to denounce the decision. At a later press conference, a youth coordinator for the St. Paul NAACP, referring to those who burned crosses, advised "black youth" to "shoot them down like a dog, because that is what they are." Given the opportunity to soften his remarks, the NAACP official denied "that his position was extreme" and said that it "was the only course open after Monday's ruling." Local government officials stood by and said nothing. Their silence encouraged a hostile, violent atmosphere, and I started to receive threats at my office and home.

Newspapers across the country reported the decision from different perspectives. Local newspapers were most hostile as they printed large pictures of the Jones family and quoted angry government officials at length. There was little attempt to explain the underlying constitutional issues. Reporters of major newspapers printed detailed and knowledgeable summaries of the Court's decision. Other journalists, who may have lacked the legal understanding required for a thorough analysis, resorted to criticism of the Court in general and Justice Scalia in particular.

Linda Greenhouse of *The New York Times* observed that the majority opinion written by Justice Scalia carried a "tone of arid absolutism." Justice Scalia described the alleged conduct in the same manner as I had—"reprehensible"—yet had not used the condemnatory language that the media expected and the concurring justices demanded. Scalia may have felt no obligation to engage in soothing rhetoric irrelevant to constitutional analysis. However, it might have been beneficial for the nation had Justice Scalia engaged in the judicial exercise cited by Bollinger in discussing the Skokie case, whereby Courts reinforce and reaffirm the general norm by acknowledging the ugliness of bigotry.

Had Justice Brennan written the opinion, he might have used the rhetoric sought by the concurring justices; yet the scrutiny given an opinion written by Justice Brennan would have been quite different. Because Justice Scalia is regarded with such suspicion by liberals, it might have been worthwhile to remind us of what all citizens gained by protecting First Amendment freedoms. As we had stated in our brief, "An unanticipated result may be enforcement against the very groups targeted for protection. The direction of the winds of political acceptability may change and such laws could be used to reduce their freedom of expression. Forcing intolerant opinions and ideas underground may result in the glorification of racist, sexist, or anti-semitic activity." As some observed, Scalia could have eliminated several concurring opinions or at least softened their bitter tone had he addressed the suspicion of other justices that he was insensitive to the pain of racial hatred.

At the beginning of the majority opinion, Justice Scalia (joined by Justices Kennedy, Souter, and Thomas and Chief Justice Rehnquist) began by footnote to disarm Justice White's position that the majority should have joined with the concurring justices to strike down the ordinance simply because it criminalized protected expression without addressing subject-matter discrimination. White suggested angrily that the majority had decided the case on a rationale that had not been "fairly included" in the issues presented to the Court. In response, Justice Scalia quoted from our petition, our briefs, and my oral argument. Justice White was so disturbed by the majority that he wrote that had we made it clear that we were requesting the Court to adopt the "majority's decisional theory" the Court "would never have granted certiorari." It takes four votes to grant certiorari, and since the majority held four votes even without Justice Thomas (who had not been on the Court when certiorari was granted), this implied that Justice White had voted for review and that at least one member of the majority had not.

Justice White was correct in suggesting that we had not focused on subject-matter discrimination. He was wrong in believing that we had not presented this "novel theory" to the Court. We had emphasized viewpoint discrimination in the law both as written and as construed, and we had stated, as Justice Scalia cited, that "denominating particular expression a 'fighting word' because of the impact of its ideological content upon the audience is inconsistent with the First Amendment." At oral argument I had emphasized that subcategories of unprotected expression could not be singled out without risking the betrayal of governmental neutrality. Punishing someone for the conduct of causing an immediate breach of the peace, without reference to their viewpoint, was permissible. Punishing another for upsetting expression based on race was not. As Akhil Reed Amar of Yale Law School has noted, "Justice White overplayed his hand by claiming that the Court 'lacks jurisdiction to decide the case in the majority rationale,' even though the questions in which certiorari were granted explicitly invoked the First Amendment and highlighted the 'content based' nature of the St. Paul ordinance, in contradistinction to 'content neutral laws' that might pass muster."

The majority opinion continued with what we had argued in interviews, in our brief, and finally at oral argument. More serious felony charges were available to prosecute the individuals who had committed such acts. The importance of these alternatives should not be overlooked. Because of the ugly and offensive factual allegations, the public and media found it hard to focus on the challenge to the ordinance itself. The opinions of the concurring justices demonstrated a similar focus on the facts alleged at the expense of a thorough evaluation of the law. Few seemed willing or able to understand that a challenge to the law did not preclude prosecution. The ordinance was a misdemeanor and provided up to ninety days' incarceration; the terroristic-threats statute was a felony and provided for up to five years in prison. The officials involved were not interested primarily in the public safety or in severely punishing the alleged participants. Every time the ugly factual allegations were recited and condemned, the public and media were misled about the actual issue involved. The use of a misdemeanor when a felony provision was available presented the contradiction of prosecutors appearing to be tough on racism while actually being soft on crime.

The opinion announced that the Court would not overturn or modify *Chaplinsky v. New Hampshire*. Although the justices refused to strike down the "injury" language of *Chaplinsky* that we believed dangerous, they did agree, as I had argued, that they need not overturn that decision to reach the result we had requested.

As the Bill of Rights entered its third century, the Court retraced the history of freedom of expression "from 1791 to the present." Agreeing that freedom of expression was not absolute in our country, the Court noted that the few recognized exceptions to that freedom, such as defamation and obscenity, had been narrowed by "our decisions since the 1960s," thus aligning the conservative Rehnquist Court with the slightly more moderate Burger Court and the liberal Warren Court, demonstrating three decades of High Court recognition of free speech.

In an observation stunning and powerful in its simplicity, the Court extended a form of protection to the narrow exceptions to freedom of expression, stating that these exceptions were not "categories of speech entirely invisible to the Constitution." While the Court did not overrule *Chaplinsky,* it acknowledged that some fighting words are "quite expressive indeed," hinting that censorship based on reflexive violence is no longer tenable. The Court distinguished the punishment of "fighting words" based on unruly conduct that may still be permissible and the impermissible punishment of "fighting words" based on the subject and viewpoint expressed.

The majority rejected the label of an "underinclusive" limitation on the First Amendment, arguing that it was a " 'content discrimination' limitation upon a State's prohibition of proscribable speech." Noting an important distinction, the majority offered examples of unprotected and protected expression. While the government may prohibit obscenity, even that conveyed in a certain manner (e.g., by telephone), it cannot prohibit obscene speech based on its offensive political message.

In the second section of the majority opinion, the Court unequivocally rejected the Minnesota Supreme Court's attempt to narrow the ordinance because of the "remaining unmodified terms" that resulted in St. Paul's imposing "special prohibitions on those speakers who express views on disfavored subjects." Writing that the ordinance went beyond content discrimination to viewpoint discrimination, the Court noted, as I had in oral argument, that the ordinance would not be applicable to expression deemed acceptable by the majority involving the given subjects (race, color, creed, religion, or gender) or intolerant expression based on other subjects. Writing for the majority, Justice Scalia noted that while Catholics could carry signs condemning their tormentors, bigots could not carry signs attacking Catholics. The majority noted that

the point of the First Amendment is that majority preferences must be expressed in some fashion other than silencing speech on the basis of its content. . . . selectivity of this sort creates the possibility that the city is seeking to handicap the expression of particular ideas. That possibility would alone be enough to render the ordinance presumptively invalid, but St. Paul's comments and concessions in this case elevate the possibility to a certainty.

Reading this passage, I recalled Justice Scalia's comment to Tom Foley before he began his argument ("Mr. Foley, if you are going to make all of these concessions, you might as well sit down now") that had elicited laughter from the audience. Presumably the audience believed that Scalia's comment was in response to Foley's answers to Justice Blackmun's questions about the neighborhood where the incident had occurred. Now it appeared Justice Scalia seriously believed that the government had already made significant "concessions."

Acknowledging the good intentions of the ordinance, the Court reminded local governments that other laws were available to enforce the "right of such group members to live in peace where they wish." The majority opinion ended with a resounding reminder to the "politicians of St. Paul" as well as to local politicians across the country:

> In fact the only interest distinctively served by the content limitation is that of displaying the city council's special hostility towards the particular biases thus singled out. That is precisely what the First Amendment forbids. The politicians of St. Paul are entitled to express that hostility—but not through the means of imposing unique limitations upon speakers who (however benightedly) disagree.

Making clear that they also found the decision of the Minnesota Supreme Court unacceptable, the concurring justices nevertheless took issue with the majority's approach. In agreement that the St. Paul ordinance was substantially overbroad, the "White Four" (Justices White, O'Connor, Blackmun, and Stevens), as Amar has referred to them, steadfastly focused on the unconstitutional impact of the law due to its overbreadth, rather than on the inherent ideological flaws of the ordinance, demonstrated by the subject-matter discrimination (race, color, creed, religion, or gender).

In an angry response to the alleged factual situation (the "expressive conduct in this case is evil and worthless"), the concurring opinion written by Justice White implied that under the majority rationale "expressions of violence . . . are of sufficient value to outweigh the social interest in order," ignoring the alternative criminal charges available. Justices White, Blackmun, and O'Connor also lamented the demise of the "purely categorical approach," concerned that the Court had now changed the rules of First Amendment analysis.

Prior to the *R.A.V.* decision, expression had been classified as protected or unprotected. Now the majority held that previously unprotected speech (i.e., obscenity, fighting words) would be protected if the law used to punish the expression singled out a subject for censorship (i.e., proscribed fighting words based on race but not on mental illness). It was an overdue recognition that the categorical approach was not protective of First Amendment interests. Now lawmakers could not make some subjects or viewpoints off-limits by classifying them as unprotected fighting words. After *R.A.V.*, the threshold question for First Amendment analysis is whether a law discriminates between viewpoints, not whether it proscribes a category of previously unprotected expression. Only Justices White, Blackmun, and O'Connor were disappointed at this revolutionary development in constitutional analysis.

Rejecting the majority's view that "the official suppression of ideas" was present in the case, the concurring justices expressed distaste and confusion over the majority opinion. They wrote that the majority's "selection of this case to rewrite First Amendment law is particularly inexplicable, because the whole problem could have been avoided by deciding this case under settled First Amendment principles."

The "White Four" then expressed agreement with the conclusion of the majority that the St. Paul ordinance was unconstitutional. Reiterating traditional overbreadth principles, the concurring justices found the ordinance substantially overbroad and agreed that as construed it "criminalizes a substantial amount of expression that—however repugnant—is shielded by the First Amendment." Acknowledging that the "words that injure" language of *Chaplinsky* is not a valid constitutional standard, the concurring justices noted that "the mere fact that expressive activity causes hurt feelings, offense, or resentment does not render the expression unprotected." One could argue that all nine justices had agreed at this point that most student speech codes were unconstitutional.

Justice White continued to express resentment toward the majority for its decision. Rejecting the notion of a betrayal of governmental neutrality, White saw no danger in the ban of fighting words based on race, a position particularly inexplicable considering his experience. For years the "fighting words" prohibition had been used disproportionately against minorities. Try as they might, the concurring justices could not remain focused on the law while allowing the ugly factual allegations to predominate. Justice White resorted to words like "evil" and "worthless" to describe such expression, Justice Blackmun referred to "hoodlums," and all the concurring justices ignored the availability of tougher criminal sanctions. While the majority may have minimized the events of that long-ago evening, the remaining justices appeared to have overcompensated, substituting vitriolic prose for constitutional analysis. If the majority seemed insensitive to the facts, the minority appeared inattentive to the underlying constitutional issues.

Four months later, on October 27, 1992, Justice Stevens presented a paper on "The Freedom of Speech" at Yale Law School. Building on his observations in *R.A.V.*, Justice Stevens expressed the belief that First Amendment freedoms and judicially created narrowing exceptions to those freedoms will not fit conveniently into a categorical framework, and that Justices White, O'Connor, and Blackmun should accept the passing of the purely categorical approach to the First Amendment. Stevens used this opportunity to demonstrate the similarities between his interpretation of the First Amendment and the majority decision in *R.A.V.* His observation that "when official power is used to prescribe what shall be orthodox in politics and matters of opinion, and to force citizens to adhere to those views, the central purpose of the Amendment is threatened" is consistent with our observation that "the result [of such restrictions] may well be the silencing of political debate, the encouraging of orthodoxy, and the endangering of the individual's right to dissent."

In the speech, as in the concurring opinion, Justice Stevens blurred the line between speech and conduct, distinguishing the burning of a cross at a public rally from burning a cross on someone's front lawn. Clearly the conduct of burning a cross on someone's front lawn is illegal and can be punished, yet the law used to punish the act must be constitutional. This is the basis for an overbreadth challenge. Justice Stevens appeared to embrace this doctrine, yet his repeated assertion that the burning of a cross on another's property is "not protected" rejects the overbreadth doctrine itself, and suggests that only someone who engages in protected conduct may challenge an unconstitutional law. The vast majority of First Amendment cases have involved citizens who have engaged in "illegal" conduct. Without their challenges, many unconstitutional laws would remain on the books threatening freedom of expression and thought, endangering "the central purpose of the amendment" and leading inexorably to orthodoxy in art, literature, music, and politics.

Justice Stevens reminded the Yale audience of the common ground the justices had with one another as well as with all those who support and defend the First Amendment: "Let us hope that whenever we decide to tolerate intolerant speech, the speaker as well as the audience will understand that we do so to express our deep commitment to the value of tolerance—a value protected by every clause in the single sentence called the First Amendment."

In the days following the opinion, other columnists began to examine the decision more closely. Stephen Chapman of the *Chicago Tribune* noted that the decision nullified many campus speech codes; Charles Krauthammer of *The Washington Post* noted that Scalia's opinion had taken dead aim at "political correctness" by refusing to create exceptions to the First Amendment for certain politically unacceptable topics. *The New Republic* applauded the decision and repeated First Amendment champion Alexander Meiklejohn's oft-quoted remark, made after the Court decided *New York Times Co. v. Sullivan,* suggesting that *R.A.V.,* like *Sullivan,* was "an occasion . . . to dance in the streets."

Returning from Athens, as my plane touched down in Minneapolis on June 28 I was unsure of public reaction to the decision. Greeted quietly by family members, I returned home to a full tape on my answering machine. I listened to the entire tape before rewinding and playing it again: there were ten messages, seven congratulations from friends and three threats. The 7–3 ratio seemed fair under the circumstances, but it was sobering to hear messages such as "You are a dead motherfucker" or "Cleary, you are going down in flames, asshole." I reviewed videotapes of local and national news coverage of the case, and was struck by how most local reporters had little understanding of the underlying constitutional issues. Don Shelby of WCCO had been the moderator of the panel at the inner-city high school the day before the Rodney King verdict. He now reminded the television audience that I had consistently noted the availability of the terroristic-threats provision to prosecutors. Mrs. Jones, who refused to be interviewed on camera, expressed her disappointment in the decision but stated that she understood that "most people, like Ed Cleary" were personally appalled by the cross-burning. I played that portion of the tape several times and was grateful for her comment. This entire experience had undoubtedly been traumatic for the Jones family, and it was a great relief to hear her words of understanding.

When I returned to my law office the next day I was not quite sure what to expect. Although there was one threat ("Lawyers should burn on crosses; you should be burned on a cross"), I had received congratulations from friends and fellow members of the local legal community. While Mike and I had received fairly consistent support from other lawyers, little had been forthcoming from a confused public.

Anthony Lewis tells the story of Harvard constitutional-law professor Thomas Reed Powell, who was approached by a student at the end of the term. The student thanked him and said that although he had found the Constitution very confusing at the beginning of the term, thanks to the professor it was now "perfectly clear." Powell's response was "Oh dear." Constitutional-law issues are complex, take a great deal of thought and insight, and are seldom capable of easy resolution. Those educated in constitutional law generally understood our position, whether or not they supported it. Once again I was reminded that we could not expect the public to understand the complex constitutional analysis of a case involving such an ugly factual situation.

Although we had not expected keys to the city, the silence was deafening. Other than congratulations from friends, other lawyers, and a few loyal supporters such as Nat Hentoff, the response was subdued. There were no awards, celebrations, or public acclaim. The ACLU not only failed to congratulate us but circulated a memorandum critical of the opinion to its affiliates. The leadership that had failed to support us at the beginning, that had later offered a lukewarm and critical section of a brief, was now undercutting the decision that they found politically unacceptable. An organization that promoted itself as a nonpartisan civil liberties organization had shown that it was neither.

The rank-and-file members of the ACLU and its many hardworking volunteer attorneys have a right to expect that their leadership is dedicated to the advancement of civil liberties as well as to the protection of civil rights. Perhaps the ACLU leadership changed direction after its loss of membership in 1977, when volunteer attorneys defended the Nazis in Skokie, Illinois. Aryeh Neier noted in 1979 that "the nation's leading free speech organization, the American Civil Liberties Union, has watched a substantial part of its own membership quitting in angry protest over the ACLU's defense of the rights of Nazis who want to march in Skokie." If so, it is particularly disappointing that the organization has retreated from such a courageous and unpopular stance, which is remembered as a truly memorable event in First Amendment advocacy.

In 1980, shortly after Skokie, the ACLU "implemented an aggressive affirmative action plan," requiring that "the 83-member national board be 50% female and 20% minority; homosexuals and people with disabilities were added to the plan." While diversifying the board may have been long overdue, "the new people were brought in with little regard to their views on civil liberties."

Sixty years earlier, the organization had been formed to champion the civil liberties of all American citizens. Time and time again the ACLU had met that mandate, at no small cost to its supporters. Now the organization had sacrificed principle for political expediency, the defense of civil liberties for the promotion of political constituencies. Having vacillated over the Fifth Amendment protection against double jeopardy after the Rodney King riots paved the way for a second trial, the ACLU was now prepared to sacrifice the First Amendment. After offering only lukewarm support in *R.A.V.*, the organization now supported enhancement laws increasing sentences for crimes motivated by bias and a broad definition of sexual harassment, including nontargeted speech deemed offensive by an observer. As Alan Dershowitz, a former ACLU board member, said, "The ACLU is caught in a tug-of-war between civil liberties and the politics of the left, and the politics of the left is winning. . . . It's a terrible tragedy."

Our nation needs a committed and nonpartisan civil liberties organization. There is already a proliferation of interest groups promoting both liberal and conservative agenda. The ACLU leadership's distrust of the *R.A.V.* opinion seemed to stem from opposition to the conservative makeup of the Court, particularly Justice Scalia. Blinded by partisanship, the leaders ignored the fact that Justice Scalia had protected symbolic expression unpopular among conservatives, as in the flag-burning cases. Perhaps the national leadership trails the regional affiliates, as "around the country, there are legal directors of some ACLU affiliates who remain more resolute in this area than most of the national officers and board. They are the ones who did cheer Justice Scalia—seeing the text of his opinion rather than the stereotype of him."

In St. Paul, the atmosphere changed from silence to open hostility. Early on the morning of August 8, 1992, I began receiving calls from friends and family who had read one of the local newspapers. As I opened the paper, my heart sank. On the editorial page was another picture of the Jones family above a headline that read, MONEY SPENT ON CROSS BURNING DEFENSE DECRIED. A long letter to the editor, at the top of the editorial page, was from a man who had called my office a week earlier to ask who had paid us "the $100,000." When I explained to him that we weren't paid, he just became angrier. The paper had printed his letter without contacting me to verify his allegations. The letter stated that public defenders were insensitive, unwilling to help "people of color," and the "citizens of Ramsey County have a right to know how more than $100,000 of taxpayers' money was spent to defend *R.A.V.*" Forgotten was the fact that Mike Cromett and I had worked hard to obtain an acquittal for an African-American man six weeks before I was assigned *R.A.V.* Some people still wanted to believe that we were racist. Nor did it seem to matter that Mike and I had contributed hundreds of hours of uncompensated time. It seemed that few were willing to believe that Mike and I had fought this long and hard because we truly believed the First Amendment was threatened. As Nat Hentoff said later, "It was a Frank Capra script without the applause at the end."

But as weeks passed, legal commentators began to analyze the opinion in a more objective manner. Of the 107 written decisions in the 1991 term, only two resulted in a majority opinion reached by these five justices with the other four joining in concurring opinions. The other case was a minor bankruptcy matter. Although all nine justices had agreed that the St. Paul ordinance was unconstitutional, the areas of agreement and disagreement in reaching that conclusion were unusual for this Court. In failing to sign on with the majority, Justice Byron White parted ways with traditional allies such as the Chief Justice; instead he formed an alliance with others, including Justice Blackmun. Justice Sandra Day O'Connor also opposed those she normally agreed with on the issues, including the other "centrist" members, Justices Kennedy and Souter. This difference of opinion among these three justices, who many observers felt now constituted an emerging center voting block on the Court, was particularly noteworthy because they were so often in agreement during the preceding term.

The only justices who voted consistently with past alliances were Justice Stevens, who often agreed with Justices Blackmun, O'Connor, and White, and Justice Scalia, who often agreed with Justices Thomas, Kennedy, and the Chief Justice, and often disagreed with Justices O'Connor, Stevens, and Blackmun.

Including the elevation of Justice Rehnquist to Chief Justice as a new appointment, the five most recent appointees to the Court had agreed on one approach, while the four older appointees had chosen a different method of analysis. The sole black individual on the Court had voted with the majority, while the only woman had voted to concur with the result but not the approach.

A review of the voting pattern revealed a fairly consistent attitude among the justices toward unpopular symbolic expression. Justices White, Stevens, and O'Connor continued to object to the majority's protective stance toward unpopular symbolic expression. Justices Scalia and Kennedy, regardless of ideology, viewed First Amendment freedoms as extending toward unpopular expression from the left or the right. Justices Souter and Thomas, replacing Justices Brennan and Marshall, voted, as had their predecessors, to protect the First Amendment. It is unknown whether they would have done so had the flag-burning decision been their case of first impression involving unpopular symbolic expression. The only two justices to switch positions from their respective votes on the flag-burning cases were Justice Blackmun and Justice Rehnquist. Perhaps the Chief Justice truly felt that flag-burning was "unique," and that other forms of unpopular expression should be protected. Justice Blackmun, it appeared, believed he was acting consistently by protecting unpopular expression on the far left while suggesting that hateful expression on the far right could be outlawed.

The unanimous result could not obscure the fact that nine justices had struggled over seven months to reach agreement on the proper analysis to the case. All nine justices had disagreed with the Minnesota Supreme Court, perhaps as soon as forty-eight hours after the argument when the first vote was taken. The decision would have been issued within two or three months, rather than seven, had the lower-court's opinion been the only focus. Instead, *R.A.V.* provided a framework for the members of the Court to examine much deeper beliefs about the meaning of free expression and the role of government.

While all nine justices agreed that the St. Paul ordinance was unconstitutional, and that the decision of the Minnesota Supreme Court should be reversed, there had been a pronounced difference in legal reasoning. Two days after the opinion was issued, Linda Greenhouse of *The New York Times* astutely observed that the division among the justices echoed an older, deeper rift among political theorists and constitutional observers concerning the meaning of freedom of expression.

Several weeks before the decision, Ronald Dworkin of NYU Law School had discussed opposing interpretations of the meaning of free expression in an article published in *The New York Review of Books*. Dworkin separated First Amendment theorists into those who embrace the instrumental, or conditional, theory (speech as a means to an end) and those who support a constitutive, or more absolute, justification for free speech (speech as an end in itself). As noted earlier, this distinction has divided First Amendment theorists into two camps. This difference of opinion was now reflected in the opinions written by members of the Court. Justices White, Blackmun, O'Connor, and Stevens advocated the narrow instrumental theory of free expression, while the majority had gone further by adopting the broader view of expression, speech as an end in itself.

Dworkin examined the majority opinion written by Justice Brennan in *New York Times Co. v. Sullivan,* the landmark free-speech case decided by the Warren Court in 1964. In Dworkin's view, Brennan's almost exclusive reliance on the instrumental theory was "dangerous for free speech in ways that have already begun to be realized." Justice Brennan may have been unable to fashion the unanimous decision in *Sullivan* without limiting his reasoning to the "special role" of political speech, providing little protection for "hate speech," since the shielding of offensive and hateful expression can hardly be justified as a means to an end. It is one thing to protect political speech; it is another matter altogether to defend a bigoted viewpoint. Freedom of expression would not truly exist until the Court recognized the right of the individual to express himself without judging the viewpoint expressed. If speech was an end in itself, then the idea conveyed was unimportant. What was important was the exercise of individual liberty. If speech was a means to an end, then freedom of expression was always contingent on the majority's determination that the viewpoint that was conveyed furthered a socially approved end.

After Justices Souter and Thomas had replaced Justices Brennan and Marshall, no one could be certain that prior case law, including *Sullivan,* would lead the Court to protect even offensive expression. In *R.A.V.* not only had the Court struck down the St. Paul ordinance but the majority had recognized that the First Amendment protected more than just political speech or acceptable opinions. It protected the right of the individual to express himself, regardless of his viewpoint.

As Dworkin had concluded weeks before the decision in an observation that could have been taken directly from the *R.A.V.* opinion, "It is the central, defining, premise of freedom of speech that the offensiveness of ideas, or the challenge that they offer to traditional ideas, cannot be a valid reason for censorship; once that premise is abandoned, it is difficult to see what free speech means."

14

"An Occasion . . . to Dance in the Streets"

The result [in *R.A.V.*] was a Supreme Court decision of landmark dimension, a declaration in favor of more speech rather than less. . . . An opinion that will probably stand as one of the Supreme Court's most far-reaching interpretations of the First Amendment.

—*The New York Times,* June 24, 1992

This is an occasion for the friends of free expression to dance in the streets. . . . In a stroke [the Court] has repelled the most serious threat to open debate that the current generation of students has experienced. . . . The *St. Paul* decision deserves to be celebrated. The Rehnquist court has not only reaffirmed but dramatically extended the principle that government may not saddle speech on the basis of its content, and that no insults, no matter how sharply they sting, may be singled out for punishment.

—*The New Republic,* July 13, 1992

R.A.V. v. St. Paul presented complex and emotional issues that split traditional allies when the bitter debate between civil rights and civil liberties advocates left the streets and the universities of the country and arrived at the hallowed chambers of the nation's highest court. Perhaps, then, it should not have come as a surprise that in writing the opinions in *R.A.V.*, the justices often engaged in angry and bitter rhetoric that at times seemed almost personal in tone. Although they were charged with preserving, protecting, and defending the Constitution, they were also members of a society that had struggled with both individual freedom and the advancement of civil rights. Their personal attitudes toward these issues colored the language of their opinions.

Rather than suggesting that the lower court had simply failed to narrow an overbroad law, the Court agreed with us that the law *as written* was incapable of meeting constitutional standards. St. Paul officials had betrayed constitutionally mandated neutrality by choosing certain subjects and viewpoints for prohibition. This result came "closest to treating the St. Paul law as the Court did the flag burning laws."

A closer examination of the opinion reveals that all nine justices agreed with our position but chose to focus on different aspects. We had presented two questions in our petition for certiorari; four of the justices had focused on our general overbreadth argument, while the majority examined the deeper question of whether it was constitutionally permissible to narrowly construe a law that was content-based (selecting certain subjects for proscription—race, color, creed, religion, or gender) in the same manner as content-neutral laws (silent on subject matter). In the first instance, politically incorrect expression on a wide range of topics would be prohibited. In the second instance, the focus would be on the act of causing an immediate breach of the peace without reference to the subject addressed.

If the unanimous result belied the diverse and often conflicting approaches of the justices, the invective used should not be allowed to overshadow that they shared "more common ground than they openly acknowledged in the heat of battle. . . . All of the Justices share . . . a commitment to basic First Amendment principles. Only after we understand these principles—the hard core of a hard-won tradition—can we appreciate the modesty of marginal disagreement in *R.A.V.*"

Viewed in the context of other landmark First Amendment cases, an analysis of the opinions in *R.A.V.* demonstrated that the justices were in agreement on a number of constitutional issues. Amar notes these areas of common ground as it pertains to the First Amendment. First, "symbolic expression is fully embraced by the First Amendment." The constitutional parallel between *R.A.V.* and the flag-burning opinions was ignored by those who focused on the disagreement between those in the majority and those concurring in *R.A.V.* The decision had been an occasion for celebration for those who treasured the First Amendment because,

> after *R.A.V.*, it would be difficult for the Court to undo *Johnson*. The *R.A.V.* majority pointedly invoked the 1989 flag case, and more importantly, reaffirmed its basic principles, fixing it as a polestar in the First Amendment firmament. The *R.A.V.* minority also regularly cited *Johnson*—with less fervor, perhaps, but with no

sign of disapproval—and accepted its basic teachings. . . . *Johnson* is no longer up for grabs.

All this is not simply big news, but good news. . . .

At oral argument, I had purposely linked the symbols banned by the ordinance in *R.A.V.* to previous symbols of political dissent, such as the red flag of *Stromberg* in the 1930s and the black armband of *Tinker* in the 1960s. The Court acknowledged that the burning flag was protected as an unpopular symbolic expression in the years immediately preceding *R.A.V.* The justices had been bitterly divided in the language of the flag-burning decisions. In struggling to resolve issues surrounding controversial expression, some members of the Court were not willing to extend First Amendment protection if personally offended by the symbolic conduct. Had Robert Bork been confirmed instead of Anthony Kennedy, the flag-burning decisions might have been decided differently. Now, in *R.A.V.*, the justices dissenting from the flag-burning decisions acknowledged the importance of protecting unpopular symbolic expression.

Only Justice Stevens seemed unrepentant in his approach to burning flags or burning crosses as he reiterated his position that the "character of expressive activity" affected its constitutional status. It is interesting to note that one of the two "liberals" on the Court seems to have been the least tolerant of unpopular symbolic expression.

The *R.A.V.* Court recognized that the earlier call by the dissenters in *Texas v. Johnson* for the elevating of a symbol (the American flag) to protected status, based on its "unique" status, would never work. The most powerful symbols, the symbols with the greatest communicative impact, cannot be protected against some uses or banned for others without undermining basic First Amendment principles. After *R.A.V.*, the Court made clear its position that unpopular symbolic expression originating from either fringe of the political spectrum would be protected and not singled out as an exception that could swallow the rule.

The second area of agreement was that "government may not regulate the physical medium with the purpose of suppressing the ideological message." Unpopular symbolic expression has been used in protest for over two hundred years. Every elementary-school student learns about the Boston Tea Party. The colonists who dumped tea in Boston harbor over two centuries ago to protest British taxation without representation certainly had alternative methods of communication available. Yet symbolic expression is often more powerful than the spoken or written word. As a consequence, government may punish flag-burning and cross-burning under general public burning restrictions, but it may not prohibit the underlying message. In *R.A.V.*, all justices agreed that "laws that restrict speech must be scrutinized to flush out illegitimate motivation." As Justice Scalia wrote for the majority, the issue is whether or not there is a "realistic possibility that official suppression of ideas is afoot."

The third area of common belief, that "political expression—especially expression critical of government—lies at the core of the First Amendment," solidified the landmark holding of *New York Times Co. v. Sullivan,* which provided for the criticism of public officials, a principle that later became the foundation for the holding in *Texas v. Johnson.* The Court agreed that protected expression could be prosecuted only when it became illegal conduct, losing its protected status. The Court reiterated that close scrutiny must be applied to prosecution of political protest. As Amar points out, both the majority and concurring opinions specifically reminded the nation that "citizen criticism of governmental officials" is the core of First Amendment activity. Even Justice Stevens, who was publicly critical of the majority decision, acknowledged that burning "a cross to announce a rally" would almost certainly be protected expression.

The critical holding of *New York Times Co. v. Sullivan* was preserved. The majority went even further, noting the importance of political speech as a means to an end (a check on the power of public officials), while acknowledging that speech was an end in itself (the individual's right to dissent from the majority, even offensively, so long as there is no intent to threaten or terrorize, which can be prohibited by other general laws). Compare the facts of *R.A.V.* with those from the famous civil rights march in Alabama, from Selma to Montgomery, three decades earlier. Participants in both events were cited for listener hostility resulting from offensive expression based on race. As long as such laws are available to government officials, those who dissent are vulnerable to selective enforcement. If charges were used that required a showing of an intent to threaten or terrorize, the factual allegations of *R.A.V.* could have been addressed, while the civil rights marchers of thirty years ago would have been safe from successful prosecution.

Use of general laws to punish criminal conduct is not a retreat from progressive principles. It is a recognition that when the government abandons its neutrality by selecting certain subjects for a preferred viewpoint, the potential for abuse against the citizenry is pronounced. Such laws not only are patronizing but may turn a disfavored viewpoint into a martyr's cause and, in the case of racism or anti-Semitism, strengthen its support.

Finally, after *R.A.V.*, "courts must guard vigilantly against . . . discrimination against disfavored viewpoints." Justice Scalia observed for the majority that the government may not regulate speech based on hostility or favoritism toward the underlying message expressed. As an example that the application of an agreed-upon principle may lead to differing results, the concurring justices failed to recognize that the law demonstrated "hostility" to a given viewpoint. Perhaps in an effort to dissociate themselves from the ugly factual allegations, these justices concluded that an intolerant or hateful viewpoint on these topics was simply not a viewpoint at all. All justices agreed in the abstract that viewpoint discrimination is a serious threat to freedom of expression, as Justice Stevens noted, "because such regulation often indicates a legislative effort to skew public debate on an issue."

Despite attempts by some groups to undercut the decision in frustration at their failure to achieve a political agenda, *R.A.V.* greatly strengthened the foundation of freedom of expression. Solidifying the holdings enunciated in the landmark cases of *New York Times Co. v. Sullivan* from 1964 and *Texas v. Johnson* from 1989, *R.A.V.* had gone even further. A conservative court had announced that it too would stand behind the First Amendment in a nonpartisan manner even while it restrictively interpreted the Fourth Amendment. Justices Souter and Thomas, replacing Brennan and Marshall, had not abandoned the First Amendment position of their predecessors on offensive symbolic expression, and, as Amar wrote, their vote was "a welcome and, one hopes, auspicious First Amendment development."

Seventy years earlier, the First Amendment had experienced a rebirth under Justices Holmes and Brandeis at that most perilous time, World War I. In the intervening years, certain exceptions had been carved from this freedom, including obscenity, libel, and "fighting words." In *R.A.V.*, the Court now acknowledged that earlier Courts, including liberal Courts, had "narrowed the scope of the traditional categorical exceptions," and that the remaining exceptions were not completely unprotected. Even expression that fit within one of these exceptions could not be punished under a law that was aimed at a subcategory of that exception. "The State may penalize obscenity, libel, fighting words, and subversive speech, so long as it uses the specific content demarcations the Court has approved for each category. But once the State chooses to penalize a subset of one of those categories, it alters the content line and raises new First Amendment questions." If government encroached on freedom of expression, it could do so only in recognition of the underlying evil addressed by the exception (maintaining public safety), without pursuing a thinly disguised political agenda (punishing only breaches of the peace caused by certain volatile topics). If it chose to punish "fighting words," it would have to do so under a law that punishes the precipitation of a fight regardless of the subject addressed. Though the *R.A.V.* Court did not throw out the fighting-words exception entirely, it remains a doctrine of questionable utility and uncertain constitutional merit.

There were those who felt that the preservation of neutral principles benefited only the established order and did little to address inequality among the citizens of this country. Recognizing that they were seeking to establish a precedent for censorship did little to inhibit such advocates because they believed their own intolerance of viewpoint justified the silencing of ugly and offensive expression.

David Cole of Georgetown Law Center has observed that "the majority will most often seek to regulate the speech of the politically powerless. . . . If an idea is unpopular, the only thing that may protect it from the majority is a constitutional norm of content neutrality." Cole, also an active member of the Center for Constitutional Rights, disagreed with the Center and supported us in the *R.A.V.* case. A well-known human-rights advocate and longtime supporter of the First Amendment, he and I were in agreement that the debate was not as simple as suggesting that those who supported free expression in this case did so at the expense of civil rights. In an article addressed to his traditional allies who had opposed his position, Cole noted:

> Speech is a powerful tool for change for those dissatisfied with their position in society, but it will remain that way only if, with vigor, we presumptively forbid the majority from suppressing speech of which it disapproves. The principle of content neutrality keeps open the possibility for political change.
>
> Whether content neutrality is an illusion or an ideal, it is all that stands between the dissenter and the majority. And as long as society remains unequal, disadvantaged minorities will find themselves far more often in dissent. To empower the majority to regulate the speech of dissenters when the majority's values happen to be aligned with our own is a terrible mistake. This once, we would do better to side with Justice Scalia.

It is this protection of the right to dissent, the "near universal agreement now, as there was not in 1919 or 1954, that political dissent may be not be subject to the coercive power of the state," that provided the core of our argument in *R.A.V. v. St. Paul.* The pragmatic foundation for this position was later summarized by Kathleen Sullivan's observation that "gearing the First Amendment for the worst of times requires practice even in the best. A benevolent government promoting messages of racial equality one day may be taken over by rogues the next, and content neutrality is an emergency preparedness device."

If "pragmatic reason will often lead to the same conclusion as First Amendment faith," what occurs when pragmatic reason and First Amendment faith are not so closely allied? On June 23, 1992, hours after the United States Supreme Court handed down its decision in *R.A.V. v. City of St. Paul,* the Wisconsin Supreme Court struck down Wisconsin's enhancement hate-crime laws, and cited *R.A.V.* as controlling precedent. Since the decision was issued soon after *R.A.V.* and quoted from the opinion at length, it seems reasonable to assume that the members of the Wisconsin Supreme Court had deliberated at length before *R.A.V.* was decided and had used the opinion to bolster their reasoning.

State of Wisconsin v. Todd Mitchell involved a statute that, though related to the St. Paul ordinance, was easily distinguishable as well. Mitchell had been convicted of aggravated battery, normally punishable by a maximum sentence of two years. Because a jury had found that Mitchell had "intentionally selected the person against whom the crime was committed because of the race of that person," the potential maximum sentence for Mitchell was increased to seven years. The statute was known as an "enhancement law"—that is, the sentence was "enhanced" because of the racial motivation of the defendant. A majority of states have such laws, which, unlike the city ordinance, require criminal conduct before the enhancement penalty may be invoked. Under the St. Paul ordinance, one could be guilty of a crime simply for expressing himself in an offensive manner. Enhancement laws present a different issue.

Mitchell was *R.A.V.* come full circle. The defendant, a nineteen-year-old black man, had left a theater where *Mississippi Burning* had been playing. The movie contained scenes of burning crosses and scenes of assaults on civil rights workers. Mitchell then became involved in an assault on a fourteen-year-old white male, Gregory Riddick, whose only crime was having been in the wrong place at the wrong time. A decision from a case involving an alleged white racist had now been used by the Wisconsin Supreme Court to throw out a law cited in order to increase the sentence of a young black felon. The law used in *Mitchell* addressing hate crime was on different constitutional ground from the St. Paul ordinance that prohibited hate speech. Many felt the majority opinion in *R.A.V.* had indicated a "sharp distinction between regulations of conduct directed at communicative content and all other attempts to penalize conduct." One of the dissenters, Justice Shirley S. Abrahamson, felt that it was the "tight nexus between the selection of the victim and the underlying crime that saves this statute," tying "discriminatory selection of a victim to conduct already punishable by state law in a manner sufficient to prevent erosion of First Amendment protection of bigoted speech and ideas." Noting that the statute was not similar to the St. Paul ordinance and that we had not challenged an enhancement charge, Judge Abrahamson dissented from the majority decision.

It was true that we had not challenged the enhancement assault law used to charge *R.A.V.;* this was because we had felt such laws were less problematic constitutionally than the St. Paul city ordinance. The state later dismissed the charge after the *R.A.V.* decision for lack of jurisdiction because R.A.V. had turned nineteen.

Several days later I received a phone call from Michael Sandberg, the Midwest civil rights director of the Anti-Defamation League of B'nai B'rith. Michael was the only *amici* lawyer to call and congratulate me—and he had opposed me! The ADL had not approved of the St. Paul ordinance, but they feared that if the ordinance was struck down, the enhancement laws would be in danger. Congratulating me, he added that he was worried about the future of enhancement laws, although he felt that they would withstand challenges. Bias motivation laws in many states were based on model legislation drafted by the ADL.

Sandberg had correctly assumed that *R.A.V.* would confuse and perhaps endanger enhancement laws. A House subcommittee in Congress held hearings later in the summer to discuss the constitutionality of federal penalty-enhancement legislation. Most constitutional law experts believed that the Court would not extend the *R.A.V.* doctrine to enhancement laws. On December 14, 1992, the Supreme Court agreed to review an appeal from the state of Wisconsin to clarify whether a decision that struck down the government's right to create special bias crimes prevented a sentence-enhancement approach. By December 1992 Ohio and Wisconsin had struck down such laws while Oregon and Florida had upheld similar provisions. The time was ripe for the United States Supreme Court to settle and clarify the remaining question left by *R.A.V.*

It appeared that hate-crime laws, which provided a penalty enhancement and separately punished certain "motives" (bias against race, religion, gender), would pass scrutiny. The larger issue was pragmatic: was this the best method to combat social evils, particularly in light of the potential cost to the First Amendment?

Edmund Burke, in his famous speech "On Conciliation with America" noted the limits of force. "If you do not succeed, you are without resource: for conciliation failing, force remains; but force failing, no further hope of reconciliation is left." In the context of social engineering within the criminal code, one commentator has accurately pointed out:

> Criminalization is the state method of persuasion of last resort. Resort to criminalization of bigoted motives indicates that we are ready to give up on the possibility that, without the threat of criminal prosecution, people will eventually come to realize that bigotry is wrong. This official acknowledgment of defeat in the quest for interethnic acceptance and respect . . . creates a symbolic message that runs counter to the self-affirming and educative value of the law.

It is doubtful that many really believe that laws of this type will increase tolerance and human understanding. As the rationale is not one of rehabilitation, presumably it is one of deterrence. It is arguable that the best method of deterring criminal activity is to ensure that those who engage in such behavior know that they risk apprehension and swift and certain punishment regardless of motive. In the Wisconsin case, if Mitchell's aggravated-battery conviction carried a maximum sentence of two years without a bias motive, and a sentence of seven years with such motive, the implication is that the criminal conduct itself is less serious (two years) than the improper motive (an additional five years). As one newspaper editorial observed:

> Why should a hoodlum who attacks someone because he hates white (or black) people . . . be punished more severely than a hoodlum who attacks someone because he hates *all* people? . . . Besides, there may be some risk that in its eagerness to condemn bias crimes as worse than others, society may send the unintended message that robbery or assault, absent a bigoted motive, isn't really so bad or doesn't terrorize others beyond immediate victims.

A reasonable and pragmatic consideration of such laws reveals their dangerousness. When a law increases the maximum penalty from two to seven years because of the improper "thought" or "motive" of the defendant, the potential for abuse in defining improper motives is obvious. Jurors often must determine the element of criminal intent that can be inferred through the actions of the defendant. Yet they may be unable to probe the heart and the mind of the defendant for evidence of bias or unacceptable thoughts, and it is dangerous to allow them to try. As *The New York Times* has noted in discussing the Wisconsin case, "If the state prevails, it is far from clear that the forces of civic order will necessarily be the ultimate victors. . . . There is no guarantee that hate-crime laws will be precise, neutrally applied instruments in the hands of prosecutors." Perhaps this is the final irony—that the groups who seek protection under these laws may often be victimized by them, just as they have been by student speech codes.

By the end of the term in July of 1992, conservatives were angry, liberals hopeful, and the media surprised by the direction of the Supreme Court. It had not overruled *Roe v. Wade* and had extended the ban on school prayer despite the vehement opposition of Justice Scalia. In *R.A.V.* the Court had refused to allow local governments to specify subject matters within an unprotected class of speech. In article after article, reporters and journalists searched for an explanation. To describe certain members of the Court they began using the same words, such as "centrist" or "moderate," when they tried to explain why the Court had not moved as far right as predicted. Only Justice Clarence Thomas developed as predicted, confirming "the worst fears of his liberal critics. . . . He is a confident, aggressive revisionist, willing to make radical legal changes. . . ."

To explain this unforeseen shift by the Court, observers quickly focused on the three justices who had voted together 71 percent of the time: Justices Sandra O'Connor, Anthony Kennedy, and David Souter. Many explanations were offered for the "powerful, if qualified, reaffirmations of some of the Court's most important modern precedents." Vincent Blasi of Columbia Law School observed that "it's easy to take potshots from the ideological extreme, but when your judgments actually determine the future of the Constitution, it tends to make you more responsible."

Perhaps other forces were at work as well. In October 1992 *The New York Times* noted that Justices O'Connor, Kennedy, and Souter had recently acknowledged publicly both their affection and gratitude to their two liberal predecessors, Justices William J. Brennan, Jr., and Thurgood Marshall. Perhaps these retired justices had influenced the three sitting members of the Court more than previously realized.

Justice Souter noted that Justice Brennan had been the author of opinions "that form our constitutional landscape today. . . . The fact is that the sight and sound and thought of our contemporary world is in a great measure the reflection of Justice Brennan's constitutional perceptions." There also may have been recognition by Justices O'Connor, Souter, and Kennedy that political ideology is an insufficient basis for striking down significant precedents.

As the Supreme Court experiences internal transformation the nation for which it functions changes as well. "More women than men are now enrolled in colleges, and by the year 2000 two out of every three new workers will be women and minorities." California's demographic research unit estimates that California will have a "minority majority" as early as 1996. Others predict that the nation will assume a majority composed of minority citizens in the mid-twenty-first century. The Census Bureau predicts that by then over 82 million people will have arrived in this country since 1991, and that as early as 2013 the Hispanic population will surpass the numbers of blacks. One newspaper notes, "This great realignment, unimaginable in almost any other nation on earth, will affect every aspect of American society." One result of this demographic realignment will be continued friction among those of different ethnic and religious backgrounds. But the transition from a predominantly white society to one considerably more diverse will be only as uneventful as we allow it to be.

By January of 1993 even the NAACP Legal Defense Fund understood the limitations of hate-crime legislation, stating that such laws don't "get at the real problem, which is profound ignorance and frustration. In the long run, making society more tolerant is both much more in keeping with our aspirational values as a country and our First Amendment concerns."

The need for harmony between different racial and religious groups will become paramount to our nation's future leaders. The cry to punish those who hold intolerant views will intensify. Now is the time to teach the need to balance individual freedom with responsibility toward others.

At the Beit Hashoah-Museum of Tolerance in Los Angeles, visitors are confronted with ugly reminders and vivid images of the history of intolerance. They are reminded that we share individual and collective responsibility for the perpetuation of such attitudes. They are cautioned never to forget the past and, in the words of Simon Wiesenthal, "Only know that hope lives when people remember."

And remember we must. Yet we also need to forget; ancient

animosities must be overcome. Parent to child, teacher to student, we can teach tolerance without resorting to indoctrination. It will be a continuing challenge to us all, but as a nation we have met such challenges before. Part of remembering is acknowledging that, historically, individual freedom has prevented abuses perpetuated by those in power.

Throughout the world, ethnic conflict and societal fragmentation have reached epidemic proportions. Whether in Bosnia, the Caucasus, Sri Lanka, Cyprus, or Northern Ireland, "both sides in an ethnic conflict will demonize and dehumanize the other side, just as warring nations do. . . . Among traumatized national groups, . . . there is an incapacity analogous to the narcissism or self-centeredness of individuals, who see themselves as having been so hurt or deprived in the past that they can attend only to their own needs, feeling little or no empathy for the hurt they inflict upon others." As one writer observed, there are

> some African-Americans who hate the Jews and some Jews who hate the Arabs, some Arabs who hate the gays and some gays who hate the Cubans and some Cubans who hate the Mexicans and some Mexicans who hate the Italians and some Italians who hate the African-Americans. And everyone's got God perched birdlike on his shoulder, whispering into his ear that his hatreds are the most just.

The lessons of history exist to guide us into the future. Our nation will become even more racially and ethnically diverse. We have seen what has happened in other countries where ethnic tensions explode into violence. But intolerant opinions will not disappear under threat of force. In our own country, some criminals will continue to be motivated by intolerance, just as others are motivated by greed, drug habits, or generalized anger. The nation must punish criminal conduct swiftly and decisively, remembering that "labels themselves have consequences, and the very act of labeling a violent incident as a crime of bias can itself fan the flames. . . ." We must preserve, protect, and defend the First Amendment both for those in power and for the powerless, all of whom benefit in a free and democratic society. Great strides need to be taken to achieve equality for all our citizens, but not at the expense of the basic right of individual thought and expression. We will not win or make tolerant the hearts and minds of others by silencing them, and when force fails, we will have accomplished little while sacrificing a great deal.

Back in St. Paul, life has not been easy for R.A.V. Silent throughout much of the case, he acknowledged again after the decision that he was a white separatist. In August 1992 he was charged by local authorities for scuffling with a police officer after one of his companions allegedly yelled "White power" to a white police officer. He was ordered to pay a fine of $100 or to do twenty hours of community service. In October the adult who had pleaded guilty to the St. Paul ordinance, Arthur M. Miller III, was indicted for the original June 21, 1990, incident for conspiring to interfere with the Jones family's right of access to housing by intimidation and the threat of force. The indictment demonstrated once again that both state and federal laws are available to punish targeted terroristic behavior without encroaching upon the First Amendment. Although the federal prosecution appears to violate double jeopardy, the Supreme Court has held that the federal government may investigate and prosecute such crimes in lieu of or in addition to state prosecutions if they fail, as seen in the Rodney King case.

The Joneses continue to live in the house on Earl Street. Thrust into the public eye, they appeared to welcome a return to privacy.

In December of 1992, another cross-burning occurred in the front yard of a black family living in a Minneapolis suburb. Local prosecutors appreciated the lesson of the R.A.V. decision and, rather than resorting to bias laws, charged the individuals with the more serious felony of terroristic threats. Both teenage defendants pleaded guilty to the offense.

A letter that I received in September of 1992 triggered a memory that had long lain dormant. Thirty years earlier, as a nine-year-old boy in the autumn of 1962, I stood next to my father in a long line at the National Archives in Washington, D.C. The room was dark and there were guards on either side of what appeared to be a mysterious platform. Although not very exciting for a nine-year-old, the hush surrounding the slowly moving line in a room so near to the United States Capitol had its effect on me and I remained quiet. All I knew was that I was going to get the opportunity to see some important historical documents. When we finally reached the platform, I saw some faded parchment under thick glass before we had to move on. Now, three decades later, a man I had never met had taken the time to send me a letter saying that he had been in Washington doing the "usual tourist stuff with the kids." He continued:

Later that day, we went to the National Archives. To get in, you have to pass through a metal detector and an x-ray setup like an airport, and inside, the Constitution is protected in a metal case and it is behind glass so thick you can barely see the document, and there is a guard standing on each side. At night, the whole thing is lowered into a vault beneath the floor.

I want you to know that as I was waiting in line there, I thought to myself that it is lawyers like you who are the real protectors of the Constitution. You should be proud.

I *was* proud. It was more credit than I deserved, and I was grateful that this attorney had taken the time to evoke a forgotten moment with my father.

Shortly after I received this letter, I drove south from St. Paul to the cemetery two miles from the farm my great-grandfather had homesteaded on March 17, 1860. The skies were clear and sunny and boys were playing baseball on a ball field adjoining the cemetery. I left my car and walked over to the section where my relatives rested. Each in his own time and in his own way had embraced both the promise and the reality of the American dream. As I approached my father's grave I walked by the resting place of Jeremiah O'Keefe, the Irish immigrant who had created a life for his family on the nearby farm; Daniel Patrick Ryan, O'Keefe's brother-in-law who had joined the Union Army at the age of eighteen and fought at Gettysburg before serving in the Minnesota Legislature; and Patrick Henry O'Keefe, Jeremiah's son, who had served as the local prosecutor during World War I and as a delegate to the Democratic National Convention that nominated Woodrow Wilson, and had inspired his nephew, my father, to dedicate his life to the law.

Lastly I came to my father's grave. The stone noted that he had been an officer in the United States Navy. He had fought for his country in some of the greatest naval battles in history. He had been a tolerant and courageous man. There were thousands of men and women like him who had lived quietly, dedicating their days to their families, never forgetting the honor of being an American citizen and understanding the responsibility such a privilege entailed.

So much had happened since he died shortly after the Minnesota Supreme Court's decision, so many events that I would have given anything to share with him. So many times I had been told "Your father would have been so proud." I would never again share a laugh with him or a knowing glance. After the decision had come down, Mike and I had received congratulations from very few members of the public. We had learned to live with the fact that we would not receive such a response. We had accepted this; but I regretted that I would never again get a pat on the shoulder from the man whose approval was so important to me, the man who had taken a nine-year-old boy to see an aging parchment under the glass.

As I turned and walked away toward the car I could have sworn I heard applause. When I looked back I realized that the noise had come from the wind whipping through the tops of the cornstalks in the field next to the cemetery. Then the breeze stopped and the only sound was the laughter of the young ballplayers down the road.

———— ■ ————

The Lessons of History

The men were dressed in dark uniforms with concealed automatic weapons. As they patrolled from the top of the building, they looked down below at the fenced-in group of mostly Jewish observers. Several towers stood starkly outlined against the threatening clouds above. Frigid gusts of wind and rain pelted the crowd below, who sat or stood in a sea of mud.

This was not Germany or Poland in 1943. The date was April 22, 1993, as I sat with others and awaited the beginning of the dedication ceremony for the United States Holocaust Memorial Museum in Washington, D.C. The armed guards were there to protect visiting dignitaries as well as the president, the vice president, and their wives. The towers were part of the museum, purposely designed to re-create the appearance of a concentration camp. The mostly Jewish crowd was confined voluntarily. On this day and in this place, the effect was chilling.

For the first time since the United States Supreme Court decided *R.A.V.,* I had returned the previous day to Washington, D.C., to observe the oral arguments before the Court in the case of *Wisconsin v. Mitchell.* As I entered the Court chamber, I was seated near the area of the room reserved for members of the media. In discussing the case with several members of the press, it became clear that they were divided regarding the probable outcome.

R.A.V. had been charged under both the ill-fated St. Paul ordinance and an "enhancement" hate-crime law similar to the Wisconsin law challenged by Mitchell. The St. Paul ordinance had been directed solely at expression. Speech or symbolic speech that aroused "anger, alarm or resentment in others" on the basis of certain subject matter could lead to prosecution. Although the allegations in *R.A.V.* had constituted criminal conduct (i.e., trespass, terroristic threats), the St. Paul ordinance had addressed not that criminal conduct but the offensive viewpoint. Consequently, we had challenged only the ordinance and not the enhancement law, believing that the Court would give much greater latitude to lawmakers to punish conduct motivated by bias, rather than allowing them to prohibit the expression of the viewpoint itself. We were a little surprised that the Wisconsin Supreme Court threw out the state's hate-crime law the day after the *R.A.V.* decision, based in part on the reasoning of the Court in *R.A.V.* The St. Paul ordinance was clearly directed at expression and more closely mirrored the speech codes prevalent on campuses throughout the nation; enhancement laws were easily distinguishable in principle, if not in spirit.

As the oral argument in *Wisconsin v. Mitchell* began on the morning of April 21, it was immediately apparent that the members of the Court saw a very clear distinction between laws aimed at expression and laws initially directed at criminal conduct.

The case had split many of the same traditional allies who had opposed each other in the *R.A.V.* case. Although we had not challenged the enhancement provision in *R.A.V.*, I was not in favor of such laws. I believed that it was a mistake to confuse the meeting of minimal constitutional standards with the formulating of wise public policy. I was disappointed to learn that the ACLU had filed a brief on behalf of the government; I could not understand how a civil liberties organization could argue for lengthening the incarceration period for defendants while minimizing the danger of governmental regulation of individual beliefs. The issue was never one of public safety; a severe sentence for one convicted of criminal conduct is not necessarily objectionable. The same sentence becomes dangerous only when it is attributed in part to the actor's beliefs, opinions, and even hatreds.

Mitchell involved a repugnant act (an assault on a defenseless individual) initiated as a result of a despicable underlying impetus—hatred based on racial identity. Yet the penalty-enhancement approach to punishment of such conduct is not limited to such egregious circumstances. By separately punishing motive, such laws open the door to increased incarceration for other unpopular opinions. Significantly, sentences for crimes against property (trespass) are enhanced in many states, as well as crimes against the person (assault). It does not take a great deal of insight to see how this practice could go awry. Increased sentences could be levied against those who "trespassed" while expressing other unpopular beliefs (e.g., abortion protesters, abortion-rights advocates, civil rights marchers, antiwar demonstrators). Selective prosecution based on majoritarian beliefs would remain a danger; the fragmentation of society would continue in the name of public safety.

As is often the case with First Amendment principles, those who argue the potential danger of such laws are accused of being First

Amendment "absolutists." Yet as I sat and listened to the argument in *Wisconsin v. Mitchell,* unintended applications of such laws seemed inevitable. Consider this exchange between a member of the Court and Attorney General James Doyle arguing on behalf of the state of Wisconsin:

> Question: What if in the draft card case the statute said that your penalty would be enhanced if you did it because of disagreement with the person's views about the Vietnam war, whether they were pro or con?

> Answer: In my view . . . that would be constitutional.

Those who believed that the Court would extend the *R.A.V.* doctrine to laws that primarily punish criminal conduct failed to consider that this was a "law and order" Court. Having acknowledged a year earlier the risk in allowing a law to endanger the First Amendment right of free expression, the Court now seemed to minimize the potential peril when a law focuses initially on criminal conduct. Chief Justice Rehnquist and Justices Scalia and Kennedy, the core of the majority in *R.A.V.,* clearly indicated by their questions to Lynn Adelman (the state senator from Milwaukee who was arguing in behalf of Mitchell) that they saw a sharp distinction between the St. Paul ordinance and the Wisconsin statute. A principled and dedicated man politically left of center, Adelman believed passionately in his cause. Since I thought the laws were probably constitutional though ill conceived, it was difficult to hear the Court sympathize with the government's argument.

Learning that Lynn Adelman's parents had tickets to the dedication ceremony the next day but would be unable to attend, I asked for and received a ticket to the museum's dedication events. The cherry blossoms had mostly faded and the weather turned ugly as the morning of April 22 dawned. As I sat in the rain waiting for the ceremony to begin I observed a large video screen showing scenes from Germany and Poland during World War II, and watched intently as the screen flashed a photograph of a Nazi book-burning rally from the 1930s; it was a stark, three-story black-and-white image of a nation sliding into the abyss six decades earlier.

The lesson seemed clear, though it has often been disregarded because of the passions of the moment. When government officials, well-meaning or evil, attempt to dictate acceptable thought, word, or opinion, a nation is in grave peril. It can happen anywhere, but it is less likely to occur when the members of a society are willing to allow all viewpoints, even discredited and unpopular ones, to be expressed. The Framers had understood this; the Court in *R.A.V.* had reaffirmed the necessity of eternal vigilance against the imposition of orthodoxy.

As each speaker reminded the audience of the necessity never to forget the horror of state-sanctioned genocide, the audience sat silently in the rain and the wind. Elie Wiesel reminded President Clinton of the horrors in Bosnia, and I recalled once again that man's inhumanity to man knows no ethnic or religious boundaries; the killing fields of Cambodia, the deserts of Iraq, and the mountains of Bosnia all serve as significant reminders of the end result of collective hatred. Yet hatred cannot be outlawed; the solution is much more complex.

As in *R.A.V. v. St. Paul,* the United States Supreme Court reached a unanimous decision in the case of *Wisconsin v. Mitchell.* That is where the similarity ended. The Court had taken over six months to reach a decision in *R.A.V.; Mitchell* was decided in less than two. The *R.A.V.* decision included a majority opinion and three concurring opinions; *Mitchell* consisted of one brief, unanimous opinion less than a quarter of the length of *R.A.V.* The collective energy of the Court appeared to have been spent on *R.A.V.; Mitchell* appeared simply to delineate the parameters of the *R.A.V.* doctrine.

In an opinion filed on June 11, 1993, and written by Chief Justice Rehnquist, the Court upheld the penalty-enhancement approach to bias crimes. The Minnesota Supreme Court had taken a position to the Court's obvious displeasure; the Wisconsin Supreme Court had taken the opposite with the same result. In summary fashion, the Court reaffirmed the holding in *R.A.V.* and gave clear notice that although *R.A.V.* would continue to stand with other landmark First Amendment cases, *Mitchell* would be relegated to that group of decisions involving failed challenges to the sentencing phase of criminal convictions:

> Nothing in our decision last Term in *R.A.V.* compels a different result here. That case involved a First Amendment challenge to a municipal ordinance prohibiting the use of " 'fighting words' that insult or provoke violence, 'on the basis of race, color, creed, religion or gender.' " . . . Because the ordinance only proscribed a class of "fighting words" deemed particularly offensive by the city . . . we held that it violated the rule against content-based discrimination. . . . But whereas the ordinance struck down in *R.A.V.* was explicitly directed at expression (i.e., "speech" or "messages")

. . . the statute in this case is aimed at conduct unprotected by the
First Amendment.

In somewhat disingenuous fashion, the Court stated that "a physical assault is not by any stretch of the imagination expressive conduct
protected by the First Amendment." No one had ever argued that
such conduct was protected. The conduct itself could be punished
severely; it was the actor's beliefs precipitating the conduct resulting
in additional punishment that opened the door to dangerous applications of such laws in the future.

R.A.V. stands for the proposition that every citizen has a right to
think what he wants and to say what he thinks. *Mitchell* further
defines that doctrine; laws are permissible that focus on criminal
conduct as a prerequisite to punishing beliefs. If convicted of criminal
conduct, one is now subject to additional punishment for one's motivation, even if that motivation is a strongly held belief.

A year earlier, a conservative Court had stood up for the First
Amendment in an emotionally charged case. Believing that they were
not retreating from this position, the Court now stated that where
government could justify its actions (maintaining the public safety)
without favoring one side of the debate (targeting those who violate
the criminal code motivated by a belief on either side of an issue), the
First Amendment was not at risk.

Yet there is a thin line between punishing motivation and penaliz-
ing dissenting opinion. The Court's focus on the governmental interest asserted allows officials to use the broad justification of law and
order as a subterfuge to suppress the expression of unpopular beliefs.
Too many criminal laws (against trespass, disorderly conduct, etc.)
lend themselves to this type of misapplication. *R.A.V.* prohibits the
direct suppression of dissenting opinion; *Mitchell* must not be allowed to indirectly undermine that critical holding. Presumably the
Court will view other laws much differently if there is, in Justice
Scalia's words from *R.A.V.*, a "realistic possibility that official suppression of ideas is afoot." The Court did not feel the Wisconsin law
constituted such a threat; it remains to be seen whether other such
laws do.

As I left the dedication ceremony for the Holocaust museum, I was
confronted by several angry protesters holding signs and screaming
anti-Semitic epithets at me. As police officers on horseback moved to
protect the crowd, I stared back at the demonstrators. Looming
behind their placards stood the familiar outline of the Jefferson Memorial. Jefferson understood that beliefs—any beliefs—will never be

genuine if held under the threat of force, and that our nation must always tolerate the dissenting voice. Over two centuries later, the struggle for individual liberty continues, and as I turned away from the demonstrators and started down the street, I recalled the inscription encircling Thomas Jefferson in his Memorial:

I have sworn upon the altar of God eternal hostility against every form of tyranny over the mind of man.

Notes

◼

Prologue

xix   "In a way . . .": Manolis Andronicas, *Delphi* (Athens: Ekdotike Athenon S.A., 1976) 7.

Chapter 1

3   Hermann Hesse, *Demian* (New York: Bantam ed., 1966), 95.
For a discussion of the events of June 21, 1990, see "The Case for Hate," *Life* (Bill of Rights issue), Fall 1991, 88.

4   Statistics are taken from St. Paul *Pioneer Press*, May 30, 1992, 1A; November 4, 1992, 17A; March 19, 1992, 8B; July 31, 1992, 14A; December 22, 1991, 14A; Twin City *Reader*, January 15–21, 1992, 8.

5   "The experience of . . .": Kenneth T. Jackson, *The Ku Klux Klan and the City, 1915–1930* (Chicago: Ivan R. Dee, Inc., 1992), 161.

6   Stephen Maxwell later had a distinguished career as the first African-American judge appointed in Ramsey County. When my father passed away in 1991, he acted as a pallbearer at the funeral.

7   For an accurate examination of the pressures and dilemmas facing public defenders nationwide, see Charles J. Ogletree, Jr., "Beyond Justifications: Seeking Motivations to Sustain Public Defenders," 106 *Harvard Law Review* 1239 (1993). Ogletree cites empathy and heroism as the primary motivations for becoming and remaining a public defender, concluding "the morality and legitimacy of our system of criminal justice depends on our ability to motivate people to defend the indigent," 1294.
For accounts of the murder trials, see Minneapolis *Star Tribune*, May 10, 1990, 5B; December 4, 1987, 1A.

8   Bias assault law: St. Paul City Ordinance section 292.01, reads as follows: Whoever, intentionally, or in reckless disregard of so doing, puts another in fear of immediate bodily harm or death by placing on public or private property a symbol, object, appellation, characterization or graffiti, including but not limited to a burning cross or Nazi swastika, which is reasonably understood as communicating threats of harm, violence, contempt or hatred on the basis of race, color, creed,

religion or gender commits an assault and shall be guilty of a misdemeanor.

R.A.V.'s comments: "The Case for Hate," *Life;* James Walsh, "Cross-burning victim, suspect discuss feelings," Minneapolis *Star Tribune,* June 24, 1992, 1B.

10 Terroristic threats statute: Minnesota Statute section 609.713 (1) provides: Whoever threatens, directly or indirectly, to commit any crime of violence with the purpose to terrorize another . . . or in reckless disregard of causing such terror . . . may be sentenced to imprisonment for not more than five years.

David H. Bennett, *The Party of Fear* (New York: Vintage Books, 1990).

"alien intruders . . .": Ibid., 2.

"the removal of aliens . . .": Ibid., 111.

"real" Americans: Ibid., 101. See also "The Case for Hate," *Life,* 88. R.A.V. is pictured wearing a T-shirt stating "Proud to be an American."

"plain American": St. Paul *Pioneer Press,* July 31, 1992, 14A.

"one-third of . . .": Bennett, *Fear,* 29.

Irish immigration: Ibid., 62.

"less than ten percent . . .": Ibid., 70.

anti-alien upheaval: Ibid., 106.

" 'Know Nothing' party . . .": Ibid., 112.

Jeremiah O'Keefe's life is discussed in *The Northwestern Chronicle,* December 9, 1898, 6.

12 foreign-born population: Bennett, *Fear,* 141.

nativist movement: Ibid., 152.

Company H: John Quinn Imholte, *The First Volunteers* (Minneapolis: Ross & Haines, Inc., 1963), 169.

"the largest battle . . .": Richard Moe, *The Last Full Measure: The Life and Death of the First Minnesota Volunteers* (New York: Henry Holt and Company, 1993), 260.

"no more gallant . . .": Ibid., 297.

"Winfield Scott Hancock . . .": Geoffrey C. Ward, Ric Burns, and Ken Burns, *The Civil War* (New York: Alfred A. Knopf, Inc., 1990), 225.

13 "When it was over . . .": Bennett, *Fear,* 155.

"You are not to . . .": Ralph Ketcham, *The Anti-Federalist Papers and the Constitutional Convention Debates* (New York: Mentor Books, 1986), 200–201.

Speech of Patrick Henry, June 5, 1788.

"Give me liberty . . .": Vincent Wilson, Jr., *The Book of the Founding Fathers* (Harrisburg, Virginia: R. R. Donnelly & Sons, Co., 1985), 30.

14 "You must first . . .": Ketcham, *Anti-Federalist,* 7.

"offenses directed to . . .": St. Paul City Council File No. 278285, *Minutes of Meeting,* March 9, 1982.

"growing problem . . .": Ibid., *Minutes of Meeting,* February 18, 1982.
"knowledgeable about . . .": Ibid., *Minutes of Meeting,* February 25, 1982. The newspaper story was written by John Camp, later a Pulitzer Prize winner in journalism for the St. Paul *Pioneer Press* and now a successful author writing under the pseudonym John Sandford.
"constitutionally sound . . .": Ibid., *Minutes of Meeting,* March 2, 1982.

15   "not covered . . .": Ibid., *Minutes of Meeting,* March 9, 1982.
"both surprised and pleased . . .": St. Paul *Pioneer Press,* December 9, 1991, 10.
"take it before . . .": ibid.
"gender" amendment: St. Paul City Council File No. 90-197, April 19, 1990. Less than two years later on February 29, 1992, the St. Paul *Pioneer Press* reported that the same council person who had moved to amend the ordinance to include gender, violated its spirit if not its language. The council member, an attorney and a woman, apparently made sexist and derogatory remarks about several of the male members of the council, who claimed that she had spoken in "reference to male anatomy." A male council member took offense, claiming the remark was "outrageous, inappropriate and unbelievable," and pointed out that if a male member had made the same comment about a female council member, he would have been severely criticized. Finally, on August 21, 1992, a sexual harassment lawsuit was filed against this council member by a former male aide calling into question whether or not she understood the amendment when she introduced it. The case was settled out of court in 1993.

16   Chinese Exclusion Act: Bennett, *Fear,* 162.
Sedition Act: Ibid., 186.
"hundreds of people . . .": Anthony Lewis, *Make No Law* (New York: Random House, 1991), 78–79.

17   Court proceedings are taken from a transcript found among my father's papers in May 1991. *In the Matter of the Petition of D.H. Exrieder, and others, for the purpose of contesting the right of P.H. O'Keefe to the office of County Attorney of Dakota County, State of Minnesota* (1919), 58, 200–202.

19   "It is an experiment . . .": *Abrams v. United States,* 250 U.S. 616, 627–631 (1919).

Chapter 2

20   Edmund Burke: Ralph Ketcham, *The Anti-Federalist Papers and the Constitutional Convention Debates* (New York: Mentor Books, 1986), 7.
"for the purpose . . .": *Thornhill v. Alabama,* 310 U.S. 88, 92 (1940). The circuit court sentenced: Ibid., 91.

21 "Those who won . . .": Ibid., 95. Compare the words of Justice Brandeis in *Whitney v. California*, 274 U.S. 357, 375. "Those who won our independence believed that the final end of the State was to make men free to develop their faculties; and that in its government the deliberate forces should prevail over the arbitrary. They valued liberty both as an end and as a means. They believed liberty to be the secret of happiness and courage to be to the secret of liberty. They believed that freedom to think as you will and to speak as you think are means indispensable to the discovery and spread of political truth. . . ."

"It is not merely . . .": Ibid., 97–98. The reluctance of the Court to trust authorities to prosecute such laws in a nondiscriminatory fashion mirrored antifederalist doctrine present in colonial America a century and a half earlier. Consider this line from Patrick Henry delivered to the Virginia Ratifying Convention on June 7, 1788: "Show me that age and country where the rights and liberties of the people were placed on the sole chance of their rulers being good men, without a consequent loss of liberty." Ketcham, *Anti-Federalist Papers*, 214.

"sword of Damocles": *Arnett v. Kennedy*, 416 U.S. 134, 231 (1974) (Marshall, J., dissenting).

22 the issue is *not* whether: *NAACP v. Button*, 371 U.S. 415, 435 (1963); *Dombrowski v. Pfister*, 380 U.S. 479, 494 (1965).

23 *Broadrick v. Oklahoma*, 413 U.S. 601 (1973).

Brockett v. Spokane Arcades, Inc., 472 U.S. 491 (1985).

"An individual whose . . .": Ibid., 503.

For a further discussion on the overbreadth doctrine, see Henry Paul Monaghan, "Overbreadth," 1981 *Supreme Court Review* 1, 8.

24 "If all mankind . . .": John Stuart Mill, *On Liberty* (originally published 1859) (New York: Bantam ed., 1993), 20.

"It is a fair summary . . .": *U.S. v. Rabinowitz*, 339 U.S. 56, 69 (1950) (Frankfurter, J., dissenting).

Stromberg v. California, 283 U.S. 359 (1931).

25 "The maintenance of the . . .": Ibid., 369.

26 *West Virginia State Board of Education v. Barnette*, 319 U.S. 624 (1943).

Tinker v. Des Moines Independent Community School District, 393 U.S. 503 (1969).

"In our system . . .": Ibid., 508–9.

Other symbolic expression: Examples of symbols banned in recent times include the Confederate flag (*Time*, March 25, 1991, 25); the Klan mask (St. Paul *Pioneer Press*, December 6, 1990, 10A); and "gang colors" (*Denver Post*, May 4, 1991, 1B). *United States v. O'Brien*, 391 U.S. 367 (1968).

27 "forges, alters . . .": Ibid., 370.

"to influence others . . .": Ibid.

addressing nude dancing: *Barnes v. Glen Theatre, Inc.*, 501 U.S. ___, 111 S.Ct. 2456 (1991).

Cohen v. California, 403 U.S. 15 (1971).

"maliciously and willfully . . .": Ibid., 16.

"the fact of the . . .": Ibid., 18.

28 "One man's vulgarity . . .": Ibid., 25, 26.

"desecration of the . . .": Robert H. Bork, *The Tempting of America* (New York: Touchstone, 1990), 127.

29 "one is not to have . . .": *Spence v. Washington,* 418 U.S. 405, 411 (n. 4), (1974).

Scalia's and Bork's voting record while on the D.C. Circuit Court of Appeals: Bork, *Tempting,* 299.

Chapter 3

31 "The case before us . . .": *Texas v. Johnson,* 491 U.S. 397, 420, 421 (1989), (Kennedy, J., concurring).

"We don't need . . .": *Street v. New York,* 394 U.S. 576, 579 (1969).

Charged with the crime: Ibid., 581.

32 "under our Constitution . . .": Ibid., 592.

"disrespect for our flag . . .": Ibid., 594.

Charged with violating: *Smith v. Goguen,* 415 U.S. 566, 570 (1974).

"statutory language . . .": Ibid., 572, 575.

33 *Spence v. Washington,* 418 U.S. 405, 407 (1974). John Hart Ely has noted that "improper use" laws are dangerous in their own right, since "orthodoxy of thought can be fostered not simply by placing unusual restrictions on 'deviant' expression but also by granting unusual protection to expression that is officially acceptable." Ely, "Flag Desecration: A Case Study in the Roles of Categorization and Balancing in First Amendment Analysis," 88 *Harvard Law Review* 1482, 1507 (1975).

"no interest the State . . .": *Spence v. Washington,* 418 U.S. 405, 414, 415.

"was not a philosopher . . .": *Texas v. Johnson,* 491 U.S. 397, 420 (1989) (Kennedy, J., concurring). Gregory Johnson attended the oral argument on *R.A.V. v. St. Paul* on December 4, 1991, and told the press that he felt the ordinance was constitutional, thus demonstrating that one who engages in far-left fringe expression is offended by one who engages in far-right fringe expression. However his attorney in that case, William Kunstler, opposed the ordinance. *The Village Voice,* January 28, 1992, 21.

the "unique" nature . . .: *Texas v. Johnson,* 491 U.S. 397, 418. The Washington Supreme Court in *Spence v. Washington* had used this rationale in upholding the conviction of Spence for his unorthodox display of the flag. However, the attorney for the state of Washington abandoned this argument and returned to a "breach-of-peace" justification that had been ignored by the lower court. 418 U.S. at 411.

Perhaps as a result of this earlier equivocation, Texas asserted both grounds as justification for the conviction of Gregory Johnson.

34 The questions of Justices Scalia, Kennedy, and O'Connor: David G. Savage, *Turning Right: The Making of the Rehnquist Supreme Court* (New York: John Wiley & Sons, Inc., 1992) 256–59.

"If there is a . . .": *Texas v. Johnson*, 491 U.S. 397, 414 (1989).

"Justice Jackson . . .": Ibid., 415.

35 "Our decision is . . .": Ibid., 419, 410. As Alan Dershowitz has pointed out, perhaps we should consider "whether it's better to live in a country where people want to burn a flag but cannot or in a country where people are free to burn the flag but do not." *Contrary to Popular Opinion* (New York: Pharos Books, 1992) 76.

United States v. Eichman, 496 U.S. 310 (1990).

"We decline the . . .": Ibid., 318.

"constitutional moments": Mark Tushnet, "The Flag-Burning Episode: An Essay on the Constitution," 61 *University of Colorado Law Review* 39, 47 (1990). Tushnet acknowledges Bruce Ackerman as the source for this label. See Ackerman, "The Storrs Lectures: Discovering the Constitution," 93 *Yale Law Journal* 1013 (1984).

"We consider . . .": Ibid., 47, 48.

37 For another viewpoint on Justice Kennedy's concurring opinion in *Texas v. Johnson*, see Tushnet, "The Flag-Burning Episode," at 43, 44, where Tushnet argues that Kennedy said, "in essence, that the Devil made him do it . . . Justice Kennedy appeared to assume personal responsibility for the outcome but in fact placed the responsibility (at the door of the Constitution)."

"your honor, on behalf . . .": Transcript, *In the Matter of the Welfare of R.A.V.: Constitutionality Hearing*, July 13, 1990, 4. A copy of the transcript is in the author's possession.

Collin v. Smith, 578 F.2d 1197 (7th Cir.), *cert. denied*, 439 U.S. 916 (1979).

38 "The Court feels . . .": Transcript, *In the Matter of the Welfare of R.A.V.: Constitutionality Hearing*, July 16, 1990, 2.

first public statement: St. Paul *Pioneer Press*, July 17, 1990, 2B.

Chapter 4

40 "There are certain . . .": *Chaplinsky v. State of New Hampshire*, 315 U.S. 568, 572 (1942).

Although none of the members of the St. Paul City Council were lawyers when section 292.02 was passed on March 9, 1982, the council was receiving legal advice from the city attorney's office. Further, two of the members of the council were attorneys when the ordinance was unanimously amended to add "gender" on April 19, 1990.

42   "creates a much more . . .": Mark C. Rutzick, "Offensive Language
      and the Evolution of First Amendment Protection," 9 *Harvard Civil
      Rights–Civil Liberties Law Review* 1, 7 (1974).
      An incident that occurred at the University of Pennsylvania in 1993
      highlighted the difficulty in punishing language that "inflicts injury"
      on others. Disciplinary proceedings were brought against a Jewish
      student who shouted innocuous names at a group of black women
      students singing and shouting late at night near his dormitory room.
      The women "perceived" the name "water buffalo" (an animal found
      not in Africa but only in Southeast Asia) "as a racial epithet" and
      claimed the student had violated the school policy against "racial
      epithets meant to 'inflict direct injury' on people." Michael de Courcy
      Hinds, "A Campus Case: Speech or Harassment?" *The New York
      Times,* May 15, 1993, 6.
      Terminiello v. Chicago, 337 U.S. 1, 4 (1949).

43   "The vitality . . .": Ibid., 4.
      "Accordingly a function . . .": Ibid., 4, 5.
      Dennis v. United States, 341 U.S. 494 (1951).
      "Public opinion . . .": Ibid., 581.

44   "Negro citizens of . . .": *Beauharnais v. Illinois,* 343 U.S. 250, 252
      (1952). See also Hadley Arkes, "Civility and the Restriction of Speech:
      Rediscovering the Defamation of Groups," 1974 *Supreme Court Re-
      view* 281.
      "If an utterance . . .": Ibid., 258, 263.
      "To begin with . . .": Harry Kalven, Jr., "Upon Rereading Mr. Justice
      Black on the First Amendment," 14 *U.C.L.A. Law Review* 428, 429
      (1967).

45   "The Court's holding . . .": *Beauharnais v. Illinois,* 343 U.S. 269, 270.
      "For here . . .": Ibid., 273.
      "No rationalization . . .": Ibid., 274, 275.

46   "Recently the Court . . .": Ibid., 285.
      Anthony Lewis, *Make No Law* (New York: Random House, 1991).
      New York Times Co. v. Sullivan, 376 U.S. 254 (1964). Compare the
      British experience with libel and the media. Since Britain has no First
      Amendment, restrictive libel laws prevent the openness Americans
      take for granted, allowing men like Robert Maxwell to hide financial
      wrongdoing until it is too late. See Arthur S. Hayes, "Britain's Libel
      Laws Helped Maxwell Keep Charges of Misdeeds from Public," *The
      Wall Street Journal,* December 9, 1991, 2B.
      Brandenburg v. Ohio, 395 U.S. 444 (1969).
      The so-called heckler's veto, as Harry Kalven, Jr., of the University of
      Chicago Law School described it, allows a member of an audience to
      silence, or "veto," the viewpoint of a speaker he disagrees with.
      several state court decisions: See *Gooding v. Wilson,* 405 U.S. 518
      (1972) and *Lewis v. City of New Orleans,* 415 U.S. 123 (1974).

47 *Collin v. Smith,* 578 F.2d 1197 (7th Cir.), *cert. denied,* 439 U.S. 916 (1978).

48 "It is, after all . . .": Ibid., 1201.
    "It would be . . .": Ibid., 1206.

49 The ADL's drafting of model "hate-crime" legislation: See Susan Gellman, "Sticks and Stones Can Put You in Jail, but Can Words Increase Your Sentence? Constitutional and Policy Dilemmas of Ethnic Intimidation Laws," 39 *U.C.L.A. Law Review* 333, 339 (1991).
    Aryeh Neier, *Defending My Enemy* (New York: E. P. Dutton, 1979).
    Loss in ACLU membership: Ibid., 10.
    "pretext of listener hostility . . .": Ibid., 119, 121.
    "The officials . . .": Ibid., 139, 140.

50 "The arguments against . . .": Ibid., 145.

Chapter 5

51 Anthony Lewis, *Make No Law* (New York: Random House, 1991), 247, 248.
    For a background on Matthew Stark and his battle on First Amendment grounds against an antipornography ordinance proposed in Minneapolis in 1983, see Donald Alexander Downs, *The New Politics of Pornography* (Chicago: University of Chicago Press, 1989), 69.
    The MCLU had come under fire locally for ignoring "major issues that would place it in conflict with the establishment, preferring more limited or acceptable issues," according to critics. "Liberty & Justice for Some," *City Pages,* March 27, 1991, 4. Ironically, much of this criticism came from those who felt the organization pursued safe civil liberty issues over controversial civil rights cases. Assisting on *R.A.V.* would have angered these critics further (as it involved a controversial civil liberty issue) while refusing to assist betrayed the mandate of the organization to safeguard civil liberties for all citizens. At this crucial point, the MCLU failed to assist us. Seven months later, it realized its mistake and offered assistance.

52 "when people's rights . . .": *USA Today,* March 31, 1993, 2A.
    "the First Amendment . . .": Brief of *amicus curiae, Anti-Defamation League of B'nai B'rith,* Minn. Supreme Court File No. C8-90-1656, 6.

53 *Marbury v. Madison,* I Cranch 1937 (1803).

54 "Like other tyrannies . . .": John Stuart Mill, *On Liberty* (New York: Bantam ed., 1993), 7.

56 *In re S.L.J.,* 263 N.W.2d 412 (Minn. 1978).
    disorderly-conduct statute: Minnesota Statute section 609.72, Subd. 1, which reads in part: Whoever does any of the following in a public or private place, knowing, or having reasonable grounds to know that it will, or will tend to, alarm, anger or disturb others . . . (3) Engages in

offensive, obscene, or abusive language or in boisterous and noisy conduct tending reasonably to arouse alarm, anger, or resentment in others.

57   The relationship between the St. Paul ordinance and laws aimed at abortion protesters was largely ignored by the media. Only the *Mac-Neil/Lehrer Newshour* (February 20, 1992) reported on the connection between these two issues in a story on the *R.A.V.* case. In *Bray v. Alexandria Women's Health Clinic,* 506 U.S. ___, 113 S.Ct. 753 (1993), the Court in a 5–4 decision held that disfavoring abortion was not invidious discrimination against women in violation of a civil rights statute. Rejecting an analogy between anti-abortion protesters and the Ku Klux Klan, Justice Scalia stated "whatever one thinks of abortion, it cannot be denied that there are common and respectable reasons for opposing it, other than hatred of or condescension toward . . . women as a class." 113 S.Ct. 760. In response, Congress proposed legislation directed at anti-abortion protesters. See Michael W. McConnell, "Free Speech Outside Abortion Clinics," *The Wall Street Journal,* March 31, 1993, A15.

In re R.A.V., 464 N.W.2d 507 (Minn. 1991).

59   "although the St. Paul . . .": Ibid., 511.

Chapter 6

63   Arthur M. Schlesinger, Jr., *The Disuniting of America* (New York: W.W. Norton and Company, 1992), 114, 115. As a member of the New York Social Studies Syllabus Review Committee, Schlesinger wrote a dissent following a debate over the New York public school curriculum. Expanding upon the theme of the dissent, Schlesinger wrote *The Disuniting of America.*

64   "The justices have . . .": David G. Savage, *Turning Right: The Making of the Rehnquist Supreme Court* (New York: John Wiley & Sons, Inc., 1992), 51, 52.

In an *Affidavit in Support of a Motion for Leave to Proceed In Forma Pauperis,* (United States Supreme Court Docket No. 90-7675), dated March 14, 1991, R.A.V. indicated that his gross income from March 1990–March 1991 was approximately $500, earned from dishwashing and maintenance work. Since this was an affidavit, he signed his full name for the notary. The press located this affidavit in the file at the United States Supreme Court and this led to the publication of his name in various newspapers on June 11, 1991. Under Minnesota law, his name was confidential because he was seventeen as of June 21, 1990.

"in forma pauperis" petitions: Also known as the "5000 series," the *in forma pauperis* docket was crowded at the time the Court decided

to accept *R.A.V.* for review. According to *United States Law Week,* June 11, 1991, the Court had 91 requests for review on this docket on June 10, 1991, and turned down 90, accepting only R.A.V.'s petition. Prior to reforms instituted in 1916 and 1922, the Court had little discretion over its calendar. It was obliged to hear cases by writ of error and on direct appeal from the federal courts. "Writs of certiorari were introduced in 1891, and greatly expanded in the reform legislation sponsored by Chief Justice Taft in 1925." Sheldon M. Novick, *Honorable Justice: The Life of Oliver Wendell Holmes* (New York: Dell Publishing, 1989), 455(n.16). As Novick points out, the Court disposed of only 60 petitions for writs of certiorari in the October 1902 term, as opposed to upwards of 5,000 per term nine decades later.

66   *Chaplinsky v. New Hampshire,* 315 U.S. 568 (1942).
For an example of the abuse of the "fighting words" doctrine, see *Lewis v. City of New Orleans,* 415 U.S. 123 (1974).

67   In regard to the passage of progressive social legislation due to freedom of expression, see Nadine Strossen, "Liberty, Equality and Democracy: Three Bases for Reversing the Minnesota Supreme Court Ruling," 18 *William Mitchell Law Review* 965, 968 (1992). Strossen quotes Benjamin Hooks, the leader of the NAACP, who stated that "the civil rights movement depended on the shield and the spear of the First Amendment."
"Imagine places . . .": William A. Henry III, "Upside Down in the Groves of Academe," *Time,* April 1, 1991, 66.
The movement toward "civility" on campus is not always aimed at students. Two teachers at City College of New York were cited for espousing "objectionable views." One incident involved a Jewish philosophy teacher accused of racist statements; the other involved a black professor cited for making anti-Semitic allegations. Both sued the college successfully, proving teachers have the "freedom to express opinions, no matter how offensive they may be to others." Maria Newman, "A Free-Speech Lesson," *The New York Times,* May 16, 1993, 20.
For an excellent volume of essays on "P.C.": covering a wide range of opinions on the subject, including the ongoing acrimonious debate between such educational organizations as the Modern Language Association (pro P.C.) and the National Association of Scholars (anti P.C.), see *Beyond P.C.: Towards a Politics of Understanding* (St. Paul: Graywolf Press, 1992).
"The radical ideas . . .": J. M. Balkin, "Some Realism about Pluralism: Legal Realist Approaches to the First Amendment," 1990 *Duke Law Journal* 375, 383.

68   For a closer examination of critical legal studies, see Richard Delgado, "The Ethereal Scholar: Does Critical Legal Studies Have What Minorities Want?" 22 *Harvard Civil Rights–Civil Liberties Law Re-*

view 301, 304 (1987). As one article noted, paraphrasing Voltaire, "those who accept censorship as a tool for 'social progress' appear to accept the motto 'I disagree with what you say and I will defend to the death my right to keep you from saying it.' " "The P.C. Police," *ABA Journal,* November 1991, 12.

For a further discussion of the "means" and "modes" of communication, see Balkin, *Realism,* 397 (". . . guarantees of formal liberty and formal equality generally favor those groups in society that are already the most powerful"). See also Rodney A. Smolla, *Free Speech in an Open Society* (New York: Knopf, 1992). Smolla points out that since the disfranchised are dependent on government funding in areas where the government controls speech, decisions such as *Rust v. Sullivan* fall disproportionately on them.

Balkin notes the continuing dispute among liberals on these issues: "We are likely to see increasing numbers of first amendment defenses raised in the years ahead. . . . the clash between the left goal of egalitarianism and the libertarian theory of the first amendment will be felt with particular poignancy. One or the other has to give way, and I suspect that for many on the left it will be libertarian theory," 423. See also David Bromwich, *Politics by Other Means: Higher Education and Group Thinking* (New Haven: Yale University Press, 1992). Bromwich refers to the right as the "culture of assent" and to the left as the "culture of suspicion," finding fault with both positions. Consider these comments from former congresswoman Barbara Jordan from Texas: "We are one, we Americans. We are one. And we reject any intruder who seeks to divide us on the basis of race and color. . . . Separatism is not the American Way. We must not allow ideas like political correctness to divide us. . . ." Daniel Henninger, "A Woman of Substance," *The Wall Street Journal,* July 15, 1992. Contrast those sentiments with the following: "America offers individual freedom and the opportunity to make something of yourself. But multi-culturalism is the exact opposite of that. . . . The bonds of national cohesion in the republic are fragile enough." Rush Limbaugh, *The Way Things Ought to Be* (New York: Pocket Books, 1992), 213. Strange bedfellows?

69 "The central tenet . . .": Arlynn Leiber Presser, "The Politically Correct Law School, Where It's Right to Be Left," *ABA Journal,* September 1991, 53.

Patricia Williams has labeled offensive racial messages "spirit murder" in support of her position that such expression can be censored. Williams, "Spirit-Murdering the Messenger: The Discourse of Fingerpointing as the Law's Response to Racism," 42 *University of Miami Law Review* 127, 129 (1987).

Matsuda's solution: Mari J. Matsuda, "Public Response to Racist Speech: Considering The Victim's Story," 87 *Michigan Law Review*

2320, 2359, 2362 (1989). The Minnesota Supreme Court cited this article in support of its observation that a "burning cross is . . . an unmistakable symbol of hatred." *In the Matter of the Welfare of R.A.V.*, 464 N.W.2d 507, 508(n.1) (1991).

As Nat Hentoff has pointed out, "No matter how affluent or influential an individual woman or black may be, he or she is, by Matsuda's definition, an outsider and therefore entitled to extra shares of free speech." "Mari Matsuda: Star of the Speech Police," *The Village Voice*, February 18, 1992, 25.

"not everyone has known . . .": Charles R. Lawrence III, "If He Hollers Let Him Go: Regulating Racist Speech on Campus," 1990 *Duke Law Journal* 432, 459 (1990).

mental and physical handicaps: Justice Scalia later pointed out this defect in section 292.02 using a similar example at the oral argument.

"With regard to what . . .": John Stuart Mill, *On Liberty* (New York: Bantam ed., 1993), 62.

71   "risk that such . . .": Nadine Strossen, "Regulating Racist Speech on Campus: A Modest Proposal?" 1990 *Duke Law Journal* 484, 489, 512 (1990).

Nadine Strossen, along with other female activists, founded the Feminists for Free Expression, a loosely knit organization of professional women who have taken issue with feminists who believe in censorship as a tool against hate speech, obscenity, etc.

"The cult of ethnicity . . .": Schlesinger, *Disuniting* 112.

"the one absolutely . . .": Ibid., 118.

"Whatever the particular . . .": Ibid., 127, 134.

72   The inconsistency of many conservatives toward freedom of expression has been noted by several commentators. See Anthony Lewis, "Bush should practice what he preaches about free speech," St. Paul *Pioneer Press*, May 29, 1992, 11A, chiding President Bush for supporting free speech on campus while proposing a constitutional amendment permitting the punishing of flag-burning; and Alan Dershowitz, making the same point: "Who is Bush to lecture us after what he did in the last campaign with the flag-burning? It's utter hypocrisy from the President and from many on the right." Presser, 54.

"magazine censored": Alan Dershowitz, *Contrary to Popular Opinion* (New York: Pharos Books, 1992) 93.

"Students from . . .": Dinesh D'Souza, *Illiberal Education: The Politics of Race and Sex on Campus* (New York: The Free Press, 1991), 156, 46–47.

"Is it unreasonable . . .": Charles Fried, "The New First Amendment Jurisprudence: A Threat to Liberty" 59 *University of Chicago Law Review* 225, 248 (1992).

Doe v. University of Michigan, 721 F. Supp. 852 (Eastern District Michigan 1989).

addendum: Ibid., 869. ("An earlier awareness of Professor Matsuda's paper certainly would have sharpened the Court's view of the issues.") Later on October 11, 1991, after the briefs had been filed, Judge Robert W. Warren of the Eastern District of Wisconsin struck down the University of Wisconsin's "rule" regulation speech on campus.

"a certain amount . . .": *City of Houston v. Hill*, 482 U.S. 451, 472 (1987).

74   For a thorough examination of the Court's procedures in selecting cases for review, see William H. Rehnquist, *The Supreme Court: How It Was, How It Is* (New York: William Morrow and Company, Inc., 1987), 263–69. "Whether or not to vote to grant certiorari strikes me as a rather subjective decision, made up in part of intuition and in part of legal judgment," 265.

75   "At 9:25 in the morning . . .": David G. Savage, *Turning Right: The Making of the Rehnquist Supreme Court* (New York: John Wiley & Sons, Inc., 1992), 52.

"a dissent would be written . . .": A justice who votes to grant review of a petition but who fails to convince at least three other justices to do the same has the right to submit a dissent. In recent years, this practice has become increasingly common among the justices. Those attorneys seeking review by the Court would be well advised to check past dissents submitted by current members of the Court in related cases. As an example, Justice Blackmun, joined by Justice White, wrote a stinging dissent when the Court failed to grant certiorari in the Skokie case (*Smith v. Collin*, 439 U.S. 916 [1978]). The anger that permeates that dissent foreshadowed the bitter tone found in the concurring opinions of Justice Blackmun and Justice White in *R.A.V.* fourteen years later.

Chapter 7

76   *The Washington Post*, June 11, 1991, A4.

"This is a very . . .": *The New York Times*, December 1, 1991, A32.

77   "Anti-war protesters . . .": *The New York Times*, June 11, 1991, A1.

78   "There is hope . . .": *The Washington Post*, June 12, 1991.

79   *The New York Times:* Linda Greenhouse, "Justices to Decide If Hate-Crime Law Curbs Free Speech," June 11, 1991, A1; *National Law Journal:* Marcia Coyle, "Hate Laws Scrutinized by Justices," December 2, 1991, 1.

80   "Federal courts . . .": William J. Brennan, Jr., "The Bill of Rights and the States: The Revival of State Constitutions as Guardians of Individual Rights," 61 *N.Y.U. Law Review* 535, 552 (1986). As Justice Brennan points out, however, ". . . state courts may not provide a level of protection less than that offered by the federal Constitution," 550.

84   *Gideon v. Wainwright,* 372 U.S. 335 (1963). For a superb account of this case, see Anthony Lewis, *Gideon's Trumpet* (New York: Random House, 1964).

Justice Brennan's quote is taken from Nat Hentoff, "The Justice Breaks His Silence," *Playboy,* July 1991, 158.

Justice Marshall's retirement: David G. Savage, *Turning Right: The Making of the Rehnquist Supreme Court* (New York: John Wiley & Sons, Inc. 1992), 417.

Alan Dershowitz's comments: WBZ Radio *1030* (Boston, Mass.), June 25, 1991.

86   Robert Bolt, *A Man for All Seasons* (New York: Vintage Books, 1960), 37, 38. A year after the brief in *R.A.V.* was filed, I came across this passage in Robert Bork's *The Tempting of America* (New York: Touchstone, 1990), 354. Apparently, Bork and I differ as to the meaning of this passage, since he would provide scant protection for unpopular symbolic expression.

"not merely a time . . .": Ibid., xiii.

87   See Cass R. Sunstein, "Pornography and the First Amendment," 1986 Duke *Law Journal* 589 (1986). Sunstein's acceptance of antipornography legislation is predicated on many of the arguments used by those in favor of hate-crime legislation.

90   "to protect the vital . . .": Patriots Defense Foundation, *amicus curiae* brief, *R.A.V. v. City of St. Paul,* U.S. Supreme Court Docket No. 90-7675, 2.

Judge Posner's quote was taken from *Kucharek v. Hanaway,* 902 F.2d 513 (7th Cir. 1990), *cert. denied* 498 U.S. 1041 (1991).

91   Lawrence's mention of powell: Charles R. Lawrence III, "If He Hollers Let Him Go: Regulating Racist Speech on Campus," 1990 Duke *Law Journal* 431, 473.

92   "in most countries . . .": Sandra Coliver, "Hate Speech Laws: Do They Work?" *Striking A Balance: Hate Speech, Freedom of Expression and Non-Discrimination,* edited by Sandra Coliver (United Kingdom: Human Rights Centre, University of Essex, 1992), 363.

93   *U.S. v. Lee,* 935 F.2d 952, *vacated,* 935 F.2d 960 (8th Cir. 1991).

94   "bring the constitutional . . .": Criminal Justice Legal Foundation, *amicus curiae* brief, *R.A.V. v. City of St. Paul,* U.S. Supreme Court Docket No. 90-7675.

The Asian-American organizations: Asian American Legal Defense and Education Fund, Asian Law Caucus, Asian Pacific American Legal Center, and National Asian Pacific American Bar Association.

Other groups sponsoring the brief from the Center for Constitutional Rights included the Center for Democratic Renewal, the National Conference of Black Lawyers, the National Council of La Raza, the International Union, United Automobile, Aerospace and Agricultural Implement Workers of America (UAW), the Y.W.C.A. of the U.S.A., the National Organization of Black Law Enforcement Executives, the National Lawyers Guild, the United Church of Christ Commission for Racial Justice, the National Institute Against Prejudice and Violence, the Greater Boston Civil Rights Coalition, and the National Coalition of Black Lesbians and Gays.

William Kunstler's position: Nat Hentoff, "This Is the Hour of Danger for the First Amendment," *The Village Voice*, January 28, 1992, 21. Kunstler told Hentoff: "I'm opposed to any ordinance like this . . . in the St. Paul case . . . I'm a strict First Amendment supporter. If this ordinance stands up, the First Amendment will be in shambles."

"every 18 seconds . . .": Brief *amicus curiae*, Center for Democratic Renewal et al., 33.

95   The Clarendon Foundation joined with the NAACP in sponsoring the brief.

96   The two cases cited: See *Gooding v. Wilson*, 405 U.S. 518 (1972), and *Lewis v. New Orleans*, 415 U.S. 123 (1974).

The story on the *Daily Variety* ad appeared in *USA Today*, July 15, 1992, 1D.

Chapter 8

98   "When men . . .": *Abrams v. United States*, 250 U.S. 616 (1919) (Holmes, J., dissenting).

"Every idea . . .": *Gitlow v. New York*, 268 U.S. 652, 673 (1925) (Holmes, J., dissenting).

99   In addition to *Schenk*, 249 U.S. 47 (1919), Holmes was a member of the Court that upheld the conviction of Eugene Debs under the Espionage Act of 1917 for having delivered a June 1918 speech in Canton, Ohio, asserting that World War I was a class war fought on behalf of the privileged by members of the working class. Debs asserted that dissent, even in times of national peril, was his right as an American citizen. He served three years of a ten-year sentence in federal prison and while incarcerated received almost a million votes for president in the 1920 election. *Debs v. United States*, 249 U.S. 211 (1919).

The efforts to dissuade Holmes are mentioned in Sheldon M. Novick, *Honorable Justice: The Life of Oliver Wendell Holmes* (New York: Laurel, 1989) 331.

Holmes's attitude toward the anarchists was consistent with that of Thomas Jefferson, who stated in his first inaugural address: "If there be any among us who would wish to dissolve this union or change its republican form, let them stand undisturbed as monuments of the safety with which error of opinion may be tolerated where reason is left free to combat it." Quoted by Justice Brandeis in *Whitney v. California*, 274 U.S. 357, 375 (n.3).

100 "unless it is eroded . . .": For an example of a constitutionally suspect effort at achieving "civility," ostensibly aimed at extending workplace safeguards against sexual harassment to the "street," see Cynthia Grant Bowman, "Street Harassment and the Informal Ghettoization of Women," 106 *Harvard Law Review* 517 (1993). Bowman argues that her proposals to silence comments made in public deemed offensive to women can be "accomplished without violence to the First Amendment," while relying on many of the failed arguments used earlier by the government in *R.A.V.* She eventually concedes that the *R.A.V.* decision makes it likely that "the Supreme Court might still strike down a street harassment regulation," noting that she felt "*R.A.V.* was wrongly decided" but then "refrain[ing] from any more extended critique of the opinion. . . ." 546, 547 (n. 152).

See "Pornography, Equality, and a Discrimination-Free Workplace: A Comparative Perspective," 106 *Harvard Law Review* 1075 (1993). The author concludes that "in the circumstances of a male-dominated workplace, pornography is an issue of power." 1092.

" 'progressive censorship' . . .": See Robert Paul Wolff, Barrington Moore, and Herbert Marcuse, *A Critique of Pure Tolerance* (New York: Beacon Press, 1969). An extension of this argument, presented to me by a former student of Professor MacKinnon's, later a law professor at Northwestern, is that since the Framers (including Madison and Jefferson) were "sexist and racist," "traditional" interpretation of the Bill of Rights is outdated. Proponents of this theory believe we should disregard the First Amendment in an effort to redefine social roles and the distribution of power.

101 "In the contemporary . . .": Hunter (citing Gary Wills), *Culture Wars* (New York: Basic Books, 1991), 246.

"Sexual dissent . . .": Kathleen M. Sullivan, "The First Amendment Wars," *The New Republic*, September 28, 1992, 36 (citing Edward de Grazia).

"pornography cannot . . .": Camille Paglia, *Sexual Personae* (New York: Vintage, 1992), 24, 25 (citing Geoffrey Hartman).

child pornography: See *New York v. Ferber*, 458 U.S. 747 (1982). Geoffrey Stone distinguishes this approach from proposed antipornography legislation on two grounds. The law in *Ferber* only minimally impacted free expression because it focused on the children involved regardless of the "message" conveyed, while proposed antipornography laws usually address the message involved (i.e., domination, etc.). In addition, children by law cannot consent to such activity, being more vulnerable than adults, making governmental involvement less objectionable. Geoffrey R. Stone, "Anti-Pornography Legislation as Viewpoint Discrimination," 9 *Harvard Journal of Law and Public Policy* 461, 472 (n.34) (1986).

Moral standards are often subjective. Consider that Charles H. Keat-

ing, Jr., a member of a commission formed to study the issue of
pornography, condemned pornography as a violation of God's law
(David A. J. Richards, "Free Speech and Obscenity Law: Toward a
Moral Theory of the First Amendment," 123 *University of Pennsylvania Law Review* 45, 89 (n.250) (1974)). Yet Keating apparently did
not see the same moral failing in the looting of a savings and loan. He
was convicted of seventeen counts of state securities fraud on December 4, 1991, the day *R.A.V.* was argued.

"So while . . .": Catharine A. MacKinnon, *Feminism Unmodified:
Discourses on Life and Law* (Cambridge: Harvard University Press,
1987), 155, 156; see also Catharine A. MacKinnon, *Only Words* (Cambridge: Harvard University Press, 1993), and Cass R. Sunstein, "Pornography and the First Amendment" 1986 Duke *Law Journal,* 589.

102 "American society . . .": David Brock, "The Real Anita Hill," *The
Wall Street Journal,* April 9, 1993, A8.

"Like the proscription . . .": *Paris Adult Theatre I et al. v. Slaton,
District Attorney, et al.,* 413 U.S. 49, 109 (1973) (Brennan, J., dissenting).

103 "cognitive content": *Cohen v. California,* 403 U.S. 15 (1971).

Beauharnais v. Illinois: 343 U.S. 250 (1952). See also *New York Times
Co. v. Sullivan,* 375 U.S. 254 (1964).

104 "To permit every . . .": *American Booksellers Ass'n Inc. v. Hudnut,*
598 F. Supp. 1316, 1337 (1984).

"the Constitution . . .": *American Booksellers Ass'n Inc. v. Hudnut,*
771 F.2d 323, 330, 331 (7th Cir. 1985), *aff'd without opinion,* 475 U.S.
1001 (1986).

"Racial bigotry . . .": Ibid., 330.

105 MacKinnon's comment is taken from Nat Hentoff, *Free Speech for
Me—But Not for Thee* (New York: HarperCollins, 1992), 351.

"The development of . . .": (Chicago: University of Chicago Press,
1989) 146, 149.

Canadian decisions: *Butler v. Her Majesty the Queen,* I. S.C.R. 452
(1992) (obscenity); *Keegstra v. Her Majesty the Queen* 3 S.C.R. 697
(hate speech).

106 *Meritor Savings Bank v. Vinson,* 477 U.S. 57 (1986).

Robinson v. Jacksonville Shipyards, Inc., 760 F.Supp. 1486 (M.D. Fla.
1991).

Harris v. Forklift Systems: 510 U.S. ___, 114 S.Ct. 367 (1993); see Paul
M. Barrett, "Sex Harassment Case to be Heard by High Court," *The
Wall Street Journal,* March 2, 1993, A4.

107 "twice as many complaints . . .": "Abused and Confused," *News-
week,* October 25, 1993, 57.

"street harassment": See Bowman, "Street Harassment and Informal
Ghettoization of Women," 106 *Harvard Law Review* 517 (1993).

"divisive even to feminists": See Katie Roiphe, *The Morning After:*

Sex, Fear and Feminism on Campus (New York: Little, Brown & Co., 1993).

"difficult to reach a consensus . . .": See Linda Greenhouse, "Plain Talk Puts Ginsburg at Fore of Court Debates, *The New York Times,* October 14, 1993, A1.

Harris v. Forklift Systems, Inc., No. 92-1168, decided November 9, 1993.

"with astonishing speed . . .": R. Gaull Silberman, "After *Harris,* More Questions on Harassment," *The Wall Street Journal,* November 17, 1993, A20.

"short, polemical . . .": Jeffrey Rosen, "Fast-Food Justice," *The New York Times,* November 16, 1993, A15.

108   "rejecting by inference . . .": Silberman, "After *Harris.*"

Teresa Harris was subjected to "repeated sexual innuendos and demeaning comments from the company's president. . . ." See Linda Greenhouse, "Court, 9–0 Makes Sex Harassment Easier to Prove," *The New York Times,* November 10, 1993, A1.

"many companies are . . .": Rosen, "Fast-Food Justice."

"epithets, slurs . . .": Silberman, "After *Harris.*"

109   "gets no stars . . .": Ellen Goodman, "Porn victims bill would chill, not clear, climate for women," St. Paul *Pioneer Press,* April 24, 1992, 11A.

"allow the victims . . .": "A Spring Chill," *City Pages,* March 4, 1992, 3.

"advocates of the . . .": "Passions over Pornography," *Time,* March 30, 1992, 52. See also "Feminists Back Anti-Porn Bill," *ABA Journal,* June 1992, 32.

"we don't permit . . .": Sullivan, "First Amendment Wars," 38. See also John Irving's essay in *The New York Times Book Review,* March 29, 1992. Opponents of the move to broadly censor pornography point out that those in favor of such censorship disingenuously confuse *correlation* (some sex offenders admit viewing of pornography) with *causation* (those who view pornography commit sex crimes). Although supporters were unsuccessful in enacting the Compensation Act by mid-1993, plans were made to reintroduce the legislation at a later date.

"if the MacKinnonites' claims . . .": Ibid., 39. This observation applies equally to the enforcement of hate-speech laws against those seeking their protection. See Alan Ellis, "A Glaring Contrast: Criminal Justice in Black and White," *The Wall Street Journal,* May 14, 1992, A15.

anti-child pornography: *New York v. Ferber,* 458 U.S. 747 (1982).

countermanding individual liberty: In June 1993, the Supreme Court held in *Alexander v. United States,* 509 U.S. ___, 113 S.Ct. 2766 (1993), that the forfeiture provisions of the Racketeer Influenced and Corrupt Organizations Act (RICO) did not violate the First Amendment as applied to the owner of numerous businesses dealing in sexually explicit materials. The petitioner, Ferris J. Alexander, an owner of adult bookstores and theaters, was convicted under federal obscenity laws based on a finding that several items sold at the stores were obscene. These convictions led to wholesale forfeitures of commercial real estate and businesses, including numerous items of protected materials (i.e., non-obscene pornography).

Chief Justice Rehnquist, writing for a 5–4 majority, minimized the chilling effect of the decision on "cautious booksellers" now forced to "practice self-censorship" for fear of losing their businesses if a controversial work is deemed obscene.

The dissent, written by Justice Kennedy, labeled the Court's decision "a grave repudiation of First Amendment principles." Adopting a speech-protective posture and citing *Near v. Minnesota*, 283 U.S. 697 (1931), the dissenters severely criticized the majority for failing to consider that "the applicability of First Amendment analysis to a governmental action depends not alone upon the name by which the action is called, but upon its operation and effect on the suppression of speech." Arguing that the majority had now approved a "new method of government control with unmistakable dangers of official censorship," Justice Kennedy noted that "any bookstore or press enterprise could be forfeited as punishment for even a single obscenity conviction."

Considered in historical perspective (i.e., earlier governmental attempts to suppress the distribution of D. H. Lawrence's *Lady Chatterley's Lover* and James Joyce's *Ulysses*), the Court's decision appears to be a serious threat to freedom of expression. Lack of sympathy for those who peddle pornography should not be allowed to obscure the fact that Justice Kennedy is correct in suggesting that the Court's focus in First Amendment cases should be on the "operation and effect" of governmental action, not on the government's proffered justification. Only by reviewing cases in this manner can the Court hope to ensure the continuation of First Amendment freedoms.

110   "Liberal doctrine . . .": Donald Alexander Downs, *The New Politics of Pornography* (Chicago: University of Chicago Press, 1989), 150.

Chapter 9

111   Studs Terkel: *Race: How Blacks & Whites Think & Feel About the American Obsession* (New York: The New Press, 1992), 13. For one viewpoint as to why the "overcoming" did not take place, see Derrick Bell, *Faces at the Bottom of the Well: The Permanence of Racism* (New York: Basic Books, 1992). Bell believes that such progress is an illusion and that white Americans will not respond to the suffering of black Americans until it is in their interest to do so. However, Bell

does cite the case of *Wallace v. Brewer*, 315 F.Supp. 431 (1970), wherein the First Amendment shielded a group of Black Muslims from an overbroad law, 41, 42.

113 For one opinion on how Justice Marshall would have approached this case, see Akhil Reed Amar, "Comment: The Case of the Missing Amendments: *R.A.V. v. City of St. Paul*," 106 *Harvard Law Review* 124, (1992). Amar speculates that Justice Marshall "would have applauded the justices' general reaffirmation of *Texas v. Johnson*." Past that point he hesitates to "put words in Justice Marshall's mouth," 161 (n.189).

"the very soul . . .": Interview with Shelby Steele, *Time*, August 12, 1991, 6. For further discussion of the liberal and conservative views toward race, see "Learning to Talk of Race" *The New York Times Magazine*, August 2, 1992, 24. The author, Cornel West, notes that "the predictable pitting of liberals against conservatives . . . reinforces intellectual parochialism and political paralysis" on the subject of race. See also E. J. Dionne, Jr., *Why Americans Hate Politics* (New York: Touchstone 1992). Dionne summarizes the challenge facing our nation's leaders in dealing with the issue of race relations: "Once again, practicality and morality are on the same side. What is needed, and desperately, is a resurgence of the language of common citizenship that animated the early civil rights movement. Such a language will necessarily involve conservative values, such as self-help and hard work, and the liberal values of generosity and tolerance. Only a combination of these values will lay the basis for a new social contract between black and white Americans," 338.

114 Maya Angelou is quoted in Ronald Dworkin, "One Year Later, the Debate Goes On," *The New York Times Book Review*, October 25, 1992, 1, 39.

"generally bad": Peter Applebone, "Racial Divisions Persist 25 Years After King Killing," *The New York Times*, April 14, 1993, 12.

115 *A Man for All Seasons:* Senator Grassley and Senator Biden both quoted passages from Robert Bolt's life of Thomas More during Senate Judiciary Committee Hearings, September 12, 1991.

117 *United States v. Lee*, 935 F.2d 952, *vacated*, 935 F.2d 960, (8th Cir. 1991).

On October 7, 1993, a badly divided Eighth Circuit Court of Appeals, sitting en banc, overturned Lee's conviction. The majority held that Lee could only be convicted of a violation of 18 U.S.C. section 241 if a jury found that "Lee's actions were done with the intent to advocate the use of force or violence and were likely to produce such action; or that Lee intended to threaten the residents . . . or at least intended to cause residents . . . to reasonably fear the use of imminent force or violence." 6 F.3d 1297, 1304 (8th Cir. 1993).

These federal provisions were later used to prosecute the adult and several of the juveniles involved in the events occurring on June 21, 1990, after the state had failed in its attempt to proceed under section 292.02.

120   *U.S. v. Eichman*, 496 U.S. 310 (1990).
      Life: "The Case for Hate," Fall 1991, 88.

123   In the months following, national news was replete with stories of intolerance among the very groups targeted in the past. African and Korean Americans in Los Angeles; African, Caribbean, and Hasidic Jewish Americans in the Crown Heights section of New York City; and even in the staid halls of the Harvard Law School, where only the third woman president of the Law Review in 106 years came under fire from feminists and minority students for alleged insensitivity.
      Dawson v. Delaware, 503 U.S. ___, 112 S.Ct. 1093 (1992). *Dawson*, an 8–1 decision with Justice Clarence Thomas dissenting alone for the first time, was indirectly related to *R.A.V.* There the Court held that it was constitutional error to admit evidence concerning Dawson's membership in a white racist prison gang, where such information was irrelevant to the punishment phase of a trial.

125   "both liberal-leaning": St. Paul *Pioneer Press*, December 9, 1991, 1D.

126   The article reporting the dissension in Foley's office: Minneapolis *Star Tribune*, December 5, 1991, 1B.
      Tom Foley confirmed this result of the moot-court argument he engaged in at the Department of Justice in Washington, D.C., on December 2, 1991, when I interviewed him on October 1, 1992.
      UWM Post v. Board of Regents of Univ. of Wis. System, 774 F.Supp. 1163, 1181 (Eastern District Wisconsin 1991). In response to this ruling, Donna Shalala, then University of Wisconsin chancellor, later secretary of health and human services in the Clinton administration, argued "we don't feel that the speech rule has anything to do with ideas." Charles Leroux, " 'Hate Speech' Enters Computer Age," *Chicago Tribune*, October 27, 1991, 4. On May 8, 1992, the U.W. board of regents adopted a redrafted speech code. After *R.A.V.* was decided, the board eventually repealed the code in December 1992. See Barry Siegel, "Fighting Words," *Los Angeles Times Magazine*, March 28, 1993. 14.

127   Sandy Nelsen was the assistant to William K. Suter, clerk of the United States Supreme Court. Her duties included working with the attorneys appearing before the Court. Minutes before *R.A.V.* was called on December 4, I had a chance to meet her and thank her for her patience. Those who visit the United States Supreme Court building in Washington, D.C., will quickly note how efficiently and professionally the employees of the Court carry out their duties. The attorneys who brief and argue the cases have the added benefit of working with the competent and considerate members of the clerk's office.
      In discussing motive in the context of free speech, I was reminded of

the language of Judge Learned Hand in a letter written to Justice Oliver Wendell Holmes in 1919: "since the cases actually occur when men are excited and since juries are especially clannish groups . . . it is very questionable whether the test of motive is not a dangerous test. Juries won't much regard the difference between the probable result of the words and the purposes of the utterer." Gerald Gunther, "Learned Hand and the Origins of Modern First Amendment Doctrine: Some Fragments of History," 27 *Stanford Law Review* 719, 759 (Appendix Doc. No. 4), 1975.

127 On December 14, 1992, the Supreme Court agreed to hear the case of *Wisconsin v. Mitchell,* a "bias motive" enhancement law case.

129 I later talked to O'Brien the night before the argument in December, in April as I awaited the decision, and finally on June 22, 1992, the day the decision came down. The longer the Court took to reach its determination, the better he felt our chances were. When I talked to him from Greece after the decision, he conceded he had been wrong with his prediction regarding the outcome and graciously offered his congratulations.

The review of the argument: "First Amendment Finds Unlikely Friends," *Legal Times,* December 9, 1991. It was the most thorough review printed of the oral argument.

131 *Sonya Live:* The acrimony did not end with this interview. Although I received a letter from CNN's home office in Atlanta on December 5, 1991, thanking me for appearing on *Sonya Live,* I soon received a letter dated December 17, 1991, from Sonya Friedman indicating that because a man at the British Consulate had been unable to confirm the banning in England of the display of the Star of David, she was "informing" the president of CNN and the president of the News Department of my "inaccuracy." I was not pleased that Ms. Friedman had failed to contact me regarding my sources for this observation before complaining. I responded with a letter dated December 23, 1991, wherein I noted my source and suggested that Ms. Friedman had lost her objectivity and was not prepared to deal with "issues of this complexity." I received an apology from a vice president of CNN on January 9, 1992. With the exception of Ms. Friedman, everyone at CNN treated me professionally and courteously.

132 Repeal of U.N. resolution: "U.N. Repeals '75 Resolution Equating Zionism to Racism," St. Paul *Pioneer Press* December 17, 1991, 1A.

Chapter 10

134 Isaiah Berlin: *The Crooked Timber of Humanity: Chapters in the History of Ideas* (New York: Vintage 1992), 19.
Salman Rushdie: "Free Speech Is Life Itself," *Time*, December 23, 1991, 50.

Chicago Tribune editorial: "The Right to Burn Crosses and Flags," December 3, 1991, 12.

Poll results: "Let Freedom Ring," *City Pages,* November 25, 1992, 3.

135   "no other forty-five . . .": David S. Broder, "Madison's Incomparable Gift," Minneapolis *Star Tribune,* December 15, 1991.

"Last spring . . .": Ellen Goodman, "To celebrate birthday of Bill of Rights, give someone a piece of your mind," St. Paul *Pioneer Press,* December 15, 1991, 25A.

"There's something stiff . . .": John McDonough, "The Bill of Rights at 100," *The Wall Street Journal,* December 13, 1991, A12.

136   "the speech and press clauses . . .": Anthony Lewis, "Staving Off the Silencers," *The New York Times Sunday Magazine,* December 1, 1991, 73.

Masses Publishing Co. v. Patten, 244 F. 535 (Southern District New York), rev'd 246 F. 24 (2nd Cir. 1917).

137   "it was a rare . . .": Gerald Gunther, "Learned Hand and the Origins of Modern First Amendment Doctrine: Some Fragments of History" 27 *Stanford Law Review* 719, 720 (1975).

Brandenburg v. Ohio, 395 U.S. 444 (1969).

"no longer the . . .": Gunther, *Learned Hand,* 755

"Learned Hand's analysis . . .": Ibid.

"the high esteem . . .": Vincent Blasi, "The First Amendment and the Ideal of Civil Courage: The Brandeis Opinion in Whitney v. California," 29 *William and Mary Law Review* 653, 681 (1988) (quoting from P. Strum, *Louis D. Brandeis: Justice for the People* (1984)).

Whitney v. California, 274 U.S. 357 (1927). By footnote in *Whitney,* Brandeis quoted Thomas Jefferson in support of his defense of freedom of expression: "We have nothing to fear from the demoralizing reasoning of some, if others are left free to demonstrate their errors and especially when the law stands ready to punish the first criminal act produced by the false reasonings; these are safer corrections than the conscience of the judge." 274 U.S. at 375 (n.3).

"freedom to think . . .": Ibid., 375.

138   later criticism of Holmes: See Stanley Ingber, "The Marketplace of Ideas: A Legitimizing Myth," 1984 *Duke Law Journal* 1. Ingber takes issue with Holmes's premise of "rational decision making" in today's society.

"noxious doctrine . . .": Blasi, *The First Amendment,* 674–75.

"Others are brave . . .": Ibid., 687 (quoting Thucydides).

"It is this quality . . .": Ibid., 689.

For a discussion of Chaffee, see generally, Gunther, "Learned Hand." See also David M. Rabban, "The Emergence of Modern First Amendment Doctrine," 50 *University of Chicago Law Review* 1207, 1348 (1984).

139   "novels and dramas . . .": Alexander Meiklejohn, "The First Amendment Is an Absolute," 1961 *Supreme Court Review* 245, 262–63.

"our citizens are . . .": Ibid., 263.

"pathological": Vincent Blasi, "The Pathological Perspective and the First Amendment," 85 *Columbia Law Review* 449, 467 (1985).

For an alternative perspective, see George C. Christie, "Why the First Amendment Should Not Be Interpreted from the Pathological Perspective: A Response to Professor Blasi," 1986 Duke *Law Journal* 683 (1986). "The correct decision in any particular case must be one that is primarily determined by the dynamics of the legal argument in that particular case rather than by a theory of the good encompassing the whole of society. . . . if one despairs of the possibility of coming up with an adequate model of consistency in the law, then one must abandon any claim for objectivity in legal decision making. Law becomes not merely politics but politics with a cynical vengeance because it is dressed in a role of hypocrisy," 694.

140   "not because people . . .": Ronald Dworkin, "The Coming Battles over Free Speech," *The New York Review of Books,* June 11, 1992, 56.

"First, morally responsible . . .": Ibid., 57.

141   Smolla: Smolla, *Free Speech in an Open Society* (New York: Alfred A. Knopf, 1992) 4, 169.

Hentoff: Hentoff, *Free Speech for Me—But Not for Thee* (New York: HarperCollins, 1992) 1.

Holmes: *Abrams v. United States,* 250 U.S. 616 (1919).

142   Bollinger, *The Tolerant Society* (New York: Oxford University Press, 1986).

"One generation . . .": Ibid., 242.

"To a society . . .": Ibid., 157–58.

143   sense of community: "Laura Jones said . . . people either have left her family alone . . . or they have been very neighborly." St. Paul *Pioneer Press,* April 20, 1992, 4A. Mrs. Jones repeated these sentiments on several occasions, including on the *MacNeil/Lehrer Newshour* on February 20, 1992, describing the cards, letters and visits her family had received in support of their right to live in the neighborhood unmolested.

"through lower educational . . .": Carl Sagan and Ann Druyan, "Real Patriots Ask Questions," *Parade* magazine, September 8, 1991, 14.

For juvenile involvement in hate crimes, see St. Paul *Pioneer Press,* December 17, 1992, 1A; *The Wall Street Journal,* December 17, 1992, A14. Studies over recent years in both Minnesota and Germany showed that juveniles (eleven to twenty in Minnesota; sixteen to twenty-one in Germany) committed over two thirds of the hate crimes reported. Clearly, the involvement of young people in such activity is not an isolated phenomenon.

144   "adults are keeping things . . .": The College of Education at the

University of Minnesota pioneered a curriculum teaching political tolerance. One teacher pointed out that ninth grade was a good time to teach tolerance because "anyone who's different gets ostracized and tacked in junior high." Nat Hentoff believes such education should start earlier—preferably at the fifth-grade level when the intellectual curiosity of students often begins.

Lincoln quote: "Bill of Rights stands 200-year test of time," St. Paul *Pioneer Press,* December 15, 1991, 24A.

Carter, "No Known Cure for the Abuse of Power," *The New York Times,* October 4, 1992, 17.

"national consensus . . .": *U.S. v. Eichman,* 496 U.S. 310, 318 (1990).

145   "any suggestion . . .": Ibid., 318.

"we have nothing to fear . . .": Hentoff, *Free Speech,* 235. In Minnesota, the "flag-burning" controversy erupted once again when the Minnesota Senate, prompted by a gallery of American Legion members, voted on March 30, 1992, to retrieve a bill from committee that would have demanded that Congress take action on a constitutional amendment "to prohibit the physical desecration" of the flag. Apparently the chance to play to the crowd on a non-issue with a resolution that would have had no actual impact was too tempting for some legislators. An opponent of the legislation attached a rider to the bill calling for passage of the equal rights amendment for women, leading the sponsor of the flag legislation to withdraw the resolution. St. Paul *Pioneer Press,* March 30, 1992, 1B, April 1992, 2B.

"Without responsible leadership . . .": Downs, *New Politics,* 67, 142.

The failure of lower courts: Ibid., 240 (n.197).

146   "The episode revealed . . .": Ibid., 91.

Berlin, *Crooked Timber,* 15.

Lewis, *Make No Law,* 247.

Errera: "In Defence of Civility: Racial Incitement and Group Libel in French Law," in *Striking a Balance: Hate Speech, Freedom of Expression and Nondiscrimination* (London: Article 19, London and Human Rights Centre, University of Essex, 1992), 156.

147   "what legitimate speech . . .": Sandra Coliver, "Hate Speech Laws: Do They Work?" Ibid., 366.

Bollinger, *Tolerant Society,* 199.

148   "Since the economic . . .": *The Wall Street Journal,* December 8, 1992.

"Germany's criminal libel law . . .": Coliver, "Hate Speech," 365.

"On paper . . .": Neier, *Defending My Enemy* (New York: E.P. Dutton, 1979) 163–64.

"Weimar Germany . . .": Ibid., 165.

New York Times Co. v. Sullivan, 376 U.S. 254 (1964).

149   "the U.S. commitment . . .": Coliver, "Hate Speech," 373.

"the use of the balancing approach . . .": Smolla, *Free Speech,* 40.

Statistics are taken from *The Wall Street Journal,* December 31, 1991. See "Japan in the Mind of America," *Time,* February 10, 1992, 19. A poll of the Japanese indicated that they envied the right of free expression of U.S. citizens more than any other facet of American life.

Chapter 11

150 William H. Rehnquist, *The Supreme Court: How It Was, How It Is* (New York: Quill, 1987), 276.

151 "once and future justices": See Bruce Fein, "A Court of Mediocrity," *ABA Journal,* October 1991, 75.

"rule of five": See Alexander Wohl, "Whose Court Is It?" *ABA Journal,* February 1992, 40.

For an examination of the Rehnquist Court's inconsistency toward the First Amendment, see Bernard Jones, "Justices Still Seeking a Consistent Voice on First Amendment," *National Law Journal,* August 19, 1991, S4.

152 "lower federal courts . . .": "Supreme Court Justices Slash Their Workload," St. Paul *Pioneer Press,* March 7, 1992, 3A. The 1991–1992 term was to produce only 108 decisions, the lowest since the 1970–1971 term. In comparison, several terms in the 1980s "produced 151 decisions each, and most yielded about 140." Ibid.

"conservative intellectuals": David G. Savage, *Turning Right: The Making of the Rehnquist Supreme Court* (New York: John Wiley & Sons, Inc. 1992), 260.

Barnes v. Glen Theatre Inc., 501 U.S. ___, 111 S.Ct. 2456 (1991).

One year after *R.A.V.* was decided, Chief Justice Rehnquist reiterated this conservative commitment to free speech, particularly on campuses across the nation, in a commencement address to students at George Mason University. "Ideas with which we disagree—so long as they remain ideas and not conduct . . . should be confronted with argument and persuasion, not suppression. . . ." "Schools should safeguard all views, Rehnquist says," St. Paul *Pioneer Press,* May 23, 1993, 6A.

153 *Rust v. Sullivan,* 500 U.S. 1753, 111 S.Ct. 1759 (1991). This "gag rule" was overturned by executive order issued by President Clinton on January 22, 1993.

154 "drenched with sweat": Rehnquist, *Supreme Court,* 283

155 Rehnquist has noted: Ibid., 281.

specific methods and strategies: See Paul M. Barrett, "Cigarette-Liability Case Should Provide Lessons on the Tactics to Use Before the Rehnquist Court," *The Wall Street Journal,* January 13, 1992, A18. See also Linda Greenhouse, "Supremely Sheltered," *The New York Times Magazine,* March 7, 1993, 84.

156   article severely criticizing: See David Carr, "One Stormy Day in
       Court," *Minnesota Lawyer,* June, 1991, 4.
       Cohen v. Cowles Media Co., 501 U.S. ___, 111 S.Ct. 2513 (1991)

158   young woman: The woman arguing on behalf of RLC was Katherian
       D. Roe of the Federal Public Defender's Office for the district of
       Minnesota. The case was *U.S. v. R.L.C.,* 503 U.S. ___, 112 S.Ct. 1329
       decided March 24, 1992, in favor of RLC.

159   *Beauharnais v. Illinois,* 343 U.S. 250. "The Framers of the Constitu-
       tion knew human nature as well as we do. They too had lived in
       dangerous days; they too knew the suffocating influence of orthodoxy
       and standardized thought. They weighed the compulsions for re-
       strained speech and thought against the abuses of liberty. They chose
       liberty." 343 U.S. at 287.
       U.S. v. Schwimmer, 279 U.S. 644 (1929). ". . . if there is any principle
       of the Constitution that more imperatively calls for the attachment
       than any other it is the principle of free thought—not free thought for
       those who agree with us but freedom for the thought we hate." 279
       U.S. at 654.
       Abrams v. U.S., 250 U.S. 616 (1919). ". . . we should be eternally
       vigilant against attempts to check the expression of opinions that we
       loathe and believe to be fraught with death . . ." 250 U.S. at 616.

160   "official censure . . .": Bollinger, *Tolerant Society,* 29.
       most majority opinions: *The Wall Street Journal,* June 28, 1991, A10.
       deserved reputation: See Howard Kohn, "Front and Center," *Los
       Angeles Times Magazine,* April 18, 1993, 14.

162   Kennedy voting record: *The Wall Street Journal,* June 28, 1991, A10.
       Kennedy's disappointing conservatives: Paul M. Barrett, "Kennedy's
       High Court Tenure Fails to Console Bork-Smitten Conservatives";
       The Wall Street Journal, February 5, 1992, B2, and Linda Greenhouse,
       "In Surprise, High Court Appears Less Solid," *The New York Times*
       May 31, 1992, 14.

164   "rarely did Rehnquist . . .": Savage, *Turning Right,* 159.

165   *Hustler Magazine, Inc. v. Falwell,* 485 U.S. 46 (1988).
       "In most constitutional . . .": Savage, *Turning Right,* 162.

166   Scalia's attitude toward freedom of the press: "Friend of the Court
       Doesn't Help Press in Cases of Libel," *The Wall Street Journal,* April
       28, 1992, A6.
       not a consensus maker: Wohl, "Whose Court Is It?" 40.
       See also Paul M. Barrett, "Despite Expectation, Scalia Fails to Unify
       Conservatives on Court," *The Wall Street Journal,* April 28, 1992, A1.

168   *Wooley v. Maynard,* 430 U.S. 705 (1977).

169   Souter's voting record: *The Wall Street Journal,* June 28, 1991, A10.
       See also *The Wall Street Journal,* February 2, 1991, A1, where the
       author observes that many court observers misjudged Souter, mistak-

ing "a person who is conservative politically for one who would be a conservative activist on the bench."

Chapter 12

173 "Oral argument . . .": Rehnquist, *Supreme Court*, 277.

174 University of Michigan speech code: *Doe v. University of Michigan*, 721 F. Supp. 852, 856 (Eastern District Michigan 1989).

175 *NAACP v. Button*, 371 U.S. 415, 435 (1963).

176 *New York v. Ferber*, 458 U.S. 747 (1982).

177 "The storm troopers . . .": Nigel Hamilton, *JFK: Reckless Youth* (New York: Random House, 1992), 271.
"very intelligent . . .": Ibid., 621.
"led a contingent . . .": Savage, *Turning Right*, 92.
"his biggest mistake . . .": *The Wall Street Journal*, March 22, 1993, A16.
White's voting record: *The Wall Street Journal*, June 28, 1991, A10.
Lewis v. New Orleans, 415 U.S. 123 (1974).

178 *Gooding v. Wilson*, 405 U.S. 518 (1972).

179 Stevens's voting record: *The Wall Street Journal*, June 28, 1991, A10.

181 Retired Justice Brennan was quoted in "Brennan Feeling Fine in Retirement," *USA Today*, December 10, 1991, 2A.

183 $1 million gift: *The Wall Street Journal*, January 22, 1992, A14.

185 Amar, "The Case of the Missing Amendments: *R.A.V. v. City of St. Paul*," 106 *Harvard Law Review* 124 (1992); Sullivan, *Foreword: The Justices of Rules and Standards*, 106 *Harvard Law Review* 24 (1992).
"outcome would have . . .": Ibid., 41.

187 See "The Demise of the *Chaplinsky* Fighting Words Doctrine: An Argument for Its Interment," 106 *Harvard Law Review* 1129 (1993). The author concludes that by "overruling *Chaplinsky,* the Court not only would eliminate a legal doctrine that manifests an anachronistic male bias, but also would eradicate a device that enables officials to use their discretionary power to harass minorities or to suppress the dissident speech," 1146.

189 "Conceived in Grecian thought . . .": Hamilton, *JFK*, 776.

Chapter 13

190 *R.A.V. v. City of St. Paul, Minnesota* 505 U.S. ___, 112 S.Ct. 2538, 2550 (1992).

191 Catholic feast day: June 22–27 is the twelfth week in ordinary time in the Catholic ecclesiastical calendar. Monday, June 22, is the memorial day for three Catholic saints. One of the three is "Thomas More, martyr."

"own safety's sake": Bolt, *Man for All Seasons,* 37, 38.

"shoot them down . . .": Charles Laszewski, "Leader Angered, Offers Prospect of Self-Defense," St. Paul *Pioneer Press,* June 23, 1992, 1A.

major newspapers: Linda Greenhouse, "High Court Voids Law Singling Out Crimes Of Hatred," *The New York Times,* June 23, 1992, A1; Ruth Marcus, "Supreme Court Overturns Law Barring Hate Crimes," *The Washington Post,* June 23, 1992, A1.

"arid absolutism": Linda Greenhouse, "2 Visions of Free Speech," *The New York Times,* June 24, 1992, A1.

192 The exchange between Justices Scalia and White: 112 S.Ct. 2542 (n.3); 112 S.Ct. 2550 (n.1).

193 "Justice White overplayed . . .": Amar, "The Case of the Missing Amendments: *R.A.V. v. City of St. Paul,*" 106 *Harvard Law Review* 124, 129 (n.38) (1992).

194 "categories of speech . . .": 112 S.Ct. 2543. As one commentator noted: "By this decision, the Court eliminated the strongest argument for the continuing vitality of *Chaplinsky's* 'inflict injury' prong." "The Demise of the *Chaplinsky* Fighting Words Doctrine: An Argument for Its Interment," 106 *Harvard Law Review* 1129, 1140 (1993).

"the point of . . .": 112 S.Ct. 2548, 2549.

195 "In fact . . .": 112 S.Ct. 2550.

For an interesting analysis of the *R.A.V.* decision and the different approaches of the justices based on "analogical reasoning" rather than "broad pronouncements about . . . free speech," see Cass R. Sunstein, "Commentary: On Analogical Reasoning," 106 *Harvard Law Review* 741, 766 (1993).

196 "selection of this case . . .": 112 S.Ct. 2559.

student speech codes: See note on "The Demise of the *Chaplinsky* Fighting Words Doctrine."

197 "evil" and "worthless": 112 S.Ct. 2553.

"hoodlums": 112 S.Ct. 2561.

"The Freedom of Speech," 102 *Yale Law Journal* 1293 (1993).

"when official power . . .": Ibid., 1309.

speech and conduct: Ibid., 1309.

198 "Let us hope . . .": Ibid., 1313.

"an occasion . . .": "Speech Therapy," *The New Republic,* 13, July 20, 1992, 7.

199 The story concerning Professor Powell is taken from *In Memoriam: Paul A. Freund,* 106 *Harvard Law Review* 16 (1992).

"the nation's leading . . .": Neier, *Enemy,* 10.

ACLU "implemented . . .": Dennis Cauchon, "Debate over Competing Principles," *USA Today,* March 31, 1993, 2A. See also Neil A. Lewis, "At A.C.L.U., Free-Speech Balancing Act," *The New York Times,* April 4, 1993, 12.

200   "around the country . . .": Nat Hentoff, "Scalia Outdoes the ACLU," *The Washington Post*, June 30, 1992.

201   minor bankruptcy matter: *Connecticut Nat. Bank v. Germain*, 112 S.Ct. 1146 (1992).
The voting pattern statistics for the 1991 term are taken from 106 *Harvard Law Review* 378–82 (1992).

202   One year after *R.A.V.* was decided, new information surfaced that indicated Justice Blackmun may have had a generally restrictive view toward *both* types of unpopular symbolic expression. The late Justice Thurgood Marshall donated a number of papers to the Library of Congress in 1991 that were made available to the public after his death in 1993. Included among the papers was a "one-sentence memo" from Justice Blackmun to Justice Brennan noting his vote in the case of *Texas v. Johnson*. Surprisingly, Blackmun cast the fifth and deciding vote, not Justice Scalia or Kennedy, and he waited until two days before the decision was issued to do so, writing that he "struggled with this difficult and distasteful little (big?) case, but I join your opinion." "Marshall Papers Reveal How Supreme Court Does Its work," St. Paul *Pioneer Press*, May 23, 1993, 2A.
Greenhouse, "2 Visions."
Dworkin, "The Coming Battles over Free Speech," June 11, 1992, 55.

203   "it is the central, defining, premise . . .": Ibid.

Chapter 14

204   "The result . . .": Greenhouse, "2 Visions."
"This is an occasion . . .": "Speech Therapy."

205   "closest to treating . . .": Kathleen M. Sullivan, "Foreword: The Justices of Rules and Standards," 106 *Harvard Law Review* 42 (1992).
"more common ground . . .": Amar, "Missing Amendments," 132.
"symbolic expression . . .": Ibid., 133.
"after *R.A.V* . . .": Ibid., 125.

206   "government may not . . .": Ibid., 137.

207   "realistic possibility . . .": 112 S.Ct. 2538.
"political expression . . .": Amar, "Missing Amendments," 140.
Justice Stevens: 112 S.Ct. 2571.

208   "courts must guard . . .": Amar, "Missing Amendments," 142.
Justice Stevens: 112 S.Ct. 2568.
"a welcome . . .": Amar, "Missing Amendments," 146 (n.127).
"The State may . . .": David Cole, "Neutral Standards and Racist Speech," 2 *Reconstruction* 1, 65, 66 (1992).

209   "the majority . . .": Ibid., 68.
"Speech is . . .": Ibid.

209   "near universal . . .": Kathleen M. Sullivan, "The First Amendment Wars," *The New Republic*, September 28, 1992, 36.

210   "gearing the First Amendment . . .": Ibid., 40.
       "pragmatic reason . . .": Ibid.
       State of Wisconsin v. Todd Mitchell 485 N.W.2d 807 (Wis. 1992).
       "intentionally selected . . .": Wisconsin Statute section 939.645, Stats.
       1989–90.
211   "sharp distinction . . .": Cole, "Neutral Standards," 66.
       Justice Abrahamson: 485 N.W.2d 818, 819.
       Ohio: *State v. Wyant*, 597 N.E.2d 450 (1992).
       Oregon: *State v. Plowman*, 838 P.2d 558 (1992).
       Florida: *Dobbins v. State*, 605 So.2d 922 (1992).
212   "If you do not . . .": *The New York Times Book Review*, January 3,
       1993, 11.
       "Criminalization . . .": Susan Gellman, "Sticks and Stones Can Put
       You in Jail, But Can Words Increase Your Sentence? Constitutional
       and Policy Dilemmas of Ethnic Intimidation Laws," 39 *U.C.L.A. Law
       Review* 333, 339 (1991). For a contrary viewpoint, see *"Hate Is Not
       Speech: A Defense of Penalty Enhancement for Hate Crimes,"* 106
       Harvard Law Review 1314 (1993).
       "Why should . . .": St. Paul *Pioneer Press*, December 24, 1992, 8A.
       "if the state prevails . . .": Linda Greenhouse, "Defining the Freedom
       to Hate While Punching," *The New York Times*, December 20, 1992,
       5. For interesting viewpoints on these issues, see Jonathan Rauch,
       Kindly Inquisitors: The New Attacks on Free Thought (Chicago:
       University of Chicago Press, 1993) and Robert Hughes, *Culture of
       Complaint: The Fraying of America* (New York Public Library/Ox-
       ford University Press, 1993).
213   "the worst fears . . .": Paul M. Barrett, "Justice Thomas Confirms
       Fears of His Critics," *The Wall Street Journal*, July 1, 1992, B4.
       "powerful, if qualified . . .": Linda Greenhouse, "Moderates on Court
       Defy Predictions," *The New York Times*, July 5, 1992, 1.
       Blasi: "A Surprising Display of Centrist Thinking," *Time*, July 6,
       1992, 16.
214   Justice Souter: Linda Greenhouse, "3 Centrist Justices Are Heirs to
       Liberal Heroes," *The New York Times*, October 25, 1992, 1.
       "More women than men . . .": David Gates, "White Male Paranoia,"
       Newsweek, March 29, 1993, 51.
       "this great realignment . . .": *The Wall Street Journal*, December 2,
       1992, A4.
       "get at the real . . .": St. Paul *Pioneer Press*, January 5, 1992, 9A.
       Wiesenthal: "A Museum of Hate," *Time*, February 15, 1993, 54.
       Parent to child: For an interesting essay on this topic, see Sara Bullard
       "Tolerance Begins in the Home," *The New York Times*, January 10,
       1993, 50.
215   "both sides in . . .": H.D.J. Greenway, "List of Historical Grievances
       Fuel Ethnic Conflicts," St. Paul *Pioneer Press*, January 5, 1993, 9A.

"some African-Americans . . .": Leonard Pitts, Jr., "Ugly Lyrics Grow Louder on Both Sides of the Atlantic," St. Paul *Pioneer Press*, December 25, 1992, 4C.

"labels themselves . . .": Greenhouse, "Defining the Freedom to Hate," 5.

219   Miller later entered a plea of guilty to federal charges and in April 1993 was sentenced to one year in federal prison. The only adult involved in the June 21, 1990, cross-burning, Miller was the only individual to be incarcerated in both federal and state institutions. In July of 1990 he pleaded guilty to a violation of section 292.02 and was sentenced to thirty days.

223   The rule allowing multiple prosecutions by both the state and federal government is known as the "dual sovereignty exception" to the constitutional prohibition against double jeopardy. Originally based on the theory that state and federal governments have different interests, the rule has come under attack as a thinly veiled attempt by the federal government to "clean up" after unsuccessful state prosecutions, as in the Rodney King case. See Ronald J. Allen, "Freedom from Double Jeopardy, Our Lost Liberty," *The Wall Street Journal*, March 17, 1993, A15.

Several juveniles involved in the June 21, 1990, incident (including R.A.V.) were convicted in January 1993 of violating 18 U.S.C. §241 and 42 U.S.C. §3631 by a federal judge sitting without a jury. Both of these provisions punish all threats aimed at the exercise of federally guaranteed rights or privileges, unlike the St. Paul ordinance which prohibited the mere expression of an unpopular viewpoint.

The individuals were referred for probable commitment to state juvenile facilities. Further details were withheld by federal authorities. Then, on April 26, 1994, a three-judge panel from the Eight Circuit denied the appeals of all the juveniles. R.A.V., whose constitutional right to a bigoted *viewpoint* had been upheld after a two-year struggle, had eventually been punished for his *conduct* in the early morning hours of June 21, 1990.

Appendix A

———— ■ ————

R.A.V. v. City of St. Paul, Minnesota
505 U.S. ___, 112 S.Ct. 2538 (1992)

Majority Opinion
(Justices Scalia, Kennedy, Souter, Thomas and Chief Justice
Rehnquist)

SUPREME COURT OF THE UNITED STATES

No. 90-7675

R. A. V., PETITIONER *v.* CITY OF ST. PAUL, MINNESOTA

ON WRIT OF CERTIORARI TO THE SUPREME COURT OF
MINNESOTA

[June 22, 1992]

JUSTICE SCALIA delivered the opinion of the Court.

In the predawn hours of June 21, 1990, petitioner and several other teenagers allegedly assembled a crudely-made cross by taping together broken chair legs. They then allegedly burned the cross inside the fenced yard of a black family that lived across the street from the house where petitioner was staying. Although this conduct could have been punished under any of a number of laws,[1] one of the two provisions under which respondent city of St. Paul chose to charge petitioner (then a juvenile) was the St. Paul Bias-Motivated Crime Ordinance, St. Paul, Minn. Legis. Code §292.02 (1990), which provides:

---

[1]The conduct might have violated Minnesota statutes carrying significant penalties. See, *e.g.,* Minn. St. §609.713(1) (1987) (providing for up to five years in prison for terroristic threats); §609.563 (arson) (providing for up to five years and a $10,000 fine, depending on the value of the property intended to be damaged); §606.595 (Supp. 1992) (criminal damage to property) (providing for up to one year and a $3,000 fine, depending upon the extent of the damage to the property).

"Whoever places on public or private property a symbol, object, appellation, characterization or graffiti, including, but not limited to, a burning cross or Nazi swastika, which one knows or has reasonable grounds to know arouses anger, alarm or resentment in others on the basis of race, color, creed, religion or gender commits disorderly conduct and shall be guilty of a misdemeanor."

Petitioner moved to dismiss this count on the ground that the St. Paul ordinance was substantially overbroad and impermissibly content-based and therefore facially invalid under the First Amendment.[2] The trial court granted this motion, but the Minnesota Supreme Court reversed. That court rejected petitioner's overbreadth claim because, as construed in prior Minnesota cases, see, *e.g., In re Welfare of S. L. J.*, 263 N. W. 2d 412 (Minn. 1978), the modifying phrase "arouses anger, alarm or resentment in others" limited the reach of the ordinance to conduct that amounts to "fighting words," *i.e.,* "conduct that itself inflicts injury or tends to incite immediate violence . . . ," *In re Welfare of R. A. V.*, 464 N. W. 2d 507, 510 (Minn. 1991) (citing *Chaplinsky v. New Hampshire*, 315 U. S. 568, 572 (1942)), and therefore the ordinance reached only expression "that the first amendment does not protect." 464 N. W. 2d, at 511. The court also concluded that the ordinance was not impermissibly content-based because, in its view, "the ordinance is a narrowly tailored means toward accomplishing the compelling governmental interest in protecting the community against bias-motivated threats to public safety and order." *Ibid.* We granted certiorari, 501 U. S. ___ (1991).

I

In construing the St. Paul ordinance, we are bound by the construction given to it by the Minnesota court. *Posadas de Puerto Rico Associates v. Tourism Co. of Puerto Rico*, 478 U. S. 328, 339 (1986); *New York v. Ferber*, 458 U. S. 747, 769, n. 24 (1982); *Terminiello v. Chicago*, 337 U. S. 1, 4 (1949). Accordingly, we accept the Minnesota Supreme Court's authoritative statement that the ordinance reaches only those expressions that constitute "fighting words" within the meaning of *Chaplinsky.* 464 N. W. 2d, at 510–511. Petitioner and his *amici* urge us to modify the scope of the *Chaplinsky* formulation,

---

[2]Petitioner has also been charged, in Count I of the delinquency petition, with a violation of Minn. Stat. §609.2231(4) (Supp. 1990) (racially motivated assaults). Petitioner did not challenge this count.

thereby invalidating the ordinance as "substantially overbroad," *Broadrick* v. *Oklahoma,* 413 U. S. 601, 610 (1973). We find it unnecessary to consider this issue. Assuming, *arguendo,* that all of the expression reached by the ordinance is proscribable under the "fighting words" doctrine, we nonetheless conclude that the ordinance is facially unconstitutional in that it prohibits otherwise permitted speech solely on the basis of the subjects the speech addresses.[3]

The First Amendment generally prevents government from proscribing speech, see, *e.g., Cantwell* v. *Connecticut,* 310 U. S. 296, 309–311 (1940), or even expressive conduct, see, *e.g., Texas* v. *Johnson,* 491 U. S. 397, 406 (1989), because of disapproval of the ideas expressed. Content-based regulations are presumptively invalid. *Simon & Schuster, Inc.* v. *Members of N. Y. State Crime Victims Bd.,* 502 U. S. ___, ___ (1991) (slip op., at 8–9); *id.,* at ___ (KENNEDY, J., concurring in judgment) (slip op., at 3–4); *Consolidated Edison Co. of N. Y.* v. *Public Serv. Comm'n of N. Y.,* 447 U. S. 530, 536 (1980); *Police Dept. of Chicago* v. *Mosley,* 408 U. S. 92, 95 (1972). From 1791 to the present, however, our society, like other free but civilized societies, has permitted restrictions upon the content of speech in a

---

[3]Contrary to JUSTICE WHITE's suggestion, *post,* at 1–2, petitioner's claim is "fairly included" within the questions presented in the petition for certiorari, see this Court's Rule 14.1(a). It was clear from the petition and from petitioner's other filings in this Court (and in the courts below) that his assertion that the St. Paul ordinance "violat[es] overbreadth . . . principles of the First Amendment," Pet. for Cert. i, was *not* just a technical "overbreadth" claim—*i. e.,* a claim that the ordinance violated the rights of too many third parties—but included the contention that the ordinance was "overbroad" in the sense of restricting more speech than the Constitution permits, even in its application to him, because it is content-based. An important component of petitioner's argument is, and has been all along, that narrowly construing the ordinance to cover only "fighting words" cannot cure this fundamental defect. *Id.,* at 12, 14, 15–16. In his briefs in this Court, petitioner argued that a narrowing construction was ineffective because (1) its boundaries were vague, Brief for Petitioner 26, and because (2) denominating particular expression a "fighting word" because of the impact of its ideological content upon the audience is inconsistent with the First Amendment, Reply Brief for Petitioner 5; *id.,* at 13 ("[The ordinance] is overbroad, *viewpoint discriminatory* and vague as 'narrowly construed'") (emphasis added). At oral argument, counsel for Petitioner reiterated this second point: "It is . . . one of my positions, that in [punishing only some fighting words and not others], even though it is a subcategory, technically, of unprotected conduct, [the ordinance] still is picking out an opinion, a disfavored message, and making that clear through the State." Tr. of Oral Arg. 8. In resting our judgment upon this contention, we have not departed from our criteria of what is "fairly included" within the petition. See *Arkansas Electric Cooperative Corp.* v. *Arkansas Pub. Serv. Comm'n,* 461 U. S. 375, 382, n. 6 (1983); *Brown* v. *Socialist Workers '74 Campaign Comm.,* 459 U. S. 87, 94, n. 9 (1982); *Eddings* v. *Oklahoma,* 455 U. S. 104, 113, n. 9 (1982); see generally R. Stern, E. Gressman, & S. Shapiro, Supreme Court Practice 361 (6th ed. 1986).

few limited areas, which are "of such slight social value as a step to truth that any benefit that may be derived from them is clearly outweighed by the social interest in order and morality." *Chaplinsky, supra,* at 572. We have recognized that "the freedom of speech" referred to by the First Amendment does not include a freedom to disregard these traditional limitations. See, *e.g., Roth* v. *United States,* 354 U. S. 476 (1957) (obscenity); *Beauharnais* v. *Illinois,* 343 U. S. 250 (1952) (defamation); *Chaplinsky* v. *New Hampshire, supra,* ("fighting words"); see generally *Simon & Schuster, supra,* at __ (KENNEDY, J., concurring in judgment) (slip op., at 4). Our decisions since the 1960's have narrowed the scope of the traditional categorical exceptions for defamation, see *New York Times Co.* v. *Sullivan,* 376 U. S. 254 (1964); *Gertz* v. *Robert Welch, Inc.,* 418 U. S. 323 (1974); see generally *Milkovich* v. *Lorain Journal Co.,* 497 U. S. 1, 13–17 (1990), and for obscenity, see *Miller* v. *California,* 413 U. S. 15 (1973), but a limited categorical approach has remained an important part of our First Amendment jurisprudence.

We have sometimes said that these categories of expression are "not within the area of constitutionally protected speech," *Roth, supra,* at 483; *Beauharnais, supra,* at 266; *Chaplinsky, supra,* at 571–572, or that the "protection of the First Amendment does not extend" to them, *Bose Corp.* v. *Consumers Union of United States, Inc.,* 466 U. S. 485, 504 (1984); *Sable Communications of Cal., Inc.* v. *FCC,* 492 U. S. 115, 124 (1989). Such statements must be taken in context, however, and are no more literally true than is the occasionally repeated shorthand characterizing obscenity "as not being speech at all," Sunstein, Pornography and the First Amendment, 1986 Duke L. J. 589, 615, n. 146. What they mean is that these areas of speech can, consistently with the First Amendment, be regulated *because of their constitutionally proscribable content* (obscenity, defamation, etc.)—not that they are categories of speech entirely invisible to the Constitution, so that they may be made the vehicles for content discrimination unrelated to their distinctively proscribable content. Thus, the government may proscribe libel; but it may not make the further content discrimination of proscribing *only* libel critical of the government. We recently acknowledged this distinction in *Ferber,* 458 U. S., at 763, where, in upholding New York's child pornography law, we expressly recognized that there was no "question here of censoring a particular literary theme. . . ." See also *id.,* at 775 (O'CONNOR, J., concurring) ("As drafted, New York's statute does not attempt to suppress the communication of particular ideas").

Our cases surely do not establish the proposition that the First

Amendment imposes no obstacle whatsoever to regulation of particular instances of such proscribable expression, so that the government "may regulate [them] freely," *post,* at 4 (WHITE, J., concurring in judgment). That would mean that a city council could enact an ordinance prohibiting only those legally obscene works that contain criticism of the city government or, indeed, that do not include endorsement of the city government. Such a simplistic, all-or-nothing-at-all approach to First Amendment protection is at odds with common sense and with our jurisprudence as well.[4] It is not true that "fighting words" have at most a *"de minimis"* expressive content, *ibid.,* or that their content is *in all respects* "worthless and undeserving of constitutional protection," *post,* at 6; sometimes they are quite expressive indeed. We have not said that they constitute *"no part of the expression of ideas,"* but only that they constitute "no *essential* part of any exposition of ideas." *Chaplinsky,* 315 U. S., at 572 (emphasis added).

The proposition that a particular instance of speech can be proscribable on the basis of one feature (*e.g.,* obscenity) but not on the basis of another (*e.g.,* opposition to the city government) is common-

---

[4]JUSTICE WHITE concedes that a city council cannot prohibit only those legally obscene works that contain criticism of the city government, *post,* at 11, but asserts that to be the consequence, not of the First Amendment, but of the Equal Protection Clause. Such content-based discrimination would not, he asserts, "be rationally related to a legitimate government interest," *ibid.* But of course the only *reason* that government interest is not a "legitimate" one is that it violates the First Amendment. This Court itself has occasionally fused the First Amendment into the Equal Protection Clause in this fashion, but at least with the acknowledgment (which JUSTICE WHITE cannot afford to make) that the First Amendment underlies its analysis. See *Police Dept. of Chicago* v. *Mosley,* 408 U. S. 92, 95 (1972) (ordinance prohibiting only nonlabor picketing violated the Equal Protection Clause because there was no "appropriate governmental interest" supporting the distinction inasmuch as "the First Amendment means that government has no power to restrict expression because of its message, its ideas, its subject matter, or its content"); *Carey* v. *Brown,* 447 U. S. 455 (1980). See generally *Simon & Schuster, Inc.* v. *Members of N. Y. State Crime Victims Bd.,* 502 U. S. ___, ___ (1991) (KENNEDY, J., concurring in judgment) (slip op., at 2–3).

JUSTICE STEVENS seeks to avoid the point by dismissing the notion of obscene anti-government speech as "fantastical," *post,* at 3, apparently believing that any reference to politics prevents a finding of obscenity. Unfortunately for the purveyors of obscenity, that is obviously false. A shockingly hard core pornographic movie that contains a model sporting a political tattoo can be found, *"taken as a whole* [to] lac[k] serious literary, artistic, political, or scientific value," *Miller* v. *California,* 413 U. S. 15, 24 (1973) (emphasis added). Anyway, it is easy enough to come up with other illustrations of a content-based restriction upon "unprotected speech" that is obviously invalid: the anti-government libel illustration mentioned earlier, for one. See *supra,* at 5. And of course the concept of racist fighting words is, unfortunately, anything but a "highly speculative hypothetica[l]," *post,* at 4.

place, and has found application in many contexts. We have long held, for example, that nonverbal expressive activity can be banned because of the action it entails, but not because of the ideas it expresses—so that burning a flag in violation of an ordinance against outdoor fires could be punishable, whereas burning a flag in violation of an ordinance against dishonoring the flag is not. See *Johnson,* 491 U. S., at 406–407. See also *Barnes* v. *Glen Theatre, Inc.,* 501 U. S. ___, ___–___ (1991) (plurality) (slip op., at 4–6); *id.,* at ___–___ (SCALIA, J., concurring in judgment) (slip op., at 5–6); *id.,* at ___–___ (SOUTER, J., concurring in judgment) (slip op., at 1–2); *United States* v. *O'Brien,* 391 U. S. 367, 376–377 (1968). Similarly, we have upheld reasonable "time, place, or manner" restrictions, but only if they are "justified without reference to the content of the regulated speech." *Ward* v. *Rock Against Racism,* 491 U. S. 781, 791 (1989) (internal quotation marks omitted); see also *Clark* v. *Community for Creative Non-Violence,* 468 U. S. 288, 298 (1984) (noting that the *O'Brien* test differs little from the standard applied to time, place, or manner restrictions). And just as the power to proscribe particular speech on the basis of a noncontent element (*e.g.,* noise) does not entail the power to proscribe the same speech on the basis of a content element; so also, the power to proscribe it on the basis of *one* content element (*e.g.,* obscenity) does not entail the power to proscribe it on the basis of *other* content elements.

In other words, the exclusion of "fighting words" from the scope of the First Amendment simply means that, for purposes of that Amendment, the unprotected features of the words are, despite their verbal character, essentially a "nonspeech" element of communication. Fighting words are thus analogous to a noisy sound truck: Each is, as Justice Frankfurter recognized, a "mode of speech," *Niemotko* v. *Maryland,* 340 U. S. 268, 282 (1951) (Frankfurter, J., concurring in result); both can be used to convey an idea; but neither has, in and of itself, a claim upon the First Amendment. As with the sound truck, however, so also with fighting words: The government may not regulate use based on hostility—or favoritism—towards the underlying message expressed. Compare *Frisby* v. *Schultz,* 487 U. S. 474 (1988) (upholding, against facial challenge, a content-neutral ban on targeted residential picketing) with *Carey* v. *Brown,* 447 U. S. 455 (1980) (invalidating a ban on residential picketing that exempted labor picketing).[5]

---

[5] Although JUSTICE WHITE asserts that our analysis disregards "established principles of First Amendment law," *post,* at 19, he cites not a single case (and we are

The concurrences describe us as setting forth a new First Amendment principle that prohibition of constitutionally proscribable speech cannot be "underinclusiv[e]," *post,* at 6 (WHITE, J., concurring in judgment)—a First Amendment "absolutism" whereby "within a particular 'proscribable' category of expression, . . . a government must either proscribe *all* speech or no speech at all," *post,* at 4 (STEVENS, J., concurring in judgment). That easy target is of the concurrences' own invention. In our view, the First Amendment imposes not an "underinclusiveness" limitation but a "content discrimination" limitation upon a State's prohibition of proscribable speech. There is no problem whatever, for example, with a State's prohibiting obscenity (and other forms of proscribable expression) only in certain media or markets, for although that prohibition would be "underinclusive," it would not discriminate on the basis of content. See, *e.g., Sable Communications,* 492 U. S., at 124–126 (upholding 47 U. S. C. §223(b)(1) (1988), which prohibits obscene *telephone* communications).

Even the prohibition against content discrimination that we assert the First Amendment requires is not absolute. It applies differently in the context of proscribable speech than in the area of fully protected speech. The rationale of the general prohibition, after all, is that content discrimination "rais[es] the specter that the Government may effectively drive certain ideas or viewpoints from the marketplace," *Simon & Schuster,* 502 U. S., at ___ (slip op., at 9); *Leathers* v. *Medlock,* 499 U. S. ___, ___ (1991); *FCC* v. *League of Women Voters of California,* 468 U. S. 364, 383–384 (1984); *Consolidated Edison Co.,* 447 U. S., at 536; *Police Dept. of Chicago* v. *Mosley,* 408 U. S., at 95–98. But content discrimination among various instances of a class of proscribable speech often does not pose this threat.

When the basis for the content discrimination consists entirely of the very reason the entire class of speech at issue is proscribable, no significant danger of idea or viewpoint discrimination exists. Such a reason, having been adjudged neutral enough to support exclusion of the entire class of speech from First Amendment protection, is also neutral enough to form the basis of distinction within the class. To illustrate: A State might choose to prohibit only that obscenity which is the most patently offensive *in its prurience*—*i. e.,* that which in-

---

aware of none) that even involved, much less considered and resolved, the issue of content discrimination through regulation of "unprotected" speech—though we plainly *recognized* that as an issue in *Ferber.* It is of course contrary to all traditions of our jurisprudence to consider the law on this point conclusively resolved by broad language in cases where the issue was not presented or even envisioned.

volves the most lascivious displays of sexual activity. But it may not prohibit, for example, only that obscenity which includes offensive *political* messages. See *Kucharek* v. *Hanaway,* 902 F. 2d 513, 517 (CA7 1990), cert. denied, 498 U. S. ___ (1991). And the Federal Government can criminalize only those threats of violence that are directed against the President, see 18 U. S. C. §871—since the reasons why threats of violence are outside the First Amendment (protecting individuals from the fear of violence, from the disruption that fear engenders, and from the possibility that the threatened violence will occur) have special force when applied to the person of the President. See *Watts* v. *United States,* 394 U. S. 705, 707 (1969) (upholding the facial validity of §871 because of the "overwhelmin[g] interest in protecting the safety of [the] Chief Executive and in allowing him to perform his duties without interference from threats of physical violence"). But the Federal Government may not criminalize only those threats against the President that mention his policy on aid to inner cities. And to take a final example (one mentioned by JUSTICE STEVENS, *post,* at 6–7), a State may choose to regulate price advertising in one industry but not in others, because the risk of fraud (one of the characteristics of commercial speech that justifies depriving it of full First Amendment protection, see *Virginia Pharmacy Bd.* v. *Virginia Citizens Consumer Council, Inc.,* 425 U. S. 748, 771–772 (1976)) is in its view greater there. Cf. *Morales* v. *Trans World Airlines, Inc.,* 504 U. S. ___ (1992) (state regulation of airline advertising); *Ohralik* v. *Ohio State Bar Assn.,* 436 U. S. 447 (1978) (state regulation of lawyer advertising). But a State may not prohibit only that commercial advertising that depicts men in a demeaning fashion, see, *e.g.,* L. A. Times, Aug. 8, 1989, section 4, p. 6, col. 1.

Another valid basis for according differential treatment to even a content-defined subclass of proscribable speech is that the subclass happens to be associated with particular "secondary effects" of the speech, so that the regulation is *"justified* without reference to the content of the . . . speech," *Renton* v. *Playtime Theatres, Inc.,* 475 U. S. 41, 48 (1986) (quoting, with emphasis, *Virginia Pharmacy Bd., supra,* at 771); see also *Young* v. *American Mini Theatres, Inc.,* 427 U. S. 50, 71, n. 34 (1976) (plurality); *id.,* at 80–82 (Powell, J., concurring); *Barnes,* 501 U. S., at ___–___ (SOUTER, J., concurring in judgment) (slip op., at 3–7). A State could, for example, permit all obscene live performances except those involving minors. Moreover, since words can in some circumstances violate laws directed not against speech but against conduct (a law against treason, for example, is violated by telling the enemy the nation's defense secrets), a particular content-based subcategory of a proscribable class of speech can be swept up incidentally within the reach of a statute directed at conduct rather than speech. See *id.*, at ___ (plurality) (slip op., at 4); *id.*, at ___ (SCALIA, J., concurring in judgment) (slip op., at 5–6); *id.*, at ___ (SOUTER, J., concurring in judgment) (slip op., at 1–2); *FTC v. Superior Court Trial Lawyers Assn.*, 493 U. S. 411, 425–432 (1990); *O'Brien*, 391 U. S., at 376–377. Thus, for example, sexually derogatory "fighting words," among other words, may produce a violation of Title VII's general prohibition against sexual discrimination in employment practices, 42 U. S. C. §2000e-2; 29 CFR §1604.11 (1991). See also 18 U. S. C. §242; 42 U. S. C. §§1981, 1982. Where the government does not target conduct on the basis of its expressive content, acts are not shielded from regulation merely because they express a discriminatory idea or philosophy.

These bases for distinction refute the proposition that the selectivity of the restriction is "even arguably 'conditioned upon the sovereign's agreement with what a speaker may intend to say.'" *Metromedia, Inc. v. San Diego*, 453 U. S. 490, 555 (1981) (STEVENS, J., dissenting in part) (citation omitted). There may be other such bases as well. Indeed, to validate such selectivity (where totally proscribable speech is at issue) it may not even be necessary to identify any particular "neutral" basis, so long as the nature of the content discrimination is such that there is no realistic possibility that official suppression of ideas is afoot. (We cannot think of any First Amendment interest that would stand in the way of a State's prohibiting only those obscene motion pictures with blue-eyed actresses.) Save for that limitation, the regulation of "fighting words," like the regulation of noisy speech, may address some offensive instances and leave other, equally offensive, instances alone. See *Posadas de Puerto Rico*, 478 U. S., at 342–343.[6]

---

[6]JUSTICE STEVENS cites a string of opinions as supporting his assertion that "selective regulation of speech based on content" is not presumptively invalid. *Post*, at 6–7. Analysis reveals, however, that they do not support it. To begin with, three of them did not command a majority of the Court, *Young v. American Mini Theatres, Inc.*, 427 U. S. 50, 63–73 (1976) (plurality); *FCC v. Pacifica Foundation*, 438 U. S. 726, 744–748 (1978) (plurality); *Lehman v. City of Shaker Heights*, 418 U. S. 298 (1974) (plurality), and two others did not even discuss the First Amendment, *Morales v. Trans World Airlines, Inc.*, 504 U. S. ___ (1992); *Jacob Siegel Co. v. FTC*, 327 U. S. 608 (1946). In any event, all that their contents establish is what we readily concede: that presumptive invalidity does not mean invariable invalidity, leaving room for such exceptions as reasonable and viewpoint-neutral content-based discrimination in nonpublic forums, see *Lehman, supra*, at 301–304; see also *Cornelius v. NAACP Legal Defense & Educational Fund, Inc.*, 473 U. S. 788, 806 (1985), or with respect to certain speech by government employees, see *Broadrick v. Oklahoma*, 413 U. S. 601 (1973); see also *CSC v. Letter Carriers*, 413 U. S. 548, 564–567 (1973).

II

Applying these principles to the St. Paul ordinance, we conclude that, even as narrowly construed by the Minnesota Supreme Court, the ordinance is facially unconstitutional. Although the phrase in the ordinance, "arouses anger, alarm or resentment in others," has been limited by the Minnesota Supreme Court's construction to reach only those symbols or displays that amount to "fighting words," the remaining, unmodified terms make clear that the ordinance applies only to "fighting words" that insult, or provoke violence, "on the basis of race, color, creed, religion or gender." Displays containing abusive invective, no matter how vicious or severe, are permissible unless they are addressed to one of the specified disfavored topics. Those who wish to use "fighting words" in connection with other ideas—to express hostility, for example, on the basis of political affiliation, union membership, or homosexuality—are not covered. The First Amendment does not permit St. Paul to impose special prohibitions on those speakers who express views on disfavored subjects. See *Simon & Schuster,* 502 U. S., at ___ (slip op., at 8–9); *Arkansas Writers' Project, Inc.* v. *Ragland,* 481 U. S. 221, 229–230 (1987).

In its practical operation, moreover, the ordinance goes even beyond mere content discrimination, to actual viewpoint discrimination. Displays containing some words—odious racial epithets, for example—would be prohibited to proponents of all views. But "fighting words" that do not themselves invoke race, color, creed, religion, or gender—aspersions upon a person's mother, for example—would seemingly be usable *ad libitum* in the placards of those arguing *in favor* of racial, color, etc. tolerance and equality, but could not be used by that speaker's opponents. One could hold up a sign saying, for example, that all "anti-Catholic bigots" are misbegotten; but not that all "papists" are, for that would insult and provoke violence "on the basis of religion." St. Paul has no such authority to license one side of a debate to fight freestyle, while requiring the other to follow Marquis of Queensbury Rules.

What we have here, it must be emphasized, is not a prohibition of fighting words that are directed at certain persons or groups (which would be *facially* valid if it met the requirements of the Equal Protection Clause); but rather, a prohibition of fighting words that contain (as the Minnesota Supreme Court repeatedly emphasized) messages of "bias-motivated" hatred and in particular, as applied to this case, messages "based on virulent notions of racial supremacy." 464 N. W.

2d, at 508, 511. One must wholeheartedly agree with the Minnesota Supreme Court that "[i]t is the responsibility, even the obligation, of diverse communities to confront such notions in whatever form they appear," *ibid.*, but the manner of that confrontation cannot consist of selective limitations upon speech. St. Paul's brief asserts that a general "fighting words" law would not meet the city's needs because only a content-specific measure can communicate to minority groups that the "group hatred" aspect of such speech "is not condoned by the majority." Brief for Respondent 25. The point of the First Amendment is that majority preferences must be expressed in some fashion other than silencing speech on the basis of its content.

Despite the fact that the Minnesota Supreme Court and St. Paul acknowledge that the ordinance is directed at expression of group hatred, JUSTICE STEVENS suggests that this "fundamentally misreads" the ordinance. *Post,* at 18–19. It is directed, he claims, not to speech of a particular content, but to particular "injur[ies]" that are "qualitatively different" from other injuries. *Post,* at 9. This is word-play. What makes the anger, fear, sense of dishonor, etc. produced by violation of this ordinance distinct from the anger, fear, sense of dishonor, etc. produced by other fighting words is nothing other than the fact that it is caused by a distinctive idea, conveyed by a distinctive message. The First Amendment cannot be evaded that easily. It is obvious that the symbols which will arouse "anger, alarm or resentment in others on the basis of race, color, creed, religion or gender" are those symbols that communicate a message of hostility based on one of these characteristics. St. Paul concedes in its brief that the ordinance applies only to "racial, religious, or gender-specific symbols" such as "a burning cross, Nazi swastika or other instrumentality of like import." Brief for Respondent 8. Indeed, St. Paul argued in the Juvenile Court that "[t]he burning of a cross does express a message and it is, in fact, the content of that message which the St. Paul Ordinance attempts to legislate." Memorandum from the Ramsey County Attorney to the Honorable Charles A. Flinn, Jr., dated July 13, 1990, in *In re Welfare of R. A. V.,* No. 89-D-1231 (Ramsey Cty. Juvenile Ct.), p. 1, reprinted in App. to Brief for Petitioner C-1.

The content-based discrimination reflected in the St. Paul ordinance comes within neither any of the specific exceptions to the First Amendment prohibition we discussed earlier, nor within a more general exception for content discrimination that does not threaten censorship of ideas. It assuredly does not fall within the exception for content discrimination based on the very reasons why the particular class of speech at issue (here, fighting words) is proscribable. As explained earlier, see *supra,* at 8, the reason why fighting words are categorically excluded from the protection of the First Amendment is not that their content communicates any particular idea, but that their content embodies a particularly intolerable (and socially unnecessary) *mode* of expressing *whatever* idea the speaker wishes to convey. St. Paul has not singled out an especially offensive mode of expression—it has not, for example, selected for prohibition only those fighting words that communicate ideas in a threatening (as opposed to a merely obnoxious) manner. Rather, it has proscribed fighting words of whatever manner that communicate messages of racial, gender, or religious intolerance. Selectivity of this sort creates the possibility that the city is seeking to handicap the expression of particular ideas. That possibility would alone be enough to render the ordinance presumptively invalid, but St. Paul's comments and concessions in this case elevate the possibility to a certainty.

St. Paul argues that the ordinance comes within another of the specific exceptions we mentioned, the one that allows content discrimination aimed only at the "secondary effects" of the speech, see *Renton* v. *Playtime Theatres, Inc.,* 475 U. S. 41 (1986). According to St. Paul, the ordinance is intended, "not to impact on [*sic*] the right of free expression of the accused," but rather to "protect against the victimization of a person or persons who are particularly vulnerable because of their membership in a group that historically has been discriminated against." Brief for Respondent 28. Even assuming that an ordinance that completely proscribes, rather than merely regulates, a specified category of speech can ever be considered to be directed only to the secondary effects of such speech, it is clear that the St. Paul ordinance is not directed to secondary effects within the meaning of *Renton.* As we said in *Boos* v. *Barry,* 485 U. S. 312 (1988), "[l]isteners' reactions to speech are not the type of 'secondary effects' we referred to in *Renton.*" *Id.,* at 321. "The emotive impact of speech on its audience is not a 'secondary effect.' " *Ibid.* See also *id.,* at 334 (opinion of Brennan, J.).[7]

---

[7]St. Paul has not argued in this case that the ordinance merely regulates that subclass of fighting words which is most likely to provoke a violent response. But even if one assumes (as appears unlikely) that the categories selected may be so described, that would not justify selective regulation under a "secondary effects" theory. The only reason why such expressive conduct would be especially correlated with violence is that it conveys a particularly odious message; because the "chain of causation" thus *necessarily* "run[s] through the persuasive effect of the expressive component" of the conduct, *Barnes* v. *Glen Theatre,* 501 U. S. ___, ___ (1991) (SOUTER, J., concurring in judgment) (slip op., at 6), it is clear that the St. Paul ordinance regulates on the basis of the "primary" effect of the speech—*i. e.,* its persuasive (or repellant) force.

It hardly needs discussion that the ordinance does not fall within some more general exception permitting *all* selectivity that for any reason is beyond the suspicion of official suppression of ideas. The statements of St. Paul in this very case afford ample basis for, if not full confirmation of, that suspicion.

Finally, St. Paul and its *amici* defend the conclusion of the Minnesota Supreme Court that, even if the ordinance regulates expression based on hostility towards its protected ideological content, this discrimination is nonetheless justified because it is narrowly tailored to serve compelling state interests. Specifically, they assert that the ordinance helps to ensure the basic human rights of members of groups that have historically been subjected to discrimination, including the right of such group members to live in peace where they wish. We do not doubt that these interests are compelling, and that the ordinance can be said to promote them. But the "danger of censorship" presented by a facially content-based statute, *Leathers* v. *Medlock,* 499 U. S. ___, ___ (1991) (slip op., at 8), requires that that weapon be employed only where it is *"necessary* to serve the asserted [compelling] interest," *Burson* v. *Freeman,* 504 U. S. ___, ___ (1992) (plurality) (slip op., at 8) (emphasis added); *Perry Education Assn.* v. *Perry Local Educators' Assn.,* 460 U. S. 37, 45 (1983). The existence of adequate content-neutral alternatives thus "undercut[s] significantly" any defense of such a statute, *Boos* v. *Barry, supra,* at 329, casting considerable doubt on the government's protestations that "the asserted justification is in fact an accurate description of the purpose and effect of the law," *Burson, supra,* at ___ (KENNEDY, J., concurring) (slip op., at 2). See *Boos, supra,* at 324–329; cf. *Minneapolis Star & Tribune Co.* v. *Minnesota Comm'r of Revenue,* 460 U. S. 575, 586–587 (1983). The dispositive question in this case, therefore, is whether content discrimination is reasonably necessary to achieve St. Paul's compelling interests; it plainly is not. An ordinance not limited to the favored topics, for example, would have precisely the same beneficial effect. In fact the only interest distinctively served by the content limitation is that of displaying the city council's special hostility towards the particular biases thus singled out.[8] That is precisely what the First Amendment forbids. The politi-

---

[8]A plurality of the Court reached a different conclusion with regard to the Tennessee anti-electioneering statute considered earlier this Term in *Burson* v. *Freeman,* 504 U. S. ___ (1992). In light of the "logical connection" between electioneering and the State's compelling interest in preventing voter intimidation and election fraud—an inherent connection borne out by a "long history" and a "wide-spread and time-tested consensus," *id.,* at ___–___ (slip op., at 14–19)—the plurality concluded that it was faced with one of those "rare case[s]" in which the use of a facially content-

cians of St. Paul are entitled to express that hostility—but not through the means of imposing unique limitations upon speakers who (however benightedly) disagree.

* * *

Let there be no mistake about our belief that burning a cross in someone's front yard is reprehensible. But St. Paul has sufficient means at its disposal to prevent such behavior without adding the First Amendment to the fire.

The judgment of the Minnesota Supreme Court is reversed, and the case is remanded for proceedings not inconsistent with this opinion.

It is so ordered.

---

based restriction was justified by interests unrelated to the suppression of ideas, *id.*, at ___ (slip op., at 19); see also *id.*, at ___ (KENNEDY, J., concurring) (slip op., at 3). JUSTICE WHITE and JUSTICE STEVENS are therefore quite mistaken when they seek to convert the *Burson* plurality's passing comment that "[t]he First Amendment does not require States to regulate for problems that do not exist," *id.*, at ___ (slip op., at 16), into endorsement of the revolutionary proposition that the suppression of particular ideas can be justified when only those ideas have been a source of trouble in the past. *Post*, at 10 (WHITE, J.); *post*, at 19 (STEVENS, J.).

Appendix B

———— ■ ————

R.A.V. *v. City of St. Paul, Minnesota*

Concurring Opinions

A. Justice White (with Justices Blackmun and O'Connor, and Justice Stevens in part);

B. Justice Blackmun;

C. Justice Stevens (with Justices White and Blackmun in part).

SUPREME COURT OF THE UNITED STATES

———

No. 90-7675

———

R. A. V., PETITIONER *v.* CITY OF ST. PAUL, MINNESOTA

ON WRIT OF CERTIORARI TO THE SUPREME COURT OF MINNESOTA

[June 22, 1992]

JUSTICE WHITE, with whom JUSTICE BLACKMUN and JUSTICE O'CONNOR join, and with whom JUSTICE STEVENS joins except as to Part I(A), concurring in the judgment.

I agree with the majority that the judgment of the Minnesota Supreme Court should be reversed. However, our agreement ends there.

This case could easily be decided within the contours of established First Amendment law by holding, as petitioner argues, that the St. Paul ordinance is fatally overbroad because it criminalizes not only unprotected expression but expression protected by the First Amendment. See Part II, *infra.* Instead, "find[ing] it unnecessary" to consider the questions upon which we granted review,[1] *ante,* at 3, the Court

———————

[1]The Court granted certiorari to review the following questions:

"1. May a local government enact a content-based, 'hate-crime' ordinance prohib-

holds the ordinance facially unconstitutional on a ground that was never presented to the Minnesota Supreme Court, a ground that has not been briefed by the parties before this Court, a ground that requires serious departures from the teaching of prior cases and is inconsistent with the plurality opinion in *Burson* v. *Freeman*, 504 U. S. ___ (1992), which was joined by two of the five Justices in the majority in the present case.

This Court ordinarily is not so eager to abandon its precedents. Twice within the past month, the Court has declined to overturn longstanding but controversial decisions on questions of constitutional law. See *Allied Signal, Inc.* v. *Director, Division of Taxation*, 504 U. S. ___ (1992); *Quill Corp.* v. *North Dakota*, 504 U. S. ___ (1992). In each case, we had the benefit of full briefing on the critical issue, so that the parties and amici had the opportunity to apprise us of the impact of a change in the law. And in each case, the Court declined to abandon its precedents, invoking the principle of *stare decisis*. *Allied Signal, Inc., supra*, at ___ (slip op., at 12); *Quill Corp., supra*, at ___ (slip op., at 17–18).

But in the present case, the majority casts aside long-established

---

iting the display of symbols, including a Nazi swastika or a burning cross, on public or private property, which one knows or has reason to know arouses anger, alarm, or resentment in others on the basis of race, color, creed, religion, or gender without violating overbreadth and vagueness principles of the First Amendment to the United States Constitution?

"2. Can the constitutionality of such a vague and substantially overbroad content-based restraint of expression be saved by a limiting construction, like that used to save the vague and overbroad content-neutral laws, restricting its application to 'fighting words' or 'imminent lawless action?' " Pet. for Cert. i.

It has long been the rule of this Court that "[o]nly the questions set forth in the petition, or fairly included therein, will be considered by the Court." This Court's Rule 14.1(a). This Rule has served to focus the issues presented for review. But the majority reads the Rule so expansively that any First Amendment theory would appear to be "fairly included" within the questions quoted above.

Contrary to the impression the majority attempts to create through its selective quotation of petitioner's briefs, see *ante*, at 3, n. 3, petitioner did not present to this Court or the Minnesota Supreme Court anything approximating the novel theory the majority adopts today. Most certainly petitioner did not "reiterat[e]" such a claim at argument; he responded to a question from the bench. Tr. of Oral Arg. 8. Previously, this Court has shown the restraint to refrain from deciding cases on the basis of its own theories when they have not been pressed or passed upon by a state court of last resort. See, *e.g., Illinois v. Gates*, 462 U. S. 213, 217–224 (1983).

Given this threshold issue, it is my view that the Court lacks jurisdiction to decide the case on the majority rationale. Cf. *Arkansas Elec. Cooperative Corp.* v. *Arkansas Public Serv. Comm'n*, 461 U. S. 375, 382, n. 6 (1983). Certainly the preliminary jurisdictional and prudential concerns are sufficiently weighty that we would never have granted certiorari, had petitioner sought review of a question based on the majority's decisional theory.

First Amendment doctrine without the benefit of briefing and adopts an untried theory. This is hardly a judicious way of proceeding, and the Court's reasoning in reaching its result is transparently wrong.

I

A

This Court's decisions have plainly stated that expression falling within certain limited categories so lacks the values the First Amendment was designed to protect that the Constitution affords no protection to that expression. *Chaplinsky* v. *New Hampshire,* 315 U. S. 568 (1942), made the point in the clearest possible terms:

> "There are certain well-defined and narrowly limited classes of speech, the prevention and punishment of which have never been thought to raise any Constitutional problem. . . . It has been well observed that such utterances are no essential part of any exposition of ideas, and are of such slight social value as a step to truth that any benefit that may be derived from them is clearly outweighed by the social interest in order and morality." *Id.,* at 571–572.

See also *Bose Corp.* v. *Consumers Union of United States, Inc.,* 466 U. S. 485, 504 (1984) (citing *Chaplinsky*).

Thus, as the majority concedes, see *ante,* at 5, this Court has long held certain discrete categories of expression to be proscribable on the basis of their content. For instance, the Court has held that the individual who falsely shouts "fire" in a crowded theatre may not claim the protection of the First Amendment. *Schenck* v. *United States,* 249 U. S. 47, 52 (1919). The Court has concluded that neither child pornography, nor obscenity, is protected by the First Amendment. *New York* v. *Ferber,* 458 U. S. 747, 764 (1982); *Miller* v. *California,* 413 U. S. 15, 20 (1973); *Roth* v. *United States,* 354 U. S. 476, 484–485 (1957). And the Court has observed that, "[l]eaving aside the special considerations when public officials [and public figures] are the target, a libelous publication is not protected by the Constitution." *Ferber, supra,* at 763 (citations omitted).

All of these categories are content based. But the Court has held that First Amendment does not apply to them because their expressive content is worthless or of *de minimis* value to society. *Chaplinsky, supra,* at 571–572. We have not departed from this principle, emphasizing repeatedly that, "within the confines of [these] given classification[s], the evil to be restricted so overwhelmingly outweighs the expressive interests, if any, at stake, that no process of case-by-case adjudication is required." *Ferber, supra,* at 763–764; *Bigelow* v. *Virginia,* 421 U. S. 809, 819 (1975). This categorical approach has provided a principled and narrowly focused means for distinguishing between expression that the government may regulate freely and that which it may regulate on the basis of content only upon a showing of compelling need.[2]

Today, however, the Court announces that earlier Courts did not mean their repeated statements that certain categories of expression are "not within the area of constitutionally protected speech." *Roth, supra,* at 483. See *ante,* at 5, citing *Beauharnais* v. *Illinois,* 343 U. S. 250, 266 (1952); *Chaplinsky, supra,* at 571–572; *Bose Corp., supra,* at 504; *Sable Communications of Cal., Inc.* v. *FCC,* 492 U. S. 115, 124 (1989). The present Court submits that such clear statements "must be taken in context" and are not "literally true." *Ante,* at 5.

To the contrary, those statements meant precisely what they said: The categorical approach is a firmly entrenched part of our First Amendment jurisprudence. Indeed, the Court in *Roth* reviewed the guarantees of freedom of expression in effect at the time of the ratification of the Constitution and concluded, "[i]n light of this history, it is apparent that the unconditional phrasing of the First Amendment was not intended to protect every utterance." 354 U. S., at 482–483.

In its decision today, the Court points to "[n]othing . . . in this Court's precedents warrant[ing] disregard of this longstanding tradition." *Burson,* 504 U. S., at ___ (slip op., at 3) (SCALIA, J., concurring in judgment); *Allied Signal, Inc., supra,* at ___ (slip op., at 12). Nevertheless, the majority holds that the First Amendment protects those narrow categories of expression long held to be undeserving of First Amendment protection—at least to the extent that lawmakers may not regulate some fighting words more strictly than others because of their content. The Court announces that such content-based distinctions violate the First Amendment because "the government may not regulate use based on hostility—or favoritism—towards the underlying message expressed." *Ante,* at 8. Should the government want to criminalize certain fighting words, the Court now requires it to criminalize all fighting words.

---

[2]"In each of these areas, the limits of the unprotected category, as well as the unprotected character of particular communications, have been determined by the judicial evaluation of special facts that have been deemed to have constitutional significance." *Bose Corp.* v. *Consumers Union of United States, Inc.,* 466 U. S. 485, 504–505 (1948).

To borrow a phrase, "Such a simplistic, all-or-nothing-at-all approach to First Amendment protection is at odds with common sense and with our jurisprudence as well." *Ante,* at 6. It is inconsistent to hold that the government may proscribe an entire category of speech because the content of that speech is evil, *Ferber, supra,* at 763–764; but that the government may not treat a subset of that category differently without violating the First Amendment; the content of the subset is by definition worthless and undeserving of constitutional protection.

The majority's observation that fighting words are "quite expressive indeed," *ante,* at 7, is no answer. Fighting words are not a means of exchanging views, rallying supporters, or registering a protest; they are directed against individuals to provoke violence or to inflict injury. *Chaplinsky,* 315 U. S., at 572. Therefore, a ban on all fighting words or on a subset of the fighting words category would restrict only the social evil of hate speech, without creating the danger of driving viewpoints from the marketplace. See *ante,* at 9.

Therefore, the Court's insistence on inventing its brand of First Amendment underinclusiveness puzzles me.[3] The overbreadth doctrine has the redeeming virtue of attempting to avoid the chilling of protected expression, *Broadrick* v. *Oklahoma,* 413 U. S. 601, 612 (1973); *Osborne* v. *Ohio,* 495 U. S. 103, 112, n. 8 (1990); *Brockett* v. *Spokane Arcades, Inc.,* 472 U. S. 491, 503 (1985); *Ferber, supra,* at 772, but the Court's new "underbreadth" creation serves no desirable function. Instead, it permits, indeed invites, the continuation of expressive conduct that in this case is evil and worthless in First Amendment terms, see *Ferber, supra,* at 763–764; *Chaplinsky, supra,* at 571–572, until the city of St. Paul cures the underbreadth by adding to its ordinance a catch-all phrase such as "and all other fighting words that may constitutionally be subject to this ordinance."

Any contribution of this holding to First Amendment jurisprudence is surely a negative one, since it necessarily signals that expressions of violence, such as the message of intimidation and racial hatred conveyed by burning a cross on someone's lawn, are of sufficient value to outweigh the social interest in order and morality that has traditionally placed such fighting words outside the First Amendment.[4] Indeed, by characterizing fighting words as a form of "de-

---

[3]The assortment of exceptions the Court attaches to its rule belies the majority's claim, see *ante,* at 8–9, that its new theory is truly concerned with content discrimination. See Part I(C), *infra* (discussing the exceptions).

[4]This does not suggest, of course, that cross burning is always unprotected. Burning a cross at a political rally would almost certainly be protected expression. Cf. *Brandenburg* v. *Ohio,* 395 U. S. 444, 445 (1969). But in such a context, the cross

bate," *ante,* at 13, the majority legitimates hate speech as a form of public discussion.

Furthermore, the Court obscures the line between speech that could be regulated freely on the basis of content (*i.e.,* the narrow categories of expression falling outside the First Amendment) and that which could be regulated on the basis of content only upon a showing of a compelling state interest (*i.e.,* all remaining expression). By placing fighting words, which the Court has long held to be valueless, on at least equal constitutional footing with political discourse and other forms of speech that we have deemed to have the greatest social value, the majority devalues the latter category. See *Burson* v. *Freeman, supra,* at ___ (slip op., at 4–5); *Eu* v. *San Francisco County Democratic Central Comm.,* 489 U. S. 214, 222–223 (1989).

B

In a second break with precedent, the Court refuses to sustain the ordinance even though it would survive under the strict scrutiny applicable to other protected expression. Assuming, *arguendo,* that the St. Paul ordinance is a content-based regulation of protected expression, it nevertheless would pass First Amendment review under settled law upon a showing that the regulation "is necessary to serve a compelling state interest and is narrowly drawn to achieve that end.' " *Simon & Schuster, Inc.* v. *New York Crime Victims Board,* 502 U. S. ___, ___ (1991) (slip op., at 11) (quoting *Arkansas Writers' Project, Inc.,* v. *Ragland,* 481 U. S. 221, 231 (1987)). St. Paul has urged that its ordinance, in the words of the majority, "helps to ensure the basic human rights of members of groups that have historically been subjected to discrimination. . . ." *Ante,* at 17. The Court expressly concedes that this interest is compelling and is promoted by the ordinance. *Ibid.* Nevertheless, the Court treats strict scrutiny analysis as irrelevant to the constitutionality of the legislation:

> "The dispositive question . . . is whether content discrimination is reasonably necessary in order to achieve St. Paul's compelling interests; it plainly is not. An ordinance not limited to the favored topics would have precisely the same beneficial effect." *Ibid.*

---

burning could not be characterized as a "direct personal insult or an invitation to exchange fisticuffs," *Texas* v. *Johnson,* 491 U. S. 397, 409 (1989), to which the fighting words doctrine, see Part II, *infra,* applies.

Under the majority's view, a narrowly drawn, content-based ordinance could never pass constitutional muster if the object of that legislation could be accomplished by banning a wider category of speech. This appears to be a general renunciation of strict scrutiny review, a fundamental tool of First Amendment analysis.[5]

This abandonment of the doctrine is inexplicable in light of our decision in *Burson* v. *Freeman, supra,* which was handed down just a month ago.[6] In *Burson,* seven of the eight participating members of the Court agreed that the strict scrutiny standard applied in a case involving a First Amendment challenge to a content-based statute. See *id.,* at ___ (slip op., at 6) (plurality); *id.,* at ___ (slip op., at 1) (STEVENS, J., dissenting).[7] The statute at issue prohibited the solicitation of votes and the display or distribution of campaign materials within 100 feet of the entrance to a polling place. The plurality concluded that the legislation survived strict scrutiny because the State had asserted a compelling interest in regulating electioneering near polling places and because the statute at issue was narrowly tailored to accomplish that goal. *Id.,* at ___ (slip op., at 17–18).

Significantly, the statute in *Burson* did not proscribe all speech near polling places; it restricted only political speech. *Id.,* at ___ (slip op., at 5). The *Burson* plurality, which included THE CHIEF JUSTICE and JUSTICE KENNEDY, concluded that the distinction between types of

---

[5] The majority relies on *Boos* v. *Barry,* 485 U. S. 312 (1988), in arguing that the availability of content-neutral alternatives " 'undercut[s] significantly' " a claim that content-based legislation is " ' *necessary* to serve the asserted [compelling] interest.' " *Ante,* at 17 (quoting *Boos, supra,* at 329, and *Burson* v. *Freeman,* 504 U. S. ___, ___ (1992) (slip op., at 8) (plurality)). *Boos* does not support the majority's analysis. In *Boos,* Congress already had decided that the challenged legislation was not necessary, and the Court pointedly deferred to this choice. 485 U. S., at 329. St. Paul lawmakers have made no such legislative choice.

Moreover, in *Boos,* the Court held that the challenged statute was not narrowly tailored because a less restrictive alternative was available. *Ibid.* But the Court's analysis today turns *Boos* inside-out by substituting the majority's policy judgment that a *more* restrictive alternative could adequately serve the compelling need identified by St. Paul lawmakers. The result would be: (a) a statute that was not tailored to fit the need identified by the government; and (b) a greater restriction on fighting words, even though the Court clearly believes that fighting words have protected expressive content. *Ante,* at 6–7.

[6] Earlier this Term, seven of the eight participating members of the Court agreed that strict scrutiny analysis applied in *Simon & Schuster,* 502 U. S. ___ (1991), in which we struck down New York's "Son of Sam" law, which required "that an accused or convicted criminal's income from works describing his crime be deposited in an escrow account." *Id.,* at ___ (slip op., at 1).

[7] The *Burson* dissenters did not complain that the plurality erred in applying strict scrutiny; they objected that the plurality was not sufficiently rigorous in its review. 504 U. S., at ___ (slip op., at 10–11) (STEVENS, J., dissenting).

speech required application of strict scrutiny, but it squarely rejected the proposition that the legislation failed First Amendment review because it could have been drafted in broader, content-neutral terms:

> "States adopt laws to address the problems that confront them. *The First Amendment does not require States to regulate for problems that do not exist." Id.,* at ___ (slip op., at 16) (emphasis added).

This reasoning is in direct conflict with the majority's analysis in the present case, which leaves two options to lawmakers attempting to regulate expressions of violence: (1) enact a sweeping prohibition on an entire class of speech (thereby requiring "regulat[ion] for problems that do not exist); or (2) not legislate at all.

Had the analysis adopted by the majority in the present case been applied in *Burson,* the challenged election law would have failed constitutional review, for its content-based distinction between political and nonpolitical speech could not have been characterized as "reasonably necessary," *ante,* at 17, to achieve the State's interest in regulating polling place premises.[8]

As with its rejection of the Court's categorical analysis, the majority offers no reasoned basis for discarding our firmly established strict scrutiny analysis at this time. The majority appears to believe that its doctrinal revisionism is necessary to prevent our elected lawmakers from prohibiting libel against members of one political party but not another and from enacting similarly preposterous laws. *Ante,* at 5–6. The majority is misguided.

Although the First Amendment does not apply to categories of unprotected speech, such as fighting words, the Equal Protection Clause requires that the regulation of unprotected speech be rationally related to a legitimate government interest. A defamation statute that drew distinctions on the basis of political affiliation or "an ordinance prohibiting only those legally obscene works that contain

---

[8] JUSTICE SCALIA concurred in the judgment in *Burson,* reasoning that the statute, "though content-based, is constitutional [as] a reasonable, viewpoint-neutral regulation of a nonpublic forum." *Id.,* at ___ (slip op., at 1). However, nothing in his reasoning in the present case suggests that a content-based ban on fighting words would be constitutional were that ban limited to nonpublic fora. Taken together, the two opinions suggest that, in some settings, political speech, to which "the First Amendment 'has its fullest and most urgent application,' " is entitled to less constitutional protection than fighting words. *Eu* v. *San Francisco County Democratic Central Comm.,* 489 U. S. 214, 223 (1989) (quoting *Monitor Patriot Co.* v. *Roy,* 401 U. S. 265, 272 (1971)).

criticism of the city government," *ante,* at 6, would unquestionably
fail rational basis review.[9]

Turning to the St. Paul ordinance and assuming *arguendo,* as the
majority does, that the ordinance is not constitutionally overbroad
(but see Part II, *infra*), there is no question that it would pass equal
protection review. The ordinance proscribes a subset of "fighting
words," those that injure "on the basis of race, color, creed, religion
or gender." This selective regulation reflects the City's judgment that
harms based on race, color, creed, religion, or gender are more pressing public concerns than the harms caused by other fighting words.
In light of our Nation's long and painful experience with discrimination, this determination is plainly reasonable. Indeed, as the majority
concedes, the interest is compelling. *Ante,* at 17.

C

The Court has patched up its argument with an apparently nonex-
haustive list of ad hoc exceptions, in what can be viewed either as an
attempt to confine the effects of its decision to the facts of this case,
see *post,* at ___ (slip op., at 1–2) (BLACKMUN, J., concurring in judgment), or as an effort to anticipate some of the questions that will
arise from its radical revision of First Amendment law.

For instance, if the majority were to give general application to the
rule on which it decides this case, today's decision would call into
question the constitutionality of the statute making it illegal to
threaten the life of the President. 18 U. S. C. §871. See *Watts* v. *United
States,* 394 U. S. 705 (1969) *(per curiam)*. Surely, this statute, by
singling out certain threats, incorporates a content-based distinction;
it indicates that the Government especially disfavors threats against
the President as opposed to threats against all others.[10] See *ante,* at
13. But because the Government could prohibit all threats and not
just those directed against the President, under the Court's theory, the

---

[9] The majority is mistaken in stating that a ban on obscene works critical of
government would fail equal protection review only because the ban would violate
the First Amendment. *Ante,* at 6, n. 2. While decisions such as *Police Dept. of
Chicago* v. *Mosley,* 408 U. S. 92 (1972), recognize that First Amendment principles
may be relevant to an equal protection claim challenging distinctions that impact on
protected expression, *id.,* at 95–99, there is no basis for linking First and Fourteenth
Amendment analysis in a case involving unprotected expression. Certainly, one need
not resort to First Amendment principles to conclude that the sort of improbable
legislation the majority hypothesizes is based on senseless distinctions.

[10] Indeed, such a law is content based in and of itself because it distinguishes
between threatening and nonthreatening speech.

compelling reasons justifying the enactment of special legislation to safeguard the President would be irrelevant, and the statute would fail First Amendment review.

To save the statute, the majority has engrafted the following exception onto its newly announced First Amendment rule: Content-based distinctions may be drawn within an unprotected category of speech if the basis for the distinctions is "the very reason the entire class of speech at issue is proscribable." *Ante,* at 9. Thus, the argument goes, the statute making it illegal to threaten the life of the President is constitutional, "since the reasons why threats of violence are outside the First Amendment (protecting individuals from the fear of violence, from the disruption that fear engenders, and from the possibility that the threatened violence will occur) have special force when applied to the person of the President." *Ante,* at 10.

The exception swallows the majority's rule. Certainly, it should apply to the St. Paul ordinance, since "the reasons why [fighting words] are outside the First Amendment . . . have special force when applied to [groups that have historically been subjected to discrimination]."

To avoid the result of its own analysis, the Court suggests that fighting words are simply a mode of communication, rather than a content-based category, and that the St. Paul ordinance has not singled out a particularly objectionable mode of communication. *Ante,* at 8, 15. Again, the majority confuses the issue. A prohibition on fighting words is not a time, place, or manner restriction; it is a ban on a class of speech that conveys an overriding message of personal injury and imminent violence, *Chaplinsky, supra,* at 572, a message that is at its ugliest when directed against groups that have long been the targets of discrimination. Accordingly, the ordinance falls within the first exception to the majority's theory.

As its second exception, the Court posits that certain content-based regulations will survive under the new regime if the regulated subclass "happens to be associated with particular 'secondary effects' of the speech . . . ," *ante,* at 10, which the majority treats as encompassing instances in which "words can . . . violate laws directed not against speech but against conduct . . ." *Ante,* at 11.[11] Again, there is a simple explanation for the Court's eagerness to craft an exception to its new First Amendment rule: Under the general rule the Court applies in

---

[11]The consequences of the majority's conflation of the rarely-used secondary effects standard and the *O'Brien* test for conduct incorporating "speech" and "nonspeech" elements, see generally *United States* v. *O'Brien,* 391 U. S. 367, 376–377 (1968), present another question that I fear will haunt us and the lower courts in the aftermath of the majority's opinion.

this case, Title VII hostile work environment claims would suddenly be unconstitutional.

Title VII makes it unlawful to discriminate "because of [an] individual's race, color, religion, sex, or national origin," 42 U. S. C. §2000e-2(a)(1), and the regulations covering hostile workplace claims forbid "sexual harassment," which includes "[u]nwelcome sexual advances, requests for sexual favors, and other verbal or physical conduct of a sexual nature" which creates "an intimidating, hostile, or offensive working environment." 29 CFR §1604.11(a) (1991). The regulation does not prohibit workplace harassment generally; it focuses on what the majority would characterize as the "disfavored topi[c]" of sexual harassment. *Ante,* at 13. In this way, Title VII is similar to the St. Paul ordinance that the majority condemns because it "impose[s] special prohibitions on those speakers who express views on disfavored subjects." *Ibid.* Under the broad principle the Court uses to decide the present case, hostile work environment claims based on sexual harassment should fail First Amendment review; because a general ban on harassment in the workplace would cover the problem of sexual harassment, any attempt to proscribe the subcategory of sexually harassing expression would violate the First Amendment.

Hence, the majority's second exception, which the Court indicates would insulate a Title VII hostile work environment claim from an underinclusiveness challenge because "sexually derogatory 'fighting words' . . . may produce a violation of Title VII's general prohibition against sexual discrimination in employment practices." *Ante,* at 11. But application of this exception to a hostile work environment claim does not hold up under close examination.

First, the hostile work environment regulation is not keyed to the presence or absence of an economic *quid pro quo, Meritor Savings Bank* v. *Vinson,* 477 U. S. 57, 65 (1986), but to the impact of the speech on the victimized worker. Consequently, the regulation would no more fall within a secondary effects exception than does the St. Paul ordinance. *Ante,* at 15–16. Second, the majority's focus on the statute's general prohibition on discrimination glosses over the language of the specific regulation governing hostile working environment, which reaches beyond any "incidental" effect on speech. *United States* v. *O'Brien,* 391 U. S. 367, 376 (1968). If the relationship between the broader statute and specific regulation is sufficient to bring the title VII regulation within *O'Brien,* then all St. Paul need do to bring its ordinance within this exception is to add some prefatory language concerning discrimination generally.

As the third exception to the Court's theory for deciding this case, the majority concocts a catchall exclusion to protect against unforeseen problems, a concern that is heightened here given the lack of briefing on the majority's decisional theory. This final exception would apply in cases in which "there is no realistic possibility that official suppression of ideas is afoot." *Ante,* at 12. As I have demonstrated, this case does not concern the official suppression of ideas. See *supra,* at 6. The majority discards this notion out-of-hand. *Ante,* at 16.

As I see it, the Court's theory does not work and will do nothing more than confuse the law. Its selection of this case to rewrite First Amendment law is particularly inexplicable, because the whole problem could have been avoided by deciding this case under settled First Amendment principles.

II

Although I disagree with the Court's analysis, I do agree with its conclusion: The St. Paul ordinance is unconstitutional. However, I would decide the case on overbreadth grounds.

We have emphasized time and again that overbreadth doctrine is an exception to the established principle that "a person to whom a statute may constitutionally be applied will not be heard to challenge that statute on the ground that it may conceivably be applied unconstitutionally to others, in other situations not before the Court." *Broadrick* v. *Oklahoma,* 413 U. S., at 610; *Brockett* v. *Spokane Arcades, Inc.,* 472 U. S., at 503–504. A defendant being prosecuted for speech or expressive conduct may challenge the law on its face if it reaches protected expression, even when that person's activities are not protected by the First Amendment. This is because "the possible harm to society in permitting some unprotected speech to go unpunished is outweighed by the possibility that protected speech of others may be muted." *Broadrick, supra,* at 612; *Osborne* v. *Ohio,* 495 U. S., at 112, n. 8; *New York* v. *Ferber, supra,* at 768–769; *Schaumburg* v. *Citizens for a Better Environment,* 444 U. S. 620, 634 (1980); *Gooding* v. *Wilson,* 405 U. S. 518, 521 (1972).

However, we have consistently held that, because overbreadth analysis is "strong medicine," it may be invoked to strike an entire statute only when the overbreadth of the statute is not only "real, but substantial as well, judged in relation to the statute's plainly legitimate sweep," *Broadrick,* 413 U. S., at 615, and when the statute is not susceptible to limitation or partial invalidation. *Id.,* at 613; *Board of*

Airport Comm'rs of Los Angeles v. *Jews for Jesus, Inc.*, 482 U. S. 569, 574 (1987). "When a federal court is dealing with a federal statute challenged as overbroad, it should . . . construe the statute to avoid constitutional problems, if the statute is subject to a limiting construction." *Ferber*, 458 U. S., at 769, n. 24. Of course, "[a] state court is also free to deal with a state statute in the same way." *Ibid*. See, *e.g., Osborne*, 495 U. S. at 113–114.

Petitioner contends that the St. Paul ordinance is not susceptible to a narrowing construction and that the ordinance therefore should be considered as written, and not as construed by the Minnesota Supreme Court. Petitioner is wrong. Where a state court has interpreted a provision of state law, we cannot ignore that interpretation, even if it is not one that we would have reached if we were construing the statute in the first instance. *Ibid.; Kolender* v. *Lawson*, 461 U. S. 352, 355 (1983); *Hoffman Estates* v. *Flipside, Hoffman Estates, Inc.*, 455 U. S. 489, 494, n. 5 (1982).[12]

Of course, the mere presence of a state court interpretation does not insulate a statute from overbreadth review. We have stricken legislation when the construction supplied by the state court failed to cure the overbreadth problem. See, *e.g., Lewis* v. *City of New Orleans*, 415 U. S. 130, 132–133 (1974); *Gooding, supra*, at 524–525. But in such cases, we have looked to the statute as construed in determining whether it contravened the First Amendment. Here, the Minnesota Supreme Court has provided an authoritative construction of the St. Paul antibias ordinance. Consideration of petitioner's overbreadth claim must be based on that interpretation.

I agree with petitioner that the ordinance is invalid on its face. Although the ordinance as construed reaches categories of speech that are constitutionally unprotected, it also criminalizes a substantial amount of expression that—however repugnant—is shielded by the First Amendment.

In attempting to narrow the scope of the St. Paul antibias ordi-

---

[12]Petitioner can derive no support from our statement in *Virginia* v. *American Bookseller's Assn.*, 484 U. S. 383, 397 (1988), that "the statute must be 'readily susceptible' to the limitation; we will not rewrite a state law to conform it to constitutional requirements." In *American Bookseller's*, no state court had construed the language in dispute. In that instance, we certified a question to the state court so that it would have an opportunity to provide a narrowing interpretation. *Ibid*. In *Erznoznik* v. *City of Jacksonville*, 422 U. S. 205, 216 (1975), the other case upon which petitioner principally relies, we observed not only that the ordinance at issue was not "by its plain terms . . . easily susceptible of a narrowing construction," but that the state courts had made no effort to restrict the scope of the statute when it was challenged on overbreadth grounds.

nance, the Minnesota Supreme Court relied upon two of the categories of speech and expressive conduct that fall outside the First Amendment's protective sphere: words that incite "imminent lawless action," *Brandenburg* v. *Ohio,* 395 U. S. 444, 449 (1969), and "fighting" words, *Chaplinsky* v. *New Hampshire,* 315 U. S., at 571–572. The Minnesota Supreme Court erred in its application of the *Chaplinsky* fighting words test and consequently interpreted the St. Paul ordinance in a fashion that rendered the ordinance facially overbroad.

In construing the St. Paul ordinance, the Minnesota Supreme Court drew upon the definition of fighting words that appears in *Chaplinsky*—words "which by their very utterance inflict injury or tend to incite an immediate breach of the peace." *Id.,* at 572. However, the Minnesota court was far from clear in identifying the "injur[ies]" inflicted by the expression that St. Paul sought to regulate. Indeed, the Minnesota court emphasized (tracking the language of the ordinance) that "the ordinance censors only those displays that one knows or should know will create anger, alarm or resentment based on racial, ethnic, gender or religious bias." *In re Welfare of R. A. V.,* 464 N.W. 2d 507, 510 (1991). I therefore understand the court to have ruled that St. Paul may constitutionally prohibit expression that "by its very utterance" causes "anger, alarm or resentment."

Our fighting words cases have made clear, however, that such generalized reactions are not sufficient to strip expression of its constitutional protection. The mere fact that expressive activity causes hurt feelings, offense, or resentment does not render the expression unprotected. See *United States* v. *Eichman,* 496 U. S. 310, 319 (1990); *Texas* v. *Johnson,* 491 U. S. 397, 409, 414 (1989); *Hustler Magazine, Inc.* v. *Falwell,* 485 U. S. 46, 55–56 (1988); *FCC* v. *Pacifica Foundation,* 438 U. S. 726, 745 (1978); *Hess* v. *Indiana,* 414 U. S. 105, 107–108 (1973); *Cohen* v. *California,* 403 U. S. 15, 20 (1971); *Street* v. *New York,* 394 U. S. 576, 592 (1969); *Terminiello* v. *Chicago,* 337 U. S. 1 (1949).

In the First Amendment context, "[c]riminal statutes must be scrutinized with particular care; those that make unlawful a substantial amount of constitutionally protected conduct may be held facially invalid even if they also have legitimate application." *Houston* v. *Hill,* 482 U. S. 451, 459 (1987) (citation omitted). The St. Paul antibias ordinance is such a law. Although the ordinance reaches conduct that is unprotected, it also makes criminal expressive conduct that causes only hurt feelings, offense, or resentment, and is protected by the First

Amendment. Cf. *Lewis, supra,* at 132.[13] The ordinance is therefore fatally overbroad and invalid on its face.

III

Today, the Court has disregarded two established principles of First Amendment law without providing a coherent replacement theory. Its decision is an arid, doctrinaire interpretation, driven by the frequently irresistible impulse of judges to tinker with the First Amendment. The decision is mischievous at best and will surely confuse the lower courts. I join the judgment, but not the folly of the opinion.

SUPREME COURT OF THE UNITED STATES

No. 90-7675

R. A. V., PETITIONER *v.* CITY OF ST. PAUL, MINNESOTA

ON WRIT OF CERTIORARI TO THE SUPREME COURT OF MINNESOTA

[June 22, 1992]

JUSTICE BLACKMUN, concurring in the judgment.

I regret what the Court has done in this case. The majority opinion signals one of two possibilities: it will serve as precedent for future cases, or it will not. Either result is disheartening.

In the first instance, by deciding that a State cannot regulate speech that causes great harm unless it also regulates speech that does not (setting law and logic on their heads), the Court seems to abandon the categorical approach, and inevitably to relax the level of scrutiny

---

[13]Although the First Amendment protects offensive speech, *Johnson* v. *Texas,* 491 U. S., at 414, it does not require us to be subjected to such expression at all times, in all settings. We have held that such expression may be proscribed when it intrudes upon a "captive audience." *Frisby* v. *Schultz,* 487 U. S. 474, 484–485 (1988); *FCC* v. *Pacifica Foundation,* 438 U. S. 726, 748–749 (1978). And expression may be limited when it merges into conduct. *United States* v. *O'Brien,* 391 U. S. 367 (1968); cf. *Meritor Savings Bank* v. *Vinson,* 477 U. S. 57, 65 (1986). However, because of the manner in which the Minnesota Supreme Court construed the St. Paul ordinance, those issues are not before us in this case.

applicable to content-based laws. As JUSTICE WHITE points out, this weakens the traditional protections of speech. If all expressive activity must be accorded the same protection, that protection will be scant. The simple reality is that the Court will never provide child pornography or cigarette advertising the level of protection customarily granted political speech. If we are forbidden from categorizing, as the Court has done here, we shall reduce protection across the board. It is sad that in its effort to reach a satisfying result in this case, the Court is willing to weaken First Amendment protections.

In the second instance is the possibility that this case will not significantly alter First Amendment jurisprudence, but, instead, will be regarded as an aberration—a case where the Court manipulated doctrine to strike down an ordinance whose premise it opposed, namely, that racial threats and verbal assaults are of greater harm than other fighting words. I fear that the Court has been distracted from its proper mission by the temptation to decide the issue over "politically correct speech" and "cultural diversity," neither of which is presented here. If this is the meaning of today's opinion, it is perhaps even more regrettable.

I see no First Amendment values that are compromised by a law that prohibits hoodlums from driving minorities out of their homes by burning crosses on their lawns, but I see great harm in preventing the people of Saint Paul from specifically punishing the race-based fighting words that so prejudice their community.

I concur in the judgment, however, because I agree with JUSTICE WHITE that this particular ordinance reaches beyond fighting words to speech protected by the First Amendment.

SUPREME COURT OF THE UNITED STATES

No. 90-7675

R. A. V., PETITIONER *v.* CITY OF ST. PAUL, MINNESOTA

ON WRIT OF CERTIORARI TO THE SUPREME COURT OF MINNESOTA

[June 22, 1992]

JUSTICE STEVENS, with whom JUSTICE WHITE and JUSTICE BLACKMUN join as to Part I, concurring in the judgment.

Conduct that creates special risks or causes special harms may be prohibited by special rules. Lighting a fire near an ammunition dump or a gasoline storage tank is especially dangerous; such behavior may be punished more severely than burning trash in a vacant lot. Threatening someone because of her race or religious beliefs may cause particularly severe trauma or touch off a riot, and threatening a high public official may cause substantial social disruption; such threats may be punished more severely than threats against someone based on, say, his support of a particular athletic team. There are legitimate, reasonable, and neutral justifications for such special rules.

This case involves the constitutionality of one such ordinance. Because the regulated conduct has some communicative content—a message of racial, religious or gender hostility—the ordinance raises two quite different First Amendment questions. Is the ordinance "overbroad" because it prohibits too much speech? If not, is it "underbroad" because it does not prohibit enough speech?

In answering these questions, my colleagues today wrestle with two broad principles: first, that certain "categories of expression [including 'fighting words'] are 'not within the area of constitutionally protected speech,'" *ante,* at 5 (WHITE, J., concurring in judgment); and second, that "[c]ontent-based regulations [of expression] are presumptively invalid." *Ante,* at 4 (Opinion of the Court). Although in past opinions the Court has repeated both of these maxims, it has—quite rightly—adhered to neither with the absolutism suggested by my colleagues. Thus, while I agree that the St. Paul ordinance is unconstitutionally overbroad for the reasons stated in Part II of JUSTICE WHITE's opinion, I write separately to suggest how the allure of absolute principles has skewed the analysis of both the majority and concurring opinions.

I

Fifty years ago, the Court articulated a categorical approach to First Amendment jurisprudence.

> "There are certain well-defined and narrowly limited classes of speech, the prevention and punishment of which have never been thought to raise any Constitutional problem. . . . It has been well observed that such utterances are no essential part of any exposition of ideas, and are of such slight social value as a step to truth that any benefit that may be derived from them is clearly outweighed by the social interest in order and morality." *Chaplinsky* v. *New Hampshire,* 315 U. S. 568, 571–572 (1942).

We have, as JUSTICE WHITE observes, often described such categories of expression as "not within the area of constitutionally protected speech." *Roth* v. *United States*, 354 U. S. 476, 483 (1957).

The Court today revises this categorical approach. It is not, the Court rules, that certain "categories" of expression are "unprotected," but rather that certain "elements" of expression are wholly "proscribable." To the Court, an expressive act, like a chemical compound, consists of more than one element. Although the act may be regulated because it contains a proscribable element, it may not be regulated on the basis of another (nonproscribable) element it also contains. Thus, obscene antigovernment speech may be regulated because it is obscene, but not because it is antigovernment. *Ante,* at 6. It is this revision of the categorical approach that allows the Court to assume that the St. Paul ordinance proscribes *only* fighting words, while at the same time concluding that the ordinance is invalid because it imposes a content-based regulation on expressive activity.

As an initial matter, the Court's revision of the categorical approach seems to me something of an adventure in a doctrinal wonderland, for the concept of "obscene antigovernment" speech is fantastical. The category of the obscene is very narrow; to be obscene, expression must be found by the trier of fact to "appea[l] to the prurient interest, . . . depic[t] or describ[e], in a patently offensive way, sexual conduct, [and] taken as a whole, *lac[k] serious literary, artistic, political or scientific value.*" *Miller* v. *California*, 413 U. S. 15, 24 (1973) (emphasis added). "Obscene antigovernment" speech, then, is a contradiction in terms: If expression is antigovernment, it does not "lac[k] serious . . . political . . . value" and cannot be obscene.

The Court attempts to bolster its argument by likening its novel analysis to that applied to restrictions on the time, place, or manner of expression or on expressive conduct. It is true that loud speech in favor of the Republican Party can be regulated because it is loud, but not because it is pro-Republican; and it is true that the public burning of the American flag can be regulated because it involves public burning and not because it involves the flag. But these analogies are inapposite. In each of these examples, the two elements (*e.g.,* loudness and pro-Republican orientation) can coexist; in the case of "obscene antigovernment" speech, however, the presence of one element ("obscenity") by definition means the absence of the other. To my mind, it is unwise and unsound to craft a new doctrine based on such highly speculative hypotheticals.

I am, however, even more troubled by the second step of the Court's analysis—namely, its conclusion that the St. Paul ordinance is an unconstitutional content-based regulation of speech. Drawing on broadly worded *dicta,* the Court establishes a near-absolute ban on content-based regulations of expression and holds that the First Amendment prohibits the regulation of fighting words by subject matter. Thus, while the Court rejects the "all-or-nothing-at-all" nature of the categorical approach, *ante,* at 6, it promptly embraces an absolutism of its own: within a particular "proscribable" category of expression, the Court holds, a government must either proscribe *all* speech or no speech at all.[1] This aspect of the Court's ruling fundamentally misunderstands the role and constitutional status of content-based regulations on speech, conflicts with the very nature of First Amendment jurisprudence, and disrupts well-settled principles of First Amendment law.

Although the Court has, on occasion, declared that content-based regulations of speech are "never permitted," *Police Dept. of Chicago* v. *Mosley,* 408 U. S. 92, 99 (1972), such claims are overstated. Indeed, in *Mosley* itself, the Court indicated that Chicago's selective proscription of nonlabor picketing was not *per se* unconstitutional, but rather could be upheld if the City demonstrated that nonlabor picketing was "clearly more disruptive than [labor] picketing." *Id.,* at 100. Contrary to the broad *dicta* in *Mosley* and elsewhere, our decisions demonstrate that content-based distinctions, far from being presumptively invalid, are an inevitable and indispensable aspect of a coherent understanding of the First Amendment.

This is true at every level of First Amendment law. In broadest terms, our entire First Amendment jurisprudence creates a regime based on the content of speech. The scope of the First Amendment is determined by the content of expressive activity: Although the First Amendment broadly protects "speech," it does not protect the right to "fix prices, breach contracts, make false warranties, place bets

---

[1] The Court disputes this characterization because it has crafted two exceptions, one for "certain media or markets" and the other for content discrimination based upon "the very reason that the entire class of speech at issue is proscribable." *Ante,* at 9. These exceptions are, at best, ill-defined. The Court does not tell us whether, with respect to the former, fighting words such as cross-burning could be proscribed only in certain neighborhoods where the threat of violence is particularly severe, or whether, with respect to the second category, fighting words that create a particular risk of harm (such as a race riot) would be proscribable. The hypothetical and illusory category of these two exceptions persuades me that either my description of the Court's analysis is accurate or that the Court does not in fact mean much of what it says in its opinion.

with bookies, threaten, [or] extort." Schauer, Categories and the First Amendment: A Play in Three Acts, 34 Vand. L. Rev. 265, 270 (1981). Whether an agreement among competitors is a violation of the Sherman Act or protected activity under the *Noerr-Pennington* doctrine[2] hinges upon the content of the agreement. Similarly, "the line between permissible advocacy and impermissible incitation to crime or violence depends, not merely on the setting in which the speech occurs, but also on exactly what the speaker had to say." *Young* v. *American Mini Theatres, Inc.,* 427 U. S. 50, 66 (1976) (plurality opinion); see also *Musser* v. *Utah,* 333 U. S. 95, 100–103 (1948) (Rutledge, J., dissenting).

Likewise, whether speech falls within one of the categories of "unprotected" or "proscribable" expression is determined, in part, by its content. Whether a magazine is obscene, a gesture a fighting word, or a photograph child pornography is determined, in part, by its content. Even within categories of protected expression, the First Amendment status of speech is fixed by its content. *New York Times Co.* v. *Sullivan,* 376 U. S. 254 (1964), and *Dun & Bradstreet, Inc.* v. *Greenmoss Builders, Inc.,* 472 U. S. 749 (1985), establish that the level of protection given to speech depends upon its subject matter: speech about public officials or matters of public concern receives greater protection than speech about other topics. It can, therefore, scarcely be said that the regulation of expressive activity cannot be predicated on its content: much of our First Amendment jurisprudence is premised on the assumption that content makes a difference.

Consistent with this general premise, we have frequently upheld content-based regulations of speech. For example, in *Young* v. *American Mini Theatres,* the Court upheld zoning ordinances that regulated movie theaters based on the content of the films shown. In *FCC* v. *Pacifica Foundation,* 438 U. S. 726 (1978) (plurality opinion), we upheld a restriction on the broadcast of *specific* indecent words. In *Lehman* v. *City of Shaker Heights,* 418 U. S. 298 (1974) (plurality opinion), we upheld a city law that permitted commercial advertising, but prohibited political advertising, on city buses. In *Broadrick* v. *Oklahoma,* 413 U. S. 601 (1973), we upheld a state law that restricted the speech of state employees, but only as concerned partisan political matters. We have long recognized the power of the Federal Trade Commission to regulate misleading advertising and labeling, see, *e.g., Jacob Siegel Co.* v. *FTC,* 327 U. S. 608 (1946), and the National Labor Relations Board's power to regulate an em-

---

[2]See *Mine Workers* v. *Pennington,* 381 U. S. 657 (1965); *Eastern Railroad Presidents Conference* v. *Noerr Motor Freight, Inc.,* 365 U. S. 127 (1961).

ployer's election-related speech on the basis of its content. See, *e.g.*,
NLRB v. *Gissel Packing Co.*, 395 U. S. 575, 616–618 (1969). It is also
beyond question that the Government may choose to limit advertisements for cigarettes, see 15 U. S. C. §1331–1340,[3] but not for cigars;
choose to regulate airline advertising, see *Morales* v. *Trans World
Airlines*, 504 U. S. ___ (1992), but not bus advertising; or choose to
monitor solicitation by lawyers, see *Ohralik* v. *Ohio State Bar Assn.*,
436 U. S. 447 (1978), but not by doctors.

All of these cases involved the selective regulation of speech based
on content—precisely the sort of regulation the Court invalidates
today. Such selective regulations are unavoidably content based, but
they are not, in my opinion, "presumptively invalid." As these many
decisions and examples demonstrate, the prohibition on content-
based regulations is not nearly as total as the *Mosley* dictum suggests.

Disregarding this vast body of case law, the Court today goes
beyond even the overstatement in *Mosley* and applies the prohibition
on content-based regulation to speech that the Court had until today
considered wholly "unprotected" by the First Amendment—namely,
fighting words. This new absolutism in the prohibition of content-
based regulations severely contorts the fabric of settled First Amendment law.

Our First Amendment decisions have created a rough hierarchy in
the constitutional protection of speech. Core political speech occupies the highest, most protected position; commercial speech and
nonobscene, sexually explicit speech are regarded as a sort of second-
class expression; obscenity and fighting words receive the least protection of all. Assuming that the Court is correct that this last class
of speech is not wholly "unprotected," it certainly does not follow
that fighting words and obscenity receive the *same* sort of protection
afforded core political speech. Yet in ruling that proscribable speech
cannot be regulated based on subject matter, the Court does just
that.[4] Perversely, this gives fighting words *greater* protection than is
afforded commercial speech. If Congress can prohibit false advertis-

---

[3]See also *Packer Corp* v. *Utah*, 285 U. S. 105 (1932) (Brandeis, J.) (upholding a
statute that prohibited the advertisement of cigarettes on billboards and street-car
placards).

[4]The Court states that the prohibition on content-based regulations "applies
differently in the context of proscribable speech" than in the context of other speech,
ante, at 9, but its analysis belies that claim. The Court strikes down the St. Paul
ordinance because it regulates fighting words based on subject matter, despite the
fact that, as demonstrated above, we have long upheld regulations of commercial
speech based on subject matter. The Court's self-description is inapt: By prohibiting
the regulation of fighting words based on its subject matter, the Court provides the
same protection to fighting words as is currently provided to core political speech.

ing directed at airline passengers without also prohibiting false advertising directed at bus passengers and if a city can prohibit political
advertisements in its buses while allowing other advertisements, it is
ironic to hold that a city cannot regulate fighting words based on
"race, color, creed, religion or gender" while leaving unregulated
fighting words based on "union membership or homosexuality."
Ante, at 13. The Court today turns First Amendment law on its head:
Communication that was once entirely unprotected (and that still can
be wholly proscribed) is now entitled to greater protection than
commercial speech—and possibly greater protection than core political speech. See *Burson* v. *Freeman,* 504 U. S. ___, ___ (1992).

Perhaps because the Court recognizes these perversities, it quickly
offers some ad hoc limitations on its newly extended prohibition on
content-based regulations. First, the Court states that a content-based
regulation is valid "[w]hen the content discrimination is based upon
the very reason the entire class of speech . . . is proscribable." In a
pivotal passage, the Court writes

> "the Federal Government can criminalize only those physical
> threats that are directed against the President, see 18 U. S. C.
> §871—since the reasons why threats of violence are outside the
> First Amendment (protecting individuals from the fear of vio-
> lence, from the disruption that fear engenders, and from the
> possibility that the threatened violence will occur) have special
> force when applied to the . . . President." *Ante,* at 10.

As I understand this opaque passage, Congress may choose from the
set of unprotected speech (all threats) to proscribe only a subset
(threats against the President) because those threats are particularly
likely to cause "fear of violence," "disruption," and actual "violence."

Precisely this same reasoning, however, compels the conclusion
that St. Paul's ordinance is constitutional. Just as Congress may
determine that threats against the President entail more severe consequences than other threats, so St. Paul's City Council may determine
that threats based on the target's race, religion, or gender cause more
severe harm to both the target and to society than other threats. This
latter judgment—that harms caused by racial, religious, and gender-
based invective are qualitatively different from that caused by other
fighting words—seems to me eminently reasonable and realistic.

Next, the Court recognizes that a State may regulate advertising in
one industry but not another because "the risk of fraud (one of the
characteristics that justifies depriving [commercial speech] of full

First Amendment protection . . .)" in the regulated industry is "greater" than in other industries. *Ante,* at 10. Again, the same reasoning demonstrates the constitutionality of St. Paul's ordinance. "[O]ne of the characteristics that justifies" the constitutional status of fighting words is that such words "by their very utterance inflict injury or tend to incite an immediate breach of the peace." *Chaplinsky,* 315 U. S., at 572. Certainly a legislature that may determine that the risk of fraud is greater in the legal trade than in the medical trade may determine that the risk of injury or breach of peace created by race-based threats is greater than that created by other threats.

Similarly, it is impossible to reconcile the Court's analysis of the St. Paul ordinance with its recognition that "a prohibition of fighting words that are directed at certain persons or groups . . . would be facially valid." *Ante,* at 13 (emphasis deleted). A selective proscription of unprotected expression designed to protect "certain persons or groups" (for example, a law proscribing threats directed at the elderly) would be constitutional if it were based on a legitimate determination that the harm created by the regulated expression differs from that created by the unregulated expression (that is, if the elderly are more severely injured by threats than are the nonelderly). Such selective protection is no different from a law prohibiting minors (and only minors) from obtaining obscene publications. See *Ginsberg* v. *New York,* 390 U. S. 629 (1968). St. Paul has determined—reasonably in my judgment—that fighting-word injuries "based on race, color, creed, religion or gender" are qualitatively different and more severe than fighting-word injuries based on other characteristics. Whether the selective proscription of proscribable speech is defined by the protected target ("certain persons or groups") or the basis of the harm (injuries "based on race, color, creed, religion or gender") makes no constitutional difference: what matters is whether the legislature's selection is based on a legitimate, neutral, and reasonable distinction.

In sum, the central premise of the Court's ruling—that "[c]ontent-based regulations are presumptively invalid"—has simplistic appeal, but lacks support in our First Amendment jurisprudence. To make matters worse, the Court today extends this overstated claim to reach categories of hitherto unprotected speech and, in doing so, wreaks havoc in an area of settled law. Finally, although the Court recognizes exceptions to its new principle, those exceptions undermine its very conclusion that the St. Paul ordinance is unconstitutional. Stated directly, the majority's position cannot withstand scrutiny.

II

Although I agree with much of JUSTICE WHITE's analysis, I do not join Part I-A of his opinion because I have reservations about the "categorical approach" to the First Amendment. These concerns, which I have noted on other occasions, see, *e.g., New York* v. *Ferber,* 458 U. S. 747, 778 (1982) (STEVENS, J., concurring in judgment), lead me to find JUSTICE WHITE's response to the Court's analysis unsatisfying.

Admittedly, the categorical approach to the First Amendment has some appeal: either expression is protected or it is not—the categories create safe harbors for governments and speakers alike. But this approach sacrifices subtlety for clarity and is, I am convinced, ultimately unsound. As an initial matter, the concept of "categories" fits poorly with the complex reality of expression. Few dividing lines in First Amendment law are straight and unwavering, and efforts at categorization inevitably give rise only to fuzzy boundaries. Our definitions of "obscenity," see, *e.g., Marks* v. *United States,* 430 U. S. 188, 198 (1977) (STEVENS, J., concurring in part and dissenting in part), and "public forum," see, *e.g., United States Postal Service* v. *Council of Greenburgh Civic Assns.,* 453 U. S. 114, 126–131 (1981); *id.,* at 136–140 (Brennan, J., concurring in judgment); *id.,* at 147–151 (Marshall, J., dissenting); 152–154 (STEVENS, J., dissenting) (all debating the definition of "public forum"), illustrate this all too well. The quest for doctrinal certainty through the definition of categories and subcategories is, in my opinion, destined to fail.

Moreover, the categorical approach does not take seriously the importance of *context*. The meaning of any expression and the legitimacy of its regulation can only be determined in context.[5] Whether, for example, a picture or a sentence is obscene cannot be judged in the abstract, but rather only in the context of its setting, its use, and its audience. Similarly, although legislatures may freely regulate most nonobscene child pornography, such pornography that is part of "a serious work of art, a documentary on behavioral problems, or a medical or psychiatric teaching device," may be entitled to constitutional protection; the "question whether a specific act of communication is protected by the First Amendment always requires some consideration of both its content and its context." *Ferber,* 458 U. S.

---

[5] "A word," as Justice Holmes has noted, "is not a crystal, transparent and unchanged, it is the skin of a living thought and may vary greatly in color and content according to the circumstances and the time in which it is used." *Towne* v. *Eisner,* 245 U. S. 418, 425 (1918); see also *Jacobellis* v. *Ohio,* 378 U. S. 184, 201 (1964) (Warren, C. J., dissenting).

at 778 (STEVENS, J., concurring in judgment); see also *Smith* v. *United States,* 431 U. S. 291, 311–321 (1977) (STEVENS, J., dissenting). The categorical approach sweeps too broadly when it declares that all such expression is beyond the protection of the First Amendment.

Perhaps sensing the limits of such an all-or-nothing approach, the Court has applied its analysis less categorically than its doctrinal statements suggest. The Court has recognized intermediate categories of speech (for example, for indecent nonobscene speech and commercial speech) and geographic categories of speech (public fora, limited public fora, nonpublic fora) entitled to varying levels of protection. The Court has also stringently delimited the categories of unprotected speech. While we once declared that "[l]ibelous utterances [are] not . . . within the area of constitutionally protected speech, *Beauharnais* v. *Illinois,* 343 U. S. 250, 266 (1952), our rulings in *New York Times Co.* v. *Sullivan,* 376 U. S. 253 (1964); *Gertz* v. *Robert Welch, Inc.,* 418 U. S. 323 (1974), and *Dun & Bradstreet, Inc.* v. *Greenmoss Builders, Inc.,* 472 U. S. 749 (1985), have substantially qualified this broad claim. Similarly, we have consistently construed the "fighting words" exception set forth in *Chaplinsky* narrowly. See, *e.g., Houston* v. *Hill,* 482 U. S. 451 (1987); *Lewis* v. *City of New Orleans,* 415 U. S. 130 (1974); *Cohen* v. *California,* 403 U. S. 15 (1971). In the case of commercial speech, our ruling that "the Constitution imposes no . . . restraint on government [regulation] as respects purely commercial advertising," *Valentine* v. *Chrestensen,* 316 U. S. 52, 54 (1942), was expressly repudiated in *Virginia Bd. of Pharmacy* v. *Virginia Citizens Consumer Council, Inc.,* 425 U. S. 748 (1976). In short, the history of the categorical approach is largely the history of narrowing the categories of unprotected speech.

This evolution, I believe, indicates that the categorical approach is unworkable and the quest for absolute categories of "protected" and "unprotected" speech ultimately futile. My analysis of the faults and limits of this approach persuades me that the categorical approach presented in Part I-A of JUSTICE WHITE's opinion is not an adequate response to the novel "underbreadth" analysis the Court sets forth today.

III

As the foregoing suggests, I disagree with both the Court's and part of JUSTICE WHITE's analysis of the constitutionality St. Paul ordinance. Unlike the Court, I do not believe that all content-based regulations are equally infirm and presumptively invalid; unlike JUS-

TICE WHITE, I do not believe that fighting words are wholly unprotected by the First Amendment. To the contrary, I believe our decisions establish a more complex and subtle analysis, one that considers the content and context of the regulated speech, and the nature and scope of the restriction on speech. Applying this analysis and assuming *arguendo* (as the Court does) that the St. Paul ordinance is *not* overbroad, I conclude that such a selective, subject-matter regulation on proscribable speech is constitutional.

Not all content-based regulations are alike; our decisions clearly recognize that some content-based restrictions raise more constitutional questions than others. Although the Court's analysis of content-based regulations cannot be reduced to a simple formula, we have considered a number of factors in determining the validity of such regulations.

First, as suggested above, the scope of protection provided expressive activity depends in part upon its content and character. We have long recognized that when government regulates political speech or "the expression of editorial opinion on matters of public importance," *FCC* v. *League of Women Voters of California,* 468 U. S. 364, 375–376 (1984), "First Amendment protectio[n] is 'at its zenith.' " *Meyer* v. *Grant,* 486 U. S. 414, 425 (1988). In comparison, we have recognized that "commercial speech receives a limited form of First Amendment protection," *Posadas de Puerto Rico Associates* v. *Tourism Co. of Puerto Rico,* 478 U. S. 328, 340 (1986), and that "society's interest in protecting [sexually explicit films] is of a wholly different, and lesser magnitude than [its] interest in untrammeled political debate." *Young* v. *American Mini Theatres,* 427 U. S., at 70; see also *FCC* v. *Pacifica Foundation,* 438 U. S. 726 (1978). The character of expressive activity also weighs in our consideration of its constitutional status. As we have frequently noted, "[t]he government generally has a freer hand in restricting expressive conduct than it has in restricting the written or spoken word." *Texas* v. *Johnson,* 491 U. S. 397, 406 (1989); see also *United States* v. *O'Brien,* 391 U. S. 367 (1968).

The protection afforded expression turns as well on the context of the regulated speech. We have noted, for example, that "[a]ny assessment of the precise scope of employer expression, of course, must be made in the context of its labor relations setting . . . [and] must take into account the economic dependence of the employees on their employers." *NLRB* v. *Gissel Packing Co.,* 395 U. S., at 617. Similarly, the distinctive character of a university environment, see *Widmar* v. *Vincent,* 454 U. S. 263, 277–280 (1981) (STEVENS, J., concurring in judgment), or a secondary school environment, see *Hazelwood School Dist.* v. *Kuhlmeier*, 484 U. S. 260 (1988), influences our First Amendment analysis. The same is true of the presence of a " 'captive audience[, one] there as a matter of necessity, not of choice.' " *Lehman* v. *City of Shaker Heights*, 418 U. S., at 302 (citation omitted).[6] Perhaps the most familiar embodiment of the relevance of context is our "fora" jurisprudence, differentiating the levels of protection afforded speech in different locations.

The nature of a contested restriction of speech also informs our evaluation of its constitutionality. Thus, for example, "[a]ny system of prior restraints of expression comes to this Court bearing a heavy presumption against its constitutional validity." *Bantam Books, Inc.* v. *Sullivan*, 372 U. S. 58, 70 (1963). More particularly to the matter of content-based regulations, we have implicitly distinguished between restrictions on expression based on *subject matter* and restrictions based on *viewpoint*, indicating that the latter are particularly pernicious. "If there is a bedrock principle underlying the First Amendment, it is that the Government may not prohibit the expression of an idea simply because society finds the idea itself offensive or disagreeable." *Texas* v. *Johnson*, 491 U. S., at 414. "Viewpoint discrimination is censorship in its purest form," *Perry Education Assn.* v. *Perry Local Educators' Assn.*, 460 U. S. 37, 62 (1983) (Brennan, J., dissenting), and requires particular scrutiny, in part because such regulation often indicates a legislative effort to skew public debate on an issue. See, *e.g.*, *Schacht* v. *United States*, 398 U. S. 58, 63 (1970). "Especially where . . . the legislature's suppression of speech suggests an attempt to give one side of a debatable public question an advantage in expressing its views to the people, the First Amendment is plainly offended." *First National Bank of Boston* v. *Bellotti*, 435 U. S. 765, 785–786 (1978). Thus, although a regulation that on its face regulates speech by subject matter may in some instances effectively suppress particular viewpoints, see, *e.g.*, *Consolidated Edison Co. of N.Y.* v. *Public Service Comm'n of N.Y.*, 447 U. S. 530, 546–547 (1980) (STEVENS, J., concurring in judgment), in general, viewpoint-based restrictions on expression require greater scrutiny than subject-matter based restrictions.[7]

---

[6]Cf. *In re Chase*, 468 F. 2d 128, 139–140 (CA7 1972) (Stevens, J., dissenting) (arguing that defendant who, for reasons of religious belief, refused to rise and stand as the trial judge entered the courtroom was not subject to contempt proceedings because he was not present in the courtroom "as a matter of choice").

[7]Although the Court has sometimes suggested that subject-matter based and viewpoint-based regulations are equally problematic, see, *e. g.*, *Consolidated Edison Co.*

Finally, in considering the validity of content-based regulations we have also looked more broadly at the scope of the restrictions. For example, in *Young* v. *American Mini Theatres,* 427 U. S., at 71, we found significant the fact that "what [was] ultimately at stake [was] nothing more than a limitation on the place where adult films may be exhibited." Similarly, in *FCC* v. *Pacifica Foundation,* the Court emphasized two dimensions of the limited scope of the FCC ruling. First, the ruling concerned only broadcast material which presents particular problems because it "confronts the citizen . . . in the privacy of the home"; second, the ruling was not a complete ban on the use of selected offensive words, but rather merely a limitation on the times such speech could be broadcast. 438 U. S., at 748–750.

All of these factors play some role in our evaluation of content-based regulations on expression. Such a multi-faceted analysis cannot be conflated into two dimensions. Whatever the allure of absolute doctrines, it is just too simple to declare expression "protected" or "unprotected" or to proclaim a regulation "content-based" or "content-neutral."

In applying this analysis to the St. Paul ordinance, I assume *arguendo*—as the Court does—that the ordinance regulates *only* fighting words and therefore is *not* overbroad. Looking to the content and character of the regulated activity, two things are clear. First, by hypothesis the ordinance bars only low-value speech, namely, fighting words. By definition such expression constitutes "no essential part of any exposition of ideas, and [is] of such slight social value as a step to truth that any benefit that may be derived from [it] is clearly outweighed by the social interest in order and morality." *Chaplinsky,* 315 U. S., at 572. Second, the ordinance regulates "expressive conduct [rather] than . . . the written or spoken word." *Texas* v. *Johnson,* 491 U. S., at 406.

Looking to the context of the regulated activity, it is again significant that the statute (by hypothesis) regulates *only* fighting words. Whether words are fighting words is determined in part by their context. Fighting words are not words that merely cause offense; fighting words must be directed at individuals so as to "by their very utterance inflict injury." By hypothesis, then, the St. Paul ordinance restricts speech in confrontational and potentially violent situations. The case at hand is illustrative. The cross-burning in this case—directed as it was to a single African-American family trapped in their

---

of N.Y. v. *Public Service Comm'n of N.Y.,* 447 U. S., at 537, our decisions belie such claims.

home—was nothing more than a crude form of physical intimidation. That this cross-burning sends a message of racial hostility does not automatically endow it with complete constitutional protection.[8]

Significantly, the St. Paul ordinance regulates speech not on the basis of its subject matter or the viewpoint expressed, but rather on the basis of the *harm* the speech causes. In this regard, the Court fundamentally misreads the St. Paul ordinance. The Court describes the St. Paul ordinance as regulating expression "addressed to one of [several] specified disfavored *topics," ante,* at 13 (emphasis supplied), as policing "disfavored *subjects," ibid.* (emphasis supplied), and as "prohibit[ing] . . . speech solely on the basis of the *subjects* the speech addresses." *Ante,* at 3 (emphasis supplied). Contrary to the Court's suggestion, the ordinance regulates only a subcategory of expression that causes *injuries based on* "race, color, creed, religion or gender," not a subcategory that involves *discussions* that concern those characteristics.[9] The ordinance, as construed by the Court, criminalizes expression that "one knows . . . [by its very utterance inflicts injury on] others on the basis of race, color, creed, religion or gender." In this regard, the ordinance resembles the child pornography law at issue in *Ferber,* which in effect singled out child pornography because

---

[8]The Court makes much of St. Paul's description of the ordinance as regulating "a message." *Ante,* at 15. As always, however, St. Paul's argument must be read in context:
"Finally, we ask the Court to reflect on the 'content' of the 'expressive conduct' represented by a 'burning cross.' It is no less than the first step in an act of racial violence. It was and unfortunately still is the equivalent of [the] waving of a knife before the thrust, the pointing of a gun before it is fired, the lighting of the match before the arson, the hanging of the noose before the lynching. It is not a political statement, or even a cowardly statement of hatred. It is the first step in an act of assault. It can be no more protected than holding a gun to a victim['s] head. It is perhaps the ultimate expression of 'fighting words.' " App. to Brief for Petitioner C-6.
[9]The Court contends that this distinction is "wordplay," reasoning that "[w]hat makes [the harms caused by race-based threats] distinct from [the harms] produced by other fighting words is . . . the fact that [the former are] caused by a *distinctive idea." Ante,* at 14 (emphasis added). In this way, the Court concludes that regulating speech based on the injury it causes is no different from regulating speech based on its subject matter. This analysis fundamentally miscomprehends the role of "race, color, creed, religion [and] gender" in contemporary American society. One need look no further than the recent social unrest in the Nation's cities to see that race-based threats may cause more harm to society and to individuals than other threats. Just as the statute prohibiting threats against the President is justifiable because of the place of the President in our social and political order, so a statute prohibiting race-based threats is justifiable because of the place of race in our social and political order. Although it is regrettable that race occupies such a place and is so incendiary an issue, until the Nation matures beyond that condition, laws such as St. Paul's ordinance will remain reasonable and justifiable.

those publications caused far greater harms than pornography involving adults.

Moreover, even if the St. Paul ordinance did regulate fighting words based on its subject matter, such a regulation would, in my opinion, be constitutional. As noted above, subject-matter based regulations on commercial speech are widespread and largely unproblematic. As we have long recognized, subject-matter regulations generally do not raise the same concerns of government censorship and the distortion of public discourse presented by viewpoint regulations. Thus, in upholding subject-matter regulations we have carefully noted that viewpoint-based discrimination was not implicated. See *Young* v. *American Mini Theatres*, 427 U. S., at 67 (emphasizing "the need for absolute neutrality by the government," and observing that the contested statute was not animated by "hostility for the point of view" of the theatres); *FCC* v. *Pacifica Foundation*, 438 U. S., at 745–746 (stressing that "government must remain neutral in the marketplace of ideas"); see also *FCC* v. *League of Women's Voters of California*, 468 U. S., at 412–417 (STEVENS, J., dissenting); *Metromedia, Inc.* v. *City of San Diego*, 453 U. S. 490, 554–555 (1981) (STEVENS, J., dissenting in part). Indeed, some subject-matter restrictions are a functional necessity in contemporary governance: "The First Amendment does not require States to regulate for problems that do not exist." *Burson* v. *Freeman*, 504 U. S. ___, ___ (1992) (slip op., at 16).

Contrary to the suggestion of the majority, the St. Paul ordinance does *not* regulate expression based on viewpoint. The Court contends that the ordinance requires proponents of racial intolerance to "follow the Marquis of Queensbury Rules" while allowing advocates of racial tolerance to "fight freestyle." The law does no such thing.

The Court writes:

> "One could hold up a sign saying, for example, that all 'anti-Catholic bigots' are misbegotten; but not that all 'papists' are, for that would insult and provoke violence 'on the basis of religion.' " *Ante,* at 13.

This may be true, but it hardly proves the Court's point. The Court's reasoning is asymmetrical. The response to a sign saying that "all [religious] bigots are misbegotten" is a sign saying that "all advocates of religious tolerance are misbegotten." Assuming such signs could be fighting words (which seems to me extremely unlikely), neither sign would be banned by the ordinance for the attacks were not "based on . . . religion" but rather on one's beliefs about tolerance. Conversely (and again assuming such signs are fighting words), just as the ordinance would prohibit a Muslim from hoisting a sign claiming that all Catholics were misbegotten, so the ordinance would bar a Catholic from hoisting a similar sign attacking Muslims.

The St. Paul ordinance is evenhanded. In a battle between advocates of tolerance and advocates of intolerance, the ordinance does not prevent either side from hurling fighting words at the other on the basis of their conflicting ideas, but it does bar *both* sides from hurling such words on the basis of the target's "race, color, creed, religion or gender." To extend the Court's pugilistic metaphor, the St. Paul ordinance simply bans punches "below the belt"—*by either party*. It does not, therefore, favor one side of any debate.[10]

Finally, it is noteworthy that the St. Paul ordinance is, as construed by the Court today, quite narrow. The St. Paul ordinance does not ban all "hate speech," nor does it ban, say, all cross-burnings or all swastika displays. Rather it only bans a subcategory of the already narrow category of fighting words. Such a limited ordinance leaves open and protected a vast range of expression on the subjects of racial, religious, and gender equality. As construed by the Court today, the ordinance certainly does not " 'raise the specter that the Government may effectively drive certain ideas or viewpoints from the marketplace.' " *Ante,* at 9. Petitioner is free to burn a cross to announce a rally or to express his views about racial supremacy, he may do so on private property or public land, at day or at night, so long as the burning is not so threatening and so directed at an individual as to "by its very [execution] inflict injury." Such a limited proscription scarcely offends the First Amendment.

In sum, the St. Paul ordinance (as construed by the Court) regulates expressive activity that is wholly proscribable and does so not on the basis of viewpoint, but rather in recognition of the different harms caused by such activity. Taken together, these several considerations persuade me that the St. Paul ordinance is not an unconstitutional content-based regulation of speech. Thus, were the ordinance not overbroad, I would vote to uphold it.

---

[10]Cf. *FCC* v. *League of Women Voters of California,* 468 U. S. 364, 418 (1984) (STEVENS, J., dissenting) ("In this case . . . the regulation applies . . . to a defined class of . . . licensees [who] represent heterogenous points of view. There is simply no sensible basis for considering this regulation a viewpoint restriction—or . . . to condemn it as 'content-based'—because it applies equally to station owners of all shades of opinion").

Index